Prophetic Times

Throughout Italy's history, prophetic voices – poets, painters, philosophers – have bolstered the struggle for social and political emancipation. These voices denounced the vices of compatriots and urged them toward redemption. They gave meaning to suffering, helping to prevent moral surrender; they provided support, with pathos and anger, which set into motion the moral imagination, culminating in redemption and freedom. While the fascist regime attempted to enlist Mazzini and the prophets of the Risorgimento in support of its ideology, the most perceptive anti-fascist intellectual and political leaders composed eloquent prophetic pages to sustain the resistance against the totalitarian regime. By the end of the 1960s, no prophet of social emancipation has been able to move the consciences of the Italians. In this Italian story, then, is our story, the world's story, inspiration for social and political emancipation everywhere.

Maurizio Viroli is Professor of Government at the University of Texas at Austin and Professor of Politics (Emeritus) at Princeton University.

Prophetic Times

Visions of Emancipation in the History of Italy

MAURIZIO VIROLI

The University of Texas at Austin

Princeton University (Emeritus)

CAMBRIDGE
UNIVERSITY PRESS

Shaftesbury Road, Cambridge CB2 8EA, United Kingdom

One Liberty Plaza, 20th Floor, New York, NY 10006, USA

477 Williamstown Road, Port Melbourne, VIC 3207, Australia

314–321, 3rd Floor, Plot 3, Splendor Forum, Jasola District Centre, New Delhi – 110025, India

103 Penang Road, #05–06/07, Visioncrest Commercial, Singapore 238467

Cambridge University Press is part of Cambridge University Press & Assessment, a department of the University of Cambridge.

We share the University's mission to contribute to society through the pursuit of education, learning and research at the highest international levels of excellence.

www.cambridge.org
Information on this title: www.cambridge.org/9781009233187

DOI: 10.1017/9781009233170

First published 2023

Printed in the United Kingdom by TJ Books Limited, Padstow Cornwall

A catalogue record for this publication is available from the British Library.

A Cataloging-in-Publication data record for this book is available from the Library of Congress
NAMES: Viroli, Maurizio, author.
TITLE: Prophetic times : visions of emancipation in the history of Italy / Maurizio Viroli, Princeton University, New Jersey.
OTHER TITLES: Tempi profetici. English
DESCRIPTION: New York, NY, USA : Cambridge University Press, 2022. | Translation of: Tempi profetici. Bari : GLF editori Laterza, 2021. | Includes bibliographical references and index.
IDENTIFIERS: LCCN 2022030547 (print) | LCCN 2022030548 (ebook) | ISBN 9781009233187 (hardback) | ISBN 9781009233200 (paperback) | ISBN 9781009233170 (epub)
SUBJECTS: LCSH: Politics and culture–Italy–History. | Political sociology–Italy–History. | National socialism and religion–History. | Italy–History–Prophecies. | Italy–Religion. | BISAC: POLITICAL SCIENCE / History & Theory
CLASSIFICATION: LCC DG442 .V5713 2022 (print) | LCC DG442 (ebook) | DDC 945–dc23/eng/20220707
LC record available at https://lccn.loc.gov/2022030547
LC ebook record available at https://lccn.loc.gov/2022030548

ISBN 978-1-009-23318-7 Hardback

To Pasquale Stoppelli and Jeffrey Tulis because "Tarde non furon mai grazie divine"

Contents

Acknowledgments

I first thought about prophecy one afternoon many years ago in Milan, at the home of Maria Teresa Fumagalli Beonio Brocchieri. Thanks to my dialogue with Maria Teresa and her excellent students, the idea for a conference was born. Held in November 2015 at the Università della Svizzera Italiana in Lugano, that conference was this work's starting point. I am very grateful to all who participated for encouraging me to undertake this long journey. Thanks to my friend Tommaso Greco, I discussed a paper on "Machiavelli the prophet" at the University of Pisa in December of the same year. I then presented the first fruits of my research to the Axel and Margaret Ax:son Johnson Foundation for Public Benefit in Stockholm, which generously financed my project. My institution, the University of Texas at Austin, has been equally generous to me. I am particularly appreciative of the sabbatical granted to me while I was bringing this project to completion.

During a conference organized by my colleague and friend Nicola Panichi, I once again discussed prophetic language and political emancipation at the Università di Urbino Carlo Bo in 2016. I am grateful to her for offering me an important opportunity to share my research hypotheses with friends and colleagues, among whom are Gianfranco Borrelli and Artemio Enzo Baldini. Under the auspices of my former Princeton student, Yiftah Elazar, I had the privilege of discussing the same topic with colleagues and scripture scholars at the Hebrew University of Jerusalem in 2017. In the same year, again in Urbino, and again thanks to Nicola Panichi and the Magnificent Rector Vilberto Stocchi, I presented the provisional results of my work and collected valuable, encouraging comments from Carlo Ossola, Raphael Ebgi, and Simonetta Bassi. Gaetano Lettieri organized a seminar on Machiavelli at which I was able to illustrate some ideas to colleagues from the Sapienza – Università di Roma and other Roman universities. I thank everyone for their comments and observations. Thanks to Lorraine and Thomas Pangle, I had the pleasure of proposing a part of this work in Austin at the Thomas Jefferson Center for the Study of Core Texts and Ideas. Here in Austin, I am honored by the friendship of Jeffrey Tulis, with whom I share civic passions and political ideals. I also discussed the use of prophetic language in history at the French and Italian Department of Dartmouth College, the Institute of Humanities and Social Sciences at the University of Peking, and at the History Department of the European University Institute in Florence.

Carlo Ossola provided me with the opportunity to lecture on prophetic language and social emancipation at the Collège de France. I extend my deepest gratitude to the colleagues with whom I had the pleasure of working during my time in Paris. My debt to Carlo is vast. I owe a special thanks to Valeria Giannetti, a Parisian friend and author of an exquisite study on Ippolito Nievo. Robert George's generous invitation to the James Madison Program in American Ideals and Institutions allowed me to interact with several colleagues from my beloved Princeton University. As always, the comments and criticism were productive. I reserve a thought of sincere gratitude for two dear friends, George Kateb and David Tubbs, whose closeness has never been lacking and who continue to welcome me with affection every time I return to Princeton.

I gave the manuscript to read, in part or in whole, to people who have passionately and caringly looked after it and who have given me important advice. My thoughts go to Antonio Ciaralli, Hilary Gatti, Tommaso Greco, Giacomo Jori, Luciano Manicardi, Pasquale Stoppelli, and Davide Susanetti. In particular, my friend Pasquale Stoppelli was involved in the heavy work of the first editing. I am very thankful to Emily C. Martin for the excellent translations from French, and to Lorenzo Manenti for pointing out important texts to me, in particular Filippo Burzio's *Profeti d'oggi*. Without the invaluable help of Robert Bucci, an American who is more Italian than me, this book would not have seen the light of day. Long-time collaborators and friends, Giorgio Volpe and Marcello Gisondi, once again assisted me with their generous assistance.

A very big thank you goes to my wife Gabriella, who also took my work to heart and followed it step-by-step, without sparing me criticism and without skimping on applause. I am indebted to her for many acute observations, as well as her suggestions and help in concluding the book with Pier Paolo Pasolini, her author.

Tempi profetici was published in Italian by Editori Laterza in 2021. I thank Giuseppe Laterza for generously allowing this revised edition to be published in English. Last but not least, I am grateful to Cambridge University Press, in particular to Robert Dreesen, for the attention and the fine care that they have dedicated to my work.

I

Introduction

Throughout Italy's history, there have been prophetic voices that have strengthened the struggle for social and political emancipation. Such voices have denounced the vices of compatriots and urged them toward redemption; they have given meaning to suffering, helping to prevent complete moral surrender; they have spoken with pathos and anger to touch the passions and set into motion the moral imagination which guides the efforts toward redemption; and finally, they have combated the tendency toward submission, thus engendering a determination to endure the efforts and sacrifices that emancipation entails.

As we read in the immense sea of literature on the subject, prophets believe that they have received an inspiration or special revelation from God.[1] The

---

[1] See Pierre Benoit, "Révélation et Inspiration," *Revue Biblique* 70 (1963): 321–370, and Brian Fitzgerald, *Inspiration and Authority in the Middle Ages: Prophets and their Critics from Scholasticism to Humanism*, Oxford: Oxford University Press, 2017. On prophecy see Carl Heinrich Cornill, *The Prophets of Israel: Popular Sketches from Old Testament History*, trans. by Sutton F. Corkran, Chicago: The Open Court Publishing Company, 1973, pp. 35–36; Abraham J. Heschel, *The Prophets*, New York: Harper & Row, 1962, pp. 10–23; Max Weber, *Ancient Judaism*, New York: Free Press, 1952; Martin Buber, *The Prophetic Faith*, New York: Harper & Row, 1949; and *Kingship of God*, New York: Harper & Row, 1967; Marcus Greil, *The Shape of Things to Come*, New York: Farrar, Straus and Giroux, 2006; Joseph Blenkinsopp, *A History of Prophecy in Israel*, Louisville (KY): Westminster John Knox Press, 1996; John J. Collins, "Temporality and Politics in Jewish Apocalyptic Literature," *Apocalyptic in History and Tradition*, edited by Christopher Rowland and John Barton, London: Sheffield Academic Press, 2002, pp. 35 and 39. On millenarianism and prophecy see Norman Cohn, *The Pursuit of the Millennium: Revolutionary Millenarians and Mystical Anarchists in the Middle Ages*, London: Maurice Temple Smith, 1970; John J. Collins, *The Apocalyptic Imagination*, New York: Crossroad, 1984 (reprint Grand Rapids: Eerdmans, 1998); and "Prophecy to Apocalypticism: the Expectation of the End," *The Encyclopedia of Apocalypticism, Vol. 1: The Origins of Apocalypticism in Judaism and Christianity*, New York: Continuum, 1998,

former is a moral enhancement that makes the prophet capable of seeing into past, present, and future times, meanings that their compatriots do not see; the latter is the inner experience of discovering truth through sensorial, imaginative, or intellectual representations. God gives prophetic light as a gift. At times He gives it even to individuals who do not exhibit outstanding moral and intellectual qualities. God does not expect their gratitude in return, but the gift comes with the mandate of total commitment to the arduous task of illuminating their compatriots. True prophets reluctantly accept God's order. They know they will not get rewards, at least not in this world. They are aware that by carrying out God's order they are likely to meet a tragic fate. Hesitation, reluctance, and fear are distinctive marks of true prophets.

The sincere persuasion that they speak to fulfill a duty they have before God gives a special force to prophets' voices. Because they feel that they are inspired, they can inspire their compatriots: They enhance their compatriots' consciences, enlighten their minds, and strengthen their hearts. In addition to their faith in divine inspiration, the power of prophets comes from their exemplary lives. Exemplary does not mean saintly. Prophets have vices, but do not share in the servile mentality, corruption, and moral emptiness of their compatriots. Together, their voices and their lives' examples accomplish the mission of

pp. 129–161; Malcolm Bull, *Apocalypse Theory and the Ends of the World*, Oxford: Basil Blackwell, 1995; John J. Collins, "Introduction: Towards the Morphology of a Genre," *Semeia* 14 (1979): pp. 1–20; Adela Y. Collins, "The Uses of Apocalyptic Eschatology," *Fourth Ezra and Second Baruch: Reconstruction After the Fall*, edited by Matthias Henze and Gabriele Boccaccini, Leiden: Brill, 2013, pp. 253–270; and "Ascents to Heaven in Antiquity: Toward a Typology," *A Teacher for All Generations: Essays in Honor of James C. VanderKam*, vol. 2, edited by Erich F. Mason, Leiden: Brill, 2012, pp. 553–572. On prophecy and social emancipation see George Shulman, *American Prophecy. Race and Redemption in American Political Culture*, Minneapolis: University of Minnesota Press, 2008; Sacvan Bercovitch, *The American Jeremiad*, Madison (WI): University of Wisconsin Press, 1978; Michael Walzer, *Exodus and Revolution*, New York: Basic Books, 1986; and *In God's Shadow: Politics in the Hebrew Bible*, New Haven: Yale University Press, 2012; David Gutterman, *Prophetic Politics and Christian Social Movements*, Ithaca (NY): Cornell University Press, 2005; Martin Buber, *The Prophetic Faith*, New York: MacMillan, 1949; and *Kingship of God*, New York: Harper & Row, 1967; Cornel West, *Prophesy Deliverance! An Afro-American Revolutionary Christianity*, Louisville (KY) and London: Westminster John Knox Press, 1982; James Darsey, *The Prophetic Tradition and Radical Rhetoric in America*, New York: New York University Press, 1997; Massimo Cacciari and Paolo Prodi, *Occidente senza utopia*, Bologna: Il Mulino, 2016. On modern and premodern prophetic movements of social emancipation see Phillip Haberkern, "Prophetic Rebellions: Radical Urban Theopolitics in the Era of the Reformations," *The Routledge History Handbook of Medieval Revolt*, edited by Justine F. Firnhaber-Baker and Dirk Schoenaers, London and New York: Routledge, 2017, pp. 349–369. See also Samuel Cohn, *Lust for Liberty: The Politics of Social Revolt in Medieval Europe, 1200–1425: Italy, France and Flanders*, Cambridge (MA): Harvard University Press, 2006; Patrick Lantschner, *The Logic of Political Conflict in Medieval Cities: Italy and Southern Low Countries, 1370–1440*, Oxford: Oxford University Press, 2015. On the emancipatory power of prophecy see Luigi Zoja, *Storia dell'arroganza*, Milan: Feltrinelli, 2010, pp. 131–143.

making their compatriots imagine more just forms of social and political life – the most important and necessary condition for emancipation.

Prophetic language has an enormous power. It touches consciences, moves imagination, and energizes the will. It has mobilized peoples against liberty. But it is also very useful to conquer and defend social emancipation. Without the transformation of consciences, without the imagination, without the determination that prophets can generate, it is almost impossible to conquer and defend liberty. It is not necessary that leaders of movements of social emancipation resort to prophetic language. Prophets, however, are especially effective. They devote all their energies and all their lives to the cause, and their total devotion instills faith in their followers and helps to generate movements that live in history. The faith that lives in history is a necessary condition for social emancipation. The journey of liberty is a never-ending journey.

The model of prophetic vision that I have summarized is taken from the *Book of Exodus*. As Michael Walzer writes, *Exodus*'s narration is different from millenarian prophecies. Millenarian prophecies imagine Christ's second coming, the descent of the New Jerusalem from heaven to earth, and the end of history. According to *Exodus*'s model, the people walk towards the Promised Land with God's help and guided by Moses, but they do so, nonetheless, with their own strength and while undergoing suffering and committing errors along the way. The Promised Land is and remains in history. It is not paradise; it is not a perpetual liberation from all things evil, from all the pains and limits of the human condition. It is a new political and social order – one that is more just with respect to the years of slavery in Egypt – that requires the people to be aware of their religious and moral duties.[2] The fundamental difference between the messianic model and the model of *Exodus* is that the first shakes the foundations of kingdoms and condemns corruption, but does not exhort an oppressed people to set out, to fight, and to suffer in order to conquer their own emancipation; the second teaches people to wait for God's intervention. For millenarian prophets, the kingdom of God will come to earth when He so desires; for the prophets inspired by *Exodus*, the New Jerusalem will only come to be if and when the people work and learn how to build it ("the kingdom will come when God ordains it").[3]

Prophets elaborate and announce visions that they see in their imagination. They see the meanings of events from God's perspective. To use the language of Scholastic philosophers, prophets see the meanings of events in the mirror of God ("*speculum Dei*"), or in the mirror of eternity ("*speculum aeternitatis*"). For instance, they see that a plague or the invasions of a foreign army are in fact punishments that God inflicts upon peoples to induce them to return to the

---

[2] Michael Walzer, *Exodus and Revolution*, New York: Basic Books, 1985, p. 17 and pp. 121–122.
[3] On the relationship between millenarianism and prophecy, see: N. Cohn, *The Pursuit of the Millennium: Revolutionary Millenarians and Mystical Anarchists in the Middle Ages*, London: Maurice Temple Smith, 1970.

right path. Prophets often rely on texts, predominantly the scriptures, but they also refer to historical accounts or to the works of philosophers and theologians. They are not copyists, though.[4] Copyists only prepare the various texts that prophets utilize. Nor are the prophets pure philologists who strive to identify and restore the true meaning of words and phrases. From these texts, instead, prophets seek to extract moral nourishment that might regenerate the spirit of their fellow citizens. The prophetic light they have received from God helps them to see; the charity that He has also bestowed on them encourages them to donate their wisdom.

When prophets succeed in persuading a fair number of their compatriots to live by the principles that their consciences dictate, and in convincing them to work together to build lasting social and political orders designed to uphold those principles, we have "prophetic times." We may call "nonprophetic" those times when prophetic voices are powerless: when very few compatriots listen to them, when they do not generate significant social movements, when they fail to generate institutional reforms. The history of Italy offers instructive examples of both prophetic and nonprophetic times.

This idea of the alternation between prophetic and nonprophetic times might suggest that I am proposing a philosophy of history. I have a great admiration for philosophies of history that identify a sense or a final goal of history – that is, if their purpose is to encourage or sustain struggles of emancipation. The last great philosophy of history, Marxism, has taught oppressed classes that the objective and necessary trends of history were on their side. And, for a while, it inspired faith in a final victory. I cannot, however, extract a philosophy of history from the story I am narrating about prophetic times. To begin with, I do not believe in the existence of God and divine Providence, the two pillars of philosophies of history. Nor do I believe in objective or necessary laws of social and political change. Therefore, I cannot assert that new prophetic times will replace our nonprophetic times. I would, of course, be happy to see new prophets capable of inspiring strong and lasting movements of social emancipation. Machiavelli, my intellectual and political mentor, writes that Italy "seems born to resuscitate dead things."[5] If he is right, we could see the rebirth of prophetic times. I would love to share his faith. However, as I explain at the end of this Introduction, I am inclined to believe that prophetic times are gone forever. If this is a philosophy of history, so be it. I prefer, however, to describe my views as modest and pessimistic beliefs.

My goal is not to explain, in the style of a social or a political scientist, the rise and decline of prophecies of social redemption. I would not know where to

---

[4] See the splendid essay by Carlo Ossola, *L'avenir de nos origines. Le copiste et le prophète*, Grenoble: Édition Jèrôme Millon, 2004, Préface, pp. 9–24.

[5] Niccolò Machiavelli, *Dell'arte della guerra*, in *Tutte le opere*, edited by Mario Martelli Florence: Sansoni, 1971, p. 389; English translation: Niccolò Machiavelli, *The Art of War*, translated, edited, and with a commentary by Christopher Lynch, Chicago and London: The University of Chicago Press, 2003, p. 164.

begin the search for an explanation. I also believe that a search for explanations would be an uninteresting effort. We simply cannot explain moral and intellectual changes, if by explaining we mean to indicate general laws or causes of some sort. I also admit that I am not examining the meaning of the concepts of prophets and prophecy from an analytical perspective. The goal of this study is just to narrate how prophetic languages have helped collective efforts of social emancipation, to explore the decline of prophetic voices during the centuries of Italy's servitude, and to offer some philosophical and political considerations on prophecy and visions of social emancipations in our times.

1.1 THE STORY

Scholars have studied, with excellent results, the emancipatory power of prophetic languages, drawing mainly from the Bible, the Puritan Revolution, the American Revolution, and the Civil Rights Movement. They have also illuminated specific aspects of the Italian prophetic tradition. No work, to my knowledge, has reconstructed the full account of the presence and impact of the prophetic languages of emancipation throughout Italian history.[6] It is worth studying the larger picture of the connections between prophecy and social

---

[6] On prophecy and social emancipation in the history of Italy see Ottavia Niccoli, *Profeti e popolo nell'Italia del Rinascimento*, Rome and Bari: Laterza, 1987; and *La vita religiosa nell'Italia moderna. Secoli XV–XVIII*, Rome: Carocci, 2008; Stephanie Toussaint, "Profetare alla fine del Quattrocento," *Studi Savonaroliani*, edited by Gian Carlo Garfagnini, Florence: SISMEL, 1996; Gabriella Zarri, "Potere carismatico e potere politico nelle corti italiane del Rinascimento," *Poteri carismatici e informali: chiesa e società medioevali*, edited by Agostino Paravicini Bagliani and André Vauchez, Palermo: Sellerio, 1992, pp. 175–191; Marjorie Reeves, *The Influence of Prophecy in the Later Middle Ages: A Study in Joachimism*, Oxford: Oxford University Press, 1969; Henri de Lubac, S.J., *La postérité spirituelle de Joachim de Flore*, vol. II, Paris: Lethielleux, 1979–1981; Cesare Vasoli, "L'influenza di Gioacchino da Fiore sul profetismo italiano della fine del Quattrocento e del primo Cinquecento," *Il profetismo gioachimita tra Quattrocento e Cinquecento: Atti del III Congresso Internazionale di Studi Gioachimiti (S. Giovanni in Fiore, 17–21 settembre 1989)*, edited by Gian Luca Podestà, Genoa: Marietti, 1991; Morton W. Bloomfield, "Recent Scholarship on Joachim of Fiore and His Influence," *Prophecy and Millenarianism: Essays in Honour of Marjorie Reeves*, edited by Ann Williams, Burnt Hill: Longman, 1980, pp. 21–52; Gian Luca Podestà, *Il tempo dell'Apocalisse: vita di Gioacchino da Fiore*, Rome and Bari: Laterza; Raoul Manselli, "L'attesa dell'età nuova ed il gioachimismo," *L'attesa dell'età nuova nella spiritualità della fine del Medioevo. Atti del III Convegno storico internazionale (Todi, 16–19 ottobre 1960)*, Spoleto: Fondazione Cisam, 1962, pp. 145–170; in the same volume see also Eugenio Garin, "L'attesa dell'età nuova e la 'renovatio,'" pp. 9–35; Debby Nirit Ben-Aryeh, *Renaissance Florence in the Rhetoric of Two Popular Preachers: Giovanni Dominici (1346–1419) and Bernardino da Siena (1380–1444)*, Florence: Brepols, 2001; Raoul Manselli, "Pietro di Giovanni Olivi ed Ubertino da Casale (a proposito della Lectura super Apocalipsim e dell'Arbor vitae crucifixae Jesu)," *Studi Medievali* IV (1965), pp. 95–122; Ovidio Capitani, "Per il significato dell'attesa della nuova età in Niccolò da Cusa," *L'attesa dell'età nuova nella spiritualità della fine del Medioevo. Atti del III Convegno storico internazionale (Todi, 16–19 ottobre 1960)*, Spoleto: Fondazione Cisam, 1962, pp. 198–216; and Cynthia L. Polecretti, *Preaching Peace in Renaissance Italy: Bernardino of*

emancipation over the centuries because it provides valuable intellectual and political insights, as I shall discuss at the end of this Introduction.

I have chosen to begin my narration with Dante (1265–1321) because I maintain that he was the first to employ prophetic language to sustain visions of political emancipation. In his *Epistles*, Dante exhorts the emperor and the kings of Italy with the words of a person who has been able to see the mind of God. In the *Divine Comedy*, he shapes the image of the prophet as a social critic who denounces the moral and political vices of his compatriots, and who exhorts them to emancipate their consciences. This image of the prophet has had an immense impact on Italian intellectual and political history. Convinced of having received divine inspiration, Dante was able to find and deliver redeeming words, even if he was perfectly aware that his contemporaries would not listen. The content of Dante's prophetic message is less relevant to my story than its form, that is, his poetry. He conveyed his prophetic messages with finest words that only great poets can find, and reinaugurated (after classical antiquity) the tradition of prophetic poetry. The chief tenet of this tradition was the belief that prophets and poets are similar figures because both have received divine inspiration, imagine new times and new social orders, and move their compatriots' imagination with the power of words.

Not all prophets of social emancipation were poets. Girolamo Savonarola was a preacher who employed a rather unrefined language and detested poets. Yet he persuaded the people of Florence to institute a republican government.[7] In his sermons, he often claimed that a republican government was the most apt to sustain true Christian life and the most fit to Florentine mores and tradition. The most distinctive trait of his preaching was its prophetic tone. He declared over and over that God had inspired him and revealed His desire for a republican government in Florence. Savonarola was the moral founding father of the first prophetic republic in history – a republic that, upon his injunction,

---

Siena and His Audience, Washington, DC: CUA Press, 2000. I shall indicate more specific bibliographical references in each chapter.

[7] Between the end of the 1400s and the first decades of the 1500s, prophetic preaching inspired and sustained radical experiences of social emancipation not only in different historical and cultural contexts – such as in Prague, Florence, and Münster – but also with strong theocratic and millenarian currents. See Phillip Haberken's excellent essay, "Prophetic Rebellions: Radical Urban Theopolitics in the Era of the Reformations," *The Routledge History Handbook of Medieval Revolt*, edited by J. F. Firnhaber-Baker and D. Schoenaers, London and New York: Routledge, 2017, pp. 349–369. On the struggles against tyranny in modern Europe, see Samuel Cohn, *Lust for Liberty: The Politics of Social Revolt in Medieval Europe, 1200–1425: Italy, France and Flanders*, Cambridge, MA: Harvard University Press, 2006; Patrick Lantschner, *The Logic of Political Conflict in Medieval Cities: Italy and Southern Low Countries, 1370–1440*, Oxford: Oxford University Press, 2015. On Italian prophetic literature between the end of the fifteenth and the early sixteenth centuries, see the excellent essay of Lorenzo Manenti, *Giorgio Luti da Siena a Lucca. Il viaggio di un mito fra Rinascimento e Controriforma*, Siena: Accademia Senese degli Intronati, 2008.

declared Christ as its king.[8] The republic that Savonarola helped to found lasted from 1494 until 1512. Savonarola's authority lasted even less, despite his prophetic charisma. By order of Pope Alexander VI, he was tried and executed by Florentine governors on May 23, 1498. His prophetic claim that God wants us to be free, and that we must therefore found and defend republican government, continued to live on in Italian religious and political imagination. As I have documented in the second and third parts of my essay, Savonarola's other chief teaching – that republican liberty necessitates a moral and religious reform that emancipates individual consciences from any form of submission to human potentates – outlived his death.

Readers of *The Prince* are familiar with Machiavelli's statement that whereas all armed prophets succeeded, all unarmed prophets failed. For Machiavelli, Savonarola was the example of unarmed prophets, while Moses served as the model for armed prophets. What readers and scholars often ignore is that Machiavelli, as a realist, was aware of the redeeming power of prophets, including unarmed ones. In adding the power of arms – as well as the power of political wisdom – to the power of prophecy, he did not at all mean to dismiss the power of prophecy. The redeemer whom Machiavelli invokes in the closing pages of *The Prince* is a person who has received from God the order of trying to liberate Italy from foreign domination, and who can count on God's friendship. The redeemer is a prophet: but must be armed. Only if we read *The Prince* within the prophetic context in which Machiavelli lived and wrote can we see that his vision of the armed prophet is a radical innovation in the history of political emancipation.

Machiavelli never claimed that he had received a special inspiration or revelation from God, as prophets do. But he wrote as if he were a prophet to whom God had revealed His mind, and who was therefore able to interpret the meaning of events. Like prophets who extract spiritual and moral nourishment from scripture, Machiavelli extracts his moral and spiritual nourishment (*"quel sapore che hanno le istorie"*) from histories as well as the scriptures: The nourishment that he hoped could resurrect Italians from their moral and political corruption. I have considered the possibility that Machiavelli's

---

[8] By republic I mean here what Savonarola meant, that is, a popular government opposed to monarchy. In the larger sense of republic as state in general or legitimate political constitution, the first prophetic republic was of course the Hebrew republic (*"respublica Hebraeorum"*) established by Moses. See Lea Campos Boralevi, "Classical Foundational Myths of European Republicanism: The Jewish Commonwealth," *Republicanism: A Shared European Heritage*, vol. 1, edited by Martin van Gelderen and Quentin Skinner, Cambridge: Cambridge University Press, 2002, pp. 247–261, and Eric Nelson, *The Hebrew Republic. Jewish Sources and the Interpretation of European Political Thought*, Cambridge, MA and London: Harvard University Press, 2010. The Italian republics of the eleventh–fourteenth centuries produced a republican Christianity based on the belief that God loves republics, but they were not founded by prophets who spoke on behalf of God. See my *As if God Existed: Religion and Liberty in the History of Italy*, Princeton and Oxford: Princeton University Press, 2012.

prophetic phrases were mere rhetorical adornments. However, the sheer number of them – to say nothing of the pathos and elegance with which they are written – precludes this possibility. They surface not only in all his political, historical, and literary works, but also in the letters where he revealed his deepest fears and hopes. I am tempted to suggest that he has concealed his prophetic inspiration behind the façade of his smile, as he loved to do with his other beliefs. But I resist the temptation, for I do not have enough textual evidence to sustain this notion. Instead, I state resolutely that Machiavelli wrote prophetic pages that have had a remarkable impact on the history of social and political emancipation.

In 1527, the year of Machiavelli's death, the Florentine aristocracy managed to put an end to the Medici regime and to institute a popular government that lasted until 1530, when it capitulated to a long siege of imperial forces. Time and again, and with ever greater fervor as the sieges became increasingly unbearable, prophets spoke in churches and in the Great Council Hall to exhort the Florentine citizens and political elite to revere the popular government as a precious gift offered by God to help them live a true Christian life. Prophets also admonished the people to regard the war's horrible hardships as God's way of testing Florentines' faith in Christ as well as their devotion to political liberty. Prominent members of the government delivered prophetic speeches to the citizens and the army to reinforce the persuasion that the Republic was under God's protection and would therefore triumph over its powerful enemies. In addition to sermons and speeches, the republican government promoted prayers and rituals of repentance to invoke God's help. The Last Florentine Republic was the most prophetic regime in Italy's history. However, neither its prophets nor the devotion of its rulers and citizens saved it. The Republic's defeat also marked the defeat of prophecy. With the defeat of prophecy, hopes and visions of emancipation also faded.

For about three centuries after the fall of the Last Florentine Republic, there were prophets who preached and advocated for radical social changes on behalf of justice and moral regeneration. The best example is Tommaso Campanella, who repeatedly asserted that God had entrusted him with the mission of redeeming Italy from tyrants and of bringing Italians back to the path of true Christian life. None of these prophets succeeded, however, in inspiring significant movements or political efforts for political emancipation. In this sense, it is fair to speak of nonprophetic times. In the second part of this work, I have tried to identify the intellectual and political changes that have rendered the Italian context utterly inhospitable and hostile to prophets in general and, accordingly, to prophets of social emancipation.

To begin with, in December 1516, the Fifth Lateran Council solemnly condemned and prohibited prophetic preaching. This prohibition did not silence prophets, but it did make their mission and their lives harder. A much more effective deterrent was the Council of Trent's (1545–1563) obligation for all baptized persons to confess at least once a year. Although individual confessors only had the power to impose light sanctions, they could count on the powerful help of inquisitors who could have transgressors imprisoned, tortured, and burned alive. Confessors and inquisitors together were able to compel believers to reveal their consciences and therefore conform to the Church's power. Politically subjugated by foreign powers, and by open or veiled domestic tyrannies, Italians in general became morally dominated and, as a result, deaf to prophetic voices. The need to protect one's conscience from ecclesiastical and secular authorities' power encouraged the proliferation of works teaching how to hide and dissimulate one's religious beliefs. Widespread social practices began to include attending Holy Mass for the sole purpose of not generating suspicion of heresy or disbelief; going to the required annual confession without believing in the value of confession; taking oaths with the secret intention of not respecting them. Truthful persons who stood up for their principles became targets of scorn and laughter. With their pretentions of announcing truths that God had revealed to them, prophets were totally out of place in Counterreformation Italy.

Around the second half of the sixteenth century, prophets of self-denial came to the forefront. As a massive body of texts addressed to religious communities and to laypeople attests, the new prophets urged the faithful to abandon vain ideas of redeeming the world to pursue instead their souls' salvation through practices of self-denial and mortification. The prophets of self-denial emphatically denied that God communicates His will to human beings. They also maintained that it is impossible to read God's mind through the scriptures. True Christians must sacrifice, humiliate, and annihilate themselves, just as Christ did on the cross. They must welcome all the defeats, pains, and sufferings that God inflicts upon them as reminders of their utter insignificance before Him. Dismissing the old humanist ideal of imitating God through charity and service for the common good, the new prophets championed practices of mortification designed to increase the faithful's awareness of their distance from God. While the Christian writers of the 1300s and 1400s had elaborated the idea that God reserves the highest ranks of paradise to founders and redeemers of republics, the prophets of self-denial preached that Christians must reject active life for an interior life of mental prayers. Glory, once the highest value of humanist moral and political theory, now belonged only to God, and, for these prophets, any attempt to seek earthly glory was conceited and futile. With this set of strokes, prophets of self-denial discredited the prophecies and prophets of social and political redemption.

The Church's effort to deafen moral consciences to prophetic voices found a powerful ally in the language of reason of state that attained a remarkable intellectual hegemony in seventeenth-century Italy. The father of the modern language of reason of state was Francesco Guicciardini (1483–1540), who framed the concept in his *Dialogo del reggimento di Firenze* (*Dialogue on the Government of Florence*, 1521). He stated that governors cannot maintain states that find guidance in a collective moral conscience illuminated by

Christian principles, as Savonarola had taught. Yet after the Sack of Rome, around 1528, the same Guicciardini retrieved transcripts of Savonarola's sermons from his father's archive. Perhaps he was searching in Savonarola's prophetic words the light that could have helped him to understand, better than the light of reason, the causes of the tragedies of the Church and Italy. Guicciardini never published the *Dialogo del reggimento di Firenze*. The author who launched the concept of reason of state and inaugurated the new intellectual tradition was Giovanni Botero. Published in Venice in 1589, his influential *Della ragion di stato* (*Of Reason of State*) argues that reason of state must be the guiding light of political action. Since reason of state teaches the means suitable for preserving existing states, prophets who advocate for the reform of political orders and mores are therefore fastidious and dangerous enemies. Prophets exhort people to listen to the voice of conscience. Supporters of reason of state regard declamations on behalf of conscience as nothing but childish illusions to be met with condescending laughter. Governing states is an affair for prudent individuals who know how the world works, not for prophets and zealots who claim to be able to redeem the world in the name of mysterious illuminations graciously granted to them by God.

Inaugurated in its modern form by Thomas More in 1516 with his *Utopia* (*De optimo statu reipublicae deque nova insula utopia*) as a language of denunciation of social injustices, utopian political language also took a conservative turn in seventeenth-century Italy. Except for Tommaso Campanella, who composed the *Città del sole* (*The City of the Sun*) in 1602 to advocate a communist theocracy, utopian literature denounced visions of social emancipation as unrealistic or plainly wrong. Utopian theories are radically different from prophetic visions. Unlike prophets, the characters of utopian narrations never declare that they have received a revelation from God. The wisdom that they impart is entirely human. They retell what they have witnessed on some remote island, with their own eyes, and without the help of any prophetic light. Whereas prophets urge their compatriots to edify a new social order through painful struggles and sacrifices, utopians say that a land of perfect justice and harmony already exists. In fact, it is ready to welcome all those who are willing to sail there and who, upon arrival, are prepared to obey the laws of the place. It is too bad that the islands of utopia exist, by definition, nowhere. Even when utopian texts indirectly suggest modest reforms in existing polities, they never issue their suggestions with any sense of moral urgency, as prophets do. To cite the obvious example, Savonarola wanted Florence to immediately put his directives into practice; Machiavelli wanted a redeemer of Italy to descend on the scene the next day, at the very latest. Utopians calmly discussed reforms to carry out at a slow pace, after careful examination, and with the greatest respect for social structures and mores. They were de facto helping the theorists of reason of state. While the theorists of reason of state were preaching the conservation of existing social orders, the utopians were inviting to imagine radically different social orders that existed, however, nowhere. Prophets had endeavored to empower imagination; utopians made every effort to make it sterile and powerless.

Despite the power of its critics and enemies, prophets of social emancipation did not entirely disappear in Counterreformation Italy. The Florentine republican Antonio Brucioli (1498–1566) wrote learned pages to exalt the value of prophecy. In the early 1540s, he courageously kept alive the tradition of republican prophecy by collecting, editing, and publishing a selection of Savonarola's sermons. Savonarola was the prophet, as Brucioli himself called him, who preached the true word of God. Whereas Brucioli wrote of prophecy and prophets, Tommaso Campanella (whom I have already cited as the author of the utopian work *The City of the Sun*) repeatedly proclaimed that he was inspired by God. Until his last days, he wrote prophetic texts announcing the return, after many tribulations and calamities, of the golden age of Christian life. Other writers persisted in composing texts interpreting Florence's history and future from a prophetic perspective. Speaking on God's behalf, they warned the Medici that God's wrath would surely befall them if they failed in carrying out their Christian duty to govern in justice. They also continued to proclaim the imminent renewal of the Church and the advent of the true Christian life. Francesco de' Ricci, in the prophetic letters that he addressed to popes and kings between 1520 and the early 1530s, announced that Florence would attain unprecedented greatness and that redemption would come after great suffering. His words were as sincere and as eloquent as Savonarola's words. His life was exemplary. Nonetheless, his vision of Florence as the New Jerusalem had lost the persuasive power to move Florentine minds and hearts. Francesco Pucci (1543–1597), a Florentine with a humanistic intellectual education, proclaimed that new prophets shall come and prove the purity of their inspiration through their deeds. With their divine authority, they shall lead the reform of religion and the republic. He was confident that such a grand deed was imminent because he had received a revelation from God and an angel. He faced a horrible death with impressive courage. Yet his voice had no impact. The conscience of Italian elites and popular classes had become deaf to prophetic exhortations. Even if they were listening, Italians had lost the moral strength to put the prophets' teachings into practice.

The most lethal blow to prophets and prophecies came, however, from seventeenth- and eighteenth-century philosophers, especially from libertine freethinkers. Their main line of attack was against the prophets' pretension of divine inspiration. The prophets' powers of predicting future events – they maintained – were the results of purely natural causes, such as the action of celestial bodies on melancholic humor. God had nothing to do with it. Surely, the most subversive and irreverent line of attack was the claim that Moses, Christ, and Muhammad were clever impostors who feigned to speak on God's behalf to fool princes and peoples and thus gain power and fame. Self-proclaimed prophets cannot boast any special wisdom on human affairs. Philosophers are to be trusted as reliable teachers of moral and political wisdom because they rely on reason. One of the most influential libertine critiques of prophets and religion was the anonymous *Treatise of the Three Impostors* published for the first time in 1719. Its author went so far as to assert that ancient peoples, much wiser than their modern counterparts, put prophets like Christ to death. Moses only escaped this punishment because he had an army to protect him. Moreover, a critical examination reveals that the scriptures are full of errors and inconsistencies, further proof that philosophers – not deceitful prophets – must lead political and social emancipation.

Many philosophers were indeed leaders of the so-called "Jacobin republics" that were born in Italy between 1796 and 1799 with the aid of French armies that were invading the peninsula. Of these republics, the Neapolitan Republic stands out for its intellectual and political importance. The shared principle of the Jacobin revolutions, as historians have called them, was that reason must guide political constitutions and deliberations. Many revolutionary leaders also believed that the newly founded republics needed a civil religion modeled after Jean-Jacques Rousseau's indications in the *Social Contract* (1762). A few Catholic priests assisted the effort of establishing the civil religion by preaching sermons in which they explained that Christianity was perfectly compatible with, indeed friendly to, republican liberty. The intellectual and moral excellence of its proponents notwithstanding, this new civil religion framed in a rational language did not touch the imagination of Italian urban plebs, not to mention those in rural areas. Among the people, much more effective was the message proclaimed by the preachers of the monarchical and Catholic Counterrevolution that eventually put a brutal end to the philosophers' republics. These preachers openly declared that God had inspired and ordered them to mobilize their compatriots to destroy the Jacobins and to defend the religion of their ancestors. While the fall of the Florentine Republic in 1530 was a defeat for the prophets of republican liberty, the fall of the Neapolitan Republic of 1799 was a defeat for the philosophers.

While the Jacobin republics collapsed, many new prophetic voices emerged in France to inspire political, national, and social redemption. Central to this prophetic movement was the belief that radical transformation was imminent. Several writers prophesied the coming of a new era, during which liberty and peace would at last triumph. Saint-Simon, on the authority of divine inspiration, foretold the advent of a religion of humanity that would realize the true principles of Christian love. Another chief work of the prophetic renaissance is *Die Erziehung des Menschengeschlechts* (*The Education of Humankind*) by Gotthold Ephraim Lessing (1729–1781). Published for the first time in Germany in 1780, it gained much wider circulation when it was translated into French by Saint-Simon's disciples and published in a volume that also contained *Le Nouveau Christianisme*. The core of Lessing's prophetic message was the belief that God reveals His will to humanity according to a precise order and measure. The chosen ones to whom He unveils His will have a duty to educate their people and all the peoples of the earth. Thanks to the efforts of the prophets, humanity shall be composed of individuals who live their lives by the principle of duty. Within the same intellectual context, Lamennais (Hugues-Félicité-Robert de Lamennais (1782–1854)), emerges as a prophet of religious and moral reform. He did not doubt that prophets can penetrate and read God's mind and see the coming of a time in which liberty and civility shall triumph over oppression and barbarism. Lamennais used a Christian language to convey his prophecies of a new temporal order. In his "salute to the future," he wrote that Christian eschatology inspires the hope for a more just society. He believed that poetry had the prophetic power of spreading the seeds of the new epoch and interpreted history as progress toward equality guided by divine Providence that shall bring about God's kingdom on Earth. Pierre Leroux (1797–1871) gave his prophecies a republican and socialist bent. George Sand (1804–1876), whose real name was Amandine Aurore Lucile Dupin, announced in her novel *Spiridion* the coming of new prophets who, like Moses and Christ, would lead humanity along the path of moral and social redemption. Yet another hero of the prophetic renaissance was Théodore Jouffroy (1796–1842). In his *Mélanges philosophiques*, published in 1833, he traced in a much-idealized fashion the different phases of the clash between old Catholic dogmas and skepticism, and sketched the prophecy of a world renovated by a new faith laboriously conquered. This faith in truth and virtue shall establish a kingdom of truth, engender in the souls an unspeakable love and enthusiasm. The writer who asserted with the greatest emphasis that God had entrusted him with a providential mission was, however, Lamartine (Alphonse Marie Louis de Prat de Lamartine, 1790–1869). Educated within a conservative milieu, he gradually elaborated republican ideas combined with rigorous Christian principles. Alexis de Tocqueville (1805–1859) too, in his *Democracy in America* (1835 and 1840), reveals a remarkable intellectual debt to the prophetic context in which he lived his youth. He did not assert that he wrote his book inspired by God. He stated, however, that the American democracy reveals God's plan.

In Italy, too, there emerged a number of prophetic poets who called Italians to commit themselves to toil and struggle for their liberty. Whereas Dante appealed to the emperor and the princes of Italy, the prophetic poets of the early nineteenth century appealed to the Italian people. Vittorio Alfieri, Ugo Foscolo, Alessandro Manzoni, and Goffredo Mameli, to cite only the most important names in my story, used the full range of prophetic themes. Combining the power of prophecy and the pathos of poetry, they infused Italian minds with the faith in a God who wanted Italy, and all nations, to be free from foreign domination. They urged Italians to lift themselves out of servile habits and, in doing so, redeem themselves. Thanks also to prophetic poets, the Risorgimento, along with the anti-fascist resistance, was the most important experience of political emancipation in Italy's history. It was a long journey (1821–1870) marked by wars, clandestine activity, resistance, exiles, and executions through which Italians attained political independence and national unity. My generation grew up with the unexamined persuasion that the Risorgimento was a failed national revolution because it did not mobilize the popular classes, was unable to give Italy a republican government, and left intolerable social injustices and privileges intact. Regardless of its limitations, the Risorgimento remains an extraordinary moral and political accomplishment that was sustained and fueled by prophetic visions and sentiments.

Among the prophetic voices of the Italian Risorgimento, Giuseppe Mazzini stands out as the most powerful as well as the most intellectually and politically innovative. Like the prophetic poets, he proclaimed that God desired the emancipation not just of Italy, but of all oppressed peoples. As early as 1826, in his reflections on Dante, Mazzini began to exemplify the model of a militant prophet who announces God's will and, more significantly, works with his compatriots to bring about his prophetic vision. Consistent with his ideal of the unity between thought and action, Mazzini dedicated his life to promoting insurrections, which were poorly designed and badly executed, founding republican associations, organizing the moral and intellectual education of the working classes, and denouncing the corruption of the Catholic Church and the covetousness of the Piedmontese kings. Like the prophets of the *Old Testament*, he exposed how moral strength and true love of liberty were lacking in his fellow Italians. But he also believed in the possibility of their liberation. To this mission he dedicated his life's efforts. Convinced that God had entrusted him with the mission to lead the emancipation of Italy and all humanity, Mazzini radically transformed the tradition of redemptive prophecy. He claimed that only a religious faith founded in the ideal of liberty can provide oppressed peoples with the moral strength required to undergo the process of emancipation.

Another distinctive aspect of Mazzini's prophetic vision was his persuasion that, in addition to republican institutions, true emancipation requires measures designed to attenuate social inequalities and to undertake the intellectual and civil education of the popular classes. Savonarola had promoted a republican government for Florence and a religious reform for Italy; on issues of social justice, though, he never went beyond the conventional exhortations to be compassionate to the poor, widows, and orphans. He never conceived, and never urged, measures of social justice. Machiavelli composed powerful prophetic pages for Italy's freedom from foreign domination; regarding social justice, he only asserted that poverty should not prevent virtuous citizens from attaining the highest political offices in the republic. Furthermore, Machiavelli presented his considerations on this subject as counsels of political wisdom – not elements of a prophetic vision, as Mazzini did.

Mazzini asserted that God wanted Italians to fight for the liberty of their country and for the liberty of all peoples, no matter how distant or different they were. Savonarola preached in defense of Florence's liberty, but justified Florence's domination over Tuscany and promised the Florentines even further greatness, if they accepted his prophetic principles. Machiavelli was a republican patriot but never connected love of one's homeland to love of humanity.

He never advocated the religious duty of defending the liberty of all nations, never considered the free association of all peoples as the fulfillment of God's plan on earth. Mazzini declared that upholding the ideal of humanity is a duty that comes directly from God, just like the duty of upholding the liberty of one's own country. No prophet before him had outlined or actively worked for a vision of emancipation that encompassed national independence, republican self-government, social justice, religious renovation, and international solidarity. Mazzini wrote a truly new chapter in the long history of redemptive prophets.

Mazzini's prophetic message was too challenging for nineteenth-century Italians, indeed probably too demanding for all peoples of all times. His words had only a minor impact on the hearts and minds of the Italians. Italy's independence and unification under the hegemony of the House of Savoy was his political defeat. When Mazzini died in Pisa on March 10, 1872, under a fake name in order to avoid arrest, he was by then a powerless prophet, the symbol of a Risorgimento that had failed to achieve true political and social emancipation of Italy. This is the conventional story told about Mazzini. But it is a wrong story, or at least an incomplete one. More than any other prophet before and after him, he inspired many Italians to devote their lives to the cause of liberty. This was an extraordinary achievement for a people that had almost lost even the memories of liberty. Yet another remarkable fact is that some of his disciples, such as Goffredo Mameli, also became prophetic poets and soldiers who bequeathed future generations a rare example of devotion to the ideal of liberty. Others, like Ippolito Nievo, kept alive Mazzini's vision of emancipation with novels that shaped the mentality of post-Risorgimento Italy. Giuseppe Garibaldi was the best example of a Mazzinian patriot. Although he and Mazzini contrasted rather sharply politically – especially regarding the role of the Savoy monarchs in the struggle for independence and national unification – Garibaldi remained faithful to Mazzini's religious vision of patriotism until his last days. In his letters and public speeches, he defended and advocated Mazzini's prophetic vision of a God who wants the liberty of all peoples. Italy became a democratic republic in 1946, some seventy years after Mazzini's death. His prophetic vision came true, at least in part. Can we really regard a prophet who left so many marks on history as a failure?

The poets and the writers who composed prophetic words, fought, and died for the cause are a distinctive feature of Italy's Risorgimento. But what is truly unique, from the perspective of intellectual history, is the prophetic opera: An artform in which splendid music enhances the power of words. Represented for the first time in 1842 – just a few years before the Risorgimento's great battles in Lombardy and the insurrections of Rome and Venice – Giuseppe Verdi's *Nabucco* offered the Italian popular classes the famous chorus "Va' pensiero." It is a hymn that contains a touching invocation to God to send prophets capable of resuscitating the moral strength that the struggle for liberty demands. Verdi himself ordered the libretto's author, Temistocle Solera, to include a prophecy of emancipation in the opera. When he composed the music of *Nabucco*, Verdi was a lonely, worn-out man, much like Machiavelli was when he wrote the prophetic words of the "Exhortation to liberate Italy" in 1513. Their stories suggest that prophetic music or words come from persons who have descended into the abyss of despair and want to resurrect themselves by devoting their best energies to the resurrection of their homeland. Prophetic inspiration comes when the hardships of life leave great human beings with nothing but their conscience as their last resource.

Political leaders, historians, poets, and writers of post-Risorgimento Italy – even those who had been fervent patriots – all announced that the times of prophets were over. Rather than prophets who mobilized the popular classes for vain and dangerous visions of emancipation, they proclaimed that the new independent and unified Italy needed science, military might, social unity. The few surviving prophets of social emancipation – like Davide Lazzaretti (1834–1878), the "prophet of Mount Amiata" – preached in remote corners of the peninsula to small communities. Prophetic voices also began to emerge within the socialist movement. Working against the prevailing winds of "scientific" or "positivist" ideology, a few organizers, and militants, like Camillo Prampolini (1859–1930), offered the movement prophetic visions intended to teach Italian workers and peasants that they could establish an earthly New Jerusalem of social justice. Unlike their positivist counterparts who believed in the objective and necessary laws of history, Prampolini and his comrades stressed that workers could attain their emancipation only if they had sincere faith in justice, that socialism is the logical consequence of Christ's message. Prampolini's ideas had a wide and lasting impact in Reggio Emilia and the surrounding areas. But they were the final reverberations of the Risorgimento's prophetic spirit, rather than signs of new prophetic times.

I had considered ending my story on this note, but then I came across the essay *The Prophets of the Risorgimento* that Giovanni Gentile published in 1923. The main ideologist of Fascism, Gentile claimed that Mussolini's regime was the fulfillment of the visions of the Risorgimento's prophets, particularly Mazzini and Gioberti. Gentile's assertion is a colossal falsification of history worthy of the fascist ideologue that he was. Mazzini dedicated his life to the ideal of an independent, united, republican Italy committed to defend the liberty of all peoples. With the king as head of state, Mussolini established a totalitarian regime that destroyed all civil and political liberty and pursued imperial domination. Fascist ideology and the fascist regime were the most blatant betrayal of Mazzini's and his followers' political ideals. To consider Mussolini a prophet is equally wrong. He was not a prophet because he did not speak or act on behalf of God. To remain under God, as prophets must remain, would have been, for him, an unacceptable limitation on his power. When he announced the fateful decision to drag Italy into war on June 10, 1940, Mussolini did not say that God had guided his decision, nor did he invoke God's help. King George VI of England invoked God's help when he declared war on Germany; the President of the United States Franklin Delano Roosevelt invoked God's help when he declared war on Japan. Mussolini did not do so because he did not need God's help.

The chief goal of the fascist political religion was to silence moral consciences. The prophets of emancipation, to the contrary, appealed to individuals' moral conscience and exhorted them to accept principles of political liberty and justice. The Italian Fascist regime feared prophets because it is impossible to control or buy persons who speak and act on behalf of God. Conversely, the anti-fascist Resistance needed prophets capable of resurrecting moral liberty. The best minds of the Italian anti-fascism, such as Piero Gobetti (1901–1926) and Carlo Rosselli (1899–1937), understood this piece of moral and political wisdom very well. In different ways, they both evoked the *Old Testament* prophets who taught that even in dark times, when chances of success are slim or nonexistent, it is necessary to resist unjust power because moral conscience so commands. Guided by his faith in the religion of liberty, Benedetto Croce (1866–1952) wrote touching pages in his *History of Europe in the Nineteenth Century* where he offered Italian anti-fascists a comforting and empowering vision of Italy's resurrection in a free and united Europe. The scholar who best understood and defended the spirit and legacy of the Italian Resistance, Piero Calamandrei (1899–1956) declared, with magnificent and inspiring words, that religious sentiment had made the anti-fascist fight possible. He also alluded to the presence of a divine voice that called the most generous of Italians to begin the armed resistance against the fascists and the German occupying forces. No anti-fascist intellectual or political leader, however, presented himself as a prophet endowed with divine inspiration or revelation. But in the early days of the Constituent Assembly in September 1946, Giorgio La Pira (1904–1977), a man of sincere Christian faith, proposed a preamble containing a declaration, "before God," of human rights for the new Republican Constitution. After a discussion of high moral and intellectual content, he withdrew his proposal as he realized that his preamble would have divided the Assembly. Had the Constituent Assembly accepted the preamble with the invocation to God, the Republic would have been, at least in principle, a republic under God, a prophetic republic radically opposed to the totalitarian ideology that venerated the "duce" as an omnipotent God.

1.2 THE (TENTATIVE) MORAL OF THE STORY

English-speaking scholars who have patiently read this Introduction thus far are probably pondering whether this story about prophetic times has some relevance outside Italy's borders. I suspect that an accurate study in the history of ideas would probably identify references to Italian prophetic texts in the literature of the Puritan Revolution, of the American Revolution, as well as in the writings and speeches of Abraham Lincoln and Martin Luther King, to mention only the most obvious cases and names. Such research, however, lies beyond the scope of my study. Hopefully, other scholars will be willing to tackle it. Here I can only suggest possible analogies and echoes of Italian prophetic times in English and American texts that have utilized prophetic language to sustain political and social emancipation.

As we read in Michael Walzer's classic work *The Revolution of the Saints*, some 800 English Protestants went to the continent as exiles in the years after the Catholic Queen Mary ascended to the throne of England. John Knox (c.1514–1572), one of the most prominent of this group, outlined conceptions of the nature of prophecy and of the role of prophets that were very similar to the ideas that Savonarola had preached in Florence. For instance, in his *Appellation from the Sentence Pronounced by the Bishops and Clergy* of 1558, Knox asserted that his duty was "to call [...] this people [...] again to the true service of God."[9] In a letter to Mrs. Bowes, he claimed that he was feeling utterly inadequate to the task, and yet, he could not fail in responding to the prophetic call: "Albeit I never lack the presence and plain image of my own wretched infirmity, yet seeing sin so manifestly abound in all estate, I am compelled to thunder out the threatenings of God against obstinate rebels."[10] Like Savonarola, Knox would have gladly fled from the prophetic task. But his conscience compelled him to discharge his duty to admonish and to correct his compatriots, princes and kings included. Indeed, Knox wrote in 1554 that "the prophet of God sometimes may teach treason against kings, and yet neither he, nor such as obey the words spoken in the Lord's name by him, offends God."[11] Knox's prophetic eloquence was more brutal and thunderous than Savonarola's, especially when he declared:

Albeit the abominable idolators triumph for a moment, yet approaches the hour when God's vengeance shall strike [and] not only their souls but their vile carcasses shall be plagued [...] Their cities shall be burnt, their land shall be laid waste, and their daughters shall be defiled, their children shall fall on the edge of the sword, mercy shall they find none because they have refused the God of all mercy.

While they may have differed in terms of boisterousness, Knox's and Savonarola's polemical targets – tyranny and religious corruption – were the same. Like Savonarola, Knox wanted to emancipate the world from Satan's domination and institute not just a good republic, but a New Jerusalem of citizens living under God's law.

Another example of the prophetic language of emancipation in the English-speaking world is, of course, Abraham Lincoln. His speeches and writings offer us copious evidence that he believed himself to be "an humble instrument in the hands of the Almighty, and of this, his almost chosen people[,]" for preserving the promise of the American Revolution, as he said in Trenton on February 21,

---

[9] Michael Walzer, *The Revolution of the Saints. A Study in the Origins of Radical Politics*, Cambridge, MA and London: Harvard University Press, 1965, p. 98.
[10] Ibid., p. 99.   [11] Ibid., p. 100.

1861.[12] Addressing a delegation of progressive friends on June 21, 1862, Lincoln restated that "he had sometime [*sic*] thought that perhaps he might be an instrument in God's hands of accomplishing a great work and he certainly was not unwilling to be." He even indicated that he was aware of the pace and timing that God had decreed for the emancipation process: "God's way of accomplishing the end which the memorialists [those who appealed to him for a proclamation] have in view may be different from theirs." George Kateb remarks that the implication of Lincoln's words was that "Lincoln's slower way was perhaps closer to God's." Kateb also stresses:

> This, like the remark at Trenton, was an untypical utterance in which Lincoln singled himself out for a special divine role. It is also worthy of notice that soon afterward, Lincoln was no longer prepared to associate God's purpose unequivocally with the Union cause or the antislavery cause, or both together; what possibly existed was not merely a discrepancy between God's means and human means to the same end. There might be a discrepancy in ends, a discrepancy as important as any could be.[13]

Yes, these phrases that I have cited in which Lincoln claims the status of a prophet may very well be "untypical." Who but a prophet, though, could claim to be an instrument of God? Who but a prophet could assert and carry the purposes that God intends for a people? Who but a prophet could declare to have understood God's design and timing? Lincoln's words were perfectly in tune with the most typical prophetic language of political emancipation whose origins and developments I have traced in my study.

As I have documented, prophets are aware that it is difficult to decipher God's plans, unless he reveals them. They also know, however, that God's plan is just. In the same vein, Lincoln wrote: "The purposes of the Almighty are perfect, and must prevail, though we erring mortals may fail to accurately perceive them in advance. We hoped for a happy termination of this terrible war long before this; but God knows best and has ruled otherwise."[14] Some two years earlier, he also assured his cabinet members that "God had decided this question [of whether to declare emancipation] in favor of the slaves."[15] Prophets know when and how God intends to punish peoples for the wrongs that they have perpetrated, or for lukewarm willingness to fight wrongs that others have perpetrated. Lincoln conveys this idea of prophetic wisdom in a letter submitted to a newspaper editor in Kentucky on April 4, 1864:

---

[12] Abraham Lincoln, "Address to the New Jersey Senate, Trenton, New Jersey, February 21, 1861," *Speeches and Writings 1859–1865*, vol. 2, edited by Don E. Fehrenbacher, New York: The Library of America, 1989, p. 209.

[13] George Kateb, *Lincoln's Political Thought*, Cambridge, MA and London: Harvard University Press, 2015, p. 180.

[14] Abraham Lincoln, "Letter to Eliza P. Gurney, September 4, 1864," *Speeches and Writings 1859–1865*, vol. 2, p. 627.

[15] *Recollected Words of Abraham Lincoln*, edited by Don E. Fehrenbacher and Virginia Fehrenbacher, Stanford: Stanford University Press, 1996, p. 474.

Now, at the end of three years struggle the nation's condition is not what either party, or any man devised, or expected. God alone can claim it. Whither it is tending seems plain. If God now wills the removal of a great wrong, and wills also that we of the North as well as you of the South, shall pay fairly for our complicity in that wrong, impartial history will find therein new cause to attest and revere the justice and goodness of God.[16]

At times, prophets are uncertain about God's plans. They have no doubts, however, that God cannot be whimsical or irrational. Lincoln states: "Both [the Union and the Confederation] *may* be, and one *must* be wrong. God can not be *for*, and against the same thing at the same time."[17] Though hesitantly, Lincoln seems prepared to admit that both parties, fighting as they are for opposite purposes, can be instrumental in God's design: "In the present civil war it is quite possible that God's purpose is something different from the purpose of either party – and yet the human instrumentalities, working just as they do, are of the best adaptation to effect His purpose. I am almost ready to say this is probably true."[18] He is reported to have said to the pastor of the First Presbyterian Church in Washington: "I believe we are all agents and instruments of Divine providence. On both sides we are working out the will of God; yet how strange the spectacle!"[19] If I were interpreting Machiavelli, I would suggest that a possible solution to this riddle – which poses, on the one hand, that one of the two parties "*must* be wrong," and, on the other, that both parties "can be instrumental to God's design" – would be to say that the party fighting for the wrong (to preserve slavery) gives the party fighting for justice (the abolition of slavery) the occasion, or the opportunity, to fight for justice and to accomplish a great redemptive goal for the whole nation.[20] I am not sure that this interpretation would work for Lincoln. For one thing, Lincoln is more hesitant than Machiavelli when he attempts to declare God's intentions. In 1862, for instance, he penned words that indicate he was unable to pierce into the darkness, that no revelation had come. The veil was still there: "God wills this contest, and wills that it shall not end yet. By his mere quiet power, on the minds of the now contestants, He could have either saved or destroyed the Union without a human contest. Yet the contest began. And having begun, He could give the final victory to either side any day. Yet the contest proceeds."[21]

---

[16] Abraham Lincoln, "Letter to Albert G. Hodges, April 4, 1864," *Speeches and Writings 1859–1865*, vol. 2, p. 586.

[17] Abraham Lincoln, "Meditation on the Divine Will," *Speeches and Writings 1859–1865*, vol. 2, p. 359.

[18] Ibid., p. 359.

[19] *Recollected Words of Abraham Lincoln*, edited by Don E. Fehrenbacher and Virginia Fehrenbacher, Stanford: Stanford University Press, 1996, p. 436.

[20] The temptation to sketch a parallel between Machiavelli's and Lincoln's political thought, and especially between their prophetic pages, is strong. I must resist it, though, and leave this suggestion to other scholars.

[21] Abraham Lincoln, "Meditation on the Divine Will," *Speeches and Writings 1859–1865*, vol. 2, p. 359.

Be that as it may, in his *Second Inaugural Address* on March 4, 1865, Lincoln spoke as a prophet capable of identifying God's designs, which otherwise are incomprehensible for human beings who do not have prophetic inspiration. Unlike other prophets whom I have studied in this work, Lincoln did not say something like "we can count on God's friendship because we are fighting for justice." Rather, he stated that God inflicted the horrors of the Civil War upon both the Union and the Confederation precisely because he wanted to end slavery:

If we shall suppose that American Slavery is one of those offences which, in the providence of God, must needs come, but which having continued through His appointed time, He now wills to remove, and that He gives to both North and South, this terrible war, as the woe due to those by whom the offence came, shall we discern therein any departure from those divine attributes which the believers in a Living God always ascribe to Him.[22]

George Kateb comments that Lincoln meant to say that "the North deserved punishment almost as much as the South because the North gladly bought the goods that slave labor produced, and in other ways invested in slavery; perhaps the guilt of the North was equal to that of the South, not lesser." Indeed, Kateb further notes how "Lincoln in his last campaign speech for the Illinois seat in the US Senate in 1858 had said that he did not express "harsh sentiments towards our Southern brethren [*sic*]" because "the only difference between them and us is the difference of circumstances."[23] As the famous last words of the Second Inaugural indicate, Lincoln's prophetic language was all but conventional: "With malice toward none, with charity for all, with firmness in the right as God gives us to see the right." While on the side of justice, Lincoln's God was also compassionate and, much better than many human beings, knew what the right path to justice on earth was. Almost a century later, speaking in the "symbolic shadow" of Lincoln on August 28, 1963, Martin Luther King delivered his "I Have a Dream" speech, the last grand prophetic speech of social emancipation. Delivered along the Potomac River, that address marks the end of a long story that began, I like to think, some four centuries before along the Arno River in Florence.

I am aware that the story I have narrated is incomplete. To acknowledge only the most evident lacuna, I have not examined prophetic iconography. The representations of the prophets and sibyls in the Duomo of Siena, as well as those of Michelangelo in the Sistine Chapel, deserve an essay longer than this whole book. I hope that other and better scholars will improve my work with

[22] Abraham Lincoln, "Second Inaugural Address," *Speeches and Writings 1859–1865*, vol. 2, p. 687.
[23] Abraham Lincoln, "Portion of Last Speech in Campaign of 1858, Springfield, Illinois," *Speeches and Writings 1832–1858*, vol. 1, edited by Don E. Fehrenbacher, New York: The Library of America, 1989, p. 827.

studies on texts that I have not considered, more convincing interpretations of the authors I have examined, and wiser reconstructions of the various historical contexts. Still, my story might provide useful materials for reflections on prophecy and social emancipation.

Would it be correct, to begin with, to assert that there has been an Italian tradition of prophets who learn from prophets? In the late fifteenth century, Savonarola almost exclusively relied on the scriptures; Giuseppe Mazzini elected Dante as his model; Croce wrote his prophetic pages looking at the achievements of the human spirit throughout history. Therefore, it would be wrong to claim the existence of a recognizable prophetic tradition of moral and social emancipation in the same sense in which we may assert, for instance, that there is a republican tradition of political thought. Prophets are solitary militants. Rather than meditating on the words of previous prophets, they listen to their conscience. They are the first to denounce injustice, they have the strength to stand alone against it. Their faith in the God who has revealed His will to them sustains them in the journey to emancipation. They do not look behind to see how many people are following.[24] They are not initiators of important traditions that outlive them, at least in the Italian case. Their wisdom dies with them. Savonarola had a fair number of followers who kept alive and treasured his memory for some decades, above all in Florence, as Lorenzo Polizzotto has evidenced.[25] Mazzini inspired a fair number of "Mazzinians" who remained active and pugnacious well into the twentieth century (a few of them still exist and resist). His voice echoed for a long time, but it was an echo that did not generate a new history; no follower ever could equal the master's charisma or have a comparable impact. Unlike philosophical or scientific doctrines, prophetic wisdom is contingent upon the persons who deliver it. It is the living voice of the prophet, indeed his whole person, that makes the prophetic message powerful.

How can we tell the difference between true and false prophets of emancipation? The task is very difficult. Good simulators can easily deceive us. We could look for help in Max Weber's theory of charismatic leadership and choose charisma as the defining quality of true prophets.[26] But charisma is not easy to describe. We could look for help in a "theory of prophecy" that would provide us with safe rules to apply to specific cases. The problem is that such a theory does not exist, and, in my opinion, there is no way of constructing

---

[24] See Carlo Ossola's "Préface," in Dag Hammarskjöld, *Jalons*, Paris: Editions du Félin, 2010, p. 18, where he cites this line that Hammarskjöld wrote in 1925–1930: "Ne surveille pas chacun de tes pas: seule qui garde loin trouve le chemin."

[25] See Lorenzo Polizzotto, *The Elect Nation: The Savonarolan Movement in Florence (1494–1545)*, Oxford: Oxford University Press, 1994.

[26] See Max Weber, *The Theory of Social and Economic Organization*, translated by A.M. Henderson and Talcott Parsons, edited and with an introduction by Talcott Parsons, Glencoe (IL): The Free Press, 1947, pp. 358–372. On Weber it is still worth reading Robert C. Tucker, "The Theory of Charismatic Leadership," *Daedalus* 97 (1968): pp. 731–756.

it since there is no way to identify objectively irrefutable marks or signs of true prophetic inspiration. We are not left, however, completely in the dark. Some light is there for us, though not in the form of indisputable, scientific criteria. It is a light that we can take from Machiavelli, who was highly skeptical about pretentions of divine inspiration and, at the same time, had the opportunity to listen to the words of Savonarola, the prophet par excellence of the time. Machiavelli's first piece of advice concerns the best way of identifying the true intentions of all human beings, prophets and nonprophets alike. He counsels that we should judge according to what we can test with our sense of touch and feeling, not merely by what the eyes can see.[27] The second piece of advice, which he framed specifically about Savonarola, is to consider the life, the doctrine, and the content of the words of those who claim to be prophets. Have the individuals who speak as prophets lived their lives with impeccable devotion to the ideals that they profess? Do they corroborate their prophetic vision with solid learning that they have attained through a long and serious study of scriptures, the history of their countries, moral philosophy, and politics? If the redemptive path they propose sounds about right to us, why should we not believe them? In this case, believing and following is more rational than not believing and remaining indifferent. The Machiavellian standards I put forth are far from safe. But they are better than nothing and, indeed, better than the available alternatives.

Prophetic messages remain powerful within specific national contexts. Prophets teach people a path of redemption that is consistent with their history and culture. Accordingly, they carefully choose words, metaphors, and examples apt to inspire their fellow citizens. All the Italian prophets of social emancipation were patriots: They praised love of country as a compassionate love for one's fellow citizens and as a devotion to the common good. Giuseppe Mazzini taught Italians to love their homeland and to stand for the liberty and dignity of all peoples. He envisaged the emancipation of Italy as the necessary step in the direction of the emancipation of humanity. For this reason, his ideas crossed the boundaries of Italy.[28] In many countries, militants of liberty listened

---

[27] See my *Redeeming The Prince: The Meaning of Machiavelli's Masterpiece*, Princeton and Oxford: Princeton University Press, 2014, pp. 81–91.

[28] The international impact of Mazzini's ideas was, as is, truly remarkable. See Colin Barr, "Giuseppe Mazzini and Irish Nationalism, 1845–70," *Giuseppe Mazzini and the Globalization of Democratic Nationalism, 1830–1920*, edited by Christopher A. Bayly and Eugenio F. Biagini, Oxford: Oxford University Press, 2008, pp. 125–144; Nick Carter, *Britain, Ireland and the Italian Risorgimento*, London: Palgrave Macmillan, 2015; Gregory Claeys, "Mazzini, Kossuth, and British Radicalism, 1848–1854," *Journal of British Studies* 28, no. 3 (Summer 1989): pp. 225–261; Rabidra K. Dasgupta, "Mazzini and Indian Nationalism," *East and West* 7, no. 1 (Spring 1956): pp. 67–70; Robert T. Handy, "The Influence of Mazzini on the American Social Gospel," *The Journal of Religion* 29, no. 2 (Spring 1949): pp. 114–123; Marcella Pellegrino Sutcliffe, *Victorian Radicals and Italian Democrats*, Woodbridge: Boydell & Brewer, 2014; Anna Procyk, *Giuseppe Mazzini's Young Europe and the Birth of Modern Nationalism in the Slavic*

to Mazzini's words and loved them. Still, his words and teachings revealed their true prophetic pathos in Italy. The national content of his prophetic vision (and of all prophetic visions) does not belittle its moral and political value at all. When prophets encourage and sustain movements of social emancipation in their own countries, they are helping the emancipation of humanity for other prophets might follow their example in different countries. With visions of emancipation framed similarly in their commitment to liberty, they shall make use of different historical and cultural references that allow their message to resonate more strongly. No single prophet can emancipate all peoples. Besides being a mere fantasy, the emancipation of all mankind under the leadership of a single prophet would not be emancipation at all. Each people must earn its own emancipation; each people needs its own prophets.

"*Cum deficit prophetia dissipabitur populus*" (*Proverbs* 29:18). The King James Version translates the Latin as, "Where there is no vision, the people perish," but I think that is more correct to render "*prophetia*" as "prophecy," or the "revelation of God's will." Probably one of the most cited phrases in the literature on the subject, this verse highlights prophets' power to unify people around common ideals and visions. In Italian history, prophets have unified their compatriots against foreign and domestic oppressors, corruption, and totalitarian domination. They have also united their compatriots in truth by persuading them to embrace the principles that they have revealed as realities coming from God.[29] Unlike totalitarian demagogues, prophets do not issue orders upon passive crowds. They encourage their fellow citizens to deliberate about principles and institutions by consulting only their individual conscience. In this way, communities are constituted by morally free individuals who hold their conscience, not the state or society, as their guide. Each member of the community freely accepts the principles that prophets have revealed precisely because they have faith in the prophets. While faith accomplishes remarkable achievements of redemption, it does not survive the prophet's death. To resume the never-ending journey of emancipation, new prophets must come to mold new communities of free individuals.

Italian history also teaches that prophetic language is especially congenial to republican theory and action. The three main prophets of political emancipation (Savonarola, Machiavelli, and Mazzini) all advocated republican liberty.

World, Toronto: University of Toronto Press, 2019; Timothy Roberts, "The Relevance of Giuseppe Mazzini's Ideas of Insurgency to the American Slavery Crisis of the 1850s," *Giuseppe Mazzini and the Globalization of Democratic Nationalism, 1830–1920*, pp. 311–322; Martin Wight, *Four Seminal Thinkers in International Theory: Machiavelli, Grotius, Kant, and Mazzini*, Oxford: Oxford University Press, 2004; *A Cosmopolitanism of Nations: Giuseppe Mazzini's Writings on Democracy, Nation Building, and International Relations*, edited by Nadia Urbinati and Stefano Recchia, Princeton: Princeton University Press, 2009.

[29] "La verité, est irruption et prophétie": Carlo Ossola's "Préface," in Dag Hammarskjöld, *Jalons*, Paris: Editions du Félin, 2010, p. 32. See also Martin Buber, *La fede dei profeti* (1942), edited by A. Poma, Casale Monferrato: Marietti, 1985, pp. 8–9.

Why have republican political theorists been so keen to resort to prophetic language? Because, I think, they know that prophetic language is an effective means to mobilize people. But this consideration clarifies only in part the reasons that have sustained the alliance between republicanism and prophecy. A more relevant cause is that redemptive prophecy is congenial to the republican conception of political liberty as absence of domination.[30] In a republican sense, we are free when we are not dependent on the arbitrary will of other individuals, whoever they are. Prophets exhort their fellow citizens to believe that true liberty means obeying God and putting His authority above any human power. They teach a vision of liberty that abhors dependence on human beings and therefore demands republican institutions and a republican way of life. When Savonarola persuaded the Florentine elite to declare Christ "king of Florence" and to place their popular government under God, he combined the tenets of prophecy and republicanism. So did Mazzini when he proclaimed that a republic accomplishes God's design in the realm of history. So did Giorgio La Pira when in 1946 he proposed the adoption of a preamble with an invocation to God for the new Republican Constitution.

But the most precious gift that prophets have offered to republican political theory is the ideal of moral liberty, that inward liberty we achieve when we choose to obey our own conscience. In modern history, the most refined and complete conception of moral liberty is Mazzini's theory of duties. All his life, he preached that duty is liberty: the liberty that we attain when we listen to the voice of our conscience, the liberty that thereby confirms we are our own masters. Individuals who have attained moral liberty do not become the servants of other human beings under any circumstances. They may be imprisoned or enslaved, but they never turn into servants who voluntarily renounce their beliefs to appease their masters. Morally free persons regard servitude as the loss of their moral identity, a loss that no material or symbolic reward can possibly compensate. Knowing how to interrogate and listen to their consciences, morally free persons have the strength to detach themselves from domination and can emancipate themselves from servitude. They understand the duties of citizenship and are willing to discharge them as they complete the long journey of emancipation. Moral liberty is precisely the sort of liberty that prophets are especially good at generating and preserving in the minds of their compatriots because they speak on behalf of God. This does not mean, of course, that only prophets can engender and sustain moral liberty. I have immaculate secularist credentials and I fervently believe that persons with moral integrity too can be effective teachers of moral liberty. Italian history

---

[30] On the republican concept of liberty see Quentin Skinner, *Liberty before Liberalism*, Cambridge: Cambridge University Press, 1988 and Philip Pettit, *Republicanism: A Theory of Freedom and Government*, Oxford: Oxford University Press, 1998.

provides to this effect countless examples.[31] I am just recognizing that prophets are particularly good as teachers of moral liberty.

Mazzini and other prophets of moral and social emancipation greatly valued moral liberty because they committed themselves to the grand mission of emancipating a morally dominated people. During the Counterreformation, as I have documented, the Catholic Church attained a vast and lasting control over Italians' individual consciences, and decimated aspirations for moral and social emancipation. Though not identical, a similar domination of individual consciences was also one of the chief goals of the fascist regime. Mussolini expected not only obedience, but also total faith in himself and in the dogmas of fascism. The emancipation of an unfree people requires prophets who teach moral truths. Which truths? Prophets state that they teach the truths that God has revealed to them. This answer is acceptable for those individuals who believe in God. For someone who does not believe in God, such as me, the claim that prophets are teachers of truth means that they teach what their conscience compels them to teach. To be effective, however, conscience needs the aid of some passions, above all compassion for the oppressed and indignation against the oppressors. These passions help prophets see injustices and give them the strength to call their fellow citizens to resist. A prophet's conscience is not the light of pure reason that illuminates and dispels darkness. Rather, it is a light that inflames the mind and warms the body.

Throughout history, there have been prophetic political leaders who have spoken the truth as they sincerely saw and felt it. Because they spoke truth that was animated by the right passions, they were able to liberate their compatriots from moral servitude. New prophetic political leaders could inspire new movements of social emancipation against the forms of domination that pervade our times.[32] Their first task would be to redeem moral emptiness. While I cannot provide data, I remain convinced that moral emptiness – that is, the absence of deeply felt and seriously examined principles – is one of the most disturbing negative features of our times. Adolf Eichmann – the symbol of the banality of evil that results from thoughtlessness, as Hannah Arendt brilliantly

---

[31] See the splendid essays by Norberto Bobbio, *Maestri e compagni*, Florence: Passigli, 1984; *Italia civile*, Florence: Passigli, 1986; "Introduzione," *Scritti di Leone Ginzburg*, Turin: Einaudi, 1964. See also Alessandro Galante Garrone, *I miei maggiori*, Milan: Garzanti, 1984.

[32] According to Fredric Jameson, "Our social order is richer in information and more literate [...] This new order no longer needs prophets and seers of the high modernist and charismatic type, whether among its cultural products or its politicians. Such figures no longer hold any charm or magic for the subjects of a corporate, collectivized, post-individualistic age; in that case, goodbye to them without regret, as Brecht might have put it: woe to the country that needs geniuses, prophets, Great Writers, or demiurges!" Fredric Jameson, *Postmodernism, or the Cultural Logic of Late Capitalism*, Durham (NC): Duke University Press, 1991, p. 15 (cited in Richard Rorty, *Achieving Our Country, Leftist Thought in Twentieth-Century America*, Cambridge (MA): London, 1998, p. 126).

portrayed – has had his revenge.[33] Maybe I am painting too bleak a picture, but my sense is that fewer and fewer persons, young and old, are able and willing to interrogate their conscience on serious moral and social issues. The great majority looks for answers from the various screens of the television, the computer, the telephone, but not from themselves. The answers they obtain are not the result of an inner meditation, of reflections on books, of dialogues with mentors and friends. They are answers that are immediately available and simple. But these answers do not fortify or strengthen the individuals who seek and accept them; they make them banal.

In my story, I have recorded examples of the domination of consciences that occurred through compulsory confession, the Inquisition, and the propaganda of the totalitarian state. Prophets of the past have spoken against these forms of domination. With the force of their words, they have been able to remedy these ills, at least in part. In our times, consciences are not dominated by the Counterreformation Church or the totalitarian state. Yet resurrecting them is a mission now much more difficult. The prophets of the past had to liberate consciences from domination; the prophets of the future, if they will come, will have to try to resuscitate lifeless consciences. They will have to inspire individuals who have no inward life, who consume their days with images, who are familiar with but few and banal words. Only a resurrection of consciences could give the people of our times a renewed sense of their dignity that, in turn, would motivate them to stand against all forms of social domination. However, my sense is that, even if new prophets of social emancipation will come and exhort their fellow citizens with the most inspiring words, very few individuals will listen. They will not listen because they are not "there"; they are never present; they are always connected to something or to someone else. Their consciences are not dominated; they are empty, or dead. Most of the time they are by themselves but not with themselves. They are all the time connected with others, never engaged in a serious inner dialogue.

From Cicero and his humanist followers, I have learned that history helps us to understand our times. I never would have imagined that writing history would help me understand who I am or why I have lived the life that I have lived. As I was writing this story about prophecy and social emancipation, I realized – for the first time in my life – that I lived my youth in prophetic times. I was eleven in 1963, when Bob Dylan sang "The times they are a-changin'." In 1964, the Italian singer Francesco Guccini wrote the song "Dio è morto" (*God is dead*) to announce that, although God died in the concentration camps, he resurrects in the minds of human beings who yearn for justice. Those prophetic times were brief. In the aftermath of the horrific fascist terrorist attack in Milan on December 12, 1969, the Italian poet and

---

[33] See Hannah Arendt, *Eichmann in Jerusalem. A Report on the Banality of Evil*, New York: Viking Press, 1964.

Nobel Prize laureate Eugenio Montale wrote in the poem *Laggiù* that prophets and prophecies shall disappear, if ever they existed (*"Spariranno profeti e profeti, / Se mai ne furono"*).[34] Between December 13 and December 14, Pier Paolo Pasolini, on the Greek island of Patmos, composed a poem that connects events and prophecy, facts and inspiration, and evokes John the Evangelist, who composed the *Apocalypse* in Patmos.[35] He interpreted the tragic events of 1969 as signs of a gloomy future.[36] His death marks the end of emancipatory prophecy. Mounting waves of corruption, vulgarity, greed, violence, and discrimination have been and are growing. There are still men and women committed to the ideal of social emancipation. But to this date they have not been able to generate and keep alive generous and lasting movements and to produce radical social reforms. If new prophets shall come and help new experiences of liberation, I shall welcome them. I am not lamenting the disappearance of prophets. I am lamenting the disappearance of prophets of emancipation. More precisely, I am lamenting the disappearance of strong movements of social emancipation. If I were to see movements of social emancipation, I would welcome them even if they were not led by prophets. I do not at all deny the possibility that new movements of social emancipation could arise without being inspired by prophets. I just doubt, however, that I will see them. The prophetic times of my youth must have left some traces, if, fifty years later, I have come to write on prophecy and social emancipation. Be that as it may, I hope that this work offers a story that I believe is worth telling and might help to revive the spirit of times that are now so distant that I suspect they never existed in truth.

---

[34] Eugenio Montale, "Laggiù (16.XII,1969)," *Satura*, 1971; now in E. Montale, *L'opera in versi*, edited by Rosanna Bettarini and Gianfranco Contini, Turin: Einaudi, 1980, p. 394.

[35] Pasolini got the news of the terrorist attack in the Banca dell'Agricoltura in Milan while he was a guest of Maria Callas in Greece at the time of the military dictatorship. A few hours later he writes the poem *Patmos*. See Pier Paolo Pasolini, *Tutte le poesie*, vol. 2, *Trasumanar e organizzar*, edited by Walter Siti, Milan: Mondadori, pp. 123–132.

[36] See Pier Paolo Pasolini, "Che cos'e questo golpe?," *Corriere della Sera*, September 14, 1974, republished in Pier Paolo Pasolini, *Scritti corsari*, Milan: Garzanti, 1975; and Pier Paolo Pasolini, "Petrolio, Appunto 103," *Romanzi e racconti*, vol. II, edited by Walter Siti and Silvia de Laude, Milan: Mondadori, pp. 1713–1723.

From Dante to the Republic of Prophets

2.1 PROPHETS AND POETS

As early as the twelfth century, prophetic voices have shaped the Italian spiritual and moral scenario. Among them, Joachim of Fiore (1135–1202), a figure whom Dante explicitly credited to be "di spirito profetico dotato," stands out. His vision of the coming of a new order (*ordo*), or state (*status*), of spiritual men had a great sentimental impact, stirred hopes of religious renewal, produced other prophecies, and inspired radical religious movements. He did not announce, however, a message of social redemption. To stress its distance from the life of activity and labor, he called the new order that he was invoking the "Virgin Church," *que requiescit in silentio heremi*. The models of his order were Elijah and Elisha, from the *Old Testament*, and Saint Benedict, "*viro utique claro miraculis, opere et sanctitate*," from his times. The symbol that he chose to describe his task was the suave dove ("*illa suavissima columba*"), and the birds that fly to heaven to contemplate the light of the sun in its fullness. The monks belonging to the spiritual order that Joachim founded distinguished themselves for their spiritual liberty and the sacred wisdom they extracted from both the Old and the New Testaments in the silence of contemplation sustained by the jubilation of psalmody.[1] Joachim assigned the new

---

[1] Marjorie Reeves, *The Influence of Prophecy in the Later Middle Ages: A Study in Joachimism*, Oxford: Oxford University Press, 1969. I am quoting from the 2011 reprint by University of Notre Dame Press, pp. 136–138. See also Henry de Lubac, S.J., *La Postérité spirituelle de Joachim de Flore*, 2 vols., Paris: Lethielleux, 1979–1981; Cesare Vasoli, "L'influenza di Gioacchino da Fiore sul profetismo italiano della fine del Quattrocento e del primo Cinquecento," *Il profetismo gioachimita tra Quattrocento e Cinquecento. Atti del III Congresso Internazionale di Studi Gioachimiti (S. Giovanni in Fiore, 17–21 settembre 1989)*, edited by Gian Luca Podestà, Genoa: Marietti, 1991, pp. 61–85; Morton W. Bloonfield, "Recent Scholarship on Joachim of Fiore and his Influence," *Prophecy and Millenarianism. Essays in Honour of Marjorie Reeves*,"

spiritual order a contemplative mission detached from the masses and was concerned with the general body of the Christian people. For this, he prophesied "the conversion of all peoples to spiritual intelligence." The new spiritual men were to be preachers of the truth (*"predicatores veritatis"*), capable of carrying out ecclesiastical reform through the spiritual change of the Church's individual members. He wanted them to act as mediators between God and the crowd of sinners who could not sustain the sunlight of a fully hermitic life. To illustrate this mediation between God and the people, he used the figure of Moses: not the Moses who led the Hebrews from Egyptian bondage to the Promised Land, but the Moses who remained on the mountaintop and told Aaron the words that were to be revealed to the people of Israel.[2]

Not even the Scholastic treatments of prophecy contain exhortations for political and social emancipation. Following the work of the Roman political leader and writer Cassiodorus, Albert the Great (1205–1280), in his authoritative treatise on prophecy (*Quaestio de prophetia*) composed between 1245 and 1248, provided the definition of prophecy as divine inspiration or revelation that would become conventional.[3] He clarifies that, although supernatural in its origin, prophetic knowledge rests on natural images that are already present in the prophet's mind. The conception of prophecy that the Fathers of the Church have constructed, however, is quite different from the philosophers' conception. For the philosophers, prophets are persons who design correct conjectures on veiled matters. Their knowledge is therefore confined within the boundaries of human capabilities. It depends on the person's ability to see and judge. According to the Fathers of the Church, prophecy is instead a gift that God freely bestows upón some individuals (*"gratia gratis data"*). It comes from divine inspiration, not from human will. As we read in the *Book of Wisdom*

---

edited by Ann Williams, Burnt Hill: Longman, 1980, pp. 21–52; Gian Luca Podestà, *Il tempo dell'Apocalisse: vita di Gioacchino da Fiore*, Bari: Laterza, 2004; Raoul Manselli, "L'attesa dell'età nuova ed il gioachimismo," *L'attesa dell'età nuova nella spiritualità della fine del medioevo, 16–19 ottobre, 1960*, Convegno del Centro di Studi sulla spiritualità medievale III, Todi, 1962, pp. 145–170; Raoul Manselli, "Ricerca sull'influenza della profezia nel basso medioevo," *Bullettino dell'Istituto Storico Italiano per il Medio Evo e Archivio Muratoriano* 82 (1970): pp. 1–12. Still essential is Eugenio Garin, "L'attesa dell'età nuova e la 'renovatio,'" *L'attesa dell'età nuova nella spiritualità della fine del medioevo, 16–19 ottobre, 1960*, Convegno del Centro di Studi sulla spiritualità medievale III, Todi, 1962, pp. 9–35.

[2] Ibid., p. 142.

[3] "Prophetia est revelatio vel inspiratio divina, rerum eventus immobili veritate denuntians"; Albert the Great, *Quaestio de prophetia*, I.1, in Albert the Great, *Quaestio de prophetia. Visione, immaginazione, dono profetico*, edited by Anna Rodolfi, Florence: Edizioni del Galluzzo, 2009. See Jean-Pierre Torrell, O.P., *Recherches sur la théorie de la prophétie au Moyen Âge XIIe – XIVe siècles*, Fribourg: Éditions Universitaires, 1992; Anna Rodolfi, "Il ruolo delle immagini sensibili nella dottrina della conoscenza profetica di Alberto Magno," *Annali del Dipartimento di Filosofia 2005*, Florence: Florence University Press, 2006, pp. 79–107; and "Sogno e profezia in Alberto Magno," *Scientia, fides, theologia. Studi di filosofia medievale in onore di Gianfranco Fioravanti*, edited by Stefano Perfetti, Pisa: ETS, 2011, pp. 193–215.

VII.27, the gift of wisdom enters the souls of the prophets and makes them "friends of God" (*"amicos Dei"*), if and only if they have the virtue of charity. In this vein, it follows that there are no prophets without charity (*"non sunt prophetae sine caritate"*). Even when it belongs to malignant men, the gift of prophecy always serves God's will, Albert the Great remarks. This means that true prophets reveal the truths that they have received exclusively for the moral and spiritual good of their nation. In his essay, however, he does not indicate social and political emancipation as the goal or purpose that prophecy must chiefly serve.[4]

Thomas Aquinas (1225–1274), the most illustrious philosopher of the Scholastic tradition, asserts, in the section *De Prophetia* of his *Summa Theologiae* IIa, IIe, that prophetic knowledge is about contingent futures, both divine and human, spiritual, and corporeal.[5] Thanks to the divine illumination they receive, prophets see the meaning of signs and vision as if they were looking at them in the mirror of God. Prophets sense that their knowledge is certain because they know it comes from God.[6] They do not just see the signs; they interpret them. Interpretation implies, on one hand, correctly judging what must be done, and on the other, inspiring the people of God to live by God's law (*Isaiah* 63:14). To assist his people, God continues to send his messengers and instructs them how to face the challenges of changing times and how to react to defeat. For these reasons, Aquinas warns his readers that prophets must be tested, not shunned.[7] Citing scripture, he reminds that "when prophecy shall fail, the people shall be scattered abroad" (*Proverbs* 29:18). This is the reason why at all times men were divinely instructed about what they were to do for the spiritual welfare of the elect."[8] Prophecy provides precious practical

---

[4] Albert the Great, *Quaestio de prophetia*, II.3, in Albert the Great, *Quaestio de prophetia. Visione, immaginazione, dono profetico*, edited by Anna Rodolfi, Florence: Edizioni del Galluzzo, 2009.

[5] Thomas Aquinas, *Summa Theologiae*, IIa, IIae, Q. 171, Art. 3; English translation by Fathers of the English Dominican Province, New York: Benziger Bros, 1947–1948. See also: Jean-Pierre Torrell's "Introduction" in Thomas Aquinas, *Somme théologique: La Prophétie*, edited by Paul Synave, O.P. and Pierre Benoit, O.P., 2nd edition, Paris: CERF, 2005; Brian Fitzgerald, *Inspiration and Authority in the Middle Ages: Prophets and their Critics from Scholasticism to Humanism*, Oxford: Oxford University Press, 2017, pp. 110–112, 115–135, 145, 235; Paul Synave and Pierre Benoit, *Prophecy and Inspiration: A Commentary on the Summa Theologica II-II, Questions 171–178*, translated by Thomas L. Sheridan and Avery R. Dulles, New York: Desclée, 1961; on the prophets as social critics see Claudio Leonardi, "Committenze agiografiche nel Trecento," *Patronage and Public in the Trecento: Proceedings of the St Lambrecht Symposium, Abtei St. Lambrecht, Styria, 16–19 July 1984*, edited by Vincent Moleta, Florence: Olschki, 1986, pp. 37–58; and "Intellectuals and Hagiography in the Fourteenth-Century," *Intellectuals and Writers in Fourteenth-Century Europe: The J.A.W. Bennett Memorial Lectures, Perugia, 1984*, edited by Piero Boitani and Anna Torti, Tubingen: Narr, Cambridge Brewer, 1986, pp. 7–21; for a general overview of Scholastic political thought see Cesare Vasoli, "Il pensiero politico della Scolastica," *Storia delle idee politiche economiche e sociali* II.2, Turin: UTET, 1983, pp. 367–462.

[6] Thomas Aquinas, *Summa Theologiae*, IIa, IIae, Q. 171, Art. 5.

[7] Thomas Aquinas, *Summa Theologiae*, IIa, IIae, Q. 174, Art. 6.   [8] Ibid.

wisdom. To accomplish the goal of guiding their peoples, prophets – illuminated by God – must display the ability to adapt their words and actions
to circumstances.

The prophets' wisdom, Aquinas remarks, especially befits free peoples.[9]
Moses, the most outstanding of all prophets, was a liberator: "He showed
himself most outstanding in boldness, for with only a rod he went down into
Egypt, not only to preach the words of the Lord, but also to scourge Egypt and
to free his people."[10] As the example of Moses eloquently instructs, prophecy
unites peoples in the justice of faith and encourages them to pursue moral
virtue.[11] God gives the gift of prophecy to those who can serve His will:

But we find discrimination in the gift of prophecy, for it is not given to everybody, even
though they have this or that disposition, but only to those whom the divine will
chooses. Nevertheless, these are not apt subjects or the best subjects simply in themselves. They are, however, apt subjects in so far as they perform the function of the
prophet to the extent which the divine wisdom judges to be fitting.[12]

Prophecy produces good out of evil men: "That God is best appears in this, that
He knows how to make good use not only of good men, but also of evil men.
Hence, if he makes evil prophets perform the good functions of prophecy, this
in no wise detracts from His supreme goodness."[13]

For Aquinas, the chief mission of prophecy is not social criticism or the
creation of new and just political orders, but the edification of the Church. The
Apostle, Aquinas remarks, proves that prophecy is more profitable than the gift
of tongues: "The object of prophecy is what is necessary for salvation. This
means that all those things that can be useful for salvation are the object of
prophecy, whether they are past, or future, or even eternal, or necessary, or
contingent. But those things which cannot pertain to salvation are outside the
matter of prophecy."[14] To buttress his interpretation, Aquinas cites
Augustine – "although our authors knew what shape heaven is, [the spirit]
wants to speak through them only that which is useful for salvation" – and the
Gospel of St. John (16:13) – "but when he, the Spirit of truth, is come, he will

---

[9] Ibid.
[10] Thomas Aquinas, *Questiones Disputatae*, in *Le questioni disputate. Testo latino dell'Edizione
leonina e traduzione italiana*, vol. II, *La verità, Questioni (10–20)*, edited by P. R. Coggi,
Bologna: Edizioni Studi Domenicano, 1992; English translation by James V. McGlynn, S.J.,
Chicago: Henry Regnery Company, 1953 (Q. 12: "Prophecy," Art. 14, Reply).
[11] "Prophecy is classified among the greatest goods since it is a free gift. For, although it does not
act as an immediate principle of meritorious action to make one live properly, the whole of
prophecy is directed to the virtuous life"; Thomas Aquinas, *Questiones Disputatae*, Q. 12,
Art. 3, Answer to difficulties, 15.
[12] Thomas Aquinas, *Questiones Disputatae*, Q. 12, Art. 5, Answer to difficulties, 4.
[13] Thomas Aquinas, *Questiones Disputatae*, Q. 12, Art. 5, Answer to difficulties, 5.
[14] Thomas Aquinas, *Summa Theologiae*, IIa-IIae, Q. 176, Art. 2.

teach you all truth." By the truth "necessary for salvation," Aquinas distinct-ively means individual salvation, not political or social emancipation.[15]

Unlike Joachim of Fiore, and unlike the Scholastic authorities, whom he knew very well, Dante Alighieri masterfully used prophetic language to announce a message of political redemption for Italy.[16] In the *Convivio*, com-posed in the early years of his exile between 1304 and 1307, he sketches an exemplary piece of prophetic interpretation of history. To rebut the argument that Rome's empire was the outcome of mere force, he outlines God's provi-dential plan for Rome, a plan that Dante himself is able to read and illustrate:

> To this we may easily reply that the election of this supreme officer [the emperor] must in the first place derive from that wisdom which provides for all men, namely God; for otherwise the election would not have been made on behalf of everyone, since prior to the officer named above there was no one who attended to the general good. And because no nature ever was or will be more tempered in the exercise of rule, stronger in its preservation, and cleverer in acquiring it than that of the Latin race (as can be seen from experience), that sacred people in whom was mingled the lofty blood of the Trojans, namely Rome, God chose this people for that office. Therefore, since this office could not be attained without the greatest virtue, and since its exercise required the greatest and most humane kindness, this was the people best disposed to receive it. Consequently, the Roman people secured it originally not by force but by divine providence, which transcends all reason.[17]

Dante's prophetic message for the political redemption of Italy is even more explicit in his Epistle to the kings and the peoples of Italy of 1310, in which he depicts Henry VII's imminent arrival in Italy as the fulfillment of a prophecy:

---

[15] Thomas Aquinas, *Questiones disputatae*, Q. 12, Art. 2, Reply. See Brian Fitzgerald, *Inspiration and Authority in the Middle Ages*, pp. 128–129.

[16] See Marjorie Reeves, "The Third Age: Dante's debt to Gioacchino Fiore," *L'età dello spirito e la fine dei tempi in Gioacchino da Fiore e nel gioachimismo medievale. Atti del II Congresso Internazionale di Studi Gioachimiti, 6–9 settembre 1984*, edited by Antonio Crocco, San Giovanni in Fiore: Centro Internazionale Studi Gioachimiti, 1986, pp. 127–139. Whereas the prophets of the "*Ecclesia spiritualis*" were longing for the "Pastor angelicus," the angelic pope, Dante connects the renovation of the Church to the vision of the "humana civilitas," a new and higher form of social and moral life that a political leader shall usher. See Raoul Manselli, "Dante e l'*Ecclesia spiritualis*," *Dante e Roma: atti del Convegno di studi, Roma 8–9–10 aprile 1965*, Florence: Le Monnier, 1965, pp. 126–127.

[17] Dante Alighieri, *Convivio*, IV. 4, 8–14; I am quoting from Dante Alighieri, *Convivio*, vol. 1, edited by Franca Brambilla Ageno, Florence: Casa Editrice Le Lettere (Società Dantesca Italiana. Edizione Nazionale), 1995, pp. 279–280; English translation by Richard H. Lansing, New York: Garland, 1990. On Dante and prophecy, see Marjorie Reeves, "Dante and the Prophetic View of History," *The World of Dante*, edited by Cecyl Grayson, Oxford: Oxford University Press, 1980, pp. 44–60; Bruno Nardi, *Dante e la cultura medievale*, Rome and Bari: Laterza, 1983 (especially ch. XI, "Dante profeta," pp. 265–326); Raffaello Morghen, *Dante profeta: tra la storia e l'eterno*, Milan: Jaca Book, 1983; see also the excellent studies published in *Poesia e profezia nel'opera di Dante, Atti del Convegno internazionale di Studi Ravenna, 11 novembre 2017*, edited by Giuseppe Ledda, Ravenna: Centro Dantesco dei Frati Minori Conventuali, 2019.

Behold now is the accepted time, wherein arise the signs of consolation and peace. For a new day is beginning to break, revealing the dawn in the East, which even now is dispersing the darkness of our long tribulation. Already the orient breeze is freshening, the face of the heavens grows rosy, and confirms the hopes of the peoples with an auspicious calm. And we too, who have kept vigil through the long night in the wilderness, shall behold the long-awaited joy. For the Sun of peace shall appear on high, and justice which, like the heliotrope, deprived of his light, had grown faint, so soon as he shall dart forth his rays, once more shall revive. All they that hunger, and thirst shall be satisfied in the light of his radiance and they that delight in iniquity shall be put to confusion before the face of his splendor. For the strong lion of the tribe of Judah hath lifted up his ears in compassion and moved by the lamentations of the multitudes in captivity hath raised up another Moses, who shall deliver his people from the oppression of the Egyptians and shall lead them to a land flowing with milk and honey.[18]

Writing like a prophet who reads God's mind, Dante brings his letter to a close exhorting the kings and the princes of Italy to open their eyes to the prophetic light he is bestowing upon them:

"Walk ye not therefore as the Gentiles walk, in the vanity of their senses, shrouded in darkness"; but open ye the eyes of your mind and behold how the Lord of heaven and of earth hath appointed us a king. This is he whom Peter, the Vicar of God, exhorts us to honor, and whom Clement, the present successor of Peter, illumines with the light of the Apostolic benediction; that where the spiritual ray suffices not, there the splendor of the lesser luminary may lend its light.[19]

In his last political work, the *De Monarchia* (1312–1313), Dante explicitly claims his special ability to see and understand God's design: "However, after the eyes of my mind had pierced to the marrow thereof, and I had come to understand by most convincing tokens that Divine Providence had affected this thing, my wonder vanished." The truth that Dante knows by virtue of divine inspiration shall liberate Italy from usurpers: "When it is proved that the Roman Empire existed by right, not only will the clouds of ignorance be cleared from the eyes of kings and princes who usurp to themselves public guidance, falsely believing that the Roman people had done so, but all mortals will know that they are free from the yoke of usurpers. Nor will the truth be revealed in the light of human reason alone, but also in the radiance of divine authority."[20]

---

[18] I am quoting from Dante Alighieri, *Opere*, vol. V, *Epistole. Ecloge. Questio de aqua et terra*, edited by Marco Baglio, Luca Azzetta, Marco Petoletti, and Michele Rinaldi, Rome: Salerno Editrice, 2016, pp. 105–109; English translation, *Dantis Alagherii epistolae. The letters of Dante*, edited by Paget Toynbee, Oxford: Clarendon Press, 1920, pp. 58–59.

[19] Dante Alighieri, *Opere*, vol. V, *Epistole. Ecloge. Questio de aqua et terra*, pp. 128–131; English translation, *Dantis Alagherii epistolae. The letters of Dante*, p. 63.

[20] Dante Alighieri, *De Monarchia*, II., I. 6–8. I am quoting from *Opere di Dante*, Volume IV, *Monarchia*, edited by Paolo Chiesa and Andrea Tabarroni, with the collaboration of Diego Ellero, Rome: Salerno, 2013, pp. 76–77; English translation, *The De Monarchia of Dante Alighieri*, edited by Aurelia Henry, Boston and New York: Houghton, Mifflin and Company, 1904, p. 70.

It is however in the Commedia that Dante expounds the prophetic visions that have had the most powerful impact on the history of political and moral emancipation. With magnificent words, he vindicates the value of moral liberty, the principle that over the centuries became the true foundation vision of political and social emancipation. In Purgatory, Virgil explains that inner liberty is the necessary premise of moral life:

They who in their reasoning went to the root of the matter / Color che ragionando andaro al fondo

took note of this innate liberty, / s'accorser d'esta innata libertate,

and, accordingly, bequeathed ethics to the world. / però moralità lasciaro al mondo.[21]

In *Paradiso*, Beatrice teaches Dante that free will is the most precious gift that God has bestowed upon human beings:

The greatest gift which God in His bounty / Lo maggior don che Dio per sua larghezza

bestowed in creating, and the most conformed to His own goodness / fesse creando, e a la sua bontate

and that which he most prizes, / più conformato, e quel ch'e' più apprezza,

was the freedom of the will, / fu de la volontà la libertate,

with which the creatures that have intelligence, / di che le creature intelligenti,

they all and they alone, were and are endowed. / e tutte e sole, fuoro e son dotate.[22]

She exhorts him to denounce the moral corruption of his times upon his return to the world:

Therefore, for the profit of the world that lives ill, / Però, in pro del mondo che mal vive,

hold your eyes now on the chariot, and what you see, / al carro tieni or li occhi, e quel che vedi,

mind that you write it when you have returned yonder. / ritornato di là, fa che tu scrive.[23]

Like the ancient prophets, Dante must speak even if he knows that his fellow human beings will dislike his words of reprobation and will rebuke him. He must speak up because it is his duty to do so. He is fully aware that if he does not reveal to his fellow human beings the truths he has learned in the world beyond, he will not be remembered by future generations:

---

[21] Dante Alighieri, *The Divine Comedy*, *Purgatorio*, XVIII, 67–69, translated, with a commentary, by Charles S. Singleton, Princeton: Princeton University Press, 1973, p. 192.

[22] Dante Alighieri, *The Divine Comedy*, *Paradiso*, V, 19–24, translated, with a commentary, by Charles S. Singleton, Princeton: Princeton University Press, 1975, pp. 48–51.

[23] Dante Alighieri, *The Divine Comedy*, *Purgatorio*, XXXII, 103–105, p. 356.

Down in the world endlessly bitter, / Giù per lo mondo sanza fine amaro,

And upon the mountain from whose fair summit / e per lo monte del cui bel cacume

My lady's eyes uplifted me, / li occhi de la mia donna mi levaro,

and after, through the heaves from light to light, / e poscia per lo ciel, di lume in lume,

I have learned that which, if I tell again, / ho io appreso quel che s'io ridico,

will have for many a savor of great bitterness; / a molti fia sapor di forte agrume;

And if I am a timid friend to the truth, / e s'io al vero son timido amico,

I fear to lose life among those / temo di perder viver tra coloro

who shall call this time ancient. / che questo tempo chiameranno antico.[24]

His ancestor Cacciaguida assuages Dante's doubts and dispels his fears by revealing to him that the most magnanimous souls of his times, as well as those of the centuries to come, will be able to understand and follow his moral teaching:

The light wherein was smiling the treasure / La luce in che rideva il mio tesoro

I had found there first became flashing / ch'io trovai lì, si fé prima corusca

as a golden mirror in the sun, / quale a raggio di sole specchio d'oro,

then it replied, "A conscience dark, / indi rispuose: 'Coscïenza fusca,

either with its own or with another's shame, / o de la propria o de l'altrui vergogna,

will indeed feel your speech to be harsh. / pur sentirà la tua parola brusca.

But none the less, all falsehood set aside, / Ma nondimen, rimossa ogne menzogna,

make manifest all that you have seen; / tutta tua visïon fa manifesta;

and then let them scratch where the itch is. / e lascia pur grattar dov' è la rogna.

For if at first taste your voice be grievous, / Ché se la voce tua sarà molesta,

yet shall it leave thereafter vital nourishment / nel primo gusto, vital nodrimento

when digested. / lascerà poi, quando sarà digesta

This cry of yours shall do as does the wind, / Questo tuo grido farà come vento,

which smites most upon the loftiest summits; / che le più alte cime più percuote;

and this shall be no little cause of honor." / e ciò non fa d'onor poco argomento.'[25]

Dante can be considered the initiator of the intellectual tradition called "poetic theology." The central tenet of this tradition is the belief that poets are akin to prophets. Like prophets, poets are endowed with a special

[24] Dante Alighieri, *The Divine Comedy, Paradiso,* XVII, 112–120, p. 194.
[25] Dante Alighieri, *The Divine Comedy, Paradiso,* XVII, 124–135, p. 194.

inspiration that permits them to detect God's plans from traces, signs, and revelations of various sorts. Like prophets, poets too can announce divine plans with appropriate and inspiring words. Their verses are to be read as oracular utterances that "need interpretation to reveal their concealed meanings."[26] As Francesco Petrarca put it in his *Epistolae rerum familiarum*, the starting point of the idea of a *theologia poetica* was Aristotle's claim that the first poets were "theologisers" [*theologisantes*].[27] The rude men of antiquity, Petrarch stresses, decided to please and praise their gods with high-sounding words and a style of speaking that was far from anything the vulgar language. Since this exquisite and artful language was called poetic, those who used it were called poets.[28] In Petrarch's understanding, poets in ancient times were inspired by the gods and had access to divine truths, an understanding to which the authority of the greatest philosophers and Christian saints also testifies. Consistent with his beliefs concerning the prophetic virtues of poets, he offered remarkable examples of prophetic poetry. In the canzone "Italia mia benché il parlar sia indarno," probably composed around 1344–1345, he laments the miserable condition of his homeland:

My Italy, though words cannot heal / Italia mia, benché 'l parlar sia indarno

the mortal wounds / a le piaghe mortali

so dense, I see on your lovely flesh, at least / che nel bel corpo tuo sí spesse veggio,

I pray that my sighs / piacemi almen che' miei sospir' sian quali

might bring some hope to the Tiber and the Arno, / spera'l Tevero et l'Arno,

and the Po, that sees me now sad and grave. / e'l Po, dove doglioso et grave or seggio.[29]

---

[26] Charles Trinkaus, *In Our Image and Likeness: Humanity and Divinity in Italian Humanist Thought*, Notre Dame: University of Notre Dame Press, 1995, pp. 688–689. On poetic theology, see *Umanisti italiani*, edited by Raphael Ebgi, Turin: Einaudi, 2016, pp. 279–287; Ronald G. Witt, "Coluccio Salutati and the Conception of the '*Poeta Theologus*' in the Fourteenth Century," *Renaissance Quarterly* XXX (1977), pp. 538–563; Raymond Marcel, "Le fureur poétique et l'Humanisme florentin," *Mélanges Georges Amati: création et vie intérieure. Recherches sur les sciences et les arts*, Paris: Centre National de la Recherche Scientifique, 1956, pp. 177–193. For the Neoplatonic context of prophetic poetry, see James Hankins, *Plato in the Italian Renaissance*, vol. 2, Leiden and New York: E.J. Brill, 1990.

[27] Francesco Petrarca, *Epistolae rerum familiarum*, vol. II, edited by Vittorio Rossi, Florence: Sansoni, 1934, p. 301.

[28] Ibid., pp. 301–302; English translation in Charles Trinkaus, *In Our Image and Likeness: Humanity and Divinity in Italian Humanist Thought*, p. 690. On Petrarch's political ideas, see Enrico Fenzi, "Per Petrarca politico: Cola di Rienzo e la questione romana in *Bucolicum Carmen V, Pietas pastoralis*," *Bollettino di italianistica* 1 (2011): pp. 49–88.

[29] Francesco Petrarca, *Canzoniere*, edited by Giancarlo Contini, Turin: Einaudi, 1964, p. 168; English translation, Petrarch, *The Complete Canzoniere*, translated by A. S. Kline, *Poetry in Translation*, 2001, p. 208.

He then appeals to God's mercy: Ruler of Heaven, I hope / Rettor del cielo, io cheggio

that the pity that brought You to earth, / che la pietà che Ti condusse in terra

will turn you towards your soul-delighting land. / Ti volga al Tuo dilecto almo paese.[30]

As he moves to the conclusion of the poem, Petrarch writes the prophecy of the resurrection of Italy's ancient virtue that shall open the path to her redemption:

By God, let this / Perdio, questo la mente

move you a little, and gaze with pity / talor vi mova, et con pietà guardate

at the tears of your sad people, / le lagrime del popol doloroso,

who place their hopes in you / che sol da voi riposo

next to God: if only you show / dopo Dio spera; et pur che voi mostriate

signs at least of pity, / segno alcun di pietate,

virtue will take up arms against fury, / vertú contra furore,

and cut short the warring because / prenderà l'arme, et fia'l combatter corto

ancient courage is not yet dead in Italian hearts. / ché l'antiquo valore ne gli italici cor' non è anchor morto.[31]

In a poem that was perhaps dedicated to Cola di Rienzo, the Roman citizen who attempted to restore Rome to its ancient glory, he portrays Italy as a "gentil donna" ("gentle lady") who awaits rescue at the hand of a husband or a father:

For more than a thousand years now / Passato è già piú che 'l millesimo anno

she has lacked those gracious spirits / che 'n lei mancâr quell'anime leggiadre

who had placed her where she was. / che locata l'avean là dov'ell'era.

Ah, you new people, proud by any measure, / Ahi nova gente oltra misura altera,

lacking in reverence for such and so great a mother! / irreverente a tanta et a tal madre!

You, be husband and father: / Tu marito, tu padre:

all help is looked for from your hands, / ogni soccorso di tua man s'attende,

for the Holy Father attends to other things. / ché 'l maggior padre ad altr'opera intende.[32]

---

[30] Francesco Petrarca, *Canzoniere*, p. 168; English translation, Petrarch, *The Complete Canzoniere*, p. 208.
[31] Francesco Petrarca, *Canzoniere*, p. 170; English translation, Petrarch, *The Complete Canzoniere*, p. 211.
[32] Francesco Petrarca, *Canzoniere*, p. 70; English translation, Petrarch, *The Complete Canzoniere*, p. 98.

In the closing verses, he shapes a prophetic vision of a redeemer:

On the Tarpeian Rock, my song, you'll see / Sopra 'l monte Tarpeio, canzon, vedrai

a knight, whom all Italy honours, / un cavalier, ch'Italia tutta honora,

thinking of others more than of himself. / pensoso piú d'altrui che di se stesso.

Say to him: "One who has not seen you close to, / Digli: Un che non ti vide anchor da presso,

and only loves you from your human fame, / se non come per fama huom s'innamora,

tells you that all of Rome / dice che Roma ognora

with eyes wet and bathed with sorrow, / con gli occhi di dolor bagnati et molli

begs mercy of you from all her seven hills" / ti chier mercé da tutti sette i colli.'[33]

In a sonnet he composed around 1350, Petrarch scourges the popes who were living in Avignon like sultans with no intention of bringing the seat of Saint Peter back to Rome, and issues the threat of divine punishment:

Babylon's idols will be scattered on the ground, / Gl' idoli suoi sarano in terra sparsi,

and her proud towers, threatening heaven, / E le torri superbe, al Ciel nemiche;

and her guards burned as they burn within. / E suoi torrer' di for, come dentr' arsi.[34]

He then offers the prophecy of a world redeemed by great souls, the friends of virtue:

Beautiful souls and friends of virtue / Anime belle e di virtute amiche

will rule the world: and we'll see it turned / Terranno 'l mondo; e poi vedrem lui farsi

all to gold and filled with ancient works. / aureo tutto, e pien de l'opre antiche.[35]

Giovanni Boccaccio (1313–1375) was another eminent advocate of the idea that poetry and prophecy are akin. In his *De genealogia deorum*, he stressed with eloquent examples that the divine art of poetry belongs to prophets:

I cannot believe that the sublime effects of this great art were first bestowed upon Musaeus, or Linus, or Orpheus, however ancient, unless, as some say, Moses and

---

[33] Francesco Petrarca, *Canzoniere*, p. 71; English translation, Petrarch, *The Complete Canzoniere*, p. 99. See Konrad Burdach, *Riforma Rinascimento Umanesimo. Due dissertazioni sui fondamenti della cultura e dell'arte della parola moderne*, translated by Delio Cantimori, preface by Cesare Vasoli, Florence: Sansoni, 1986, pp. 92–93 and p. 95. On the date of composition, see Anna Maria Voci, "Per l'interpretazione della canzone 'spirto gentil' di Francesco Petrarca," *Romanische Forschungen* 91 (1979): 281–288; on Petrarch and Cola di Rienzo, see Mario Emilio Cosenza, *Francesco Petrarca and the Revolution of Cola di Rienzo*, Chicago: University of Chicago Press, 1913.

[34] Francesco Petrarca, *Canzoniere*, p. 184; English translation, Petrarch, *The Complete Canzoniere*, p. 227.

[35] Francesco Petrarca, *Canzoniere*, p. 184; English translation, Petrarch, *The Complete Canzoniere*, p. 227.

Musaeus were one and the same [...]. Rather, it was instilled into most sacred prophets dedicated to God. For we read that Moses, impelled by what I take to be this poetic longing, at dictation of the Holy Ghost, wrote the largest part of the *Pentateuch* not in prose but in heroic verse. In like manner, others have set forth the great works of God in the metrical garments of letters, which we call poetic. And I think the poets of the Gentiles in their poetry – not perhaps without understanding – followed in the steps of these prophets.[36]

Boccaccio established a line of intellectual continuity and compatibility between the pagans – who were not inspired by the Holy Spirit – and Moses, who was indeed inspired by God. He was a poet, a prophet, and the redeemer of the Hebrews.

In his *Comento sopra la Comedia*, Cristoforo Landino (1424–1498) remarked that for the greatness of their eloquence and the divinity of their sapience, poets amply outshine all other writers ("nessuna generazione di scrittori trovarsi, e quali o per grandeza d'eloquentia, o per divinità di sapientia, per alchuno tempo a poeti pari sieno stati"). For this reason, Aristotle, whose eminence is second only to that of Plato, rightly believed that in ancient times theologians and poets were one and the same. On the contrary, whoever does not believe that poetry is a divine art deserves to be regarded as less than a man. Poets alone invoke God's help. They do so because they are aware that poetry comes from divine inspiration. If we investigate the matter carefully, we cannot fail to notice the strong analogy between the poet and the prophet ("non piccola similitudine troverremo essere fra 'l poeta et el propheta"). The Latin writers, in fact, used the same word ("vates" from "vi mentis") to indicate both the prophet and the poet. The Greeks derived the word "poet" from "poiein," a verb that indicates not only God's power to create out of nothing, but also human beings' ability to create out of existing matters and forms.[37] The poets, moreover, are prophets because they have the special ability to read God's plans and design. Inspired by God, they can then reveal these plans to their fellow human beings.

---

[36] Giovanni Boccaccio, *De genealogia deorum*, XIV, 8. I am quoting from *Tutte le opere di Giovanni Boccaccio*, VII–VIII, tomo secondo, edited by Vittore Branca, Milan: Mondadori, 1998, pp. 1410–1411; English translation, Charles G. Osgood, *Boccaccio on Poetry*, Princeton: Princeton University Press, 1930, pp. 45–46.

[37] "Il perché e Latini vollono che 'vates', decto 'a vi mentis', da vementia et concitatione di mente, fossi comune nome all'uno et all'altro. Et e Greci dixono poeta da questo verbo 'poiein', el quale è in mezo tra 'creare', che è proprio di Dio quando di niente produce in essere alchuna chosa, et 'fare', che è de gl'huomini in ciaschuna arte quando di materia et di forma compongono. Imperoché benché el figmento del poeta non sia al tutto di niente, pure si parte dal fare et al creare molto s'appressa. Et è Idio sommo poeta, et è el mondo suo poema. Et chome Idio dispone la creatura, in el visibile et invisibile mondo che è sua opera, in numero, misura, et peso, onde el profeta: 'Deus omnia facit numero, mensura et pondere'; chosi e poeti chol numero de' piedi, con la misura delle syllabe brievi et lunghe, et col pondo delle sententie et de gl'affecti, constituiscono el lor poema": Cristoforo Landino, *Comento sopra la Comedia*, Proemio: 53–65, vol. I, edited by Paolo Procaccioli, Rome: Salerno, 2001.

2.2 SAVONAROLA'S REPUBLICAN PROPHECY

As we shall see, early Humanism's intellectual tradition of poetic theology had a widespread and lasting impact on Italian ideas and movements of political emancipation. Yet the most powerful prophetic voice of Renaissance Italy – the friar Girolamo Savonarola, born in Ferrara in 1452 and executed in Florence on May 23, 1498 – was neither a poet nor a humanist.[38] He was a Dominican preacher who exhorted his fellow citizens to reform their consciences in accordance with Christ's example and to live their lives by the principles of charity and justice. At the same time, he taught them to found and defend republican self-government, the system most apt to encourage an authentic Christian life and, therefore, to pave the path to eternal salvation.[39] His biographer, Roberto Ridolfi, has written that Savonarola indeed became a preacher and a prophet to correct the moral and religious corruption of his times.[40] Because he

[38] See Mario Martelli, "Savonarola poeta," *Una città e il suo profeta. Firenze di fronte al Savonarola*, edited by Gian Carlo Garfagnini, Florence: SISMEL, 2001.

[39] Before Savonarola, Bernardino da Siena (1380–1444) and Giovanni Dominici (1356–1419) openly claimed in their sermons that God had inspired them. They thundered against factional strife, sodomy, injustice, usury, tyranny; invoked peace, celebrated Christian piety, preached the beauty of pardon. They did not provide, however, a vision of political and moral redemption comparable to Savonarola's. See Debby Nirit Ben-Aryeh, *Renaissance Florence in the Rhetoric of Two Popular Preachers: Giovanni Dominici (1346–1419) and Bernardino da Siena (1380–1444)*, Florence: Brepols, 2001. Similar considerations hold also for Pietro di Giovanni Olivi (1248–1298) and Ubertino da Casale (1259–1329) who wrote prophetic pages and lived their lives waiting for the new times and the redemption to come in humility and patience; see Raoul Manselli, "Pietro di Giovanni Olivi ed Ubertino da Casale (a proposito della *Lectura super Apocalipsim* e dell'*Arbor vitae crucifixae Jesu*)," *Studi Medievali* IV (1965), pp. 95–122. Niccolò da Cusa (1401–1464), in his prophetic work *Conjectura de ultimis diebus* (1446), announces the coming redemption ("*appropinquantem redemptionem nostram*"), by which he means the restoration of the unity and majesty of the Church. See Ovidio Capitani, "Per il significato dell'attesa dell'età nuova in Niccolò da Cusa," *L'attesa dell'età nuova nella spiritualità della fine del Medioevo. 16–19 ottobre 1960*, Todi: Presso l'Accademia Tudertina, pp. 198–216.

[40] See Roberto Ridolfi, *Studi savonaroliani*, Florence: Olschki, 1935, p. viii. In his classic work *Savonarola and Florence. Prophecy and Patriotism in the Renaissance* (Princeton: Princeton University Press, 1970, p. 312), Donald Weinstein has written: "As for Savonarola himself, the statesman was born of the prophet and the reformer, as he himself acknowledged; what was important was to get the Florentines started on the work of religious and constitutional reform; God would see to it that they were richly rewarded. Nowhere in his sermons or in his writings does he concern himself with the details of the new order (an omission, it may be observed, which is characteristic of millenarians of all times)." See also Cesare Vasoli, "L'attesa della nuova era in ambienti e gruppi fiorentini del Quattrocento," *L'attesa dell'età nuova nella spiritualità della fine del Medioevo. Convegni del centro di studi sulla spiritualità medievale*, Todi: Accademia Tudertina, 1962, pp. 370–432; and "L'influenza di Gioacchino da Fiore sul profetismo italiano della fine del Quattrocento e del primo Cinquecento," *Il profetismo gioachimita tra Quattrocento e Cinquecento. Atti del III Congresso Internazionale di Studi Gioachimiti San Giovanni in Fiore, 17–21 settembre 1989*, edited by Gian Luca Podestà, Genoa: Marietti, 1991, pp. 61–85; and *Filosofia e religione nella cultura del Rinascimento*, Naples: Guida, 1988;

connected religious, moral, and political reform, it is no exaggeration to claim that Savonarola's principles marked a turning point both in the history of prophecy and in the history of republicanism.

2.2.1 The Mission of the Prophet

Savonarola openly proclaimed that he had received prophetic light directly from God.[41] Repeatedly, he asserted that he was an instrument of God, and

and *Tra "maestri" umanistici e teologi: studi quattrocenteschi*, Florence: Le Lettere, 1991; and *Civitas Mundi: Studi sulla cultura del Cinquecento*, Rome: Edizioni di Storia e Letteratura, 1996; and *Quasi sit Deus': Studi su Marsilio Ficino*, Lecce: Conte, 1999; *Christianity and the Renaissance: Image and Religious Imagination in the Quattrocento*, edited by Timothy Verdon and John Henderson, Syracuse, NY: Syracuse University Press, 1990; David S. Peterson, "Religion, Politics, and the Church in Fifteenth-Century Florence," *Girolamo Savonarola: Piety, Prophecy, and Politics in Renaissance Florence*, edited by Donald Weinstein and Valerie R. Hotchkiss, Dallas: Bridwell Library, 1994; Gian Carlo Garfagnini, "La predica savonaroliana per una società in crisi," *Savonarola rivisitato [1498–1998]*, edited by Massimiliano G. Rosito, Florence: Città di Vita, 1998; and "Alle origini dell'impegno politico savonaroliano: la profezia," *Una città e il suo profeta. Firenze di fronte a Savonarola*, edited by Gian Carlo Garfagnini, Florence: SISMEL, 2001; and "Il messaggio profetico di Savonarola e la sua recezione. Domenico Benivieni e Gianfrancesco Pico," *Studi savonaroliani. Verso il V centenario*, edited by Gian Carlo Garfagnini, Florence: SISMEL, 1996; Guidobaldo Guidi, "La politica e lo stato nel Savonarola," *Studi savonaroliani. Verso il V centenario*, edited by Gian Carlo Garfagnini, Florence: SISMEL, 1996; Claudio Leonardi, "Girolamo Savonarola profeta di San Marco," *La chiesa e il convento di San Marco a Firenze*, vol. 1, Florence: Giunti, 1989; and "La crisi della cristianità medievale, il ruolo della profezia e Girolamo Savonarola," *Verso Savonarola. Misticismo, profezia, empiti riformistici fra medioevo ed Età moderna. Atti della III Giornata di Studi (Poggibonsi, 30 aprile 1997)*, edited by Gian Carlo Garfagnini and Giuseppe Picone, Florence: SISMEL, 1999; and "La spiritualità del Savonarola: l'arte del ben morire," *Una città e il suo profeta. Firenze di fronte al Savonarola*; and "Savonarola e la politica nelle prediche sopra l'*Esodo* e nel *Trattato circa el reggimento e governo della città di Firenze*," *Savonarola e la politica*, edited by Gian Carlo Garfagnini, Florence: SISMEL, 1997; and "La profezia di Savonarola," *Girolamo Savonarola. L'uomo e il frate. Atti del XXXV Convegno storico internazionale (Todi, 11–14 ottobre 1998)*, Spoleto: Centro Italiano di Studi sull'Alto Medioevo, 1999; Nicolai Rubinstein, "Savonarola on the Government of Florence," *The World of Savonarola. Italian Elites and Perceptions of Crisis*, edited by Stella Fletcher and Christine Shaw, Aldershot and Burlington: Ashgate, 2000; Mario Turchetti, "Savonarola: la tirannide secondo un profeta," *Savonarola. Democrazia tirannide profezia, Atti del Seminario (Pistoia, 23–24 maggio 1997)*, edited by Gian Carlo Garfagnini, Florence: SISMEL, 1998; Armando Felice Verde, "Savonarola lettore e commentatore del testo sacro," *Una città e il suo profeta. Firenze di fronte al Savonarola*.

[41] "Verum in his, que predico, non erro. Et gratia Dei sum quod sum": Girolamo Savonarola, *Compendio di rivelazioni e Dialogus de veritate prophetica*, Testo volgare e latino del *Compendio*, edited by Angela Crucitti, Rome: Angelo Belardetti, 1974, pp. 8–9. See also Girolamo Savonarola, *Prediche sopra i Salmi*, 2 volumes, edited by Vincenzo Romano, Rome: A. Belardetti, 1969–1975, p. 41. On Savonarola's prophetic visions and ideas see Felice Armando Verde, "Savonarola lettore e commentatore del testo sacro," *Una città e il suo profeta. Firenze di fronte al Savonarola*; Paolo Viti, "Savonarola e i libri," *Una città e il suo profeta. Firenze di fronte al Savonarola*; Gian Carlo Garfagnini, "Alle origini dell'impegno politico

compared his own prophetic power with that of the Apostles.[42] When he deemed it necessary, he revealed his prophetic visions in detail.[43] He had very little interest, if any at all, in the acclaimed late medieval prophets. The scriptures and, even more so, direct communication with God were the only sources of his prophetic light.[44] Proud to assert his prophetic illumination, Savonarola mercilessly denounced the poets' false pretensions of possessing prophetic powers. Whereas poets seek worldly fame and pursue beauty, true prophets must devote their best energies to reform the world. In his *Apologeticus de ratione poeticae artis*, published for the first time in 1492, he flatly asserted that "the works of the poets are not divine, not moral but animal: no I should rather call them diabolical."[45] True preachers of the word of God have nothing in common with pagan poets and orators.

Prophets do not seek glory. Their mission is to spread the truth. For Savonarola, prophets must not try to "track down stylistic devices, but rather the truth which, as St. Augustine says in *On Christian Doctrine*, is eloquent because it was written by God, and describes his mysteries."[46] Poets are not inspired prophets:

savonaroliano: la profezia," *Una città e il suo profeta. Firenze di fronte al Savonarola*; Claudio Leonardi, "La crisi della cristianità medievale, il ruolo della profezia e Girolamo Savonarola," *Verso Savonarola. Misticismo, profezia, empiti riformistici fra medioevo ed Età moderna. Atti della III Giornata di Studi (Poggibonsi, 30 aprile 1997)*, edited by Gian Carlo Garfagnini and Giuseppe Picone, Florence: SISMEL, 1999; and "La profezia di Savonarola," *Girolamo Savonarola. L'uomo e il frate, Atti del XXXV Convegno storico internazionale (Todi, 11–14 ottobre 1998)*, Spoleto: Centro Italiano di Studi sull'Alto Medioevo, 1999; Giorgio Cadoni, "*Tale stato non può stare così...*," *Savonarola e la politica*, edited by Gian Carlo Garfagnini, Florence: SISMEL, 1997.

[42] "Tu sarai solamente instrumento e io sarò il maestro, che farò lo edilizio. Che instrumento si sia, io non me ne curo, o nobile o ignobile": Girolamo Savonarola, *Prediche sopra Aggeo con il Trattato circa il reggimento e governo della città di Firenze*, edited by Luigi Firpo, Rome: Angelo Belardetti, 1965, p. 329. See also *Prediche sopra i Salmi*, vol. 1, p. 113: "Vedrete ... che'l lume che Dio ha mandato oggi in terra per rinnovare la sua Chiesa, è quel medesimo che mandò ancora in quelli tempi [the times of the Apostles], e vedrete che questa è la vera via della salute e di salire in cielo."

[43] "Vidi dunque ne l'anno 1492, la notte precedente a l'ultima predicazione che io feci quello avvento in Santa Reparata, una mano in cielo con una spada, sopra la quale era scritto: '*Gladius Domini super terram cito et velociter*', e sopra la mano era scritto: '*Vera et iusta sunt iudicia Domini*'": Girolamo Savonarola, *Compendio di rivelazioni: testo volgare e latino e Dialogus de veritate prophetica*, p. 12 (Latin text, p. 138).

[44] Ibid., p. 43.

[45] I am using Stanley Meltzoff's translation in *Botticelli, Signorelli and Savonarola. Theologia Poetica and Painting from Boccaccio to Poliziano*, Florence: Olschki, 1987. The *Apologeticus* is a polemical response to a letter in defense of poetry (*Carmen de Christianae Religionis Vitae Monasticae foelicitate. Ad Hieronymum Ferrariensem, theologum Ordinis fratrum Praedicatorum insignem*) that Ugolino Verino (1438–1516), a Christian humanist who supported republican government, addressed to Savonarola in 1490. For the date of composition and a fine description of Savonarola's manuscript, see p. 49.

[46] Ibid., p. 51.

they are liars, as the proverb says, and they lie and make up stories about gods as well as men full of lustfulness, and the most silly and unspeakable intercourse of gods and men. They nourish the tender minds of the young with their lies and juvenile, wicked, and lustful tales of gods, and fill their pure and unprotected intellects first with falsehoods and then with the filthy, abominable superstitions of idolatry, and inflame their lusts of the flesh, always prone to evil, adding fire to fire and subjugating the whole body and soul, to the servitude of the devil. The art that our poets now preserve is a most deadly plague for youth.[47]

Savonarola urged Christian princes to ban poets and burn their books.[48] The very notion that poets could have prophetic powers, and that prophecy could hide under the allegories of pagan poems, was utterly unacceptable to him. Insofar as aural allurements might be used to transpose the argument into poetry, he claims, these delights would detract from the truth and present the danger of distracting both poet and listener from truth to sensuous delights and vanities. The beauty of poetry is the source of its evil, the devil's bait. The same was true of parables. These fictions signify, beyond the literal sense, what Christ meant, but this does not at all imply that pagan stories can or should be read in that way. Savonarola proved that ancient writers could not prefigure events allegorically: "only God knows the future, and only His providence knows the inescapable."[49]

Equally severe were Savonarola's attacks against astrologers. Pretending to know the future from the movements of stars and planets means boasting to possess a knowledge that can only belong to God.[50] Astrology offends both divine providence and free will. As God's creatures, human beings are free from celestial influences and powers.[51] True prophets have no use for astrology. Interpreted with the help of God's grace and of Christian charity, the scriptures provide all the wisdom that prophets need. Human philosophy and eloquence are redundant. Prophets must trust in a supernatural knowledge that is entirely different from the philosophic schools, and yet, at the same time, not mystical at all. Prophetic knowledge is similar, though not identical, to the knowledge of the theologian who sees divine mysteries by way of inward illumination, as if in a mirror.[52] The only virtue that prophets truly need is to be "full of God (*"Deo plenus"*), to be enriched by the grace of the Holy Spirit and charity (*"gratia*

---

[47] Ibid., p. 51.   [48] Ibid., p. 52.   [49] Ibid., pp. 54–55.

[50] "E breviter la Sacra scrittura dimostra che cognoscere le cose future contingente è prophetia divina: e però solo Dio le conosce, e quelli a' quali lui si degna revelarle. [...] E però quelli che seguono questa superstizione divinatorie peccano gravemente, usurpandosi la proprietà divina falsamente"; G. Savonarola, *Compendio di rivelazioni: testo volgare e latino e Dialogus de veritate prophetica*, pp. 3–125 (Italian); 127–245 (Latin).

[51] See Gian Carlo Garfagnini, "La polemica antiastrologica del Savonarola ed i suoi precedenti tomistici," *Filosofia scienza astrologia nel Trecento europeo*, edited by Graziella Federici Vescovini and Francesco Baroncelli, Padua: Il Poligrafo, 1992, p. 157.

[52] Girolamo Savonarola, *Scritti filosofici*, edited by Gian Carlo Garfagnini and Eugenio Garin, Rome: Angelo Belardetti, 1982, vol. I, p. 207.

Spiritus sancti et caritate et divina Sapientia").[53] To accomplish their mission and to transfer themselves entirely in God (*"conversio ad Deum"*), they must distance themselves from the world and from human wisdom (*"aversio a mundo"*).[54]

Prophetic knowledge is grounded upon God's power to see all events as present in time.[55] We may attain it not by deriving conclusions from principles, but rather through a direct comprehension of principles themselves. It is a light that God instills in whom he wants – a light that permits prophets to share, for a brief period, God's eternal wisdom.[56] "God speaks in the heart of the prophets," we read in *Psalm* 84:9. Since prophetic knowledge is "divinely inspired" (*"divinitus inspirata"*), it does not need words and sentences.[57] Like mental prayer, it is made possible by the union of the mind with God

---

[53] Giulio Cattin, *Il primo Savonarola. Poesie e prediche autobiografiche dal codice Borromeo*, Florence: Olschki, 1983, p. 13.

[54] Armando F. Verde, O.P., *Lo Studio Fiorentino. 1473–1503. Ricerche e documenti*, IV: *La vita universitaria*, vol. 2, Florence: Olschki, 1985, p. 979.

[55] "Le cose future e quelle che sono del libero arbitrio, che possono essere e non essere, solamente Iddio le sa e quella creatura a chi Iddio le vuole rivelare, come abbiamo detto. E però io ti dico che l'astrologia, per volere indovinare, è cagione di molte superstizione e eresie," Sermon of January 13, 1495, in *Prediche sopra i Salmi*, vol. I, pp. 38–39.

[56] "Li profeti avevono ancora di questo lume di Dio [...] E pertanto questo lume è una participazione della eternità, el quale Iddio comunica a chi e' vuole." *Prediche sopra i Salmi*, vol. I, p. 40.

[57] Girolamo Savonarola, *Sermoni sopra il salmo "Quam bonus,"* edited by Claudio Leonardi, Rome: Angelo Belardetti, 1999, pp. 1–14. While respectful of the prophets, Savonarola had no esteem for prophetesses. In sermons from 1496 and 1497, he affirmed that scripture indeed attests that God also gives his prophetic light to women. Not all prophetesses are to be despised and rejected. However, Savonarola adds that, when God entrusts humans with the power of prophecy, he does so because he wants them to spread his message in the world. Since women cannot speak in church or in public, God prefers to give this prophetic light to men (*Prediche sopra Ruth e Michea*, edited by V. Romano, Rome: Angelo Belardetti, 1962, vol. II, pp. 92–93; Adriana Valerio, "La predica sopra Ruth, la donna, la riforma dei semplici," *Una città e il suo profeta: Firenze di Fronte al Savonarola*, edited by Gian Carlo Garfagnini, Florence: SISMEL, 2001, pp. 261–262; see also Adriana Valerio: "L'altra rivelazione: L'esperienza profetica femminile nei secoli XIV–XVI," *Donne, potere e profezia*, edited by Adriana Valerio, Naples: D'Auria, 1995, pp. 136–162; "Il profeta e la parola: La predicazione di Domenica da Paradiso nella Firenze post-Savonaroliana," *Studi savonaroliani: verso il V centenario*, edited by Gian Carlo Garfagnini, Florence: SISMEL, 1996, pp. 299–307. When the prophetess Suor Maddalena harshly attacked Savonarola in 1497, his followers urged him to confront her in a public debate. Savonarola sidestepped the issue by saying that the nun would do better if she devoted herself to sewing and other womanly tasks, and that her superiors should have forbidden her from leaving the convent and preaching. In his twenty-third sermon on Ezekiel, Savonarola explained that the mother of Christ had surely received God's prophetic light, but, because she was aware that spreading the word of God was an exclusively male prerogative, she avoided speaking in public on religious matters. Those women who want to spread their prophetic revelations publicly – out of lust for vainglory – must follow St. Paul's golden precept: *mulieres in ecclesia taceant.* See Tamar Herzig, *Savonarola's Women: Vision and Reform in Renaissance Italy*, Chicago and London: Chicago University Press, 2008.

(*"unione della mente con Dio"*).[58] Through the prophetic light they have received from God, prophets understand the meaning of past, present, and future events and perceive what God intends to teach when He intervenes in history. In his sermons, Savonarola often explains his method of prophetic interpretation. Let us take, for instance, his *Sermons on the Psalms*. He states that, if you see that the leaders of the Church and of the republic are full of vices, God's scourge is imminent. The scriptures, he clarifies, clearly help us to comprehend the meaning of this fact when they recount how God allowed King David to sin to punish the people. If you see that good people leave the city, you can be sure, once again, that God's scourge is imminent, as inferred from the story of Lot, who left Sodom just before God's punishment befell that wretched city. At times, Savonarola declares that he has recognized God's intentions by himself and without citing the scripture. For example, when the chiefs of the republic expelled the best and the wisest citizens from their council, he asserted that this clearly meant, yet again, that God's scourge would be imminent. The narrations and the conclusions change, but Savonarola's prophetic method is always the same: he understands the meaning of facts because God has gifted him with the light of prophecy.[59]

Prophets need no words to communicate with God. Yet, they must find the right way of teaching their fellow citizens the truth God has revealed to them. To inspire they must resort to both human and divine reason, and moderate their tongue to speak not with the tone of a lord but with the tone of a father.[60] When the occasion requires it, however, Savonarola makes use of an authoritative attitude and issues precise orders concerning divine worship and religious practices (*"come padre vostro io vi dico e impongo"*).[61] He also knows how to present himself as a compassionate mother who understands that at times it is right to forgive.[62] Prophets must be able to persuade their fellow citizens to make the right choice for their community. Their chief duty is to fight religious and moral corruption, to oppose injustice, to resist political and social oppression. As servants of God, their task must be to change the beliefs, the

---

[58] "E, benchè voglia dir bene le parole con la intelligenzia delle sentenzie, nientedimeno el cuore suo è fisso a Dio, non discorrendo né per parole né per sentenzie, ma elevando la mente sopra di sé. E questa attenzione è ottima e alcuna volta leva tanto l'anima in alto che si dimentica tutte le cose umane e se medesima." Girolamo Savonarola, *Trattato in difesa e commendazione dell'orazione mentale*, edited by Mario Ferrara in *Operette spirituali*, vol. 1, Rome: Belardetti, 1976, p. 167.

[59] Girolamo Savonarola, *Prediche sopra i Salmi*, vol. I, pp. 42–45.

[60] Ibid., p. 62. "I have said all these things for reasons both divine and human, with moderation and tempering my tongue. I have begged you; I cannot command you, for I am not your lord, but your father. Do it, Florence, I pray to God for you, that He may enlighten you"; English translation from *Selected Writings of Girolamo Savonarola. Religion and Politics, 1490–1498*, translated and edited by Anna Borelli and Maria Pastore Passaro, New Haven and London: Yale University Press, 2006, p. 76.

[61] Girolamo Savonarola, *Prediche sopra Aggeo*, p. 74.

[62] Girolamo Savonarola, *Prediche sopra i Salmi*, vol. I, edited by Vincenzo Romano, Rome: A. Belardetti, 1969–1975, pp. 57–58.

institutions, and the mores of their times.[63] Composed when he was twenty, the canzone *De ruina mundi* eloquently documents the passions and concerns that motivated Savonarola to embrace the life of the prophet:

If your providence were not, as I believe it to be, / truly infinite, Lord of the world; / nor could I ever / believe otherwise, for I know it so through experience; I would then feel even colder than snow, / seeing that the world is upside down / and that every virtue and every good custom / have now died out: / I cannot find one virtuous person / or even one who is ashamed of his own vices. / But there are those who deny you, those who say that you are dreaming. [...] Here people esteem those who are God's enemies; / Cato is now a beggar; / power has fallen into pirate hands; / St. Peter's crumbles down; / here lust and all kinds of spoils abound, so much so that I do not know how heaven is not confused. / Do you not see how arrogant / that insolent fool is and how he overflows with vices, / so much that my heart is consumed by great disdain? / Behold! Look at that catamite and his pimp / dressed in cardinal's red – an actor / whom commoner follow and whom the blind world adores! / Does it not at all offend you / that this lustful pig enjoys himself / with adulterers and parasites, and that he usurps / the high praises due to you, / while your faithful ones are banished from one city to another? / Happy now are those who live by stealing; / more so, those who feed on the blood of others; / those who rip off widows and their orphans still in swaddles; / those who run to bring ruin to the poor! / Noble and virtuous are those souls / who obtain more and more with fraud or with force; / those who scorn heaven and Christ, / and who always think about how to crush others; / the world honors those / who have books and papers filled with treacheries, / those who know best the art of all wrongdoing. /The world is so oppressed by every vice / that, by its own devices, it will never be released from such a burden: / [...] oh! How much pain do you feel, Brutus, and you, Fabricius, / if you have noticed this other great ruin! / As if what Cataline, / Sulla, Marius, Caesar, and Nero did was not enough! / But here men and women, / everyone strives to inflict harm upon others: / the time of piety and chastity has passed. / Absent virtue, you never raise your wings, / cry the populace and the blind, wicked people. / Now lust is called philosophy: / everyone even turns their back on doing good. / No longer are there those who follow along the right path, / such that the virtue left in me remains frozen. / However, a hope / does not allow this virtue to leave me completely, / for I know that in the next life / well-seen will be those noble souls / whose wings rose them to a more gracious life. / Song, be careful, / do not entrust yourself to those dressed as prelates; / flee from palaces and loggias; / keep your thoughts only among few people, / because you will be the enemy of the whole world.[64]

[63] See Roberto Ridolfi, *Studi savonaroliani*, Florence: Olschki, 1935, p. vii.

[64] "Se non che pur è vero e così credo / Rettor del mondo, che infinita sia / Toa providenzia; nè già mai potria / Creder contra, perché ab experto el vedo; / Talor seria via più che neve fredo, / Vedendo sotto sopra volto el mondo, / Et esser spenta al fondo / Ogne vitute et ogni bel costume. / Non trovo un vivo lume, / Né pur chi de' soi vizii se vergogni: / Chi te nega, chi dice che tu sogni. / [...] Quivi se estima chi è de Dio nemico; / Catone va mendico; / Ne le man di pirata è gionto el scetro: / A terra va San Pietro; / Quivi lussuria et ogni preda abunda: / Che non so come il ciel non si confunda. / Non vedi tu il satirico mattone / Quanto è superbo, et è di vizii un fiume? / Che di gran sdegno il cor mi si consume. / Deh! Mira quel cinedo e quel lenone / Di porpora vestito, un istrione / Che'l vulgo segue e il cieco mondo adora! / Non ti vien sdegno ancora / Che quel lussurioso porco gode, / E le toe alte lode / Usurpa, assentatori e parasciti; / E i

Revulsion against moral and religious corruption, as well as the firm determination to emend it, prompted Savonarola to join the Dominican order. He wrote to his father:

Foremost, the reason which moves me to enter into religion is this: first the great misery of the world, the wickedness of men, acts of violence and adultery, theft, arrogance, idolatry, grievous blasphemies: so much so that a time has come in which we no longer can find anyone who does good, and wherein I, many times a day, have sung this verse crying: *Oh!* *Escape these cruel lands, escape this greedy shore* (*Heu fuge crudeles terras, fuge littas avarum*) [*Aeneid* III.44]. And for this, I could not endure the great sickness of the blind peoples of Italy; and all the more so as I saw virtues fade to nothing and vices be promoted.[65]

To be a prophet and to carry out the mission of Italy's moral and religious regeneration effectively, he left his family and his native city, mindful that "*nemo propheta in patria*," as the Gospel of Jesus teaches.[66] Even if he felt himself to be but a humble friar inept for such a grand task, he began to preach for the redemption of Florence through submission and obedience to God's will. While he would have gladly liked to abandon his prophetic task – and its respective labors and its resultant persecutions – in order to withdraw to the quiet of a cloister, he understood that he could not disobey God and refuse the gift of prophecy he had received. He found some consolation, though, in the consideration that people would understand that all the glory belongs to God, should the moral and religious reformation for which he was advocating at last triumph.[67]

---

toi di terra in terra son banditi? / Felice or mai chi vive di rapina, / E chi del'altrui sangue più se pasce, / Chi vedoe spoglia e soi pupilli in fasce, / E chi di povri corre a la ruina! / Quella anima è gentil e peregrina / Che per fraude o per forza fa più acquisto, / Chi spreza il ciel cum Cristo / E sempre pensa altrui cacciar al fondo; Colui onora el mondo / Che ha pien di latrocinii libri e carte / E chi d'ogne mal far sa meglio l'arte. / La terra è sì oppressa da ogne vizio, / Che mai da sé non leverà la soma: / [...] O quanta doglia hai Bruto e tu Fabrizio, / Se hai intesa questa altra gran ruina! / Non basta Catilina, / Non Silla, Mario, Cesaro o Nerone: / Ma quivi omini e done, / Og'om si sforza dargli qualche guasto. / Passato è il tempo pio e il tempo casto. / Virtù mendica mai non alzi l'ale: / Grida il vulgo e la cieca gente ria. / L'usura si chiama or filosofia; / Al far bene ogn'om volta pur le spale: / Non è chi vada or mai per dritto cale, / Tal che'l valor se agiaza che me avanzia. / Se non che una speranzia / Pur al tutto, nol lassa far partita, / Ch'io scio che in l'altra vita / Ben si vedrà qual alma fo gentile, / E chi alzò l'ale a più legiadro stile. / Canzion, fa che sia acorta, / Che a purpureo color tu non te apoggie; / Fugi palazi e le logie, / E fa che toa ragion a pochi dica: / Chè a tuto el mondo tu sarai nemica"; Girolamo Savonarola, *De ruina mundi*, in Giulio Cattin, *Il primo Savonarola. Poesie e prediche autobiografiche dal codice Borromeo*, pp. 207–212. English translation by Robert Bucci.

[65] *Le lettere di Girolamo Savonarola, ora per la prima volta raccolte e a miglior lezione ridotte da Roberto Ridolfi*. Florence: Olschki, 1933, p. 1.

[66] G. Savonarola to his mother of January 25, 1490, in *Le lettere di Girolamo Savonarola, ora per la prima volta raccolte e a miglior lezione ridotte da Roberto Ridolfi*, p. 12. On Savonarola and his family, see Roberto Ridolfi, "La fuga dalla casa paterna: gli scritti consolatorî," *Studi savonaroliani*, edited by Roberto Ridolfi, Florence: Olschki, 1935.

[67] "E di più, per volontà di Dio, da me se' stata fatta partecipe de' secreti di Dio delle cose future [...] io, per la salute tua e perché così ha voluto Dio, mi sono esposto agli obbrobrii, alle derisioni, alle murmurazioni di molti per tuo amore, e mai non t'ho lasciato, e così sono qua

Prophetic light does not make prophets just. To be just, Savonarola admonished, prophets must always respect the virtue of charity.[68] They must also remain humble before God.[69] Charity and humility give prophets the moral force they need to be immune from the corruption of their times, and to be strong in their faith even amidst the hatred, mockery, and contempt of their fellow citizens.[70] Prophets must teach all their fellow citizens, even when they do not listen. They must be the voice of the most miserable, lowly, and disconsolate who have no voice. From their prophetic light, they receive an extraordinary moral strength that, in turn, gives their fellow citizens the power to accomplish their redemption. Since prophets are under God's protection, their redemptive mission survives even after their death.[71] If necessary, God will send new prophets to accomplish the redemptive mission. The individuals who start their journey of emancipation may be reassured that one day, with God's help, they shall reach the Promised Land.

Prophecy aids the natural light that helps human beings in their search for true happiness. This, Savonarola tirelessly affirmed, is the most precious gift that prophecy bestows upon human beings.[72] By itself, human intelligence is not an adequate guide for our moral and political choices. It needs the counsel

---

per te e non per me, né per alcuna mia utilità, ma perché Dio ha voluto così e ha preso uno uomo vile e inetto a far questo officio, acciò che lui mostri d'essere lui quello che fa e non uno fraticello. Non potrei io, se io volessi, lasciarti e fuggire tante persecuzioni e tante fatiche"; *Prediche sopra Aggeo*, pp. 16–17.

[68] See G. Savonarola, *Prediche sopra i Salmi*, vol. I, pp. 59–60, and *Prediche sopra Giobbe*, vol. 1 edited by Roberto Ridolfi, Rome: Angelo Belardetti, 1957, pp. 213–214.

[69] See G. Savonarola, *Prediche sopra Amos e Zaccaria*, edited by Paolo Ghiglieri, Rome: Angelo Belardetti, 1971–1972, vol. II, pp. 56–157, and *Prediche sopra Giobbe*, vol. I, pp. 213–214.

[70] Girolamo Savonarola, "*A tutti gli eletti di Dio e fedeli cristiani*, Florence, May 8, 1497," *Lettere e Scritti apologetici*, edited by Roberto Ridolfi, Vincenzo Romano and Armando F. Verde, Rome: Angelo Belardetti, 1984, pp. 259–260. See also Armando F. Verde, *Lo Studio Fiorentino. 1473–1503. Ricerche e documenti*, IV: *La vita universitaria*, vol. 2, pp. 1052–1055 and 1139–1145.

[71] Girolamo Savonarola, *Lettere e Scritti apologetici*, pp. 251–252.

[72] "Quanto sia necessaria la profezia alla salute umana, dilettissimi in Cristo Iesù, si cognosce per molte ragione, Primo, perché è necessario alla salute umana la fede della provvidenzia di Dio, bisogna che credino li uomini che Dio abbi provvidenzia, perché credendo quella hanno dua sproni, cioè d'amore e di timore, e non è cosa che faccia più fede della provvidenzia di Dio delle cose umane che fa la profezia, perché li profeti dicono tanto tempo innanzi le cose future che non le può sapere se non Dio [...]. Secondo, è necessaria per dare argumento alla fede, perché cognoscendo li uomini che tutto quello che è fatto circa la fede è stato profetato, si vengono a fortificare più nella fede, perché li profeti non attendono ad altro che a provare e magnificare la fede. Terzio, è necessaria per la gubernazione della Chiesa, perché vengano casi e difficultà singulari che bisogna che vi sia altro che lume naturale a solverle [...] Quarto, per certi particulari, *idest* tribulazioni che vengono, perché li uomini per quella profezia si consolano [...] Quinto per distinguere li buoni dalli cattivi, perché la mescolanza delli cattivi fa molti errori, ma *immediate* che la profezia viene si scoprono e' cattivi a contradire e li buoni si veggono [...] Sesto, per la conversione de' peccatori, perché vedendo che le cose predette vengono si convertono [...] Settimo, per laude di Dio [...] Ora tu hai veduta la provvidenzia di Dio e cognosciuto li buoni e li cattivi e tiepidi che si sono scoperti, si che adunque vogliamo seguitare

of grace and prophecy.[73] Instead of trusting our intelligence, he warns, we should elect Christ's life as our model.[74] With Christ's guidance, along with the help of God's revelations, prophets can successfully fight tyranny, the mortal enemy of Christian life.

2.2.2 The New Jerusalem

Like the Scholastic writers before him, Savonarola maintains that tyranny deprives peoples of their liberty, dignity, and prosperity. Its chief vice is the religious and moral corruption that perverts individual consciences and renders people unfit to live a truly Christian life.[75] Though veiled, the Medici family's domination was also a form of tyranny. After the expulsion of the Medici from Florence, he proclaimed in December 1494: "You are frightened by no one now, but when you had a head or tyrant, you know that the law of the tyrant is his will, that's how the tyrant is: every time he thinks you've done the slightest thing he doesn't like, he doesn't want to see you anymore."[76] Savonarola stressed that the religious life of the Florentines had degenerated in a sequel of empty and insincere rituals under the tyranny of the Medici.[77] The evil of tyranny is especially acute in Christian cities – and above all in Florence – where

---

nel dichiarare li profeti perché è molto utile"; Girolamo Savonarola, *Prediche sopra Ezechiele*, vol. 1, edited by Roberto Ridolfi, Rome: Angelo Belardetti, 1955, pp. 3–5.

[73] "Girolamo Savonarola, *Prediche sopra Aggeo*, p. 301.

[74] "Ha posto dunque Dio la beatitudine dell'uomo in questo Crucifisso, e certamente, se beatitudine alcuna si trova in questo mondo, la non è altro che assomigliaria a questo Crucifisso e imitare, in quanto l'uomo può, la vita, e' modi e li costumi di questo Crucifisso. Cristo ci ha dato la sua legge evangelica, della quale nessuna si trovò mai la migliore né la più perfetta. [...] ma noi veggiamo questa sua legge esser per tutto, e massime in Firenze, lacerata e disprezzata dagli uomini cattivi e perversi, che non si vogliono accostare a questa legge di Cristo, né vivere secondo quella. Però è venuto Dio per medicare Firenze e per fare che la sua legge si osservi, e che la città viva ad un altro modo, e che ella faccia nuova reformazione, come io t'ho detto nelli sermoni nostri precedenti"; Girolamo Savonarola, *Prediche sopra Aggeo*, pp. 302–303.

[75] Girolamo Savonarola, *Prediche sopra Aggeo*, pp. 456–457. In his earlier work *De politia et regno* (1480), however, Savonarola had advised that it is better to tolerate the tyrant than to rebel against him, particularly if his tyranny is mild. See Girolamo Savonarola, *Compendium philosophiae moralis*, in *Scritti filosofici*, vol. II, p. 469. In his sermons on Aggeus, Savonarola strongly warned the Florentines to mistrust princes; see Girolamo Savonarola, *Prediche sopra Aggeo*, p. 447.

[76] Girolamo Savonarola, *Prediche sopra Amos e Zaccaria*, vol. I, pp. 229–230.

[77] "Non ti ricorda, Firenze, che non sono molti anni, come tu stavi nelle cose di Dio e della fede? Non eri tu in molte cose come eretica? Non sai tu che t'ha fatto toccare la fede si può dire con mano? Tu ti stavi in quelle tue cerimonie estrinseche e parevati essere santa, e Dio t'ha demostrato quanto tu erravi e che quelle non vagliano cosa alcuna senza la purità del cuore e che la vita cristiana consiste in altro che in cerimonie"; Girolamo Savonarola, *Prediche sopra Aggeo*, p. 11. As early as April 6, 1461, Savonarola launched a severe critique of Florence moral and political corruption in which he openly accuses the republic's leader (Lorenzo the Magnificent) of being a tyrant, of protecting arrogant and powerful men, denying justice to the poor, deliberating unjust wars, selling public honors, allowing magistrates to abuse their

citizens are strongly inclined to live according to Christian piety.[78] Because they corrupt the conscience of the Christian people, the wrath of God shall infallibly fall upon tyrants and crooked prelates.

The chief tenet of Savonarola's redemptive vision was the principle of moral liberty, the liberty of the person who has accepted God's law and lives by it. This radical transformation of individual consciences was for him the necessary condition to accomplish a moral and religious reform that could aptly sustain and protect the Christian way of life. He wanted to make Florence a New Jerusalem under God's protection.[79] Spiritual goods (*bona spiritualia*), Savonarola stressed, are more important than temporal goods. If a community pursues the former, it shall also attain the latter; if it puts temporal goods above spiritual goods, it shall miss them both.[80] Savonarola openly challenged the Florentine mentality that puts political power and social status above spiritual goods. He insisted that the true reform Florence needed was, in the first place, spiritual.[81] In the proper order of reform, the most important step must be the fear of God.[82] If the Florentines shall at last rediscover and obey the law of God, they shall be able to establish a political and social order that shall reflect the celestial Jerusalem.[83]

powers, fomenting the division of citizens. See Pasquale Villari, *La storia di Girolamo Savonarola e de' suoi tempi*, vol. I, Florence: Le Monnier, 1887, p. xxxiv.

[78] See Donald Weinstein, *Savonarola and Florence*, p. 299.

[79] Roberto Rusconi, "Profezia e profeti in Occidente, dal secondo medioevo alla prima età moderna. Dallo scrittoio alla piazza ovvero dalla penna alla spada," *Carisma profetico: fattore di innovazione religiosa*, edited by Giovanni Filoramo, Brescia: Morcelliana, 2003, p. 141.

[80] "Rinnovatevi prima dentro, se volete bene rinovarvi nelle cose esteriore, e se volete fare le buone leggi, acconciatevi prima co' la legge di Dio, perché tutte le buone leggi dependano dalla legge eterna, all'osservanzia della quale si ricerca la grazia dello Spirito Santo. Adunque bisogna che tu sia illuminato da Dio, Firenze, d'altro lume che del naturale, perché el lume naturale non è per sé sufficiente a reggere e governare el popolo cristiano [...]. E' bisogna, Firenze, che tu ti riduca al culto divino, perché gli stati de' veri cristiani si reggano con l'orazione e col ben fare, e non è vero quel che dicano e' pazzi e cattivi, che lo stato non si regge co' paternostri. Questo è detto di tiranni e non di veri prìncipi. Le tirannie si reggono a cotesto modo, ma durano poco. Vivete adunque da cristiani e venite alle predicazioni, dove s'impara el ben vivere cristiano; chi non vuole udire il verbo di Dio fa in prima ingiurie a Dio e, secundario, dà scandalo al popolo. E però andate alle prediche ad imparare, e saperete meglio reggervi secondo Dio"; Girolamo Savonarola, *Prediche sopra Aggeo*, pp. 133–135.

[81] Girolamo Savonarola, *Prediche sopra Aggeo*, p. 284.

[82] "Io ti ho detto quattro cose [Firenze], se non le farai, guai a te: prima, il timore di Dio; secundo, il bene commune; terzio, la pace universale; quarto, la reforma. Voi avete cominciato a rovescio, cioè a la reforma, che era l'ultima. Seguitate almeno a rovescio, e fate questa pace; ché, se non la fate, sarà la ruina vostra"; Girolamo Savonarola, *Prediche sopra i Salmi*, vol. I, p. 32. See also *Trattato del governo di Firenze*, in *Prediche sopra Aggeo con il Trattato circa il reggimento e governo della città di Firenze*, p. 436.

[83] Girolamo Savonarola, *Prediche sopra Aggeo*, pp. 416–417. See also Donald Weinstein, *Savonarola and Florence*, pp. 302–303. To render his message attractive, Savonarola promised his fellow Florentines that the more the community is spiritual, the more it becomes prosperous and powerful. In this regard, see Girolamo Savonarola, *Prediche sopra Aggeo*, pp. 216–217.

The other major tenet of Savonarola's prophetic vision was his persuasion that the reform of consciences requires a political reform that institutes a well-ordered popular government.[84] The example that the Florentines ought to follow was the ancient government of Israel:

> Your government then, Florence, is like that of a judge of the Israelites. I have distinguished government into three types: royal, optimates and popular [...] and I have with reasons shown you that this government of the people is more natural and proper to you than all the others. So I want to tell you that although the government of the Hebrews was popular because the people ruled and the judge didn't command but advised, yet it could be called royal because it depended on the mouth of one person, that is God's, because God was the one who ruled them, because through the mouth of the judge and prophet they were counseled by God what they had to do, and so it was royal, and it was also optimates because God allowed the best to advance and be elected and govern. So, Florence, your time will come if you do what I have said. You will find good government and do well. God will always send someone to enlighten you and you will not be able to do badly.[85]

In the ancient *respublica Hebreorum*, Savonarola stressed, God ruled de facto through the mouths of his prophets. It was a republic of God and of prophets, and for this reason it was the best.[86] He taught his fellow Florentines that they must openly acknowledge popular government as a gift from God, a sign of his friendship. Naturally, he also cautioned them that God would immediately withdraw his friendship should his law be disobeyed.[87] Savonarola wanted the citizens of Florence to regard the Consiglio Maggiore (Great Council) as the republic's soul, hence as the object of their profound devotion. Citizens must feel it their duty before God to make the republican government ever more perfect. They must believe that God has given Florence the Great Council because he cares for the condition of the city.[88]

2.2.3 Christ King of Florence

A fundamental tenet of the republican ideology since the thirteenth century was the belief that God (or Christ, or the Virgin, or all three) loves and protects popular governments because they are the most apt to encourage true Christian life.[89] Savonarola restated this conventional belief. But he restated it with a prophetic voice, as a truth that he had received from God. He persuaded the Florentines that they ought to elect Christ as their king, if they wanted to make their popular government perfect, truly be capable of accomplishing God's

---

[84] Girolamo Savonarola, *Prediche sopra Ruth e Michea*, pp. 248–249.
[85] Girolamo Savonarola, *Prediche sopra Ruth e Michea*, pp. 106–108.
[86] Girolamo Savonarola, *Prediche sopra i Salmi*, vol. I, p. 58.   [87] Ibid.
[88] Girolamo Savonarola, *Prediche sopra Aggeo*, pp. 476–477.
[89] I have discussed this subject in *As if God Existed. Religion and Liberty in the History of Italy*, Princeton: Princeton University Press, 2012, pp. 18–51.

design on earth. On December 27, 1494, four days after the institution of the Republic's highest legislative body, the Great Council, Savonarola thundered:

One can't deny that those states that are governed by one head alone are best, but he must be perfect [...]. So, what would you like, Florence, what head, what king can we give you to keep you quiet? I've told you before that it's not better everywhere, or in every country, for one head to rule, and St Thomas says, too, that in Italy princes become tyrants – come on, Florence, God wants to satisfy you and give you one head and one king to govern you. And this is Christ. Take Christ for your king and stay under his law and with it he will govern you [...]. Let Christ be your Captain [...] be with Christ and don't seek another head.[90]

The proclamation of Christ king of Florence was Savonarola's prophetic masterpiece and a remarkable innovation in the history of prophecy and political liberty. To declare Christ king of Florence meant to accept the solemn commitment to obey his example. As long as Christ is the king of Florence, no citizen can make himself king, and the republic is therefore safe.[91] All the citizens must always have before their eyes the example of Christ and that of the apostles, who reformed the religion of their times through sufferings and tribulations. The condition of Florence and of Italy, Savonarola remarked, resembles that of the Hebrews before the advent of Christ. Just as Christ and few apostles reformed the Hebrew religion and instilled a new faith in the hearts of people, the new prophets sent by God, like Christ himself, will bring about the renovation of the Church and accomplish the political reform. It is one thing to be under God; another to have Christ as a king. While God remains on high in heaven, Christ as a king is a tangible presence. The governors of Florence wrote his name in large letters in the hall of the Great Council. Whereas Italian republics before the Florentine republics regarded themselves as sacred republics, the Florentine Republic of 1494 was the first prophetic republic. A prophet helped to found it; the prophetic vision of Christ as its king was supposed to keep it eternal and perfect.

For Savonarola, the presence of Christ at the core of the republic's symbolic space was necessary to win the war against Satan, the enemy of the moral and political redemption.[92] Since Satan is aware that prophetic light, when combined with faith, leads human beings to rediscover true Christian life, he mobilizes all his guiles and forces to suffocate it.[93] He fights against the prophets of redemption because he is envious of the glory that redemption

---

[90] Girolamo Savonarola, *Prediche sopra Ruth e Michea*, p. 422.
[91] Girolamo Savonarola, *Prediche sopra Aggeo*, pp. 409–428. According to Weinstein, Savonarola retained elements of his earlier monarchism when he announced, in his sermon of December 28, 1494, that Christ and only Christ must be the king of Florence. I do not agree with this interpretation. Savonarola exhorted his fellow Florentines to elect Christ as king of Florence precisely to bar the road to a true prince. See *Savonarola and Florence*, p. 294.
[92] Girolamo Savonarola, *Lettere e Scritti apologetici*, p. 244.   [93] Ibid., p. 266.

brings to God.[94] To be able to defend good government, citizens must follow the example of Christ and have their conscience and their love of country be their guides.[95] In perfect agreement with classical republican tradition, Savonarola remarks that serving the common good is the wisest way to secure one's liberty and one's private goods. It is also the right way of serving God and, at the same time, showing gratitude for the precious gift of republican government.[96] However contradictory it might sound, true liberty is service: serving God and the common good.[97] Only a true prophet inspired by God can help citizens see the truth and the value of these principles of republican political wisdom. Without true prophets, the republic cannot be born, cannot live, cannot resurrect.

In addition to paying taxes, serving in the militia, and attending public rituals, republican liberty demands that citizens have the courage to speak truth when they sit on councils.[98] If they serve as representatives or as officers of the republic, they must set aside all private loyalties and interests to serve only the common good. They must have the moral strength to guarantee justice to

---

[94] Ibid., p. 239.

[95] Girolamo Savonarola, *Prediche sopra Amos e Zaccaria*, vol. I, pp. 256–257.

[96] "Così io dico a voi: il padre è il vostro comune, e però ciascuno è obligato ad aiutarlo. E se tu di': – Io non ho utile nessuno dal commune -, sappi che tu non puoi dire così, perché lui ti conserva la tua roba, la tua famiglia e li figliuoli, perché se lui perdesse, perderesti ancora tu ogni cosa. Doverresti andare là e dire: – Ecco qua cinquanta ducati, eccone cento, eccone mille-: così fanno e' buoni cittadini che amano la patria loro. Tu dirai: – Se noi abbiamo avere tante grazie, non bisogna fare altro -. Io ti rispondo che non si vuole tentare Iddio, ma lui vuol che tu facci le provisioni umane e che poi la prima confidenzia tu abbia in lui. Se tu non seminassi nulla nel tuo giardino e solo dicessi: – Iddio vi farà nascere delle erbe e quello che mi bisogna-, questo saria uno tentare Iddio [...]. Dico adunque così: che adesso che avete qualche tribulazione, doverresti mettere tutti la roba per adiutare la città, e insino alle donne doverriano dar via il superfluo per adiutare la patria. Adiutatela adunque tutti gagliardamente e non vi curate di metterci la roba, ché io vi conforto stamani di novo che al tempo suo verrà tanta la roba che direte: – Io non ne voglio più -; e verrà tempo che arete tanta gloria e tante cose a governare che direte: – Non ne vogliàno più; perché non possiamo governare tanto – [...] Se tu non hai a morire, tu debbi ad ogni modo dar della roba adesso per adiutare la patria, perché tu sarai ristorato poi, e passate le tribulazioni arai più roba che tu non vorrai"; Girolamo Savonarola, *Prediche sopra Amos e Zaccaria*, vol. III, pp. 335 e 404.

[97] "Bisogna esser solleciti al bene commune e sempre ricordarsi de' beneficii di Dio e ringraziarlo; così debba fare el buono e vero cittadino che ama la sua città. Cittadino vuol dire uomo libero della città sua e non vuol dire servo: '*qui facit peccatum servus est peccati*'; chi fa peccato si domanda servo del peccato, e però non è libero, né vero cittadino, e '*servus non manet in domo Domini in aeternum*', non starà sempre el servo nella casa del padrone, ma sì el figliuolo; fa adunque d'essere vero figliuolo e vero cittadino e non servo, se tu vuoi stare nella casa del Signore per sempre. Chi è servo, è non libero, è servo di quella cosa che lui ama, come si vede nello avaro che ama e' danari, e quasi servo e non signore di quelli. 'Servi Domino', servi al tuo creatore, 'cui servire regnare est', e allora ti chiamerai veramente libero e vero cittadino della tua città"; Girolamo Savonarola, *Prediche sopra Aggeo*, p. 145.

[98] Girolamo Savonarola, *Prediche sopra Ruth e Michea*, vol. II, pp. 136–137.

all.[99] Because popular government functions under God, good citizens must not hesitate to punish the enemies of liberty for peace's sake.[100] When circumstances so require, however, they can be compassionate and follow the chief Christian virtue, charity. Only the voice of the prophet instills in citizens' hearts the moral strength needed to discharge the heavy duties of liberty. Florence was blessed to have such a prophet.

On many occasions, Savonarola claimed that the Christian principle of charity inspired his prophetic preaching.[101] In full agreement with Thomistic tradition, he interpreted charity as moral strength. In the third *Predica sopra Aggeo*, he explained that charity "renders man valiant and able to accomplish great things for love of God." To extol charity's power, he almost literally repeats Saint Paul's words: "Charity minds not persecutions, or opprobria, or scourges, she minds not death; charity fears nothing at all; charity is stronger than death is; charity separates man from all the things of the world more than death does; death takes away from you the things of the world, against your will; charity takes them away in accordance with your will, and the entire world cannot triumph over charity."[102]

Savonarola reiterates that human beings must act well "for God's honor, and then for zeal towards the fatherland and the common good"; he even affirms that "if you have no charity, you are no true Christian."[103] Egoism diminishes "when everyone can have what is common to all, and you are content that everyone has his lot, and therefore every good citizen is bound to love the common good." Charity unifies the people and the Church, just like the mortar "that conjoins and binds the stones together."[104] Aware that he could accomplish such an extraordinary achievement only with the help of God, and

---

[99] "Fate uomini che non guardino in viso a persona, e che per l'onore di Dio e che per il bene commune, non abbino rispetto a parenti, né abbino alcun altro respetto, e impaccinsi solamente di quello che è officio loro." Girolamo Savonarola, *Prediche sopra Ruth e Michea*, vol. II, pp. 435–436.

[100] Girolamo Savonarola, *Lettere e Scritti apologetici*, pp. 249–250. Savonarola cites the *Exodus* to claim that great tribulations befall the people if they are hesitant to inflict the just punishment against the enemies of its redemption; see also p. 251.

[101] "È inumano ed empio, e dispiace moltissimo a Dio, che raccomanda soprattutto la carità, che si trascuri il bene supremo e comune, quando si può in qualche modo procurarlo. A questo popolo che vacilla pericolosamente, poiché solo recentemente si è proclamato libero, era necessario proporre cose utili e indispensabili a comporre le questioni, a fugare gli odî, i contrasti i tumulti, le stragi incombenti, volute da molti, con il sovvertimento di tutta la città"; Girolamo Savonarola, *Compendio di rivelazioni e Dialogus de veritate prophetica*, p. 93.

[102] Girolamo Savonarola, *Prediche sopra Aggeo*, pp. 422–423.   [103] Ibid.

[104] Girolamo Savonarola, *Prediche sopra Aggeo*, pp. 51, 102, 245. See Lorenzo Polizzotto, *The Elect Nation: The Savonarolan Movement in Florence (1494–1545)*; Guidobaldo Guidi, *Lotte, pensiero e istituzioni politiche nella repubblica fiorentina dal 1492 al 1512*, 3 vols., Florence: Olsckhi, 1992. On the Florentines' "civil" religiosity and charity, see Arnaldo D'Addario, *Aspetti della Controriforma a Firenze*, Rome: Pubblicazioni degli Archivi di Stato, 1972.

by speaking and behaving as his loyal and humble prophet, Savonarola sought a radical moral transformation in Florence for the sake of instituting and preserving republican liberty. Can a prophet offer attractive rewards for the citizens who loyally serve the common good? Savonarola reiterates that good magistrates obtain from God both glory in this world and eternal life as rewards for their virtue. Savonarola insists that those rulers who govern for the common good are similar to God, recognized by Him, and therefore loved by Him more than the other human beings:

All creatures being similar to God, they all are loved by Him; but since some are more similar to Him than others, these – those who are more similar – are loved by God more: and inasmuch as the ruler is much more similar to God than the ruled, it is obvious that if he rules justly, he is more loved and rewarded by God because he is exposed to greater danger and more tiring efforts of mind and body than ordinary citizens.[105]

Conventional wisdom would have us believe that redemptive prophecy and political realism are mutually exclusive. Prophets offer visions of emancipation that radically contrast the institutions and prevalent mores that they wish to leave behind. They generate the hatred of the social elites they challenge, as well as the resentment of some of the very fellow citizens whom they intend to redeem. Others do not understand the prophets' words, and yet others lack the moral courage to act upon them. As a result, time and again prophets meet a tragic fate. Moreover, political realists – who know too well the weaknesses of their peoples and how difficult it is to persuade them to begin a long journey of emancipation – ridicule prophets. Savonarola's story would apparently confirm this conventional wisdom. After a brief period of glory, he lost the support of his compatriots and, unable to defend himself against Pope Alexander VI and against his enemies in Florence, met his end on the scaffold.

This is but one part of the truth. The whole truth is that Savonarola's sermons reveal a significant political realism. An eloquent example is found in his assertion that political constitutions must be congenial to the geography, the mores, and the history of the peoples they are designed for. Savonarola outlined his theory of political regimes in his sermon of December 14, 1494. The text deserves to be quoted in full:

Every people and place, which tends toward its natural good, requires governance, and these types of government are distinct and different in several ways. Some are ruled by a single leader, others by several persons, still others are ruled by the whole people together. Regulation and governance by a single leader, when that leader is good, is better than any other government, or the very best, and more easily achieves unity. The reason is this: because it is more difficult to unify the many than the few, and, wherever power is more united, it has more strength, and because power is more easily concentrated and unified in one than in many, therefore, the government of one is better than

---

[105] Girolamo Savonarola, *Prediche sopra Aggeo*, pp. 467–468.

that of many, when he who rules the others is good. But when that one leader is wicked, there is no worse government and form of rule since the worst is the opposite of the best. Nonetheless, divers, and various governments have been invented in accordance with the diversity of men and countries. In the warm part of this hemisphere, men are more pusillanimous than in other places because they are less sanguine, and thus, in those places, the people easily let themselves be ruled by a single leader, and they readily obey him and willingly subject themselves to him. In the cold northern part, where people are more sanguine and less intellectual, they are likewise steadfast and submissive to their one lord and head. But in the middle part, such as Italy, where both the sanguine and the intellectual abound, men do not remain patiently under a single leader; rather, each of them would like to be the leader who governs and rules over others and can command and not be commanded. From this, then, arise the dissension and discord among the citizens of the city, where one wants to make himself great and dominate the others. Experience has repeatedly demonstrated this; both at the time of the Romans and every day since, one has seen and sees examples of this in the cities of Italy; even in your own city you have seen and experienced this many times in our own days. Therefore, it is the counsel of the holy Doctors that, in these places where it seems that the nature of man will not endure a superior, government by the majority is better than that of a single leader, and one could say that this is especially appropriate for the city of Florence, where the sanguine and intelligence aplenty abound in the nature of men. But this government by the many must take care to be well regulated; otherwise, you would always be embroiled in dissension and partisanship, for in a few years restless men will divide themselves and become sectarian, and one faction will expel the other and make it rebel against the city, and so, it is necessary to think carefully about the form you have to choose.[106]

He taught his supporters that the work of instituting a new popular political order and edifying the New Jerusalem must be a gradual evolution from imperfection to perfection.[107] The Florentines must be patient, proceed slowly, and even pause, if necessary. But they must not yearn for the restoration of the Medici regime or forget that their mission is to transform Florence into a radically new city that lives by God's law, a New Jerusalem.[108] He also affirmed that, at times, to be a good Christian might not be sufficient to be a good citizen. Good Christians might be too simpleminded and lack judgment.[109] Like a true political realist thinker, he claimed that moral goodness

---

[106] Girolamo Savonarola, *Prediche sopra Aggeo*, pp. 210–212; English translation from *Selected Writings of Girolamo Savonarola. Religion and Politics, 1490–1498*, translated and edited by Anne Borelli and Maria Pastore Passaro, New Haven and London: Yale University Press, 2006, pp. 151–152.

[107] Girolamo Savonarola, *Prediche sopra i Salmi*, vol. II, p. 129.   [108] Ibid., pp. 117–118.

[109] "E Romani pagani furono signori di tutto el mondo, non per altro se non perché amorono el ben commune [...] Nota che non si debbe eleggere quello che è più santo, quando è troppo semplice: altro è buon cristiano, altro è buono cittadino che ama la republica. Ma se avessi bontà cristiana con questo, sarebbe meglio. Terzio, *roborare patientia*. Confortatevi e roboratevi nella pazienza, state fissi in orazione, esercito mio: pazienzia longanime, tollerare el male, massime quando el bene non vien presto. Tutte le cose naturale bisogna che abbino pazienzia,

often is not enough to found and preserve good republican governments. He also went as far as to say that, when they sit in office, citizens must be prepared to tolerate or perpetrate an evil in view of the greater good.[110]

Because he was a realist, Savonarola knew that establishing a New Jerusalem was an extraordinary task. Only a prophet who could count on God's friendship could lead the change. His model was Moses, the prophet par excellence who led the Hebrews out of Egyptian bondage to the Promised Land. Even if he was a friend of God, Moses did not hesitate to resort to armed violence to punish his own people when they rebelled against God's law. Savonarola not only approved of Moses' severity and cruelty, but he also explicitly compared himself to him.[111] Unlike Moses, however, Savonarola could not resort to armed violence. Even if he could have, he would not have. He was a prophet of moral and social emancipation who wanted to count only on the power of his prophetic words. Although he accomplished his redemptive vision only for a short time and only in part, Savonarola's prophetic legacy remains a landmark in the history of emancipation.

Savonarola's sermons motivated Marsilio Ficino (1433–1499), the most prominent philosopher of his times, to reflect upon the nature of prophecy and the mission of prophets. In a letter to Giovanni Cavalcanti of December 12, 1494 a few days after Savonarola's momentous homily on *Haggai*, he remarked that prophets are like "divine doctors" whom God in his infinite mercy sends to redeem peoples in times of despair. The prophets' wisdom, as Plato teaches us, is a sort of divine furor (*"furore divino"*) much more powerful that human sapience. When plagues and other calamities are God's punishments for people's vices, the prophets, inspired by God, teach people to redeem themselves through penance, prayers, and confession. The best evidence that God inspires prophets, Ficino concluded, was Savonarola. When Florence was in

---

perché è troppo grande la sapienzia di Dio che le conduce"; Girolamo Savonarola, *Prediche sopra i Salmi*, vol. II, pp. 238–239.

[110] "Così nel reggimento d'una repubblica, benché vi siano le leggi fatte ad utilità degli uomini, e per il bene delle anime, nondimeno alcune cose si permettano che in sé non sono buone, com'è il meretricio, ma per conservare il ben comune e fuggire uno maggior male. Così nelle città sono di molte sorte d'uomini, ma non vi è sì vile uomo che non sia utile a qualche cosa, e però la città comporta e tiene e opera ognuno secondo il grado di quelli. [...] L'uomo animale si convince colle ragioni animali, il che si può fare con simili per vincerli quando si vede che sono dediti alla vanagloria, e con quella si placano; e a questo modo *etiam* si permette qualche cosa, *etiam* non così buona, per evitare un maggior male [...] e però il prudente rettore e governatore, gli mette questi tali in qualche ministerio e officio molte volte per il meglio, e così permette uno manco male per uno maggior bene"; Girolamo Savonarola, *Prediche sopra Giobbe*, vol. II, pp. 66–68.

[111] Girolamo Savonarola, *Prediche sopra Giobbe*, pp. 64–67. See also Allison Brown, "Savonarola, Machiavelli, and Moses: a Changing Model," *Florence and Italy. Renaissance Studies in Honour of Nicolai Rubinstein*, edited by Peter Denley and Caroline Elam, London: Westfield College (University of London Committee for Medieval Studies), 1988, p. 60.

danger of being devastated by the French army that had invaded Italy in 1494, Savonarola, with the help of God, saved the city.[112] The text that best illustrates the prophetic longing for moral and social redemption in late fifteenth-century Florence is however the *Oracolo del nuovo secolo* by Giovanni Nesi (1456–1506), a fervent follower of Savonarola. In this work he extols the value and power of prophetic wisdom.[113] Everyone, he maintains, would love to live in the republic envisaged by the prophets in which political virtues and spiritual virtues shall reign and provide all citizens the most delightful beatitude. He combines Plato, whom he calls "the greatest prophet" ("*grandissimo profeta*"), and Virgil to design the luminous and comforting vision of the New Jerusalem and the return of the golden age.[114] Andrea Cattani was referring to Savonarola, reader of the Studio fiorentino, in his *Opus de intellectu et causis mirabilium effectuum* of 1502. He outlines here the model of the ideal prophet who not only announces God's plans but is also a founder, thanks to his outstanding virtue, of new and more just political and social orders and higher forms of moral life.[115]

---

[112] See Marsilio Ficino, *Epistolae*, Venice 1495, cc. 196r–197r. See also Raphael Ebgi, *Umanisti italiani. Pensiero e destino*, Torino: Einaudi, 2006, pp. 523–524. After Savonarola's death, Ficino wrote a violent attack against him. See *Apologia di Marsilio Ficino a favore dei molti fiorentini ingannati dall'Anticristo Girolamo di Ferrara, sommo degli ipocriti, al Collegio dei Cardinali*, in *Umanisti italiani, Pensiero e destino*, Torino: Einaudi, 2006, pp. 527–531; English translation, *Selected Writings of Girolamo Savonarola*, pp. 355–359. See also Amos Edelheit, *Ficino, Pico and Savonarola: The Evolution of Humanist Theology 1461/2–1498*, Leiden and Boston: Brill, 2008.

[113] Giovanni Nesi, *Oraculum de novo saeculo*, Florence: Lorenzo Morgiani, 1497. See also Giovanni Nesi, *Oracolo del fiorentino Giovanni Nesi a Giovanfrancesco Pico della Mirandola, illustre principe di Concordia*, in *Umanisti italiani*, pp. 491–492. On Nesi see Cesare Vasoli, "Giovanni Nesi tra Donato Acciaioli e Girolamo Savonarola," *I miti e gli astri*, Napoli: Guida, 1977, pp. 51–128.

[114] *Umanisti italiani*, p. 493.

[115] "Refert Avicenna quasdam humanas animas esse ita elatas, nobiles [...] ut non solum in propria corpora alterationibus et transmutationibus in eis factis agant, verum etiam in aliena et absque medio [...]. Difficile enim est huiusmodi hominem invenire, nam in paucis invenitur materia huiusmodi hominis temperamentum recipiens, ita ut alii divinum quid in eo esse percipiant, quo ille ab ipsis differat, et hic est ille homo quem prophetam vocamus, cuius offitium est universi conservandi gratia iura atque praecepta instituere, nec non et miracula facere [...] tali anima praeditus homo aegros in pristinam valitudinem mirabiliter potest reducere [...] potestque etiam elementa ipsa permutare [...] et pro ipsius voluntate contingunt pluviae et grandines et fulmina [...]. Multa etiam quae naturae cursum ac seriem excedunt valet efficere [...] potest etiam talis homo pro eius voluntate hominibus parare discordiam atque concordiam, suaque vi in proelio potest hostes expellere [...] potest ulterius talis homo orationibus et suplicationibus ac sacrificiis ex forti sua imaginatione super improborum urbes Dei flagellum convertere ac efficere." Andrea Cattani da Imola, *Opus de intellectu et de causis mirabilium effectuum*, Florence (after 1502), tract. III, fol. e6r-v.

2.3 PROPHETIC MACHIAVELLI

Savonarola's prophetic voice left lasting marks in the moral and political life of sixteenth-century Florence.[116] But Florence was not a unique case. Between 1494 and 1530, prophets, diviners, and clairvoyants crowded the public squares, streets, churches, and courts of Italy. The intellectual and social elite, as well as the popular classes, were eagerly listening to their words.[117] As Ottavia Niccoli succinctly notes, prophecy during the Renaissance was "a generalized culture that had profound ties to the political and religious events of the period [...] disseminated very broadly through different channels," a "living experience," an important part of "townspeople's practical knowledge."[118] Niccolò Machiavelli lived his entire life during these prophetic times. Did he repudiate the prophetic spirit, or did he revive and reinterpret it? Put differently, did he repudiate prophecy, or did he take it seriously and write as a prophet of political redemption? I intend to discuss these interpretive issues focusing first on Machiavelli's assessment of prophecies and prophets, then on his own prophetic language, and lastly on the relationship between prophecy and his political realism.

2.3.1 On Prophets and Prophecies

If we consult scholarly literature, the answer to the question I have posed is negative. Prevailing wisdom maintains that Machiavelli was the intellectual and political alternative to Savonarola. The origin of this view is probably Francesco De Sanctis, one of the most distinguished historians of Italian literature (1817–1883). In a conference held in 1872, he remarked that once the attempt at religious reform advocated by Savonarola proved to be in vain, what remained was the scientific path that Machiavelli indicated: "the Renaissance

---

[116] See Lorenzo Pollizzotto, *The Elect Nation: The Savonarolan Movement in Florence (1494–1545)*; Cesare Vasoli, "Il messaggio profetico di Savonarola e la sua recezione. Domenico Benivieni e Gianfrancesco Pico," *Studi Savonaroliani. Verso il V centenario*, edited by Gian Carlo Garfagnini, Florence: SISMEL, 1996.

[117] Eugenio Garin, *L'età nuova. Ricerche di storia della cultura dal XII al XVI secolo*, Naples: Morano, 1969, pp. 96–97.

[118] Ottavia Niccoli, *Profeti e popolo*, Rome and Bari: Laterza; English translation from *Prophecy and People in Renaissance Italy*, Princeton: Princeton University Press, 1990, pp. xi and xii. See also Stephanie Toussaint, "Profetare alla fine del Quattrocento," *Studi Savonaroliani*, edited by Gian Carlo Garfagnini, Florence: SISMEL, 1996, p. 168; Gabriella Zarri, "Potere carismatico e potere politico nelle corti italiane del Rinascimento," *Poteri carismatici e informali: chiesa e società medioevali*, edited by Agostino Paravicini Bagliani and André Vauchez, Palermo: Sellerio, 1992, pp. 175–191; Felix Gilbert has remarked: "By the time Machiavelli had written *The Prince* and was working at the *Discourses on Livy*, prophecy and prophets were held in the highest respect by the most enlightened and open-minded members of the church's elite" (Felix Gilbert, "Contarini on Savonarola: An Unknown Document of 1516," *Archiv für Reformationsgeschichte* 59 (1968): pp. 145–150); see also Felix Gilbert, "Cristianesimo, Umanesimo e la bolla 'Apostolici Regiminis' del 1513," *Rivista Storica Italiana* 79 (1967): pp. 976–990.

came, and science truly believed that it was capable of restoring life: the science was called Machiavelli, Campanella, and Sarpi; and the life was Cesare Borgia, Leo X, and Philip II." Both Machiavelli and Savonarola wanted to reform Italy. Savonarola relied upon enthusiasm for reform; Machiavelli relied upon science. For De Sanctis, Savonarola failed because he wanted to replace social indolence with the indolence of monasteries; Machiavelli failed because science lacked the power of redemption.[119] Yet in his highly influential *History of Italian Literature*, De Sanctis glorified Machiavelli as the prophet of Italy's unity and independence:

Developed, corrected, simplified, and in part realized, Machiavellism is the program of the modern world, and the great nations are the nations that come nearest to realizing it. Let us be proud of our Machiavelli. Whenever a part of the ancient building crumbles, let there be glory to Machiavelli, and whenever a part of the new is built, let there be glory to Machiavelli! Even as I am writing these words [1870], the bells are ringing far and wide, unceasingly, saying that the Italians are in Rome: the temporal power is falling, the people are shouting, "Long live the unity of Italy!" Let there be glory to Machiavelli![120]

An even more impressive documentation of the impact Machiavelli's prophetic words had on the militants of Italian liberty is the book that Luigi Russo (1892–1961) published in 1945 and dedicated to Nello Rosselli and Leone Ginzburg, two anti-fascist martyrs. Russo explained that the profound significance of Machiavelli's lesson had been truly kept alive by men like Alfieri and Mazzini, who understood that the problem of liberty in Italy was first and foremost a question of moral reform.[121] Savonarola is vindicated by Italian history, Russo wrote, "when the unity of the peninsula, an abstract prophecy at the turn of the sixteenth century, became a concrete standard at the end of the eighteenth century and in the nineteenth century, only because pure politics became also poetic and religious agitation, and the friar's prophetic pathos returned in the words of an Alfieri and a Mazzini." For Russo, political action that becomes prophecy and poetry in order to redeem peoples and found states was not the antithesis of the politics that Machiavelli had theorized, but rather its truest expression:

After a cold dissertation on the arts of the lion and the fox, at the end of the short treatise, he steals the colors, the images, and the style of his much satirized adversary [Savonarola], and speaks as a prophet, himself describing such biblical notions as a sea

---

[119] Francesco De Sanctis, *Conferenze su Machiavelli, L'arte, la scienza e la vita: nuovi saggi critici, conferenze e scritti vari*, edited by Maria Teresa Lanza, Turin: Einaudi, 1972, pp. 56–57.

[120] Francesco De Sanctis, *Storia della letteratura italiana*, edited by Niccolò Gallo, Turin: Einaudi-Gallimard, 1996, pp. 511–512; English translation, *History of Italian Literature*, edited by Joan Redfern, New York: Harcourt, 1931, pp. 584–585.

[121] Luigi Russo, *Machiavelli*, Bari: Laterza, 1949. The dedication, dated 1945, reads: "I dedicate this book to the memory of my friends Nello Rosselli and Leone Ginzburg, my close companions in our literary labors and our political beliefs, at a time when their tragic sacrifice begins to appear to be illuminated by the light of liberty and peace."

that has parted, a cloud that showed the path, a stone that has poured forth water, the heavens that have rained down manna, and he calls to his aid the voice of a poet; because he knew that "many times poets are filled with divine and prophetic spirit."[122]

Machiavelli becomes a prophet because he knows that "without prophetic pathos, without moral renewal, without civil conscience," a principality – and to a greater degree, a republic – will remain a mere utopia, nothing more than yet another imaginary republic. Political realism obliges Machiavelli to speak like the prophet of a God who commands his followers to love their country and to be strong in order to defend it.[123]

De Sanctis and Russo's works are milestones in scholarly literature. They do not provide, however, compelling evidence that Machiavelli wrote as a prophet or indeed was a prophet. To make some progress, we must examine whether prophets – individuals who have received inspiration or revelations from God – have a place in Machiavelli's vision of the cosmos. The first impression is that they have none. To begin with, his conception of history is cyclical and does not contemplate God's final triumph in the world. Nations and states endlessly swing between the domination of virtue and the domination of laziness:

Virtue makes countries tranquil, / and from Tranquillity, laziness next emerges, / and Laziness burns the towns and villages. / Then, after a country has for a time been subject to disorder, / Virtue often returns to live there once again / Such a course she who governs us permits and requires, / so that nothing beneath the sun / ever will or can be firm. / And it is and always has been and always will be, / that evil follows after good, good after evil.[124]

The heavens have an immense power on human affairs: "You see the stars and the sky, you see the moon, you see the rest; / sometimes you see the sky cloudy, sometimes shining and clear, and likewise nothing on earth remains in the same condition always. / From this result peace and war; on this depend the hatreds among those whom one wall and one moat shut up together."[125] In the *Decennale primo*, a narration of the events that occurred in Italy from 1494 to 1504, Machiavelli declares: "I shall sing Italian hardships for those two lustres now just over, / under planets hostile to her good."[126] In the dedicatory letter to Alamanno Salviati, he states that Italy's misfortunes were caused by fate, whose power cannot be contrasted: "I know that you will

---

[122] Ibid., p. 8.   [123] Ibid., p. 5.
[124] Niccolò Machiavelli, *L'Asino*, in *Tutte le opere*, edited by M. Martelli, Florence: Sansoni, 1971, p. 967; English translation, *Machiavelli. The Chief Works and Others*, vol. II, edited by Allan Gilbert, Durham, NC: Duke University Press, 1969, p. 763.
[125] Niccolò Machiavelli, *L'Asino*, in *Tutte le opere*, p. 961; English translation, *The Chief Works and Others*, pp. 757–758.
[126] Niccolò Machiavelli, *Decennale primo*, in *Tutte le opere*, p. 940; English translation, *The Chief Works and Others*, vol. III, p. 1445.

sorrow for her and for me, seeing her borne down by such misfortunes and me trying to include so many great things within such narrow limits. I am sure also that you will excuse us both: her because of fate's necessity and me because of the short time allowed me for such avocation."[127] The heavens exert either benign or malignant influence over individual persons as well. In *L'Asino* (*The Golden Ass*), Circe's good handmaiden explains to the unfortunate protagonist of the story, none other than Machiavelli himself, that: "Not yet has Heaven altered its opinion, nor will alter it, while the Fates keep toward you their hard purpose. / And those feelings which you have found so hostile and so adverse not yet are purged; / but when their roots are dry, and the Heavens show themselves gracious, times happier than ever before will return."[128]

To read heavens' signs is a job for astrologers, not for prophets. In fact, Machiavelli turns to astrologers when he must offer his counsel on important matters. In June 1509, he received a detailed response from the astrologer Lattanzio Tedaldi concerning the best time for Florentine commissioners to enter into Pisa after a long siege and to take possession of the city.[129] When he sensed looming tragedy for Italy in November 1526, he had no hesitation in revealing to the skeptic Guicciardini that he had consulted an astrologer.[130] If it was a matter of special importance, he wasn't picky about the difference between the Christian God and the pagan gods:

And if God does not help us out in the south, as He has already done in the north, then there are few remedies left to us. For, just as He interfered with the reinforcements from the Germans for the northerners [the lansquenets who were marching south upon Rome] with the destruction of Hungary, so he will have to interfere with the reinforcements from Spain with the destruction of the fleet; hence we shall be in need of Juno to go and pray Aeolus on our behalf and promise him the countess and every lady Florence has, so that he might set loose the winds in our behalf.[131]

Along with the heavens, Fortune too has great power on human actions. While the heavens govern orderly and necessary movements, Fortune is the mistress of chance and contingent events. She mercilessly exerts her immense power over terrestrial affairs in an arbitrary manner, with neither law nor reason: "She often keeps the good beneath her feet; the wicked she raises up; and if ever

---

[127] Niccolò Machiavelli, *I Decennali*, in *Tutte le opere*, pp. 939; 292; English translation, *The Chief Works and Others*, vol. III, p. 1444.

[128] Niccolò Machiavelli, *L'Asino*, in *Tutte le opere*, p. 962; English translation, *The Chief Works and Others*, vol. II, p. 758.

[129] Lattanzio Tedaldi to Niccolò Machiavelli, June 5, 1509, in *Tutte le opere*, p. 1107; English translation, *Machiavelli and His Friends. Their Personal Correspondence*, translated and edited by James B. Atkinson and David Sices, DeKalb: Northern Illinois University Press, 1996, p. 180.

[130] Niccolò Machiavelli to Francesco Guicciardini, November 5, 1526, in *Tutte le opere*, p. 1247; English translation, *Machiavelli and His Friends. Their Personal Correspondence*, p. 408.

[131] Niccolò Machiavelli to Bartolomeo Cavalcanti, October 6, 1526, in *Tutte le opere*, p. 1254; English translation, *Machiavelli and His Friends. Their Personal Correspondence*, p. 405.

she promises you anything, never does she keep her promise."[132] She is happy especially when she strikes down magnanimous citizens like Antonio Giacomini Tebalducci, one of the few valorous military commanders serving the Florentine Republic: "For his native city this man bore much, and long he sustained with great justice your army's dignity. / Covetous of honor, generous with money, and capable of such virtue he is, that he merits honor much higher than I give him. / Now neglected and scorned he lies in his house, poor, old, and blind. So greatly displeasing to Fortune is he who does well."[133] Fortune is as ferocious as she is discerning. She clearly distinguishes between the good (whom she punishes with servitude, infamy, and sickness) and the wicked (whom she rewards with power, honor, and wealth). When she wishes to come to the aid of great undertakings, she selects a man capable of seizing the opportunity that she proffers. Equally so, when she wishes to send a nation or a republic into ruin, she supports ambitious men suited to the task. If there is someone who might be able to hinder her plans, she either kills him or deprives him of all the means that would allow anything to work in his favor.[134] Nobody, including prophets, can read her mind. Only an "*ordinata virtù*" can resist her.[135]

While Machiavelli acknowledges God as the creator of the universe, he also does not entirely rule out the pagan idea of the eternity of the world.[136] He also hints at an occult power concealed in the heavens: "A hidden power which up above is nurtured, / Among the stars rotating in the sky, / And is not friendly to the human nature, / To give us war and strip us of sweet peace, / To take all happiness and calm away."[137] Rather than making use of the heavens and Fortune, Machiavelli's God seems to compete with them for the honor of influencing the world's events. In the closing of one of his earliest writings, the *Words to Be Spoken on the Law for Appropriating Money* (*Parole da dirle sopra la provvisione del danaio facto un poco di proemio et di scusa*) of 1503, Machiavelli remarks that the heavens "do not wish or are not able to support

---

[132] Niccolò Machiavelli, *Di Fortuna*, in *Tutte le opere*, pp. 976–979; English translation, *Niccolò Machiavelli. The Chief Works and Others*, vol. II, p. 745.

[133] Niccolò Machiavelli, *Decennale secondo*, in *Tutte le opere*, p. 951; *Niccolò Machiavelli. The Chief Works and Others*, vol. III, p. 1458.

[134] Niccolò Machiavelli to Giovan Battista Soderini, September 13–21, 1506, in *Tutte le opere*, pp. 1082–1083; English translation, *Machiavelli and His Friends. Their Personal Correspondence*, pp. 134–136.

[135] Niccolò Machiavelli, *Il Principe*, XXV, in *Tutte le opere*, p.295; English translation, *The Prince*, edited by Harvey C. Mansfield, Chicago and London: Chicago University Press, 1998. p. 98.

[136] Niccolò Machiavelli, *Discorsi sopra la prima deca di Tito Livio*, II.5, in *Tutte le opere*, pp. 154–155; English translation, *Discourses on Livy*, edited by Harvey C. Mansfield, Chicago: Chicago University Press, 1996, pp. 138–140; see also Gennaro Sasso in *Machiavelli e gli antichi e altri saggi*, vol. I, Milan: Riccardo Ricciardi, 1987, pp. 167–376.

[137] Niccolò Machiavelli, *Dell'ambizione*, in *Tutte le opere*, pp. 983–987; English translation, *Niccolò Machiavelli. The Chief Works and Others*, vol. 2, pp. 735–739; see Anthony Parel, *The Machiavellian Cosmos*, New Haven: Yale University Press, 1992, pp. 54–59.

a city that is determined to fall in any case."[138] But in the *Florentine Histories* (*Istorie fiorentine*), it is God who intervenes, not the heavens: "But God, who in such extremities has always had a particular care for it, made an un-hoped-for accident arise that gave the king, the pope, and the Venetians something greater to think about than Tuscany." In the same book, Machiavelli again attributes to the heavens a similar intervention in human affairs: "Since the heavens willed that things prepare for future evil, he [the Duke of Athens] arrived in Florence precisely at the time when the campaign at Lucca had been lost completely." In yet another passage, he chooses to cite Fortune: "And although the nobility had been destroyed, nonetheless fortune did not lack for ways to revive new trials through new divisions."[139] Even if God is not the only power intervening in human affairs, for Machiavelli it is undeniable, as I shall document, that God intervenes either directly or by way of revelations and inspirations through prophets. Furthermore, God has bequeathed human beings the gift of free will.[140] Because God reveals his will and human beings are free to obey or resist it, prophets have indeed a place in Machiavelli's worldview. They have the power to inspire human will. Within the limits imposed by Fortune, the heavens, and occult powers, human will is the decisive force in political life, especially when peoples attempt to attain their emancipation from servitude and corruption.

Nonetheless, Machiavelli is skeptical about human beings' possibility of predicting future events. The most eloquent example is his letter to Giovan Battista Soderini in September 1506. After a long discussion on the rules for successful political action, Machiavelli states:

And truly, anyone wise enough to adapt to and understand the times and the pattern of events would always have good fortune or would always keep himself from bad fortune; and it would come to be true that the wise man could control the stars and the Fates. But such wise men do not exist in the first place, men are shortsighted; in the second place, they are unable to master their own natures; thus it follows that Fortune is fickle, controlling men and keeping them under her yoke.[141]

---

[138] "La Fortuna non muta sententia, dove non si muta ordine; né e cieli vogliono o possono sostenere una cosa che voglia ruinare ad ogni modo"; Niccolò Machiavelli, *Parole da dirle sopra la provvisione del danaio facto un poco di proemio et di scusa*, in *Tutte le opere*, p. 13; English translation, *Niccolò Machiavelli. The Chief Works and Others*, vol. 3, p. 1443.

[139] Niccolò Machiavelli, *Istorie fiorentine*, VIII. 19, II. 33; II. 42; English translation, *Florentine Histories*, edited by Laura Banfield and Harvey C. Mansfield, Princeton: Princeton University Press, 1988, pp. 341, 90, 104.

[140] Niccolò Machiavelli, *Il Principe*, in *Tutte le opere*, p. 297. Machiavelli takes up from Dante the idea that free will is the greatest gift that God has given human beings: "Lo maggior don che Dio per sua larghezza / fesse creando, e a la sua bontade / piú, e quel ch'e' piú apprezza, / fu de la volontà la libertate; / di che le creature intelligenti, / e tutte e sole, fuoro e son dotate"; *Paradiso*, V. 19–24.

[141] "Et veramente, chi fussi tanto savio che conoscessi e tempi et l 'ordine delle cose et adcomodassisi ad quelle, harebbe sempre buona fortuna o e' si guarderebbe sempre da la trista, et verrebbe ad essere vero che 'l savio comandassi alle stelle e a' fati. Ma, perché di questi savi non si truova, havendo li huomini prima la vista corta, et non potendo poi comandare alla natura loro, ne

At times, Machiavelli becomes sarcastic about prophets' pretenses to predict the future. The best example is his letter to Francesco Vettori of December 19, 1513. Here he mercilessly ridicules Frate Francesco da Montepulciano (he died in 1513, we do not know when he was born), a pupil of Savonarola who had considerable fame as a prophet:

In this city of ours – a magnet for all the world's pitchmen – there is a friar of Saint Francis who is half hermit and who, to increase his standing as a preacher, professes to be a prophet; and yesterday morning in Santa Croce, where he preaches, he said "*many things great and wonderful*: that before much time elapses, so that whoever is ninety years of age will be able to see it, there will be an unjust pope created against a just pope, and he will have false prophets with him, he will create cardinals, and he will divide the Church. *Item*, that the king of France was to be crushed and someone from the House of Aragon was to be master of Italy. Our city would go up in flames and be sacked, the churches would be abandoned and would crumble, the priests dispersed, and we would have to do without divine services for three years. There would be pestilence and widespread famine; in the city, not ten men would remain; on farms, not two would remain. That for eighteen years there has been a devil in a human body, and he has said mass. That well over two million devils were unleashed to supervise the above-mentioned activities. That they would enter many dying bodies and not allow those bodies to putrefy so that false prophets and clerics might resuscitate the dead and be believed. These activities demoralized me so much yesterday that I was supposed to go this morning to see La Riccia [his lover], but I did not go; I am not at all sure whether, had I been supposed to go see Riccio, I would have been concerned. I myself did not hear the sermon, for I do not observe such practices, but I have heard it told about in this manner throughout all of Florence."[142]

segue che la Fortuna varia et comanda ad li huomini, et tiègli sotto el giogo suo." Niccolò Machiavelli to Giovan Battista Soderini, September 13–21, 1506, in *Tutte le opere*, p. 1083; English translation, *Machiavelli and His Friends. Their Personal Correspondence*, p. 135.

[142] "E' si trova in questa nostra città, calamita di tutti i ciurmatori del mondo, un frate di S. Francesco, che è mezzo romito, el quale, per haver più credito nel predicare, fa professione di profeta; et hier mattina in Santa Croce, dove lui predica, dixe multa magna et mirabilia: che avanti che passassi molto tempo, in modo che chi ha 90 anni lo potrà vedere, sarà un papa iniusto, creato contro ad un papa iusto, et harà seco falsi profeti, et farà cardinali, et dividerà la Chiesia; item, che il re di Francia si haveva adnichilare, et uno della casa di Raona ad predominare Italia. La città nostra haveva a ire a fuoco et assacco, le chiese sarebbono abbandonate et ruinate, i preti dispersi, et tre anni si haveva a stare senza divino offitio. Moria sarebbe et fame grandissima; nella città non haveva a rimanere 10 huomini nelle ville non harebbe a rimanere dua. Era stato 18 anni un diavolo in uno corpo humano, et detto messa. Che bene dua milioni di diavoli erano scatenati per essere ministri della sopradetta cosa, et che egli entravano in di molti corpi che morivano, et non lasciavano putrefare quel corpo, acciò che falsi propheti et religiosi potessono fare resuscitare morti, et essere creduti. Queste cose mi sbigottirono hieri in modo, che io haveva andare questa mattina a starmi con la Riccia, et non vi andai; ma io non so già, se io havessi hauto a starmi con il Riccio, se io havessi guardato a quello. La predica io non la udi', perché io non uso simili pratiche, ma la ho sentita recitare così da tutto Firenze"; Niccolò Machiavelli to Francesco Vettori, December 19, 1513, in *Tutte le opere*, pp. 1161–1162; English translation, *Machiavelli and His Friends. Their Personal Correspondence*, p. 267.

Vettori too, in his letter of December 24, is skeptical about Francesco Da Montepulciano and about preachers in general.[143] On the prophets announcing the end of the world, Machiavelli says more in his letter to Vettori of February 4, 1514 in which he invokes God's intervention: "There is nothing to tell you about from these parts except prophecies and proclamations of calamities; if the prophets are telling lies, may God annihilate them; if they are telling the truth, may He convert it into good."[144]

In *De' romiti*, a later poem composed around 1519, Machiavelli derides the prophecies of imminent floods and cataclysms that were spreading terror in Italy. If the floods shall come, he reassures, there will be fine opportunities for erotic amusements:

> And they declare above all that the stars
> are overflowing with so many waters
> that the world, as great as it is, will wholly be covered.
> Therefore, gracious and fair ladies,
> if ever it pleased you to serve
> anything that is above you,
> let not one of you come forward to make defense against us.
> It is true that the sky is clear
> and promises us a glad carnival:
> but any man who tries to oppose us speaks falsely.[145]

[143] Francesco Vettori to Niccolò Machiavelli, December 24, 1513, in *Tutte le opere*, p. 1164.

[144] Niccolò Machiavelli to Francesco Vettori, February 4, 1514, in *Tutte le opere*, p. 1168; English translation, *Machiavelli and His Friends. Their Personal Correspondence*, p. 278. Francesco da Meleto also claimed to have received inspiration from the Holy Spirit, but he also relied on arithmetic calculations. He predicted that the renewal of the Church and the conversion of the Jews would begin in 1517. He wrote *Convivio de' Segreti della Scrittura* no later than 1513, and in *Quadrivium temporum prophetatorum* he restates that the conversion of the Jews would begin in 1517 and that the religion of Muhammad would be extinct by 1536. He presented the *Quadrivium* to Leo X, but his prophetic visions were met with a cold reception in the Curia. He was forced to retract his words and recant. Nothing more was heard of him after his conviction. On Francesco da Meleto, see: Salvatore Bongi, "Francesco da Meleto un profeta fiorentino a' tempi del Machiavello," *Archivio storico italiano* 3 (1889), pp. 62–70; Donald Weinstein, *Savonarola and Florence: Prophecy and Patriotism in the Renaissance*, Princeton: Princeton University Press, 1970, pp. 353–363; Cesare Vasoli, "La profezia di Francesco da Meleto," *Umanesimo e ermeneutica*, Padova: Cedam, 1963, pp. 27–80; and "L'attesa dell'età nuova nella spiritualità della fine del medioevo," *Convegni del centro di studi sulla spiritualità medievale*, vol. III, Todi: Accademia Tudertina, 1962, pp. 370–432; Stefano Dall'Aglio, "L'altra faccia dello pseudoprofeta Francesco da Meleto scrivano della SS. Annunziata di Firenze," *Bibliothèque d' Humanisme et Renaissance* LXVII (2005): pp. 343–351.

[145] "E voglion sopratutto che le stelle /influssin con tant' acque, / che 'l mondo tutto quanto si ricuopra. / Per questo, donne graziose e belle, /se mai servir vi piacque, / alcuna cosa che vi sia di sopra; / nessuna se ne scuopra / per farci alcun riparo; / però che 'l cielo è chiaro / e ci promette un lieto carnovale: / ma chiunque crede apporsi, dice male." Niccolò Machiavelli, *De' romiti*, in *Tutte le opere*, p. 991; English translation, *Machiavelli. The Chief Works and Others*, vol. II, p. 881.

There is nothing to worry about, Machiavelli assures. He knows better than astrologers and self-appointed prophets:

> Do not fear other harm;
> That will be which is wont to be.
> Heaven wishes to save us;
> And besides, he who sees the devil in very truth,
> Sees him with smaller horns and not so black.[146]

To the (alleged) prophets of doom, Machiavelli either responds with irony or invokes God's intervention. One may consider His judgment inconsistent. But so was Machiavelli, now grave and serious, now playful, and irreverent. He believed that his way of life was the right one. He was never remorseful about his way of balancing lightness and gravity. To the contrary, he was proud of it.[147]

Other texts do eloquently show that Machiavelli indeed took prophecies and prophets very seriously. The oldest reference is in his transcription of the comedy *Andria* written by Terentius (185–159 BC). This transcription was a juvenile exercise completed around 1495, as Pasquale Stoppelli has established.[148] In Machiavelli's copy, the servant Davos replies to an obscure sentence of his master Simo with these words: "*Io son Davo, non propheta, vel non il frate*" ["I am Davo, not the prophet that is the friar (Savonarola)]. Terentius' text reads: "*Davus sum, non Oedipus.*" The fact that Machiavelli renders "Oedipus" with "propheta" indicates that he believes prophets to be persons capable of unveiling the hidden meanings of words and signs – just as Savonarola was able, or at least pretended, to understand God's revelations.[149] In the *Discourses on Livy*, Machiavelli explicitly admits the possibility of

---

[146] "Non temete altro danno, / e fia quel ch'esser suole. / Il ciel salvar ci vuole: / e poi, chi vede il diavol daddovero, / lo vede con men corna e manco nero"; Niccolò Machiavelli, *De' romiti*, in *Tutte le opere*, pp. 990–991; English translation, *Machiavelli. The Chief Works and Others*, vol. II, p. 881.

[147] "Chi vedesse le nostre lettere, honorando compare, et vedesse le diversità di quelle, si maraviglierebbe assai, perché gli parrebbe hora che noi fussimo huomini gravi, tutti vòlti a cose grandi, et che ne' petti nostri non potesse cascare alcuno pensiero che non havesse in sé honestà et grandezza. Però dipoi, voltando carta, gli parrebbe quelli noi medesimi essere leggieri, inconstanti, lascivi, vòlti a cose vane. Questo modo di proccedere, se a qualcuno pare sia vituperoso, a me pare laudabile, perché noi imitiamo la natura, che è varia; et chi imita quella non può essere ripreso"; Niccolò Machiavelli to Francesco Vettori, January 31, 1515, in *Tutte le opere*, p. 1168; English translation, *Machiavelli and His Friends. Their Personal Correspondence*, p. 312.

[148] Pasquale Stoppelli, "Nota Introduttiva' ad *Andria*," *Teatro. Andria, Mandragola, Clizia*, edited by Pasquale Stoppelli, Rome: Salerno Editrice, 2017, pp. 3–16. See also, in the same volume, "Introduzione. Preliminari su Machiavelli comico," pp. ix–xx.

[149] Pasquale Stoppelli, "Nota Introduttiva," p. 12. In another, later, transcription of *Andria* that Stoppelli has assigned to around the mid-'20s, Machiavelli drops "vel non el frate," and keeps only "Io son Davo, non profeta."

predicting future events by reading "celestial signs."[150] His tentative explanation of this possibility reveals that with the prophetic tradition he shared the persuasion that: "it could be that since, as some philosophers hold, the air about us is full of intelligences – and these through their natural abilities foreseeing future things and having compassion on men – these spirits warn men with such signs, so they can prepare for resistance. At any rate, however it is, so the truth seems to be; and always after such events strange and new things happen to countries."[151]

Machiavelli knew well and fully endorsed the intellectual tradition of prophetic poetry that had a chief role in the intellectual context of his times, as I have indicated. The most relevant documentation that evidences his belief in the poets' special prophetic powers is in the *Istorie fiorentine*, specifically the chapter in which he narrates the failed conspiracy of Stefano Porcari in Rome.

Living at that time was a Messer Stefano Porcari [early 1400–1453], a Roman citizen, noble by blood and by learning, but much more so by the excellence of his spirit. This man desired, according to the custom of men who relish glory, to do or at least to try something worthy of memory; and he judged he could do nothing else than try to see if he could take his fatherland from the hands of prelates and restore it to its ancient way of life, hoping by this, should he succeed, to be called the new founder and second father of that city. The dissolute manners of the priesthood and the discontent of the Roman barons and people, and some verses encouraged him to look for a happy termination of his enterprise.[152]

---

[150] "Donde ei si nasca io non so, ma ei si vede per gli antichi e per gli moderni esempii, che mai non venne alcuno grave accidente in una città o in una provincia, che non sia stato, o da indovini o da rivelazioni o da prodigi o da altri segni celesti, predetto. E per non mi discostare da casa nel provare questo, sa ciascuno quanto da frate Girolamo Savonerola fosse predetta innanzi la venuta del re Carlo VIII di Francia in Italia; e come, oltre a di questo, per tutta Toscana si disse essere sentite in aria e vedute genti d'armi, sopra Arezzo, che si azzuffavano insieme. Sa ciascuno, oltre a questo, come, avanti alla morte di Lorenzo de' Medici vecchio, fu percosso il duomo nella sua più alta parte con una saetta celeste, con rovina grandissima di quello edifizio. Sa ciascuno ancora, come, poco innanzi che Piero Soderini, quale era stato fatto gonfalonieri a vita dal popolo fiorentino, fosse cacciato e privo del suo grado, fu il palazzo medesimamente da uno fulgure percosso. Potrebbonsi, oltre a di questo, addurre più esempli, i quali, per fuggire il tedio, lascerò. Narrerò solo quello che Tito Livio dice, innanzi alla venuta de' Franciosi a Roma: cioè, come uno Marco Cedicio plebeio riferì al Senato avere udito di mezza notte, passando per la Via nuova, una voce, maggiore che umana, la quale lo ammuniva che riferissi a' magistrati come e' Franciosi venivano a Roma"; *Discorsi sopra la prima deca di Tito Livio*, I.56, in *Tutte le opere*, p. 139; English translation, *Discourses on Livy*, p. 113.

[151] "Sendo questo aere, come vuole alcuno filosofo, pieno di intelligenze, le quali per naturali virtù preveggendo le cose future, ed avendo compassione agli uomini, acciò si possino preparare alle difese, gli avvertiscono con simili segni. Pure, comunque e' si sia, si vede così essere la verità; e che sempre dopo tali accidenti sopravvengono cose istraordinarie e nuove alle provincie"; *Discorsi sopra la prima deca di Tito Livio*, I.56, in *Tutte le opere*, p. 139; English translation, *Discourses on Livy*, p. 114.

[152] "Viveva in quelli tempi un messer Stefano Porcari, cittadino romano, per sangue e per dottrina; ma molto più per eccellenza di animo, nobile. Desiderava costui, secondo il costume degli

The verses to which Machiavelli refers are from a canzone by Petrarch that ends with this prophetic vision:

Atop Mount Tarpeio, Oh ! canzone, you will see / Sopra il monte Tarpeio, canzon, vedrai

A knight whom all Italy honors / Un cavalier che Italia tutta onora,

More thoughtful of others than of himself. / Pensoso più d'altrui che di se stesso.[153]

Machiavelli tells us that these words inspired Stefano Porcari because he believed that poets are oftentimes filled with divine and prophetic spirit. In this light, Porcari maintained that he was the man destined to be the "executor of so glorious an undertaking." Petrarch's prophecy did not come true. Stefano Porcari was captured and executed. He lacked political judgment, Machiavelli remarks. But he also recognizes that prophetic poetry has the power to inspire redeemers.[154]

To reconstruct Machiavelli's beliefs on prophecy and prophets, we must revisit his considerations on Savonarola, the prophet par excellence.[155] In the well-known letter of March 9, 1498 to Ricciardo Becchi, the Florentine orator

---

uomini che appetiscono gloria, o fare, o tentare almeno, qualche cosa degna di memoria; e giudicò non potere tentare altro, che vedere se potesse trarre la patria sua delle mani de' prelati e ridurla nello antico vivere, sperando per questo, quando gli riuscisse, essere chiamato nuovo fondatore e secondo padre di quella città. Facevagli sperare di questa impresa felice fine i malvagi costumi de' prelati e la mala contentezza de' baroni e popolo romano; ma sopra tutto gliene davano speranza quelli versi del Petrarca, nella canzona che comincia: 'Spirto gentil che quelle membra reggi', dove dice: 'Sopra il monte Tarpeio, canzon, vedrai Un cavalier che Italia tutta onora, pensoso più d'altrui che di se stesso'. Sapeva messere Stefano i poeti molte volte essere di spirito divino e profetico ripieni; tal che giudicava dovere ad ogni modo intervenire quella cosa che il Petrarca in quella canzona profetizzava, ed essere egli quello che dovesse essere di sì gloriosa impresa esecutore; parendogli, per eloquenzia, per dottrina, per grazia e per amici, essere superiore ad ogni altro romano"; Niccolò Machiavelli, *Istorie fiorentine*, VI.29, in *Tutte le opere*, p. 785; English translation, *Florentine Histories*, pp. 263–264.

[153] Francesco Petrarca, "Spirto gentil che quelle membra reggi," in Francesco Petrarca, *Canzoniere*, p. 71; English translation from *The Complete Canzoniere*, 2001.

[154] Niccolò Machiavelli, *Istorie fiorentine*, VI.29, in *Tutte le opere*, p. 785; English translation, *Florentine Histories*, pp. 263–264.

[155] Of the very large bibliography on Savonarola and Machiavelli see at least Gennaro Sasso, *Niccolò Machiavelli, Il pensiero politico*, Bologna: Il Mulino, 1993, pp. 25–40; Mario Martelli, "Machiavelli e Savonarola," *Savonarola. Democrazia tirannide profezia, Atti del terzo Seminario di studi (Pistoia, 23–24 maggio 1997)*, edited by Gian Carlo Garfagnini, Florence: SISMEL-Edizioni del Galluzzo, 1998, pp. 67–89; Innocenzo Cervelli, "Savonarola, Machiavelli e il libro dell'*Esodo*," *Savonarola. Democrazia tirannide profezia*, pp. 243–298; Giorgio Cadoni, "Qualche osservazione su Machiavelli e Savonarola," *La Cultura* 2 (2007): pp. 263–278; Vivien Gaston, "The Prophet Armed. Machiavelli, Savonarola, and Rosso Fiorentino's Moses Defending the Daughters of Jethro," *Journal of the Warburg and Courtauld Institutes* 51 (1988): pp. 220–225; Marcia L. Colish, "Republicanism, Religion, and Machiavelli's Savonarolan Moment," *Journal of the History of Ideas* LX (1999): pp. 597–616.

at the papal court, Machiavelli unmasks the political strategy that guided Savonarola's interpretation of the *Book of Exodus*. Machiavelli openly denounces Savonarola as a liar:

The next morning, still expounding Exodus and coming to that passage where it says that Moses slew an Egyptian, he said that the Egyptian represented evil-doers and Moses the preacher who slew them by exposing their vices. Then he said, "O Egyptian, I want to stab you." And it was your books, O priests, whose pages he leafed through, treating you in such a way that not even dogs would have eaten any of it. Then he added – and this is what he was driving at – that he wanted to give the Egyptian another stab wound, a big one. He said that God had told him that there was someone in Florence who sought to make himself a tyrant, and he was engaged in dealings and schemes to succeed, and that the desire to drive out the friar, to excommunicate the friar, and to persecute the friar meant nothing else than to seek to create a tyrant, and that the laws ought to be obeyed. And he made so much of this that later that day people speculated publicly about someone who is about as close to being a tyrant as you are to Heaven. Afterward, since the Signoria had written to the pope in his behalf and he realized that he no longer needed to be afraid of his adversaries in Florence, instead of trying, as he once had, solely to unite his party through hatred of his adversaries and through frightening them with the word "tyrant," he has changed coats now that he understands that he no longer needs to act in this way. So, he urges them to the union that was initiated, and he no longer mentions either the tyrant or the wickedness of the people; he seeks to set all of them at odds with the Supreme Pontiff and, turning toward him and his attacks, says of the pope what could be said of the wickedest person you might imagine. Thus, in my judgment, he acts in accordance with the times and colors his lies accordingly.[156]

Along with the texts that I have thus far discussed, this letter does not lend sufficient evidence to the claim that Machiavelli despised and scorned prophets in the name of a sound political realism. These documents merely indicate that

---

[156] "L'altra mattina poi exponendo pure lo Exodo et venendo a quella parte, dove dice che Moyses amazò uno Egiptio, dixe che lo Egiptio erono gli huonini captivi, et Moyses el predicatore che gli amazava, scoprendo e vitii loro; et dixe: O Egitio io ti vo' dare una coltellata; et qui cominciò a squadernare e libri vostri, o preti, et tractarvi in modo che non n'harebbono mangiato e cani; dipoi soggiunse, et qui lui voleva capitare, che volea dare all'Egiptio un'altra ferita et grande, et dixe che Dio gli haveva detto, ch'egli era uno in Firenze che cercava di farsi tyranno, et teneva pratiche et modi perché gli riescissi: et che volere cacciare el frate, scomunicare el frate, perseguitare el frate, non voleva dire altro, se non volere fare un tyranno; e che s' osservassi le leggi. Et tanto ne disse, che gli huomini poi el di feciono pubblicamente coniectura d'uno, che è tanto presso al tyranno, quanto voi al cielo. Ma havendo dipoi la Signoria scripto in suo favore al papa, et veggiendo non gli bisognava temere più degli adversarii suoi in Firenze, dove prima lui cercava d'unire sola la parte sua col detextare gli adversarii et sbigottirgli col nome del tyranno, hora, poi che vede non gli bisognare più, ha mutato mantello, et quegli all'unione principiata confortando, né di tyranno, né di loro scelerateze più mentione faccendo, d'inna-glienirgli tucti contro al sommo pontefice cerca, et verso lui e' suoi morsi rivoltati, quello ne dice che di quale vi vogliate sceleratissimo huomo dire si puote; et cosi, secondo el mio iudicio, viene secondando e tempi, et le sua bugie colorendo"; Niccolò Machiavelli to Ricciardo Becchi, March 9, 1498; in *Tutte le opere*, p. 1011; English translation, *Machiavelli and His Friends. Their Personal Correspondence*, p. 10.

he was good at identifying false prophets. His remarks on armed and unarmed prophets in *The Prince* also point in the same direction:

From this comes the fact that all armed prophets were victorious and the unarmed came to ruin. For, besides what has been said, people are fickle by nature: it is easy to convince them of something, but difficult to hold them in that conviction. Therefore, affairs should be managed in such a way that when they no longer believe, they can be made to believe by force. Moses, Cyrus, Theseus and Romulus could not have made their institutions respected for long if they had been unarmed; as in our times happened to Brother Girolamo Savonarola, who was ruined in his new institutions when the populace began to believe in them no longer, since he had no way of holding steady those who had believed, nor of making the unbelievers believe.[157]

Here Machiavelli criticizes unarmed prophets because they cannot be successful redeemers. He is not dismissing prophets, nor is he disparaging their role as leaders of political redemption. After all, an armed prophet is still a prophet.

Machiavelli does not at all deny the possibility that human beings with extraordinary moral and intellectual virtues are indeed inspired by God or talk to God. In the case of Savonarola, he admits that Savonarola was quite possibly talking to God:

To the people of Florence it does not appear that they are either ignorant or coarse; nonetheless, they were persuaded by Friar Girolamo Savonarola that he spoke with God.

---

[157] Niccolò Machiavelli, *Il Principe*, VI; English translation, Niccolò Machiavelli, *The Prince*, p. 24. Machiavelli criticized Savonarola for failing to impose respect for a law that he himself had sustained in *Discourses on Livy*, I. 45. In the essay "Prophetic Statebuilding: Machiavelli and the Passion of the Duke" (*Representations* 115 (2001): pp. 1–19, [p. 16]), John P. Mccormick argues that Machiavelli intended "allegorically" to propose the myth of the armed prophet who redeems peoples and protects the weak through the "parable" of Ramiro de Lorqua's execution as ordered by Cesare Borgia ("And because he knew that severity in the past had brought about some hatred against himself, in order to purify his image in the minds of the people and to win them over, he wanted to show that, if any cruelty had been undertaken, it did not come from him, but from the bitter nature of his minister. Under this pretense, one morning he had Ramiro executed in Cesena and left him in the piazza with the block and a bloody knife at his side": *The Prince*, chapter VII). But there is nothing prophetic at all about Cesare Borgia. Seeing allusions to prophetic meaning in Cesare Borgia's actions is a forced reading of Machiavelli's narrative. Why would Machiavelli resort to veiled allegories in order to express one of his most fundamental concepts – the armed prophet – that he had already formulated with clear and eloquent words in chapter VI of *The Prince*? Cesare Borgia is not a prophet, but a man who, having become a prince "thanks to his father" and with "the arms of others," demonstrated great *virtù*. Moses and Savonarola are the only prophets in *The Prince*. John T. Scott states: "Attending to the important role of Savonarola in *The Prince* also enables us to better appreciate how Machiavelli's political vision weds realism, in the form of attention to 'the effectual truth of the thing,' and a kind of idealism, in the form of a prophetic call to action based on imagining what is possible through the exercise of virtue" ("The Fortune of Machiavelli's Unarmed Prophet," *The Journal of Politics* 80 (2018): pp. 615–629 [p. 628]); see also Thomas Berns, "Prophetic Efficacy: The Relationship between Force and Belief," *The Radical Machiavelli. Politics, Philosophy and Language*, edited by Filippo Del Lucchese, Fabio Frosini, and Vittorio Morfino, Leiden and Boston: Brill, 2015, pp. 207–218.

I do not wish to judge whether it is true or not, because one should speak with reverence of such a man; but I do say that an infinite number believed him without having seen anything extraordinary to make them believe him. For his life, learning, and the subject he took up were sufficient to make them lend faith.[158]

In fact, Machiavelli explicitly wrote that Moses was speaking to God: "And although one should not reason about Moses, as he was a mere executor of things that had been ordered for him by God, nonetheless he should be admired if only for that grace which made him deserving of speaking with God."[159] Machiavelli wanted his readers to believe that the sanctity of life, learning, and eloquence were the requisite qualities incarnated in those individuals who can help generate grand political action: that is to say, individuals to whom the masses could look for inspiration. For Machiavelli, prophets must be armed if they want to accomplish the work of founding new political orders and redeeming peoples. But an armed prophet is still a prophet, as I have stressed, a friend of God who can instill in his people the determination to fight for their political and moral redemption. If there have been prophets – armed or unarmed – others, like Moses and Savonarola, might come to carry out the mission of political and moral redemption. Machiavelli was indeed hoping that other prophets might come to lead the redemptive struggle: "No one, therefore, should be terrified that he cannot carry out what has been carried out by others, for as was said in our preface, men are born, live, and die always in one and the same order."[160]

2.3.2 Machiavelli's Prophetic Words

With his typical irony, Machiavelli likes to pose as a prophet. On November 20, 1502, in his report to the Signori of Florence on the conversations he held with the Duke Caesar Borgia in Urbino, Machiavelli writes:

I said to him that I had always felt convinced that he would be victorious, and that if on the first day of my arrival I had written down my view of these matters, and he were to

---

[158] "Al popolo di Firenze non pare essere né ignorante né rozzo: nondimeno da frate Girolamo Savonarola fu persuaso che parlava con Dio. Io non voglio giudicare s'egli era vero o no, perché d'uno tanto uomo se ne debbe parlare con riverenza: ma dico bene, che infiniti lo credevano sanza avere visto cosa nessuna straordinaria, o da farlo loro credere; perché la vita sua, la dottrina e il suggetto che prese, erano sufficienti a fargli prestare fede"; Niccolò Machiavelli, *Discorsi sopra la prima deca di Tito Livio*, ch. XI, in *Tutte le opere*; English translation, *Discourses on Livy*, p. 36.

[159] "E benché di Moisè non si debba ragionare, sendo suto uno mero esecutore delle cose che gli erano ordinate da Dio, tamen debbe essere ammirato solum per quella grazia che lo faceva degno di parlare con Dio"; Niccolò Machiavelli, *Il principe*, ch. VI, in *Tutte le opere*, ch. VI; English translation, Niccolò Machiavelli, *The Prince*, pp. 22–23.

[160] "Non sia, pertanto, nessuno che si sbigottisca di non potere conseguire quel che è stato conseguito da altri; perché gli uomini, come nella prefazione nostra si disse, nacquero, vissero e morirono, sempre, con uno medesimo ordine"; Niccolò Machiavelli, *Discorsi sopra la prima deca di Tito Livio*, in *Tutte le opere*, I.11; English translation, *Discourses on Livy*, p. 36.

read it now, it would seem to him like prophecy; and that one of the reasons that had made me think thus was that he was alone, and had to deal with a combination of several adversaries; but that it was easy for him to break the ties that united them.[161]

Machiavelli enjoys when a friend calls him "prophet," even if he knows that it is in jest. Soon after Florence conquered Pisa with the help of the soldiers of the militia that Machiavelli had so tenaciously wanted, Filippo Casavecchia, a friend of his who held minor offices under the republican government, wrote on June 17, 1509: "Every day I discover you to be a greater prophet than the Hebrews or any other nation ever had."[162] Although the institution of the militia was the specific occasion that prompted his words, Casavecchia was more generally praising Machiavelli's characteristic wisdom in dealing with the political problems of the Florentine Republic: "I do not believe your ideas will ever be accessible to fools, and there are not enough wise men to go around: you understand me, even if I am not putting it very well."[163] Casavecchia called Machiavelli a prophet because, like the prophets of the *Old Testament*, he was severely criticizing his fellow citizens' vices while also indicating a path of repentance, even if they were not willing to listen and learn.

So far, I have examined Machiavelli's considerations on prophets and prophecy. Did he also write prophetic pages? Textual evidence clearly shows that he did. Albeit in different works and for different purposes, Machiavelli demonstrates an impressive mastery of the language of prophecy. After a long lamentation on the miserable condition of Italy in the tercets *Of Ambition* (*Dell'Ambizione*), which he composed in 1509, Machiavelli prophesies that those new wars and tragedies will distress Tuscany. The only hope is that divine grace will assist the Florentine people or that they will at last be able to provide themselves with better political orders:

---

[161] Niccolò Machiavelli, in *Tutte le opere*, p. 452; English translation, Niccolò Machiavelli, *The Historical Political and Diplomatic Writings of Niccolò Machiavelli*, vol. III, translated by Christian E. Detmold, Boston: James R. Osgood and Company, 1882, p. 217. See also Mario Martelli's "Introduzione" to *Tutte le opere*, p. xxii.

[162] "Ogni in dì vi scopro el maggiore profeta che avessino mai li ebrei o altra generazione"; Filippo Casavecchia to Niccolò Machiavelli, June 17, 1509, in *Tutte le opere*, p. 1108; English translation, *Machiavelli and His Friends. Their Personal Correspondence*, p. 182. James Harrington (1611–1677), an eminent Christian and republican reformer, put Machiavelli close to the prophets when he wrote that he was the only modern political writer to have rediscovered the "ancient prudence" revealed to humanity "by God himself" in order to establish and preserve governments founded on the common interest and the rule of law. See James Harrington, "The Commonwealth of Oceana," *The Political Works of James Harrington*, edited by John G. A. Pocock, Cambridge: Cambridge University Press, 1977, pp. 161 and 178.

[163] "Nicolò, questo è un tempo, che se mai si fu savio, bisogna esere ora. La vostra filosofia non credo che abbi a eser mai capacie a' pazzi, e' savj non son tanti che bastino: voi m'intendete, benché non abbi sì bello porgere." Filippo Casavecchia to Niccolò Machiavelli, June 17, 1509, in *Tutte le opere*, p. 1108; English translation, *Machiavelli and His Friends. Their Personal Correspondence*, p. 182.

I see Ambition, with that swarm

Which Heaven at the world's beginning allotted her,

Flying over the Tuscan mountains;

And already she has scattered so many sparks

Among those people swollen with envy

That she will burn their towns and their farmsteads

If grace or better government does not bring her to naught.[164]

In the short poem *By the Blessed Spirits* (*Canto degli spiriti beati*), probably composed in March 1513, Machiavelli evokes the prophetic theme of the return to the golden age along with the resurrection of ancient virtue: "May fear leave you, / may enmities and rancors, / avarice, pride, and cruelty; / in you may the love of just and true honors resurrect, / and may the world return to that first age. / So to you will be open the roads to heaven, / leading to the blessed folk, / and the flames of virtue will not be extinguished."[165] An even more striking prophetic statement is in the *Second Decennale* (*Decennale second*), a composition in verses (left unfinished) in which Machiavelli summarizes the political events that agitated Italy between 1504 and 1514. Here Machiavelli intends to narrate: "The lofty events and insane actions / that in ten succeeding years have occurred / since, falling silent, I laid down my pen, / the shifts in kingdoms, empires and states brought to pass in Italian lands only, / by divine wisdom foreordained, / I shall sing."[166] In *The Ass* (*L'Asino*), another unfinished poem composed around 1517–1519, Machiavelli issues from the mouth of Circe's damsel a prophecy that concerns the future of the main character who is in fact none other than Niccolò in disguise:

And those humors [my translation] which you have found / so hostile and so adverse / not yet, not yet are purged; / but when their roots are dry, / and the Heavens show themselves gracious, / times happier than ever before will return; / and so pleasant and

---

[164] "Io sento Ambizion, con quella scola / ch'al principio del mondo el ciel sortille, / sopra de' monti di Toscana vola; / e seminato ha già tante faville / tra quelle genti sì d'invidia pregne, / ch'arderà le sue terre e le sue ville, / se grazia o miglior ordin non la spegne." Niccolò Machiavelli, *Dell'ambizione*, in *Tutte le opere*, p. 987; English translation, *Machiavelli. The Chief Works and Others*, vol. II, p. 739.

[165] "Dipàrtasi il timore, / nimicizie e rancori, / avarizia, superbia e crudeltade: / risurga in voi l'amore / de' giusti e veri onori, e torni il mondo a quella prima etade: / così vi fien le strade / del ciel aperte a la beata gente, / né saran di virtù le fiamme spente"; Niccolò Machiavelli, *Degli spiriti beati*, in *Tutte le opere*, p. 990; English translation, *Machiavelli. The Chief Works and Others*, vol. II, p. 880.

[166] "Gli alti accidenti e fatti furiosi, / che in dieci anni seguenti sono stati, / poi che, tacendo, la penna riposi, / le mutazion di regni, imperi e stati, successe pur per l'italico sito, / dal consiglio divin predestinati / canterò io"; Niccolò Machiavelli, *Decennale secondo*, in *Tutte le opere*, p. 950; English translation, *Machiavelli. The Chief Works and Others*, vol. III, p. 1457.

delightful they will be / that you will get joy from the memory / of both past and future affliction. / Perhaps you will yet take vainglory [my translation] / in retelling to various peoples the long account of your sufferings. / But before these stars show themselves / propitious toward you, you will have to travel / to explore the world, covered with a different skin, / because that Providence which supports the human species / wants [my translation] you to bear / this affliction for your greater good.[167]

Writing as a prophetic poet, Machiavelli announces the return of the golden age and the triumph of virtue; he affirms that the dramatic vicissitudes of 1504–1514 were "predestined by God's counsel," and he proclaims that Providence wants us to endure afflictions for our greater good.

His most powerful prophetic text, however, is the *"Exhortatio ad capessendam Italiam"* that closes *The Prince*, the (wrongly) alleged manifesto of political realism.[168] At the outset of the chapter, Machiavelli reveals that he has pondered greatly whether times were ripe for the coming of a redeemer capable of emancipating Italy from its miserable condition of servitude. And he concluded that the times were indeed set to welcome a redeemer.[169] As the text

---

[167] "Non ha cangiato il cielo opinione / ancor, né cangerà, mentre che i fati / tengon ver te la lor dura intenzione. / E quelli umori i quai ti sono stati / cotanto avversi e cotanto nimici, / non sono ancor, non sono ancor purgati; / ma come secche fien le lor radici / e che benigni i ciel si mostreranno, / torneran tempi più che mai felici; / e tanto lieti e giocondi saranno, / che ti darà diletto la memoria / e del passato e del futuro danno. / Forse ch' ancor prenderai vanagloria / a queste genti raccontando e quelle / de le fatiche tue la lunga istoria. / Ma prima che si mostrin queste stelle / liete verso di te, gir ti conviene / cercando il mondo sotto nuova pelle; / ché quella Provvidenza che mantiene / l'umana spezie, vuol che tu sostenga / questo disagio per tuo maggior bene"; *L'Asino*, in *Tutte le opere*, p. 962; English translation, *Machiavelli. The Chief Works and Others*, vol. II, p. 962.

[168] On the prophetic meaning of *The Prince* see Gaetano Lettieri, "Nove tesi sull'ultimo Machiavelli," *Humanitas* 72 (2017): pp. 1034–1089, especially at p. 1044 and p. 1045, n.21. See also Mario Martelli, "Da Poliziano a Machiavelli: sull'epigramma 'Dell'Occasione' e sull'occasione," *Interpres* 2 (1979): pp. 230–254; and "La logica provvidenzialistica e il capitolo XXVI del 'Principe'," *Interpres* 4 (1981–1982): pp. 262–383; and "Firenze," *Letteratura italiana. Storia e geografia*, II, *L'età moderna*, I, Turin: Einaudi, 1988, pp. 132–140; Gennaro Sasso, "Il 'Principe' ebbe due redazioni?," *La Cultura* 29 (1981): pp. 52–109; and "Del ventiseiesimo capitolo del 'Principe', della provvidenza e di altre cose," *La Cultura* 22 (1984): pp. 249–309. See also Hans Baron, "The 'Prince' and the Puzzle of the Date of Chapter 26," *Journal of Medieval and Renaissance Studies* 21 (1991): pp. 84–102 (written in 1968); Tullio Pandolfi, "Gian Matteo Giberti e l'ultima difesa della libertà d'Italia negli anni 1521–1525," *Archivio della Reale società Romana di storia Patria* 31 (1911): pp. 131–237, in particular pp. 147–148. Cfr. Giorgio Inglese, "'Italia' come spazio politico in Machiavelli," *The Radical Machiavelli*, edited by Filippo Del Lucchese, Fabio Frosini, and Vittorio Morfino, Leiden and Boston: Brill, 2015, pp. 73–80.

[169] "Considerato, adunque, tutte le cose di sopra discorse, e pensando meco medesimo se, al presente, in Italia correvano tempi da onorare uno nuovo principe, e se ci era materia che dessi occasione a uno prudente e virtuoso di introdurvi forma che facessi onore a lui e bene alla università degli uomini di quella; mi pare concorrino tante cose in benefizio di uno principe nuovo, che io non so qual mai tempo fussi più atto a questo." Niccolò Machiavelli, *Il Principe*, XXVI, in *Tutte le opere*; English translation, *The Prince*, pp. 101–102.

shows, he interpreted the signs of the times by comparing the condition of Italy with that of those peoples of antiquity who had attained redemption: "It was necessary that Italy be reduced to the condition in which she is at present, which is more enslaved than the Hebrews, more servile than the Persians, more dispersed than the Athenians, without a head, without order, beaten, despoiled, torn, pillaged, and having endured ruin of every sort."[170] He then proceeds to indicate the path of Italy's redemption and points to the *Exodus* as the paradigm to follow, and to Moses as the model leader he hopes that God will send as the answer to Italy's prayers: "Here there is very great readiness, and where there is great readiness, there cannot be great difficulty, provided that your house keeps its aim on the orders of those whom I have put forth. Besides this, here may be seen extraordinary things without example, brought about by God: the sea has opened; a cloud has escorted you along the way; the stone has poured forth water; here manna has rained; everything has concurred in your greatness."[171] What Machiavelli *sees* in his times are not facts, but signs that reveal God's plan for Italy. He does not write "look" ("*guardate*"), or "consider" ("*considerate*"), but "*specchiatevi*" ("look at yourself in a mirror"). Looking in the mirror is a typical metaphor of prophetic literature used to indicate prophets' special gifts to understand representations of God's plan in history.[172]

Another turn of phrase that reveals Machiavelli's debt to prophetic language is his remark that in the past he had believed that someone was "ordered by God" for Italy's "redemption." To write that someone "was ordered by God" is the language of a prophet.[173] Machiavelli calls the redeemer "an Italian

---

[170] "Più stiava che gli Ebrei, più serva ch' e' Persi, più dispersa che gli Ateniesi; sanza capo, sanza ordine; battuta, spogliata, lacera, corsa; ed avessi sopportato d'ogni sorte ruina"; Niccolò Machiavelli, *Il Principe*, XXVI, in *Tutte le opere*; English translation, *The Prince*, p. 102.

[171] "Qui è disposizione grandissima; né può essere, dove è grande disposizione, grande difficultà, pur che quella pigli degli ordini di coloro che io ho proposti per mira. Oltre di questo, qui si veggano estraordinarii sanza esemplo condotti da Dio: el mare si è aperto; una nube vi ha scorto el cammino; la pietra ha versato acqua; qui è piovuto la manna; ogni cosa è concorsa nella vostra grandezza"; Niccolò Machiavelli, *Il Principe*, XXVI; English translation, *The Prince*, p. 102.

[172] See for instance Thomas Aquinas, *Summa Theologiae*, IIa, IIae, Q.171, Art. 5 and G. Savonarola, *Scritti filosofici*, vol. I, p. 207.

[173] In December 1512, a few months before Machiavelli began to work on *The Prince*, Agostino Nifo completed the short tract *De prophetia*, published in 1523 in his *Parva naturalia*. Against peripatetic philosophers who attributed prophecy to natural causes, Nifo claimed that prophecy comes from divine inspiration and from a suspension of external senses or intense contemplation. He stresses his idea of the Christian prophet as an individual who can predict the future and perform miracles. The purpose of prophetic instincts ("*instinctus propheticus*") that God freely bestows on human beings ("*gratis a deo donatus*"), Nifo explains in the conclusion of his tract, is the soul's happiness and the life in accordance with virtue ("*pro animi foelicitate, beneque vivendi ratione*"). I am quoting from *Parva Naturalia Augustini Niphi Medices philosophi suessani*, Venetiis, Hieronymus Scotus, 1550, folios 114vb and 118vb. Ten years later, in his *De regnandi peritia*, where he rewrites and criticizes large sections of *The Prince*,

spirit": that is, a man inspired (*inspiratus*) by God and to whom God has given the virtue necessary to accomplish His plan in history.[174] Machiavelli seems so confident to be able to read God's mind that he has no hesitation in promising God's friendship to the redeemer of Italy he invokes: "nor was God friendlier to them than to you" ("*nè fu a loro Dio più amico che a voi*"). God will be a friend to Italy's redeemer because Italy's redemption is just: "their undertaking [of Moses, Cyrus and Theseus] was not more just than this one." To have God as a friend means that He will help the people who fight for justice, not that He will fight in their place. God cannot bring about their emancipation by way of a miracle because, if he did, he would deprive the Italians of the free will that He has bequeathed to them as his most precious gift: "God does not want to do everything, so as not to take free will from us" ("*Dio non vuole fare ogni cosa per non ci torre el libero arbitrio*"). A political emancipation that is not the outcome of moral change, sufferance, and sacrifice, is not emancipation at all. It does not bring glory ("*quella parte di quella gloria che tocca a noi*").[175]

Nifo, consistent with his interpretation of prophecy as a divine gift for the soul's happiness, ignores chapter XXVI where Machiavelli invokes a prophet who could redeem Italy. On the *De Prophetia* see the "Introduction" by Valeria Sorge to Agostino Nifo, *Sui sogni*, Milan-Udine: Mimesis Edizioni, 2016, pp. 7–60.

[174] On the meaning of spirit in the *Old Testament*, see Spinoza's analysis in *Tractatus teologico-politicus*, I. 21–22.

[175] Alison McQueen is right when she states that "Exodus politics and messianic or apocalyptic politics are not easily separable" (*Political Realism in Apocalyptic Times*, Cambridge: Cambridge University Press, 2018, p. 86). In fact, prophecy, apocalypse, and eschatology (an essential term for determining an apocalyptic style of writing) are rather slippery and sometimes even ambiguous. What interests this discussion is whether, as McQueen states, chapter XXVI of *The Prince* has traces that resemble the apocalyptic genre. Messianism and apocalypticism are a particular type of prophecy. However, apocalypticism is a recognized and detailed genre. Even in its broadest and most comprehensive form, the apocalyptic genre has boundaries, and eschatology certainly falls within these boundaries. If we consider the two subgenres of the apocalyptic genre – the journey to the other world and the historical apocalypse – we can conclude that neither *The Prince* nor Machiavelli's thought in general belong to the first subgenre. There is no suggestion of traveling to the world beyond. There is no trace of the historical apocalypse (which does not coincide with the end of the world and time, but rather with the victory of the chosen people) in chapter XXVI of *The Prince* or in any other Machiavellian text. The end times, or the ultimate victory, are part of a linear vision of time that does not belong to Machiavelli. His vision of time is cyclical in nature. In chapter XXVI of *The Prince*, there is no hint of a word that indicates rebirth (a concept that, while not found in *The Prince*, is used by Machiavelli in other contexts, for example in the *Art of War*: "this province seems born to bring life to that which is dead"). Chapter XXVI of *The Prince* speaks of redemption, of liberation. It invokes *a* redeemer, not the Redeemer. Once again, there is no trace of supernatural or final events in the text, but rather events of an entirely human renewal in the realm of history, a return won with the reinvigoration of "ancient virtue in Italian hearts." Not even Italy can be reborn. Even though it may be "without order – beaten, stripped, torn, overrun" – it is still not dead. In Machiavelli, there is no reference to the apocalyptic genre: there is no revelation of a superhuman mediator to a human recipient; there is no vision; there is no dream; there are no symbols to interpret. As for McQueen's thesis that "the book of Revelation draws heavily on the narratives and images of Exodus [...], as does Savonarola's

Never in the *Exhortatio* or in any other work does Machiavelli write that God has inspired him. This marks a major difference with the prophetic tradition. But he does indicate that he has received divine inspiration from the great men of antiquity (*"gli antiqui uomini"*) who have attained immortality because of their accomplishments in this world (*"sono stati Iddii"*) – among whom, Moses, Cyrus and Theseus, the great founders and redeemers whom he extols as his heroes in the "Exhortation."[176] They disclosed to him "the reason for their actions" (*"le ragioni delle loro azioni"*), and inspired the vision of redemption that Machiavelli then revealed to his fellow compatriots.[177] Moved by great men who have become like God, Machiavelli borrows Petrarch's verses to deliver a prophecy of emancipation:

Virtue will seize arms

Against furor, and the battle will be brief:

For ancient valour

Is not yet dead in Italian hearts.[178]

While the closing of *The Prince* is surely Machiavelli's most inspired and inspiring prophecy of redemption, it is not the only one to be found in his works. In the *Discourses on Livy*, he describes his own endeavor as an intellectual effort designed to encourage young readers to imitate the virtue of ancient times and to shun the corruption of the modern era:

And truly, if the virtue that then used to reign and the vice that now reigns were not clearer than the sun, I would go on speaking with more restraint, fearing falling into this deception of which I accuse some. But since the thing is so manifest that everyone sees it, I will be spirited in saying manifestly that which I may understand of the former and of

apocalypticism," I would like to note that this does not imply that Machiavelli uses the figure of Moses and the story of *Exodus* with messianic and apocalyptic interpretations. Savonarola is one thing; Machiavelli is quite another. Whenever Machiavelli mentions Moses (eleven times in all, six of which are in *The Prince*), Machiavelli speaks of him as the liberator of an oppressed people and as the founder of a state and associates him with other such founders while emphasizing his particular "grace." Machiavelli never suggests anything else. On the apocalyptic genre, see also: *Rivista di storia del cristianesimo: Apocalisse come genere, un dibattito ancora attuale?* 1 (2020), edited by Enrico Norelli, Brescia: Morcelliana; and Alfonso De Petris, *Riletture dell'Apocalisse: Riconsiderazioni sull'idea del Regno*, Florence: Olschki, 2007.

[176] Niccolò Machiavelli, *Discursus Florentinarum rerum post mortem iunioris Laurentii Medices*, in *Tutte le opere*, p. 30; English translation, *Machiavelli. The Chief Works and Others*, vol. I, pp. 113–114.

[177] Niccolò Machiavelli to Francesco Vettori, December 10, 1513, in *Tutte le opere*, p. 1160; English translation, *Machiavelli and His Friends. Their Personal Correspondence*, p. 264.

[178] "Virtù contro a furore / prenderà l'arme, e fia el combatter corto; / ché l'antico valore / nell'italici cor non / è ancor morto"; Niccolò Machiavelli, *Il Principe*, XXVI; English translation, *The Prince*, p. 105. See Francesco Bausi, "Petrarca, Machiavelli, il *Principe*," *Niccolò Machiavelli: politico, storico, letterato: Atti del Convegno di Losanna, 27–30 settembre 1995*, edited by Jean-Jacques Marchand, Rome: Salerno Editrice, 1996, pp. 41–58.

the latter times, so that the spirits of youths who may read these writings of mine can flee the latter and prepare themselves to imitate the former whenever time and fortune may give them opportunity for it.

He then adds this telling remark: "For it is the duty of a good man to teach others the good that you could not work because of the malignity of the times and of fortune. So that when many are capable of it, someone of them more loved by heaven may be able to work it."[179] The prophetic model is clearly visible: first, he denounces the moral corruption of his times; next, he declares that it is his duty, as a good man, to announce the wisdom that could redeem a people from corruption; last, aware that he will not see it come to pass, he entrusts this redemption to someone who might be able to carry it out with the help of God's love ("*più amato dal cielo*").

Machiavelli has written as if he believed he was able to discern the meanings of God's, or the heavens' ("*i cieli*"), intervention in history. In the *Discourses on Livy*, for instance, he pens that the heavens "inspired in the breast of the Roman Senate" the sound counsel that brought infinite good to Rome by advising senators to elect Numa as successor to Romulus "so that those things omitted by him might be ordered by Numa."[180] Even though he is the source of Machiavelli's commentary, Livy does not mention divine or celestial inspiration at all. Rather, he simply remarks: "When they heard the name of Numa, although the Roman fathers [the senators] perceived that the balance of power

---

[179] Niccolò Machiavelli, *Discorsi sopra la prima deca di Tito Livio*, in *Tutte le opere*, II.1; English translation, *Discourses on Livy*, p. 125.

[180] Niccolò Machiavelli, *Discorsi sopra la prima deca di Tito Livio*, in *Tutte le opere*, II.1; English translation, *Discourses on Livy*, p. 134. We find the idea that the heavens help extraordinary individuals in their efforts to change people's way of life and to found new laws in the works of the philosopher Pietro Pomponazzi (1462–1525). The movements and the configurations of the stars, he wrote in his *De incantationibus* (completed in 1520 and published for the first time in 1556), determine the coming of new prophets who institute new laws. See Pietro Pomponazzi, *De incantationibus*, edited by Vittoria Perrone Compagni and L. Regnicoli, Florence: Olschki, 2011, pp. 933–941). In the *Apologia* (1518), Pomponazzi claims that the prophets help humankind to regenerate itself after natural cataclysms and calamities. It is nature, he writes, that produces this kind of prophet. They are, however, instruments of the divinity ("le santis-sime leggi [...] sono date dagli enti divini attraverso i profeti"). The task of the prophets, moreover, is to restore justice in human society. See Pietro Pomponazzi, *Apologia*, II.7, edited by Vittoria Perrone Compagni, Florence: Olschki, 2011, pp. 237–239. On Pomponazzi and prophecy see Vittoria Perrone Compagni, "'Evidentissimi avvertimenti dei Numi': Sogni, vati-cini, profezie in Pomponazzi," *Annali del Dipartimento di Filosofia (Nuova Serie)* XVII (2011): pp. 21–59. The eminent philosopher, doctor, and mathematician Girolamo Cardano (1501–1576) also held that the heavens use prophets to bring about radical changes in the mores and the laws of peoples. See Guido Giglioni, "Voci della sibilla e voci della natura: divinazione oracolare in Girolamo Cardano," *Bruniana & Campanelliana* 11 (2005): pp. 365–387. Ibid., p. 93 and Valeria Sorge, *Tra contingenza e necessità. L'ordine delle cause in Pietro Pomponazzi*, Milan and Udine: Mimesis, 2010.

would incline to the Sabines if a king were chosen from them, yet none of them ventured to prefer himself, or any other member of his party, or, in fine, any of the citizens or fathers, to a man so well known, but unanimously resolved that the kingdom should be offered to Numa Pompilius."[181] It is Machiavelli who wishes to see in Numa's election a celestial intervention that encouraged the Romans to provide themselves with the religious institutions that so admirably contributed to future greatness.

In the *Art of War*, the only major political text published during his lifetime, Machiavelli repeats the core of the prophetic message of the "Exhortation." First, he forcefully deplores the lamentable condition of Italy's corruption, oppression, and servitude, all of which has been caused by the malignity and cowardice of Italian princes:

The common belief of our Italian princes, before they felt the blows of Transalpine war, was that a prince needed only to think of a sharp reply in his study, to write a fine letter, to show quickness and cleverness in quotable sayings and replies, to know how to spin a fraud, to be adorned with gems and with gold, to sleep and eat with greater splendor than others, to be surrounded with wanton pleasures, to deal with subjects avariciously and proudly, to decay in laziness, to give positions in the army by favor, to despise anybody who showed them any praiseworthy course, and to expect their words to be taken as the responses of oracles. It did not enter the minds of these wretches that they were preparing themselves to be the prey of whoever attacked them.[182]

Next, as in the "Exhortation," Machiavelli outlines a prophetic vision of Italy's redemption: "By Italy's condition I do not wish you to be dismayed or terrified, because this land seems born to resuscitate [my translation] dead things [*"nata per risuscitare le cose morte"*], as she has in poetry, in painting."[183]

In the *Istorie fiorentine*, Machiavelli explicitly writes that God intervened to help Florence: "But God, who in such extremities has always had a particular care for it, made an unhoped-for accident arise that gave the king, the pope, and the Venetians something greater to think about than Tuscany." He also writes that "Since the heavens willed that things prepare for future evil, he [Gualtieri

---

[181] Livy, *Ab urbe condita*, I.18.

[182] "Credevano i nostri principi italiani, prima ch'egli assaggiassero i colpi delle oltramontane guerre, che a uno principe bastasse sapere negli scrittoi pensare una acuta risposta, scrivere una bella lettera, mostrare ne' detti e nelle parole arguzia e prontezza, sapere tessere una fraude, ornarsi di gemme e d'oro, dormire e mangiare con maggiore splendore che gli altri, tenere assai lascivie intorno, governarsi co' sudditi avaramente e superbamente, marcirsi nello ozio, dare i gradi della milizia per grazia, disprezzare se alcuno avesse loro dimostro alcuna lodevole via, volere che le parole loro fussero responsi di oraculi; né si accorgevano i meschini che si prepravano ad essere preda di qualunque gli assaltava"; Niccolò Machiavelli, *Dell'arte della guerra*, in *Tutte le opere*, p. 388; English translation, *Machiavelli. The Chief Works and Others*, vol. I, p. 724.

[183] Niccolò Machiavelli, *Dell'arte della guerra*, in *Tutte le opere*, p. 389; English translation, *Machiavelli. The Chief Works and Others*, vol. I, p. 726.

di Brienne, duke of Athens] arrived in Florence precisely at the time when the campaign at Lucca had been lost completely."[184]

In another chapter of the *Florentine Histories*, he interprets a whirlwind that devastated the Tuscan countryside as a clear warning from God:

Thereupon, when arms had been put away by men, it appeared that God wished to take them up Himself: so great was a windstorm that then occurred, which in Tuscany had effects unheard of in the past and for whoever learns of it in the future will have marvelous and memorable effects. [...] Without doubt, God wanted to warn rather than punish Tuscany; for, if such a storm had entered a city among many and crowded houses and inhabitants, as it did enter among few and scattered oaks and trees and houses, without doubt it would have made ruin and torment greater than that which the mind can conjecture. But God meant for then that this small example should be enough to refresh among men the memory of His power.[185]

In this case, too, as he has done with the Senate's appointment of Numa as second king of Rome, Machiavelli adds a prophetic interpretation to the story he is narrating. The sources that Machiavelli has used for his narration of the tempest are Giovanni Rucellai's *Zibaldone* and Filippo di Cino Rinuccini's *Ricordi storici*.[186] Neither interprets the facts as a sign of God's will to show his power.[187] In another chapter of the *Florentine Histories*, he speaks of the fire that burned the Church of Santo Spirito during the visit of the Duke of Milan in 1471. Without discounting it, Machiavelli cites the popular belief that the fire was God's punishment for the corrupt manners of the Duke's court:

At that time was seen a thing never before seen in our city: this being the season of Lent, in which the Church commands that one fast by not eating meat, his court, without respect to Church or God, all fed on meat. And because many spectacles were held to

---

[184] Niccolò Machiavelli, *Istorie fiorentine*, in *Tutte le opere*, pp. 831 and 681; English translation by Laura F. Banfield and Harvey C. Mansfield, *Florentine Histories*, Princeton: Princeton University Press, 1998, p. 341 and p. 90.

[185] "Posate le armi dagli uomini, parve che Iddio le volessi prendere egli, tanta fu grande una tempesta di venti che allora seguì, la quale in Toscana fece inauditi per lo adietro e a chi per lo avvenire lo intenderà maravigliosi e memorabili effetti [...] Volle senza dubio Iddio più tosto minacciare che gastigare la Toscana; perché se tanta tempesta fusse entrata in una città, infra le case e gli abitatori assai e spessi, come l'entrò fra querce e arbori e case poche e rare, sanza dubio faceva quella rovina e fragello che si può con la mente conietturare maggiore. Ma Iddio volle, per allora, che bastasse questo poco di esempio a rinfrescare infra gli uomini la memoria della potenzia sua"; *Istorie fiorentine*, VI. 34, in *Tutte le opere*, p. 789. See also Felix Gilbert, "Florentine Political Assumptions in the Period of Savonarola and Soderini," *Journal of the Warburg and Courtauld Institutes* 20 (1957): pp. 187–214.

[186] See Niccolò Machiavelli, *Opere storiche*, vol. 2, edited by Alessandro Montevecchi and Carlo Varotti with Gian Mario Anselmi, Rome: Salerno Editrice, 2010, p. 610.

[187] See *Giovanni Rucellai e il suo Zibaldone*, edited by Alessandro Perosa, London: The Warburg Institute, University of London, 1960, pp. 78–82; *Ricordi storici di Filippo di Cino Rinuccini dal 1282 al 1460 colla continuazione di Alamanno e Neri suoi figli fino al 1506: seguiti da altri monumenti inediti di storia patria estratti dai codici originali ... con documenti ed illustrazioni*, edited by Giuseppe Aiazzi, Florence: Stamperia Piatti, 1840, p. lxxxvi.

honor him, among which was represented the giving of the Holy Spirit to the Apostles in the Church of Santo Spirito, and because that church burned down as a result of the many fires that are made in such solemnities, it was believed by many that God, angered against us, had wished to show that sign of his wrath.[188]

His main source is probably the *Libri de temporibus suis* that the Dominican friar Giovanni di Carlo (1428–1503) compiled around 1480. The chronicler writes that the fire was a remarkable and great punishment that followed the most impious event of many sacrilegious actions (*"multa impie obsceneque confecta"*) that the Florentine perpetrated on the occasion of the visit of the Duke of Milan. Machiavelli wants to see in the same facts a prophetic meaning. He cites approvingly the popular opinion that the fire was a just punishment that God inflicted on the Florentines because of the serious sins they had perpetrated.[189]

[188] "Dove si vide, cosa in quel tempo nella nostra città ancora non veduta, che, sendo il tempo quadragesimale, nel quale la Chiesa comanda che sanza mangiar carne si digiuni, quella sua corte, sanza rispetto della Chiesa o di Dio, tutta di carne si cibava. E perché si feciono molti spettaculi per onorarlo, intra i quali, nel tempio di Santo Spirito, si rapresentò la concessione dello Spirito Santo agli Apostoli, e perché per i molti fuochi che in simile solennità si fanno, quel tempio tutto arse, fu creduto da molti Dio, indegnato contro di noi, avere voluto della sua ira dimostrare quel segno"; *Istorie fiorentine*, VII.28, in *Tutte le opere*, p. 811; English translation, *Florentine Histories*, pp. 306–307. On the interpretations of natural cataclysms see Gerrit J. Schenk, "Dis-astri.Modelli interpretativi delle calamità naturali dal medioevo al Rinascimento," *Le calamità ambientali nel tardo Medioevo: realtà, percezioni, reazioni*, edited by Michael Matheus, Florence: Florence University Press, 2010, pp. 23–75.

[189] Here is the transcription of Giovanni Di Carlo's text: "Accidit autem prodigii cuiusdam loco ut cum quadragesime sanctissimum tempus instaret, cives vero quo ducis animum oblectarent, festum quod apud heremitarum templum hactenus celebrari soleba‹n›t intempestive fieri procurassent. Eo vigilia prima perfecto, cum omnes abiissent, forte quidpiam ignis quo crebro in eo festo utuntur in eo templo remansit. Cepit ergo in tempeste noctis silentio ignis arida fomenta comperiens coalescere ac sensim tam maximus ignis accendi ut omne templum ingens flamma consumeret. Tanta vero flammarum vis fuit ut eius fulgor per multa spatia longius corruscarunt. Et quamvis multi concurrerent remedium tamen nullum potuit adhiberi. Quippe cum vetustissimum esset templum totumque ab interiori parte assibus pene celatum ut primum flamma emersit totum confestim miro modo absumpsit. Ferebatur autem in ea hominum permixtione multa impie obsceneque confecta cum invicem se viri ac mulieres comprimerent. Itaque inpiissimam rem statim talis tantaque ultio secuta est ut usque ad interiora omnia templi vorax flamma penetraret arasque et civium sepulcra commineret atque in cinerem pene omnia reducta perirent. Erat vero et concrepantis ignis et in ruinam omnia contrahentis tumultus ingens. Concursantium quoque et advenientium strepitu et vocibus pulverisque magnitudine omnia miscebantur. Decebat sane ut eius violationem templi non alia quam ignis ultio expiaret. Proinde malum aliquid maximum imminere civitati augurabantur omnes, quoniam et iam pridem Iustine proruisset porta, nuper Misericordie domus fuisset exusta, nunc vero ut fere aliud nil superesset quo tutaremur Sancti Spiritus templum ignibus conflagrasset"; Giovanni di Carlo, *Libri de temporibus suis*, Rome: Biblioteca Apostolica Vaticana, Vat. Lat. 5878, 118v–119. I sincerely thank Antonio Ciaralli and Pasquale Stoppelli for having transcribed and corrected the text of the manuscript.

We also find visible traces of prophetic language in the "Exhortation to Penitence," a work that Machiavelli composed for a religious confraternity probably in 1525.[190] The example he therein indicates is "David the prophet," who humbly repented before God's infinite mercy: "O Lord, I, imprisoned in the depths of sin, with a voice humble and full of tears have called upon you, O Lord, for mercy; and I pray you that in your infinite goodness you may be willing to grant it to me." As in the past, Machiavelli again writes as if he were able to read God's mind:

Consider, then, how all things made and created are made and created for the benefit of man. You see first of all the huge extent of the land, which, in order that it could be inhabited by men, he did not allow to be wholly covered over with water but left in part exposed for their use. Then he made to grow on it so many animals, so many plants, so many grasses, and whatever upon it is produced, for their benefit; and not merely did he wish that the earth should provide for their living but commanded the waters also to support countless animals for their food. But let us leave these earthly things; let us raise our eyes to the sky; let us consider the beauty of the things we see. Of these, part he has made for our use, part in order that, as we observe the glory and the marvelous workmanship of these things, upon us may come a thirst and a longing to possess those other things that are hidden from us.[191]

Machiavelli also looked with a prophetic eye at the tragic events that led to Italy's complete servitude. Upon receiving news of the fall of the Dukedom of Milan under the domination of the Emperor Charles V in October 1525, Machiavelli borrowed the prophecies of Ugo Capeto from Dante's *Purgatory*: "I see the fleur-de-Lys of Alagna return, and in his Vicar" ("*Veggio 'n Alagna tornar lo fiordaliso / e nel vicario suo, etc.*"). Commenting on the reality of the situation, he then remarks: "thus is it imposed from above" ("*Sic datum desuper*").[192] Machiavelli meant to tell Guicciardini that no remedy was possible because the fall of Milan and the consequent defeat of the Pope were both

---

[190] See Gaetano Lettieri, "Nove tesi sull'ultimo Machiavelli," pp. 1045–1051. Luigi Lazzerini proposes a later date in "Machiavelli e Savonarola. L' 'Esortazione alla penitenza' e il 'Miserere,'" *Rivista di storia e letteratura religiosa* 44 (2008): pp. 385–402, and also in *Teologia del miserere. Da Savonarola al Beneficio di cristo 1490–1543*, Torino: Rosenberg & Sellier, 2013, pp. 85–100. For an accurate review of the studies, and for a suggestive interpretative hypothesis, see Emanuele Cutinelli-Rendina's "Nota introduttiva" to the *Esortazione alla penitenza*, in Niccolò Machiavelli, *Scritti in poesia e in prosa*, edited by A. Corsaro, P. Cosentino, E. Cutinelli-Rendina, F. Grazzini, and N. Marcelli, Rome: Salerno Editrice, 2012, pp. 403–409. See also Francesco Bausi, *Machiavelli*, Rome: Salerno Editrice, 2005, pp. 319–320.

[191] Niccolò Machiavelli, *Exortatione alla penitenza*, in *Tutte le opere*, p. 933; English translation, *The Chief Works and Others*, vol. I, pp. 171–172.

[192] Niccolò Machiavelli to Francesco Guicciardini, post October 21, 1526, in *Tutte le opere*, p. 1224; English translation, *Machiavelli and His Friends. Their Personal Correspondence*, p. 371. Dante's verses are from *Purgatorio* XX 86–87: "Veggio in Alagna intrar lo fiordaliso / e nel vicario suo Cristo esser catto. / Veggiolo un'altra volta essere deriso; / veggiolo rinnovellar l'aceto e 'l fiele, / e tra vivi ladroni esser anciso."

decided by God. Yet, as rumors spread of a popular uprising against the imperial troops in Lombardy in May 1526, Machiavelli addressed a most passionate and desperate exhortation to Guicciardini and the Pope to fight the invaders. His words evoke the "Exhortation" with which he had closed *The Prince*, thirteen years before. Once again, he emphasized how God had offered Italy a unique opportunity to emancipate itself from foreign domination and urged, for the love of God, to combat the barbarians.[193] This time too he spoke in vain. To see that his prophetic words have real impact on the mind of the Italians, we must wait for the beginnings of the Risorgimento, almost three centuries later, as I shall analyze in the fourth part of this study.

2.3.3 Reality and Dreams: An Antichristian Prophet?

How can we trust the sincerity of Machiavelli's prophetic words, given his anti-Christian and possibly even atheistic pronouncements? I am confident that many readers, who have patiently followed my argument thus far, have also considered this fundamental question. If Machiavelli did not believe in the Christian God, we must take all his prophetic words as rhetorical ruses intended to persuade his readers to embrace the beliefs that he was urging them to embrace. This is quite possible. As I have argued elsewhere, Machiavelli was a master of the *ars rhetorica*, and therefore perfectly capable of writing prophetic words even if he did not believe in prophetic inspiration.[194] Yet, I find much more persuasive the idea that Machiavelli did, in fact, believe in the existence of God: that he was not at all anti-Christian, and his prophetic pronouncements were perfectly consistent with his own beliefs about God and Christianity.

[193] "Questa occasione per l'amor di Iddio non si perda, et ricordatevi che la fortuna, i cattivi nostri consigli, et peggiori ministri harieno condotto non il re, ma il papa in prigione: hannonelo tratto i cattivi consigli di altri et la medesima fortuna. Provvedete, per l'amor di Iddio, hora in modo che S. S.tà ne' medesimi pericoli non ritorni, di che voi non sarete mai sicuri sino a tanto che gli Spagnuoli non siano in modo tratti di Lombardia, che non vi possino tornare. Mi pare vedere lo imperadore, veggendosi mancare sotto il re, fare gran proferte al papa, le quali doverrieno trovare gli orecchi vostri turati, quando vi ricordiate de' mali sopportati, et delle minacce che per lo addietro vi sono state fatte, et ricordatevi che il duca di Sessa andava dicendo, quod pontifex sera Caesarem ceperat timere. Hora Iddio ha ricondotto le cose in termine, che il papa è a tempo a tenerlo, quando questo tempo non si lasci perdere. Voi sapete quante occasioni si sono perdute: non perdete questa né confidate più nello starvi, rimettendovi alla Fortuna et al tempo, perché con il tempo non vengono sempre quelle medesime cose, né la Fortuna è sempre quella medesima. Io direi più oltre, se io parlassi con huomo che non intendesse i segreti o non conoscesse il mondo. Liberate diuturna cura Italiam, extirpate has immanes belluas, quae hominis, preter faciem et vocem, nichil habent"; Niccolò Machiavelli to Francesco Guicciardini, May 17, 1526, in *Tutte le opere*, p. 1232; English translation, *Machiavelli and His Friends. Their Personal Correspondence*, pp. 386–387.

[194] Maurizio Viroli, *Machiavelli's God*, translated by Anthony Shugaar, Princeton and Oxford: Princeton University Press, 2010, pp. 89–153.

To begin with, even Machiavelli's most severe condemnations of Christian religion are not anti-Christian. He surely declares that "our religion" bears a heavy burden of responsibility for having suffocated the love of republican liberty in modern times. So too has it rendered "the world weak" and "given it in prey to criminal men, who can manage it securely, seeing that the collectivity of men, so as to go to paradise, think more of enduring their beatings than of avenging them." Machiavelli also exalts pagan education which taught the young to esteem the honor of the world and to place in it "the highest good"; beatified only men who were "full of worldly glory, as were captains of armies and princes of republics"; and celebrated "greatness of spirit," strength of body, and "all other things capable of making men very strong." In the same chapter of the *Discourses* where he pens these words, however, he adds an important qualification concerning the moral and political value of Christian religion. The Christian religion's principles are not wicked, Machiavelli explains, rather the Church's interpretation of those principles is wicked: "And although the world appears to be made effeminate and heaven disarmed, it arises without doubt more from the cowardice of the men who have interpreted our religion according to idleness and not according to virtue."[195]

A return to the principles of the Christian religion is thus needed. He writes in *The Discourses*: "If such religion [Christian religion] had been maintained by the princes of the Christian republic as was ordered by its giver, the Christian states and republics would be more united, much happier than they are." Within the Christian tradition, Machiavelli found and extolled the idea of a God he loved and needed, a God who teaches us to love our fatherland and liberty. As for Machiavelli's alleged atheism, I find no conclusive evidence in his whole corpus. The text that proponents of an atheistic Machiavelli often cite is *Discourses* II. 5 ("*Che la variazione delle sètte e delle lingue, insieme con l'accidente de' diluvii o della peste, spegne la memoria delle cose*"), where Machiavelli seems to assert that the world is eternal and not created. If the world was not created there is, of course, no Creator. Against the notion that Machiavelli did not believe in God, I wish to put forth the wise words that Sebastian de Grazia wrote in *Machiavelli in Hell*. Scattered throughout the works of Machiavelli, "like poppies in a field of chickpeas, [there] are many references to God." Niccolò's God is "the creator, the master deity, providential, real, universal, one of many names, personal, invocable, thankable, to be revered, a judge, just and forgiving, rewarding and punishing, awesome, a force transcendent, separate from but operative in the world."[196] To De Grazia's words, I fondly and lovingly add that Machiavelli explicitly wrote that God did create the world: "Hardly had God created stars and light, / Heaven and

---

[195] Niccolò Machiavelli, *Discorsi sopra la prima deca di Tito Livio*, II.2, in *Tutte le opere*, pp. 149–150; English translation, pp. 131–132.

[196] Sebastian de Grazia, *Machiavelli in Hell*, Princeton: Princeton University Press, 1989, p. 58.

elements and man (the one / He made lord over all such beauties bright)."[197] I also add that in his private correspondence, where Machiavelli reveals his innermost beliefs, he thanks God for having saved his life. He writes to his nephew Giovanni Vernacci:

> I have received several letters from you, most recently one from last April in which, among other things, you complain that you have not received any letters from me. My answer is that since your departure I have had so much trouble that it is no wonder I have not written to you. In fact, if anything, it is a miracle that I am alive, because my post was taken from me and I was about to lose my life, which God and my innocence have preserved for me. I have had to endure all sorts of other evils, both prison and other kinds. But, by the grace of God, I am well, and I manage to live as I can – and so I shall strive to do, until the heavens show themselves to be more kind.

Equally telling are the words that Machiavelli's son, Ludovico, wrote to his father in a letter dated May 22, 1527: "God help me. I send you my regards as always. God keep you always from ill. Give my regards to Madonna Marietta and tell her to pray God for me; greet the entire family."[198] Would Ludovico ever have written those words to an atheist father? In a dramatic letter dated May 17, 1526, Machiavelli calls upon God three times in order to persuade Francesco Guicciardini (and the pope) to wage an open war against the horde of landsknechts that had crossed over the Alps: "For the love of God, let us not lose this opportunity"; "for the love of God, see to it now with such measures that His Holiness does not fall back into these same perils"; "now God has brought things to such a pass that, if this moment is not lost, the pope is in time to take the emperor."[199] He again invokes God, twice, in his last letter, which was written to Vettori and dated April 18, 1527: "And for the love of God, since this treaty cannot be made, if indeed you are unable to make it, break the negotiations off immediately"; "but whoever profits from war, as these soldiers do, would be crazy to extol peace. Yet God will grant them more war than we would like."[200] Machiavelli's invocations and expressions of gratitude to God are too many, and too powerful, to be interpreted as insincere rhetorical statements. Machiavelli's God loves justice more than any other virtue. ("*Questa sola virtù è quella che in fra tucte l'altre piace a Dio*").[201] To see justice in the world, God inspires prophets.

---

[197] Niccolò Machiavelli, *Dell'ambizione*, in *Tutte le opere*, p. 984; English translation, *Machiavelli. The Chief Works and Others*, vol. II, p. 735.

[198] Lodovico Machiavelli to Niccolò Machiavelli, May 22, 1527, in *Tutte le opere*, p. 1252; English translation, *Machiavelli and His Friends. Their Personal Correspondence*, p. 418.

[199] Niccolò Machiavelli to Francesco Guicciardini, May 17, 1526, p. 1232; English translation, *Machiavelli and His Friends. Their Personal Correspondence*, pp. 386–387.

[200] Niccolò Machiavelli to Francesco Vettori, April 18, 1527, in *Tutte le opere*, pp. 1251–1252; English translation, *Machiavelli and His Friends. Their Personal Correspondence*, pp. 417–418.

[201] Niccolò Machiavelli, *Allocuzione fatta ad un magistrato*, in *Tutte le opere*, p. 36.

How can Machiavelli's prophetic side coexist with his realism? To answer this question, I must first stress that he was a special sort of political realist. The truest example of political realism, Francesco Guicciardini, considered Machiavelli to be a political thinker too keen to generalize and interpret political events through abstract models and examples taken from antiquity. With subtle irony, in a letter of May 1521, Guicciardini reproached Machiavelli for his inclination to discuss general forms of government such as monarchy, aristocracy, and republic. In his notes on the *Discourses on Livy*, he called it a mistake to cite the example of the ancient Romans – as Machiavelli did many times – because each situation is unique and contingent. According to Guicciardini, political decisions should not be made by way of abstract models but using discretion (*discrezione*): a highly refined form of political prudence that is not based on general rules, that cannot be learned in books, and that very few men have by nature or are able to attain after long practice.[202]

For Guicciardini, Machiavelli was also often inclined to suggest highly unusual and surely risky – although perhaps effective – courses of political action. During the dramatic political and military crisis of 1525–1527 that led to the Sack of Rome, for instance, Machiavelli proposed to Guicciardini and Pope Clement VII that the only way to save Italy and preserve the integrity of the Papal States was to arm the peoples of Romagna and mobilize them against the invasion of the imperial troops. To arm and organize the subjects of Romagna in a militia, Guicciardini replied, would be "one of the most useful and praiseworthy works that His Holiness could undertake," if only it were possible. Given the conditions of the Papal States in Romagna, however, such a course of action was very dangerous. The peoples were torn by chronic political hostilities, and the Church had neither partisans nor friends there. Those who wished to live well and peacefully disliked the Church because they wanted a government that would protect them; troublemakers and evil men disliked the Church because they saw disorder and war as a chance to settle accounts and see to their own interests. Machiavelli's proposal was fascinating, but it did not pass the scrutiny of a genuine political realist.

What really distinguishes Machiavelli's realism from the realism of Guicciardini (and many others like him) was the persuasion that at times "rare and marvelous men" appear on the world's stage (perhaps sent by God) to accomplish grand things such as unifying scattered peoples, emancipating nations, and resurrecting political liberty. For Machiavelli, as we have seen, men like Moses, Cyrus, Theseus, and Romulus were real, and he believed that others like them might come. Guicciardini could not have even conceived the possibility of composing an exhortation such as that of *The Prince*. Having

---

[202] Francesco Guicciardini, *Ricordi*, in *Opere di Francesco Guicciardini*, vol. I, edited by Emanuella Lugnani Scarano, Turin: UTET, 1983, pp. 759–760 and p. 804; English translation, Francesco Guicciardini, *Maxims and Reflections of a Renaissance Statesman*, translated by Mario Domandi, Gloucester (MA): Peter Smith, 1970, p. 69 and p. 42.

explained, in the most realistic manner, what a new prince should do to preserve a principality, Machiavelli, instead, openly invoked a redeemer to liberate Italy from the barbarians. He stressed that such an extraordinary achievement would be possible, indeed easy, because times were ripe for it. But he was imagining a grandiose event that existed only in his heart and in his mind. No other political writer of his time, or of later centuries, combined strict adherence to the rule that the knowledge of political reality comes before political imagination, with a powerful political imagination and a poetic proclivity to forge political myths.

Myths inspire, impel action, and sustain commitment. They are political forces. Because he is a true realist, Machiavelli creates them when he feels inspired to, and sees the need for them. At the same time, he believes that human beings judge political matters by looking at leaders' real accomplishments: "In the actions of all men, and especially of princes, where there is no tribunal to which to appeal, one must consider the final result," he writes in *The Prince*.[203] To be a realist does not mean to be either audacious or cautious, but to be wise enough to pursue the kind of political conduct that is in tune with the context of the times at hand. In crazy times, a political decision that normally would be insane is in fact the right thing to make. As he explained in a very important letter written to Giovan Battista Soderini in September 1506, very different modes of action lead to the same results, whereas identical modes of action lead to opposite outcomes. Scipio succeeded in Spain by governing his army mildly and by providing an outstanding example of personal integrity. On the contrary, Hannibal succeeded in Italy by displaying the most inhumane cruelty against his own soldiers. Had Scipio used Hannibal's methods in Spain, he would have failed. Had he behaved like Scipio, Hannibal too would have met the same fate. As Machiavelli explains, the key element to be considered in this case, and in general, is the ability to act as the times and the mood of the people require (*"riscontro"*).[204]

Surprising as it might seem, Machiavelli regarded Savonarola, the prophet par excellence, as the example of a religious reformer and founder of a new political order who masterfully put into practice the realist principle of adapting political conduct to changing circumstances. He highlights this prophetic quality in the letter to Ricciardo Becchi of March 9, 1498 that I have already cited.[205] More than twenty years later, in a letter to Francesco Guicciardini of

---

[203] Niccolò Machiavelli, *Il Principe*, XV, in *Tutte le opere*, p. 284; English translation, *The Prince*, p. 71.

[204] Niccolò Machiavelli to Giovan Battista Soderini, September 13–21, 1506, in *Tutte le opere*, pp. 1082–1083; English translation, *Machiavelli and His Friends. Their Personal Correspondence*, pp. 134–136.

[205] Niccolò Machiavelli to Ricciardo Becchi, March 9, 1498, in *Tutte le opere*, p. 1011; English translation, *Machiavelli and His Friends. Their Personal Correspondence*, p. 10.

May 17, 1521, from Carpi, Machiavelli restates that one of Savonarola's distinctive qualities was to understand the variations of the political context and change his political action accordingly.[206] The Italian word that Machiavelli chooses to describe Savonarola is "*versuto,*" which comes from the Latin verb "*vertere,*" indicating the ability to change, alter, or turn one's conduct. When he was attributing to Savonarola the ability to change his words and actions according to shifting conditions, he was bestowing on him words of praise. The example of Savonarola shows that the same person can be both a prophet and a realist. For Machiavelli, only a leader who is both a prophet and a realist could accomplish the redemption of Italy.

Another equally distinctive principle of Machiavelli's realism – that founders and redeemers are often compelled to be cruel to accomplish their mission – is consistent with Savonarola's prophetic teaching. In the sermons of March 18 and July 12, 1495, Savonarola praised Moses' severity against the Israelites when he found them worshiping the golden calf. Savonarola stressed that the founding of new political orders requires a "severe justice" ("*severa iustizia*"). Machiavelli in the *Discourses on Livy* approvingly cites the same episode of the *Book of Exodus*: "And whoever reads the Bible judiciously will see that since he wished his laws and his orders to go forward, Moses was forced to kill infinite men who, moved by nothing other than envy, were opposed to his plans."[207] Furthermore, Machiavelli tellingly adds:

Friar Girolamo Savonarola knew this necessity very well; Piero Soderini, gonfalonier of Florence, knew it too. The one was not able to conquer it because he did not have the authority to enable him to do it (that was the friar) and because he was not understood well by those who followed him, who would have had authority for it. Not therefore because of him did it remain undone, and his sermons are full of accusations of the wise of the world, and of invectives against them, for so he called the envious who were opposed to his orders.[208]

We do not have enough textual evidence to claim that Machiavelli drew inspiration from Savonarola's sermons for his views that founders and redeemers must be capable of being cruel and deceitful. What Machiavelli's texts do clearly indicate is that the realist positions that have brought the most severe reprobation against him from Christian quarters were perfectly congenial with the story of the *Exodus*. If "the greatest good to be done and the most pleasing

---

[206] Niccolò Machiavelli to Francesco Guicciardini, May 21, 1521, in *Tutte le opere*, p. 1203; English translation, *Machiavelli and His Friends. Their Personal Correspondence*, p. 336.

[207] "E chi legge la Bibbia sensatamente, vedrà Moisè essere stato forzato, a volere che le sue leggi e che i suoi ordini andassero innanzi ad ammazzare infiniti uomini, i quali, non mossi da altro che dalla invidia, si opponevano a' disegni suoi"; Niccolò Machiavelli, *Discorsi sopra la prima deca di Tito Livio*, III.30, in *Tutte le opere*, p. 237; English translation, *Discourses on Livy*, p. 280.

[208] "Niccolò Machiavelli, *Discorsi sopra la prima deca di Tito Livio*, III.30, in *Tutte le opere*, p. 237; English translation, *Discourses on Livy*, p. 280.

to God is that which one does to one's fatherland,"[209] if no enterprise is in God's eyes more just than the redemption of one's fatherland,[210] if God loves justice and mercy,[211] it is perfectly consistent to assume – in full agreement with the prophetic tradition – that God is willing to pardon, and even rewards, founders and redeemers who are forced to enter into evil.[212]

Totally inconsistent with the prophetic tradition is, however, the belief that founders and redeemers go to hell and not to paradise. This is what Machiavelli revealed in the narration that became famously known as "Machiavelli's dream." The story of "Machiavelli's dream" has come down to us in different versions. The common content can be reported as follows. To the relatives and the friends who were around his bed, he said that he had had a dream in which he had seen a band of a few poorly dressed men, ragged and miserable in appearance, who told him that they were on their way to Paradise because it is written *Beati pauperes, quoniam ipsorum est regnum caelorum*. He then saw a very large crowd of men full of majesty and gravity. They resembled a Senate discussing serious matters of state. Among them he recognized Plato, Seneca, Plutarch, Tacitus, and others of the same kind. He asked them who they were, and they replied that they were the damned, the souls of men that had been sentenced to Hell because *Sapientia huius saeculi inimica est Dei*. After telling his friends of his dream, Machiavelli remarked he very much preferred to be with the second crowd to discuss with them matters of state than to be with the miserable blessed who were going to Paradise.[213]

---

[209] Niccolò Machiavelli, *Discursus Florentinarum rerum post mortem iunioris Laurentii Medices*, in *Tutte le opere*, p.30; English translation, *The Chief Works and Others*, vol. I, pp. 113–114.

[210] Niccolò Machiavelli, *Il Principe*, XXVI, in *Tutte le opere*, p. 297; English translation, *The Prince*, p. 103.

[211] "Questa sola virtù [la giustizia] è quella che in fra tucte l'altre piace a Dio. [...] Idio ama et la iustitia et la pietà"; *Allocuzione fatta ad un magistrato*, in *Tutte le opere*, pp. 36–37.

[212] Niccolò Machiavelli, *Il Principe*, XVIII, in *Tutte le opere*, p. 270; English translation, *The Prince*, p. 70.

[213] The first source we have is a letter of Giambattista Busini to Benedetto Varchi that reveals that Machiavelli narrated "his very celebrated dream" on his deathbed, but the letter indicates nothing of the dream's content. The first written narration of the content of Machiavelli's dream is in *La salut d'Origene*, a text composed in 1629 by the French Jesuit Estienne Binet (1569-1639). Here is the citation: "On arrive à ce detestable poinct d'honneur, où arriua Machiavel sur la fin de sa vie: car il eut cette illusion peu deuant que rendre son esprit. Il vit un tas de pauures gens, comme coquins, deschirez, affamez, contrefaits, fort mal en ordre, et en assez petit nombre; on luy dit que c'estoit ceux de Paradis, desquels il estoit escrit, *Beati pauperes, quoniam ipsorum est regnum coelorum*. Ceux-cy estans retirez, on fit paroistre un nombre innombrable de personnages pleins de grauité et de majesté: on le voyoit comme un Senat, où on traitoit d'affaires d'Estat, et fort serieuses; il entrevit Platon, Aristate, Senèque, Plutarque, Tacite, et d'autres de cette qualité. Il demanda qui estoient ces Messieurs-là si venerables: on luy lit que c'estoient les damnez, et que c'estoient des ames reprouuées du Ciel, *Sapientia huius saeculi inimica est Dei*. Cela estant passé, on luy demanda desquels il vouloit estre. Il respondit qu'il aymoit beaucoup mieux estre en enfer avec ces grands esprits, pour deuiser avec eux des affaires d'Estat, que d'estre avec cette vermine de ces belistres qu'on luy

Even if we know of "Machiavelli's dream" from indirect sources, I believe that the story is authentic. The first consideration that leads me to believe it is authentic is that it fits perfectly with Machiavelli the man. One of the distinctive features of Niccolò's character was his propensity to face the most dramatic and painful experiences of life (both personal and political) with jokes, pranks, and wit. Many sources document his inclination to face tragedies with irony. In a letter to Francesco Guicciardini in October 1525, for instance, he correctly predicts the end of Italy's independence. For Machiavelli, who loved his fatherland more than his soul, it was a tragic political event. It meant the failure of all his efforts beginning at least with the composition of the "Exhortation to liberate Italy." In the same letter, immediately after his disconsolate political comment, he speaks of the imminent Carnevale and petitions Guicciardini to find an apartment close to the friars of Modena for Barbera, the singer for *Mandragola*. Machiavelli wanted to be sure that the view of the attractive singer would make the friars go mad, and he then asks to give his regards to "the Maliscotta," another lady he liked.[214] No words of grief or sorrow or despair came from his pen, not because he was not feeling grief, sorrow and despair, but because he wanted, as usual, to cover them with playful words. To tell an irreverent story as he was facing death was perfectly consistent with the way he lived his entire life.[215]

auoit fait voir. Et à tant il mourut, et alla voir comme vont les affaires d'Estat de l'autre monde." With minimal variation, the story attained a wider international circulation thanks to Pierre Bayle, who reported it in the *Dictionnaire*: "On arrive à ce detestable poinct d'honneur, où arriva Machiavel sur la fin de sa vie: car il eut cette illusion peu devant que rendre son esprit. Il vit un tas de pauvres gens, come coquins, deschirez, affamez, contrefaits, fort mal en ordre, & en assez petit nombre: on luy dit que c'estoi ceux de Paradis, desquels il estoit escrit: *Beati pauperes, quoniam ipsorum est regnum caelorum.* Ceux-ci stans retirez, on fit paroitre un nombre innombrable de personnages pleins de gravité de majesté: on les voyoit comme un Senat, où on traitoit d'affaires d'Estat, & fort sérieuses; il entrevit Platon, Seneque, Plutarque, Tacite, & d'autres de cette qualité. Il demanda qui estoient ces Messieurs-là si vénérables; on lui dit que estoient les damnez, & que c'estoient des ames reprouvées du Ciel, *Sapientia huius saeculi inimica est Dei.* Cela estant passé, on lui demanda desquels il vouloit estre. Il respondid qu'il aimoit beaucoup mieux estre avec eux pour deviser avec eux des affaires d'estat, que d'estre avec cette vermine de ces belistres qu'on luy avoit fait voir. Et à tant il mourut, & alla voir comme vont les affaires d'Estat de l'autre monde"; Pierre Bayle, *Dictionnaire historique et critique*, Amsterdam, 1740, edited by P. Brunel, vol. 3, p. 248.

[214] "Facciamo una volta un lieto carnesciale, et ordinate alla Barbera uno alloggiamento tra quelli frati, che, se non inpazzano, io non ne voglio danaio, et raccomandatemi alla Maliscotta, et avvisate a che porto è la commedia, et quando disegnate farla." Niccolò Machiavelli to Francesco Guicciardini, post-October 1525, in *Tutte le opere*, p. 1224; English translation, *Machiavelli and His Friends. Their Personal Correspondence*, p. 32.

[215] "Ma perché il pianto a l'uom fu sempre brutto, si debbe a' colpi de la sua fortuna voltar il viso di lagrime asciutto"; *L'Asino*, in *Tutte le opere*, p. 961; English translation, *Machiavelli: The Chief Works and Others*, vol. II, p. 757. In January 1513, the Medici government imprisoned Machiavelli with the serious charge of conspiracy. He could have been executed. Yet while he was in prison, he composed poems full of irony and mockery. See my *Niccolò's Smile: A Biography of Machiavelli*, New York: Farrar, Straus and Giroux, 2000, pp. 138–140.

Another fact that invites me to take seriously the narration of the dream is that it appears to be an elaboration on *Inferno* IV, the canto in which Dante describes his encounter with the great spirits of antiquity. Now in Limbo, the first circle of Dante's hell, these great spirits did not sin (*"non peccaro"*) but were not admitted to paradise *"perché non ebber battesimo, / chè porta della fede che tu credi; e s'e' furon dinanzi al Cristianesimo, / non adorer debitamente a Dio."* Machiavelli alludes to this canto in the famous letter of December 10, 1513, where he writes: "when evening comes, I return home and enter my study; on the threshold I take off my workday clothes, covered with mud and dirt, and put on the garments of court and palace. Fitted out appropriately, I step inside the ancient [my translation] courts of the ancients where, solicitously received by them, I nourish myself on that food that alone is mine and for which I was born."[216] Courts are a part of castles, and in that canto, the great men of antiquity are gathered in a castle:

We came to the foot of a noble castle, / *Venimmo al piè d'un nobile castello,*

seven times encircled by lofty walls / *sette volte cerchiato d'alte mura,*

and defended round by a fair stream. / *difeso intorno d'un bel fiumicello.*

This we crossed, as on solid ground, / *Questo passammo come terra dura;*

and through seven gates I entered with these sages. / *per sette porte intrai con questi savi:*

We came to a meadow of fresh verdure. / *giugnemmo in prato di fresca verdura.*[217]

Like in Machiavelli's dream, the great men of antiquity display authority, gravity, and solemnity. They speak in a manner appropriate for discussions on matters of statecraft. It is an exalting vision.

Where there were people with grave and slow-moving eyes / *Genti v'eran con occhi tardi e gravi,*

and looks of great authority; / *di grande autorità ne' lor sembianti:*

they spoke seldom and with gentle voice. / *parlavan rado, con voci soavi.*

Then we drew to one side, / *Traemmoci così da l'un de' canti,*

into an open place which was luminous and high, / *in loco aperto, luminoso e alto,*

so that we could see all of them. / *sì che veder si potien tutti quanti.*

There before me, on the enameled green, / *Colà diritto, sovra 'l verde smalto,*

---

[216] "Rivestito condecentemente entro nelle antique corti degli antiqui huomini, dove, da loro ricevuto amorevolmente, mi pasco di quel cibo, che *solum* è mio, et che io nacqui per lui"; in *Tutte le opere*, p. 1160; English translation, *Machiavelli and His Friends. Their Personal Correspondence*, p. 264.

[217] Dante Alighieri, *The Divine Comedy, Inferno*, IV.106–111; English translation by Charles E. Singleton, *The Divine Comedy, Inferno*, Princeton: Princeton University Press, 1970, pp. 42–43.

the great spirits were shown to me, / *mi fuor mostrati li spiriti magni,*

so that I glory within me for having seen them. / *che del vedere in me stesso m'essalto.*[218]

Yet another reason that compels me to believe in the veracity of Machiavelli's dream is that it is consistent with beliefs and ideas he had expressed in his works and letters. The view that humility opens the way to paradise is one of the Christian beliefs that he severely criticizes.[219] The idea that the finest of people can be found in hell is in the *Mandragola*: "On the other hand, the worst you can get from it is that you'll die and go to Hell. But how many others have died! And in Hell how many worthy men there are! Are you ashamed to go there?"[220] It is for this reason that Machiavelli denies access to the very distinguished echelons of Hell to Pier Soderini, the chief Gonfalonier of the Republic of Florence. He was unable to enter into evil and consequently failed to save the popular government: "That night when Piero Soderini died, his spirit went to the mouth of Hell. Pluto roared: 'Why to Hell Silly spirit, go up into Limbo with all the rest of the babies.'"[221] The best evidence of the dream story's authenticity is by far its finale, when Machiavelli asserts that he wanted to join the grave and solemn men who were going to Hell. Had he not revealed in the letter of December 10, 1513 that his paradise, his perfect happiness, and true salvation, was to be in the company of the great men of antiquity and to converse with them about matters of statecraft?[222]

With his dream, Niccolò was subverting one of the most widespread assumptions of the political culture of his times, namely the belief that those citizens who devote their best energies to serve their fatherland ascend to heaven and enjoy perennial glory. The source of this interpretation of great statesmen's destiny was Macrobius's *Commentary on the Dream of Scipio.*

---

[218] Dante Alighieri, *The Divine Comedy, Inferno,* IV.112–120, p. 43.

[219] "La nostra religione ha glorificato più gli uomini umili e contemplativi, che gli attivi. Ha dipoi posto il sommo bene nella umiltà, abiezione, e nel dispregio delle cose umane: quell'altra lo poneva nella grandezza dello animo, nella fortezza del corpo, ed in tutte le altre cose atte a fare gli uomini fortissimi. E se la religione nostra richiede che tu abbi in te fortezza, vuole che tu sia atto a patire più che a fare una cosa forte. Questo modo di vivere, adunque, pare che abbi renduto il mondo debole, e datolo in preda agli uomini scelerati; i quali sicuramente lo possono maneggiare, veggendo come l'università degli uomini, per andarne in Paradiso, pensa più a sopportare le sue battiture che a vendicarle"; Niccolò Machiavelli, *Discorsi sopra la prima deca di Tito Livio,* II.2, in *Tutte le opere,* p. 149; English translation, *Discourses on Livy,* p. 131.

[220] "Da l'altro canto, el peggio che te ne va è morire ed andarne in inferno: e' son morti tanti degli altri! e' sono in inferno tanti uomini da bene! Ha'ti tu a vergognare d'andarvi tu?"; Niccolò Machiavelli, *Mandragola,* in *Tutte le opere,* p. 882; English translation, *Machiavelli. The Chief Works and Others,* vol. II, pp. 804–805.

[221] "La notte che morì Pier Soderini, l'anima andò de l'inferno a la bocca; gridò Pluton: – 'Ch' inferno? Anima sciocca, va su nel limbo fra gli altri bambini'"; Niccolò Machiavelli, *Epigrammi,* in *Tutte le opere,* p. 1005; English translation, *Machiavelli. The Chief Works and Others,* vol. III, p. 1463.

[222] Niccolò Machiavelli to Francesco Vettori, December 10, 1513, in *Tutte le opere,* p. 1160; English translation, *Machiavelli and His Friends. Their Personal Correspondence,* p. 264.

Macrobius was an erudite, probably a senator of the fifth century and a native of Sicily or Spain. He composed the *Commentary* around 430 and dedicated it to his son Eustachius, or Eustatius. The crucial passages that interest us are in chapters 8–10 of Book I. Here Macrobius comments on the following words that Publius Cornelius Scipio Africanus says to his nephew Scipio Africanus the Younger:

> That you may be more zealous in safeguarding the commonwealth, Scipio, be persuaded of this: all those who have saved, aided, or enlarged the commonwealth have a definite place marked off in the heavens where they may enjoy a blessed existence forever. Nothing that occurs on earth, indeed, is more gratifying to the supreme God who rules the whole universe than the establishment of associations and federations of men bound together by principles of justice [*iure sociati*], which are called commonwealths [*civitates*]. The governors and protectors of these [*rectores et servatores*] proceed from here and return hither after death.[223]

In Machiavelli's dream, founders, governors, and redeemers go instead to Hell. As he was approaching death, he wanted to bequeath his conviction that founders and redeemers must not be afraid of entering into evil if doing so is necessary. Because they work for justice, God loves them more than all other human beings. He shall not punish them with hellfire but shall reward them with perennial glory.[224] To convey this belief that he regarded as most precious, Machiavelli decided to narrate and explain a dream, just as many prophets before him had done.

2.4 THE REPUBLIC OF THE PROPHETS (1527–1530)

On the wave of the dismay following the Sack of Rome (May 1527), the Florentine aristocrats forced the Medici to leave Florence and established a new popular government modeled after that of 1494–1512.[225] After fifteen years of Medici rule, the institution of the new republican government stirred great hopes for a moral and civil rebirth of Florence, as well as great fears of returning under the Medici's regime. To sustain hope and give citizens the courage necessary to face the powerful enemies of the Republic, the political

---

[223] Macrobius, *Commentary on the Dream of Scipio*, edited by W. H. Stahl, New York: Columbia University Press, 1952, p. 120. For the Latin text, I have used the *Commento al Somnium Scipionis*, edited by Mario Regali, Pisa: Giardini, 1983.

[224] "Io credo che il maggiore onore che possono avere gli uomini sia quello che voluntariamente è loro dato dalla loro patria: credo che il maggiore bene che si faccia, e il più grato a Dio, sia quello che si fa alla sua patria"; *Discursus florentinarum rerum*, in *Tutte le opere*, p. 30; English translation, *Machiavelli. The Chief Works and Others*, vol. I, pp. 113-114; "Questa sola virtù [la giustizia] è quella che in fra tucte l'altre piace a Dio. [...] Idio ama et la iustitia et la pietà"; *Allocuzione fatta ad un magistrato*, in *Tutte le opere*, pp. 36-37.

[225] See Rudolf von Albertini, *Firenze dalla repubblica al principato. Storia e coscienza politica*, Turin: Einaudi, 1970, pp. 104-178.

elite worked very hard to rediscover and teach Savonarola's prophetic language and the old republican religion. Prophecy pervaded the moral and spiritual life of the Last Florentine Republic. A single prophetic voice, that of Savonarola, dominated the moral and intellectual scenario of the Republic of 1494–1512; in the Last Florentine Republic, many prophetic voices spoke. It is no exaggeration to say that it was a republic of prophets, probably the first in history.

The most prominent prophetic voice was the Dominican Benedetto da Foiano (1490?–1531). The popular government called upon him to take the office of Prior in Santa Maria Novella and to preach to the Florentines. Venerable for his age and for his imposing figure, eloquent and learned, he attracted great masses of people to listen to his sermons, and he had a considerable influence on political deliberations. During the siege of Florence (1529–1530), he talked in the exceedingly crowded hall of the Great Council. The historian Benedetto Varchi recounts that the preacher, in the most classic prophetic style, declared:

by reference to passages of the scripture, both in the Old and in the *New Testament*, when, how, and by whom could the city of Florence survive so many misfortunes, and then enjoy her most desired liberty and happiness; and he said this with such grace and such eloquence that he made all the listeners cry and rejoice, from moment to moment, according to his rhetorical intention [...]. In the end, with unspeakable gestures and words, saying *cum hoc et in hoc vinces* [with this and under this you win] he gave the Gonfalonier a standard, one side of which had a victorious Christ with soldiers lying on the ground, and the other a red cross, ensign of the Commune of Florence.[226]

Prophets inspired the deliberations and the rituals of the Republic. On June 26, 1529, the Signoria passed a law intended to promote the peace, moral reform, and unity of the city. The text opens with a preface that solemnly declares the magnificent and excellent Florentine dignitaries' intentions as:

wishing with all their forces to confirm and establish the present free and popular government, and knowing the judgment of Holy Scripture to be very true, which affirms that the effort and the diligence of men in the government and custody of the city is wholly in vain, unless it is guarded and defended by divine goodness through its infinite compassion and remembering the most precious gift of the most holy liberty granted to this most devoted people by work of God, and how it has been freed from so many serious dangers up to the present day, and hoping to be defended in future by His Majesty from all the sinister dangers and accidents which are to be seen overhanging the city, if it is well based and established on the four-square and immovable rock of Jesus Christ; and recalling that we are admonished by the Holy Spirit, speaking through the mouth of Moses: "If you will hear my voice and will observe my pact and obey my Commandments, you will be my people chosen among all other peoples," and wishing

---

[226] Benedetto Varchi, *Storia fiorentina*, Book XI, Ch. 24, edited by Gaetano Milanesi, Florence: Le Monnier, 1857, pp. 226–227.

to benefit from such a promise and so great a reward as the certain and infallible truth and testimony and the most evident sign of the good disposition and devoted spirit of the whole Florentine people towards His Majesty.[227]

The most eloquent effort to instill a republican faith in the hearts of the citizens of Florence was, however, the Great Council's deliberation of June 25, 1529, that proclaimed Christ the "king of Florence." It was a tribute to Savonarola's memory made in the hope that religious sentiment would have worked the miracle of saving the city from its enemies. A few days later, in the same spirit, the Signoria placed on the altar of the Sala dei Cinquecento books in which citizens could affix their signatures in a solemn oath of faith sworn to Christ and to the republican regime.

On November 2, 1529, when the siege had caused devastating effects on the life of Florence's citizens, the Signoria solemnly issued another decree that alone suffices to make us understand the pervasive impact of prophetic preaching:

considering how much, for every human action, one must first of all seek always divine aid, and hoping that the troops of the army, inasmuch as it will be accompanied by prayers and divine help, victory and all other good effects will always follow, we therefore publicly proclaim and notify to all those who are unable and unfit to the army – like priests, friars, monks, nuns, children and women of any age – that whenever our soldiers will have to fight the enemies and we, from the palace, will give a sign, will hail-mary ring the great bell of the palace [...] all the people mentioned [...] are expected and obliged to kneel down both in chuches or monasteries and in their homes and pray and continue to pray while the battle lasts, and pray the Almighty God that He shall give strength and virtue to the arms of the soldiers and to the Florentine army, and shall give victory against the enemies of the city of Florence, in the hope that, through the infinite mercy of our lord, King of our city, and through the intercessions of His Holy Mother, our city will obtain such a grace.[228]

Beginning with the Gonfalonier, all citizens were requested to swear an oath of loyalty to the "sacred foundations of this just, political, and popular government upon the firm and irremovable rock of Jesus Christ." No one could ever become a member of the Great Council without first taking this oath. In order to reinforce the republican religion, the Signoria also deliberated that every November 9 be a solemn holiday in commemoration of "the day in which God the Almighty restored the welfare of this republic" – that is to say, the day in which the Medici had been expelled from the city in 1494. Another day also to be celebrated in perpetuity with solemn festivities (including a parade of the Florentine army) was May 16, the day of the foundation of the popular

[227] John N. Stephens, *The Fall of the Florentine Republic 1512–1530*, Oxford: Clarendon Press, 1983, pp. 216–217.
[228] Cecil Roth, *The Last Florentine Republic*, New York: Russell & Russell, 1968, pp. 203–204.

government in 1527, when "our immortal king was pleased to restore Christian religion and free us from the exceedingly hard yoke of tyranny."[229]

The prophetic rhetoric of the Republic's governors moved the hearts of the Florentines. Citizens who were participating in public deliberations readily promised to observe the Christian religion, and to preserve with utmost devotion the popular government and its "most holy liberty," the special gifts bestowed upon them by Divine Majesty. To make what had been established by the law effective, the Signoria decreed that a crown of thorns would be affixed to the door of Palazzo Vecchio as a symbol that the people's will be subject only to Christ, their "true and immortal king." The Signoria took very strict measures against those who would curse or offend God in whatever way. The Signoria also admonished that, since Christ was the king of Florence, whoever would rebel against the popular government would have betrayed not just fellow citizens but also God. Such an individual would have incurred punishment both before the magistrates of the popular government and before God at the last judgment.[230]

Prominent magistrates committed themselves to teach the new faith to their fellow citizens. To this effect, they largely borrowed traditional prophetic themes. An eloquent example is the oration that Francesco Carducci (1465–1530) delivered to the Florentine army in 1529 as he assumed the office of Gonfalonier. Carducci insisted upon the conventional idea that God loves liberty, and on the citizen's duty to work with all means possible to defend it: "It was God's work that tyranny was expelled from this city, in contrast with the wishes of many, and it will be God's work to keep tyranny away, despite the will of more than a few: but we cannot conclude from this that we may or should feel that we are secure and can do nothing." At the conclusion of the oration, he stressed that the citizens who devote their best energies to the common good become similar to God and attain perpetual glory on earth as well as eternal beatitude in heaven:

I cannot think of anything that is more welcome to God nor more desirable to men than to work in such a way that those who write histories will have our names placed in their books, and the things that we have done, either through prudence or valor, celebrated in bright and perpetual inks; for this is nothing other than avoiding death and preserving oneself alive for a long age; indeed, nothing other than never dying at all, and eternally living in glory. What the Gentile philosophers and theologians wrote is therefore not completely wrong, nor actually far from our own most true and most holy religion: that after death the souls of those who have administered republics well and loyally live a sempiternal and blessed life, separate from all the others, in the highest and brightest region of Heaven. For no praise is greater or finer among mortal beings, nor can any

---

[229] Ibid., pp. 218–219.
[230] John N. Stephens, *The Fall of the Florentine Republic 1512–1530*, pp. 216–219. See also Michael Walzer, *The Revolution of the Saints: A Study on the Origins of Radical Politics*, Cambridge (MA): Harvard University Press, 1965.

praise make men more godlike, than to do good to the other men, and be the cause of the liberty and safety of their republics.[231]

In a solemn speech of February 5, 1529, Piero Vettori (1499–1585), yet another eminent citizen, had no hesitation in interpreting the institution of the militia as the providential outcome of divine inspiration (*"istinto divino"*). He devoutly thanked God for his unfailing love and care for Florence:

> O glorious and supreme God, you who have always particularly cared about this city of yours, one can clearly see that you do not want to destroy this poor people, as you have reignited in these valiant soldiers' hearts that ancient virtue which for long had been hidden and buried. This is a sign that the ancient valor that cured this beloved country of yours from its own mortal wounds and freed it from the shameful sores of servitude could rise again; for you have generated such frank souls and such resolute hearts in this beautiful youth that they throw themselves in any danger in order to save our sweet liberty and unleash a just wrath against the enemies. I certainly do not see adequate rewards that can be found for such merits, but the most beautiful will be given them from God the Almighty and their own virtue, nor will this fatherland fail to recognize them with great benefit, a fatherland that can never ever forgot any merit or service she received.

Since serving in the army is a religious duty, those who would use arms to "oppress the good and serve their own personal hatreds and interests" would therefore "gravely offend the Almighty God." Mindful that perjurers would face an inescapable punishment, all citizens who served in the army had to take a solemn oath before God; mindful that no cause was more just nor more saintly than defending sweet liberty and the blessed life of the citizens, the soldiers of the army could serenely trust in victory, for "Jesus Christ of the armies" would be their infallible guide. When facing danger, they should be comforted by the thought that those who die for the fatherland have waiting for them a "chair among the blessed spirits where they will then enjoy eternally the face of their Redeemer."[232]

Bartolomeo Cavalcanti (1503–1562) explicitly asserted that he was speaking on behalf of Christ, the king of Florence, when he declared that faith in Christ must be a source of hope and discipline for the soldiers of the Republic:

> Your King [Christ] desires nothing more from you than that your souls be inflamed with his love, and joined together and bound by the most holy bond and the indissoluble knot of charity. O Florentine people, this religion is such that, if it will reign among you, you not only will be always defended by him [Christ] – as his devoted and faithful servant – as

---

[231] See Benedetto Varchi, *Storia fiorentina*, Book VIII, 26, vol. I, pp. 417–418.

[232] See *Oratione di Piero Vettori, fatta alla militare ordinanza fiorentina l'anno M.D.XXIX il dì 5 febbraio*, in Rudolf von Albertini, *Firenze dalla Repubblica al principato. Storia e coscienza politica*, pp. 418–424.

well as freed from your enemies, but you also will be exalted victorious and triumphant above all other peoples: otherwise let none of us confide in their own virtue and hope to achieve successfully anything; because our works will turn out wrong, if we are devoid of the light of divine religion, which guides us along the right path; the daring will be reckless, if it depends upon confidence not of divine help but of our own valor; the forces will be weak if they are not supported by the immense power of our King; and ultimately any hope will be vain unless based on him who governs the universe.[233]

On another occasion, Cavalcanti evoked Savonarola's admonition to never forget that political liberty is a gift from God that is to be defended with utmost devotion and without succumbing to the vices of pride and vainglory:

On that day, 16 May 1527, the tyranny of the Medici left, and not because they were expelled, but out of the great fear that God instilled in them in order to fulfill the prophecy, uttered through the prophet Friar Girolamo, which stated: "The next time that you regain your liberty, you will regain it from God, and not through your own industry and strength, lest the citizens grow proud in the glory of that liberty, as they did the first time, in the year 1494, when they were unwilling to recognize it as a gift from God, as it was; and they therefore lost it."[234]

Utterly hostile to republican zealots and highly skeptical of prophets, even the realist Francesco Guicciardini had to recognize that Savonarola's prophetic language provided the Republic's defenders with extraordinary devotion and astonishing valor. In this regard, his commentary is a precious source. I must cite it in full:

The Pious say that faith can do great things, and, as the gospel tells us, even move mountains. The reason is that faith breeds obstinacy. To have faith means simply to believe firmly to deem almost a certainty things that are not reasonable; or, if they are reasonable, to believe them more firmly than reason warrants. A man of faith is stubborn in his beliefs; he goes his way, undaunted and resolute, disdaining hardship and danger, ready to suffer any extremity. Now, since the affairs of the world are subject to chance and to a thousand and one different accidents, there are many ways in which the passage of time may bring unexpected help to those who persevere in their obstinacy. And since this obstinacy is the product of faith, it is then said that faith can do great things. In our own day, the Florentines offer an excellent example of such obstinacy. Contrary to all human reason, they prepared for an attack by the pope and the emperor, even though they had no hope of help from any quarter, were disunited, and burdened with thousands of other difficulties. And they have fought off these armies from their walls for seven months, though no one would have believed they could do it for seven days. Indeed, the Florentines have managed things in such a manner that, were they to win, no one would be surprised; whereas earlier everyone had considered them lost. And this

[233] See *Orazioni politiche del Cinquecento*, edited by Manlio Fancelli, Bologna: Zanichelli, 1941, p. 18.
[234] Ibid., p. 18. See also Donato Giannotti, "Della Repubblica Fiorentina," *Opere politiche e letterarie di Donato Giannotti*, vol. I, edited by Filippo Luigi Polidori, Florence: Le Monnier, 1850, p. 229.

obstinacy is largely due to the faith that they cannot perish, according to the prediction of Brother Jerome of Ferrara.[235]

In the *History of Italy*, which he worked on between 1537–1540, Guicciardini gives yet another eloquent account of prophetic preaching's power to instill in Florentines' hearts, thanks to God's help, a deep faith in the final victory of the cause of republican liberty:

Thus the Florentines were abandoned of all help divine or human, and the famine spread without any hope whatever of further alleviation. Nevertheless, the stubbornness of those opposed to an accord, grew even greater. For they were driven by ultimate desperation: unwilling that their own downfall should occur without the slaughter of their country, and no longer seeking means whereby they or other citizens might die to save their country, but that their country might perish together with them. They were also followed by many who were convinced that the miraculous help of God was bound to reveal itself, but not until matters were brought to such a pitch that almost no courage remained. And there was danger lest the war end with the utter extermination of the city, because the magistrates shared in that stubbornness, as did almost all those who held the reins of public authority in their hands. Thus no place remained for the others who felt otherwise but dared not express their opposition for fear of the magistrates and armed threats.[236]

---

[235] "Quello che dicono le persone spirituali che chi ha fede conduce cose grandi, e come dice lo Evangelo, chi ha fede può comandare a' monti ecc., procede perché la fede fa ostinazione. Fede non è altro che credere con opinione ferma, e quasi certezza le cose che non sono ragionevole; o, se sono ragionevole, crederle con più resoluzione che non persuadono la ragione. Chi adunque ha fede diventa ostinato in quello che crede, e procede al cammino suo intrepido e resoluto, sprezzando le difficultá e pericoli, e mettendosi a sopportare ogni estremitá. Donde nasce che essendo le cose del mondo sottoposte a mille casi e accidenti, può nascere per molti versi nella lunghezza del tempo aiuto insperato a chi ha perseverato nella ostinazione; la quale essendo causata dalla fede, si dice meritamente: chi ha fede ecc. Esemplo a' dí nostri ne è grandissimo questa ostinazione de' Fiorentini, che essendosi contro a ogni ragione del mondo messi a aspettare la guerra del papa ed imperadore, sanza speranza di alcuno soccorso di altri, disuniti e con mille difficultá, hanno sostenuto in sulle mura giá sette mesi gli eserciti, e' quali non si sarebbe creduto che avessino sostenuto sette dí; e condotte le cose in luogo che se vincessino, nessuno più si ne maraviglierebbe, dove prima da tutti erano giudicati perduti; e questa ostinazione ha causata in gran parte la fede di non potere perire secondo le predizioni di Fra Ieronimo da Ferrara"; Francesco Guicciardini, *Ricordi*, pp. 725–726; English translation, *Maxims and Reflections of a Renaissance Statesman*, pp. 39–40.

[236] "Così abbandonati i fiorentini da ogni aiuto divino e umano, e prevalendo la fame senza speranza alcuna che potesse più essere sollevata, era nondimeno maggiore la pertinacia di quegli che si opponevano allo accordo: i quali, indotti dalla ultima disperazione di non volere che senza l'eccidio della patria fusse la rovina loro, né trattandosi più che essi o altri cittadini morissino per salvare la patria ma che la patria morisse insieme con loro, erano anche seguitati da molti che avevano impresso nell'animo che gli aiuti miracolosi di Dio si avessino a dimostrare, ma non prima che condotte le cose a termine che quasi più niente di spirito vi avanzasse"; Francesco Guicciardini, *Storia d'Italia*, edited by Emanuella Lugnani Scarano, Turin: UTET, 2013, pp. 2404–2405; English translation, Francesco Guicciardini, *The History of Italy*, translated and edited by Sidney Alexander, New York and London: The Macmillan Company and Collier-Macmillan, 1969, p. 1530.

Prophecies and prophets did not save the Republic from its powerful internal and external enemies. Besieged by overwhelming imperial forces, Florence surrendered on August 12, 1530. As the Republic was closer to its death, attacks on prophets became more and more sarcastic. The best evidence is the dialogue between Francesco Capponi and Piero Vettori that Francesco's older brother, Luigi Guicciardini (1478–1551), composed in 1530. Capponi restated the conventional views of republican prophecy, in particular the belief that God would not fail to rescue Florence since she is sincerely devoted to Him. Florence's victory over her powerful enemies, Capponi assures, is as certain as if Savonarola himself had predicted it. To Francesco Capponi's excited words, Piero Vettori replies that over the last years many prophecies have proved wrong. Only fools still trust prophets. It is much safer to place trust only in reason.[237] In another dialogue he wrote around 1530, *Del Savonarola* (*Of Savonarola*) Luigi Guicciardini ridiculed prophecies as merely superstitious opinions that would bring about the complete devastation of Florence.[238] In this dialogue, Francesco Zati's attempt to defend prophecy is so weak that it verges on pathetic. When our enemies shall march on Florence, God's angels, he reassured, shall come to defeat them and save us.[239] "At what time shall the

---

[237] Critics of prophets and prophecies appeared also in the years of the Medici's regime. One of the earliest signs of mistrust of prophecies of social emancipation is the *Dialogo della mutatione* that Bartolomeo Cerretani, a pro-Medici moderate, wrote around 1520. The protagonists of the dialogue, Lorenzo and Girolamo, both fervent followers of Savonarola, set off on a journey to Germany to meet "Martino Luter," and they explained to Giovanni Rucellai, whom they chanced to meet near Modena, the reasons for their pilgrimage: "To you, as our brother, our desire need not remain secret: we are going to Germany, attracted by the fame of a Venerable Religious there whom they call Brother Martino Luter, whose writings have been published in Italy and especially in Rome, as I know you are aware, and which suggest that this man must be in his way of life, his doctrine, and his religion very admirable, and it strikes us that his conclusions are quite proper and in keeping with the opinions and way of life of the early church militant." Upon hearing these words from the wayfarers, Rucellai responded: "Ah, then, you are victims of the same superstition as you were before with Fra' Girolamo from Ferrara." In the mentality of the Florentine pilgrims, Martin Luther overlapped with their memory of the monk who had been burnt at the stake twenty years earlier and became the prophet of a *renovatio* that some yearned for, others feared, and still others mocked. "Don't you have in Rome," asks Girolamo, "a great fear of this renewal of the church out of love for your temporal possessions?" Even if "everyone is calling for a *renovatio*," Giovanni Rucellai responded, "and your nuns and peasants and friars and other two-bit prophets talk about it all the time these days, everyone laughs at it in Rome, and you are living on dreams." Bartolomeo Cerretani, *Dialogo della mutatione di Firenze*, edited by Raul Mordenti, Rome: Edizioni di Storia e Letteratura, 1990, pp. 18–19.

[238] Luigi Guicciardini, *Del Savonarola ovvero Dialogo tra Francesco Zati e Pieradovardo Giachinotti il giorno dopo la battaglia di Gavinana*, Florence: Olschki, 1959, pp. 129–130.

[239] "O quanto, credimi, resterai admirato quando per qualunque si vedrà (nota bene quello hora ti affermo) le bandiere delli inimici al vento spiegate, con li tamburi et con le squadre ordinate et armate, salire, con irreparabile celerità (sforzati che haranno et bastioni) continuamente in su le nostre mura, et parte di loro furiosamente drento entrando, perseguitare in questa et in quella strada e nostri increduli Cittadini, spaventati et interamente privi d'ogni humana speranza

angels come to rescue us?" ("*a che ora arriveranno gli angeli a salvarci?*"), Pieradovardo Giachinotti sarcastically replies. Fasting, prayers, confessions, processions, and charity to the poor shall not save the Republic from the ultimate tragedy. Only political prudence and virtue could.[240] You are prepared to accept the final devastation of Florence, Pieradovardo insists, rather than admitting that your prophet Savonarola was wrong. What our religion teaches us is quite the opposite, namely to defend ourselves with prudence and courage rather than waiting for God to fight for us.[241]

With the fall of the Last Florentine Republic, the times of prophets of political emancipation seemed to be over. As we shall see, some prophets continued to speak of moral renewal and political emancipation. Their voices, however, were not able to inspire the Italian social elite, let alone the popular classes. To see the resurrection of effective prophecies of moral and social emancipation in Italy, we must wait almost three centuries, as I shall discuss in chapter 4. In the meantime, the decline of prophets marked the times of Italy's moral and political subjection.

---

impetuosamente fuggire la morte. Alhora dico, et non prima, appariranno visibilmente li Angeli, con la presenza del nostro sancto propheta, togliendo facilmente, con le spade sanguinose in mano, alli arditi et già vittoriosi inimici la vita; et con tanto angelico furore consumandoli, et subito discostandoli dalle nostre innocentissime mura, talmente che quelli di drento, vedendo con tanto celeste favore molti delli inimici morti et li Cittadini miracolosamente salvarsi, ripiglieranno l'ardire et le forze, et con l'armi in mano vendicando le ricevute ingiurie, alhora et in quello instante dico, et non prima, apertamente per ciascuno si confesserà (succedendo, come indubitabilmente aspetto, tanta vittoria) quanto iniustamente fussi condutto il nostro innocente padre al crudelissimo suo martirio. Tu non mi vuoi ancora credere: persuaditi horamai (io lo dirò pure) che tanta ruina, tanti nostri gravissimi danni (secondo che molti valenti nostri expositori affermono) supportiamo solamente per parte di penitenza della sua miseranda et iniustissima morte. Tu scuoti il capo così ridendo, eh? Ah, come ci sta bene ogni flagello!"; Luigi Guicciardini, *Del Savonarola ovvero Dialogo tra Francesco Zati e Pieradovardo Giachinotti il giorno dopo la battaglia di Gavinana*, pp. 131–132.
[240] Ibid., pp. 136–137.   [241] Ibid., pp. 137–138.

3

The Decline of Prophecy and Italy's Bondage

In chapter XXIX of *Leviathan* (1651), "Of Those Things that Weaken or Tend to the Dissolution of a Commonwealth," Hobbes puts to rest the belief that prophets can claim for themselves the authority of judging the sovereign's actions:

> It hath been also commonly taught that faith and sanctity are not to be attained by study and reason, but by supernatural inspiration or infusion. Which granted, I see not why any man should render a reason of his faith; or why every Christian should not be also a prophet; or why any man should take the law of his country rather than his own inspiration for the rule of his action. And thus, we fall again into the fault of taking upon us to judge of good and evil; or to make judges of it such private men as pretend to be supernaturally inspired to the dissolution of all civil government.

In chapter XXXII, he instructs his readers to be very skeptical about new prophets, especially when they announce religious reforms: "Out of the Holy Scripture that there be two marks by which together, not asunder, a true prophet is to be known. One is the doing of miracles; the other is the not teaching any other religion than that which is already established. Asunder, I say, neither of these is sufficient." Since "miracles now cease, we have no sign left whereby to acknowledge the pretended revelations or inspirations of any private man; nor obligation to give ear to any doctrine, farther than it is conformable to the Holy Scriptures, which since the time of our Saviour supply the place and sufficiently recompense the want of all other prophecy." We no longer have prophets, Hobbes reassures us, and we do not need them at all.

In his *Theological-Political Treatise* (*Tractatus Theologico-Politicus*) written in 1670, Baruch Spinoza wrote eloquently in praise of *Old Testament* prophets:

> So that is what obliges us also to believe Scripture – i.e., believe the prophets – namely their teaching, confirmed by signs. We see that the prophets commended loving kindness

and justice above all and were not "up to" anything else; which shows us that when they taught that men become blessed by obedience and trust they were honestly speaking from a true heart. Because they reinforced this with signs, we're convinced that in their prophecies they weren't just flailing around. We are further confirmed in this when we notice that every moral doctrine they taught fully agrees with reason. It's no coincidence that the word of God in the prophets agrees completely with the word of God speaking in us through reason. (XV. 7)

At the same time, though, he also approvingly notes the Hebrews' practice of submitting new prophets to sovereign scrutiny and, like Hobbes, remarks that the prophets' pretension to judge laws has caused civil wars (*"magna bella civilia"*; XVIII. 4). Even more explicitly than Hobbes, Spinoza states that there are no prophets in his times (*"hodie nullos, quod sciam, habemus prophetas"*; I.6).

The fact that two political theorists as different as Hobbes and Spinoza reached similar conclusions on prophets is an illuminating sign of the decline of prophecy in the seventeenth century. Italian intellectual history confirms the theory of the end of prophecy, even if historians disagree on whether and when the prophetic spirit and hopes that pervaded the late medieval and early Renaissance period declined and faded away. Ottavia Niccoli has pinpointed 1530 as the approximate time of the "end of prophecy."[1] Federico Chabod claims, instead, that the rural and urban popular classes in the Dukedom of Milan were disposed to listen to prophets announcing the imminent end of the world and denouncing the corruption of the Church well into the sixteenth century. The strength of prophecy, he observes, was largely due to its ability to frighten peoples and, at the same time, to indicate "a possible way of redemption for their souls" (*"una via di salvezza per l'anima"*).[2] Adriano Prosperi argues that the "end of prophecy" was in fact a protracted process that was neither definitive nor ever complete.[3] To know God's design, Prosperi also remarks, has always been a permanent aspiration with revolutionary consequences.[4]

In her splendid book, *The Anointment of Dionisio: Prophecy and Politics in Renaissance Italy*, Marion Leather Kuntz argues that prophecy had by no means become an "almost insignificant factor after 1530" (p. xi), and instead had a remarkable effectiveness "among various strata of society well after the middle of the Sixteenth Century."[5] It is true that prophets preached with great

---

[1] Ottavia Niccoli, 'The End of Prophecy," *Journal of Modern History* 61 (1989): pp. 667–682.

[2] Federico Chabod, *Per la storia religiosa dello Stato di Milano durante il dominio di Carlo V. Note e documenti*, Bologna: Zanichelli, 1938, pp. 81–95.

[3] Adriano Prosperi, *America e apocalisse e altri saggi*, Rome: Istituti editoriali e poligrafici internazionali, 1999, p. 347.

[4] Ibid., p. 350.

[5] Marion Leather Kuntz, *The Anointment of Dionisio: Prophecy and Politics in Renaissance Italy*, University Park, PA: The Pennsylvania State University Press, 2001, p. 245.

doctrine and eloquence in Italy's churches and squares even after 1530. Some of them found an audience with republican princes and rulers. Perhaps the most significant example is Guillaume Postel (1510–1581), a Frenchman who was active in Venice, the Levant, Paris, and Vienna between 1545 and 1555. Postel proclaimed himself *"propheta, comprehensor et congregator mundi."*[6] He invoked a universal council that was to establish *harmonia mundi cordialis* and inaugurate the kingdom of God on earth where human beings would find joy and peace. He announced the advent of a divine mediator who would make the law of God be reborn in human hearts, and who would guide people to live in humility, piety, and good works.[7] The foundation of a happy republic is God. A republic is happy and holy when its citizens' interior life is holy, when the Father lives in their hearts. Only then will wars and political upheavals end, and will the world live in peace. The God of hosts, Guillaume proclaimed, wants the earthly world to be a mirror of the heavenly kingdom.[8]

In his redemptive vision, Postel points to Mother Giovanna, the "Venetian Virgin," as an example of Christian life. She devoted all her strength to assisting the poor and the sick, and convinced some Venetian aristocrats to build a place to welcome them. According to Postel, Venice was able to enjoy God's protection and become the New Jerusalem thanks to Mother Giovanna's work.[9] It was the Virgin of Venice who revealed to him that God desires to see all creatures gathered as one flock under one shepherd, that everyone can receive forgiveness, and that the redemption of humankind begins with good works. As faithful servants of the one true God, citizens of the universal monarchy will live according to the laws of nature and reason. Restored to their true nature, they will live as cosmopolitans. Postel called himself "cosmopolitus." Because he created everything with infinite power, wisdom, and goodness, God thus wants his law to rule the world: one mind, one spirit. In order to carry out his project, Postel appealed to the sovereigns of Europe. He trusted above all in the king of France, Francis I. He was convinced that it would be possible to establish God's kingdom on earth and to revive the laws of God and reason in people's hearts.[10] But his hopes turned out to be naïve illusions. Tried in Rome in 1555, Postel was thrown into prison, where he remained until 1559. He ended his days banished in the convent of Saint-Martin-des-Champs. Dionisio Gallo also met a similar fate. A French friar who preached between 1565 and 1567 in Turin, Florence, Rome, Ferrara, and Venice, Dionisio not only obtained the protection of princes and aristocrats, but he also aroused the

---

[6] Marion Leather Kuntz, "Guillaume Postel and the World State: Restitution and the Universal Monarchy, Part II," *History of European Ideas* 4 (1983): p. 455.

[7] Marion Leather Kuntz, "Guillaume Postel and the World State: Restitution and the Universal Monarchy, Part I," *History of European Ideas* 4 (1983): p. 302.

[8] Ibid., p. 304.   [9] Ibid., p. 309.

[10] Marion Leather Kuntz, "Guillaume Postel and the World State: Restitution and the Universal Monarchy, Part II," *History of European Ideas* 4 (1983): p. 454.

interest of the people. In the wake of a long tradition, his prophetic sermons invoked the reform of the Church, the fight against heresy, and the conversion of Turks, Jews, and all infidels. His preaching also expressed matters of social and political emancipation. He admonished leaders to accept subservience to the law.[11] He called for princes and clergy to commit themselves concretely to helping the poor; he went so far as to claim that a third of the Church's goods should go to the poor. He envisioned a league of Christian princes that would facilitate the triumph of God's law on earth.[12] He repeatedly underscored the necessity to educate both the laity and the religious in good schools that needed to be established in all cities. On several occasions, he stated that civil and religious magistrates were to be chosen only for their virtue.

While his vision dwells on general themes, it nonetheless lacks precise directions for reform. "Dionisio's utopian program was long on generalities and short on specific implementation."[13] Despite the attention that Dionisio received from leaders and the people, his prophetic word did not succeed in giving life to significant movements of social emancipation; it did not produce institutional and political reforms. On several occasions, Dionisio proclaimed that he had received divine revelation directly from the Venetian Virgin. His prophetic discourse took up themes that were typical of Savonarola's style of preaching. While Savonarola adapted his message to the political tradition and mentality of Florence, Dionisio merely presented the same project to the leaders and Republic of Venice. Savonarola succeeded in persuading the Florentines to establish a popular government and to strive to make Florence the New Jerusalem; Dionisio was unable to move either princes or republics. Although he had placed his hopes for religious and social reform in the Republic of Venice's rulers, they sent him away to Ferrara in a litter after hearing his proposals. Nothing was heard of him again.[14] Savonarola's prophetic message left important and lasting traces in Italian intellectual and social life; Dionisio's message was immediately forgotten.

---

[11] Marion Leather Kuntz, *The Anointment of Dionisio: Prophecy and Politics in Renaissance Italy*, pp. 44–45.

[12] Ibid., pp. 213–214 and p. 236.   [13] Ibid., p. 213.

[14] Ibid., p. 256. About prophetic visions of the sixteenth and seventeenth centuries, Marjorie Reeves has written a most valuable passage for the story that I am trying to reconstruct: "There is little need to press home further the point that expectation of the *renovatio mundi* remained a continuing hope right through to the seventeenth century. It was fostered wherever fervent groups gathered round their special prophet or leader; it was fed by oracles and prophecies from many periods of history; it was reinvigorated through the printing press. There were in it, certainly, elements which looked back to a past Golden Age, to the pristine glory of the Apostolic Church. But what is abundantly clear is that this last age was not really conceived as a renewal, so much as the ultimate goal of all history. It sprang, not from a cyclical view of history, but a linear one which directed men's aspirations towards a positive end within history." Marjorie Reeves, *The Influence of Prophecy in the Later Middle Ages: A Study in Joachimism*, Notre Dame: University of Notre Dame, 2011, p. 502. See also Brendan Dooley, *Morandi's Last Prophecy and the End of Renaissance Politics*, Princeton and Oxford: Princeton University Press, 2002.

After the Battle of Lepanto (October 7, 1571), prophetic texts spread throughout the Mediterranean region and announced the advent of the much-desired religious unity of Europe and the Mediterranean, the destruction of Islam, and the conquest of Jerusalem and Constantinople. The universal Christian Empire could finally be born thanks to the defense of Old Rome and the conquest of New Rome (Constantinople). The king of Spain, Philip II, would become the Emperor of the East. Under his enlightened government, the conversion of the Jews to Christianity and the unification of the Eastern Church with the Church of Rome would finally take place. After surprising Turkish victories in the naval battles of La Goleta and Tunis in September 1574, prophetic texts were printed in Venice and announced the Ottoman conquest of Rome, the defeat of the Christian princes, the conversion of the Ottomans to Christianity, and their universal empire until the end of time.[15] Copied by a Spaniard on December 4, 1575 and then sent to the Council of State in Madrid, one of these texts related the prophecy of Guido Latino, who died in 1194. According to this prophecy, the Ottoman conquest of Constantinople in 1453 was a sign of God's will to punish the Catholic Church. Furthermore, the Turks would also take Rome and force many Christians to flee. Even though the pope would bestow all imperial honors and privileges on the Venetians, and despite any efforts made by Venice, the Ottomans would still defeat the Christian fleet and kill the pope. Only then, after liberating Rome from all corrupt priests and cardinals, would Jesus send "a holy man" to lead the Christian Church and perform miracles. Having witnessed "very great miracles" and having heard the preaching of this holy man, the Ottoman Sultan would then become a true Christian and receive the Holy Spirit; he would nullify all the laws of Muhammad, would govern the whole world together with the holy man, would give back to Venice all its territories, and the whole world would then live in peace and perfection. All of this was to take place before the year 1580. The style of these texts is certainly prophetic, but it does not express a message of political and social emancipation. It does not encourage commitment and dedication to a cause; it invites people to wait in hope. The establishment of the new order of peace finds a protagonist not in the people, but in a holy man who works in agreement with the emperor. This message does not envisage the transformation of consciences. Rather than heralding a new age, it announces the end of time in a manner that has strong undertones of messianism.

In Counterreformation Italy, however, prophetic voices urging religious and political reforms did not disappear. But those few prophetic voices that survived in the interstices of social life were no longer capable of inspiring

---

[15] Giampaolo Tognetti, "Venezia e le profezie sulla conversione dei Turchi," *Venezia e i Turchi: scontri e confronti di due civiltà*, edited by Anna Della Valle, Milan: Electa, 1985; John Martin, *Venice's Hidden Enemies: Italian Heretics in a Renaissance City*, Berkeley, CA: University of California Press, 1993.

significant social movements or bringing about relevant political changes. The only prophetic voices that had some impacts were found within religious communities, as they encouraged the pursuit of individual perfection through the annihilation of one's own will and passions to attain complete unity with God. The political domination of Spain, the Church's determination to control individual consciences, the language of reason of state, utopian literature, and the libertine critique of religion also all reinforced a mentality that was indifferent, or even unfriendly, to prophetic language. The visible consequence of these intellectual and moral changes was the decline of the hopes and aspirations for political emancipation and religious reform: a moral surrender that strengthened Italy's political subjection.

3.1 THE DOMINATION OVER CONSCIENCES

When the Medici pope Clement VII placed the iron crown on Charles V and proclaimed him Holy Roman Emperor in Bologna on February 24, 1530, Spain accomplished its almost complete political domination of Italy. By that time, the Church of Rome had already launched its attack against prophecy as it sought to achieve a solid domination over the conscience of Italians. Issued in one of the last sessions of the Fifth Lateran Council on December 19, 1516, the Bull "*Supremae Maiestatis*" denounced prophets with very harsh words. Those prelates who no longer preached the way of the Lord through virtue and who invented miracles, as well as new and false prophecies and other frivolities, were deemed to be hardly distinguishable from old wives who recount tales that cause the greatest scandals. The Church was determined to wipe out this "dangerous and contagious and mortal disease so that not even its memory [would remain]."[16]

The Church's determination was not sufficient to eradicate prophetic voices and prophetic hopes. From the *Dialogo della mutatione*, a work composed around 1520 by the moderate Medicean Bartolomeo Cerretani, we learn that "nuns and peasants and monks and petty prophets" ("*monache e contadini e frati et altri profetucoli*") still believed in the imminent renovation of the Church.[17] As Lorenzo Polizzotto has shown, the Savonarolan movement remained alive until the fourth decade of the sixteenth century. And as we have

---

[16] The Council ruled that some persons might receive divine revelation, but revelations and prophecies must be submitted to the Church's authorities for approval. The Church reiterated its attack against all forms of divination in the Bull *Coeli et terrae* (1586). See Jean Hardouin, *Acta conciliorum et epistolae decretales ac constitutiones summorum pontificum*, vol. IX, 1576c, Paris: Ex typographia regia, 1715; Hefele-Hargenröther-Leclerq, *Histoire des Concils d'après les documents originaux*, Paris: Letouzey et Ané, 1917, pp. 404–420. On the prohibition of prophecy by the Lateran Council, see Delio Cantimori, *Eretici italiani del Cinquecento e Prospettive di storia ereticale italiana del Cinquecento*, edited by Adriano Prosperi, Turin: Einaudi, 2009, pp. 23–25.

[17] Bartolomeo Cerretani, *Dialogo della mutatione di Firenze*, pp. 4–5.

seen, the Last Florentine Republic generated strong prophetic sentiments and hopes.[18] A more effective line of attack against prophecy and prophets was the obligation restated by the Council of Trent (1545–1563) that required all baptized persons to go to confession at least once a year. The annual confession compelled the faithful to expose their consciences to the Church.[19] The Church was able to know and control the minds and hearts of believers: a knowledge and a grasp rendered even more effective given the repentants' duty to reveal all their sinful actions and thoughts with complete sincerity. The invisible, inner world of the conscience became utterly visible.

Under no circumstance could the confessor reveal what he had heard in the confessional. The seal of secrecy was "*de iure divino*": not even the pope had the power to remove it.[20] Believers were free to choose their own confessors.[21] Despite this aura of personal protection, the mandatory confession compelled believers to reveal their conscience to another person invested with the power to open or close the gates of eternal salvation. To penetrate an individual's conscience, the confessional was much more effective than civil courts. Except for a few cases (like the sin of heresy), confessors granted absolution to penitent sinners; on the other hand, civil courts might have well inflicted severe punishments for confessed crimes. Moreover, confessors often presented themselves as benevolent fathers, friends, and confidants – just the opposite of the stern, impartial, and severe judges of the civil courts. Believers were thus much keener to open their consciences to a confessor than to a judge. As Michele Ghislieri (1504–1572), a pupil of the dreadful inquisitor Giovanni Pietro Carafa (1476–1559), asserted, a confessor believes everything sinners say while a judge suspects that defendants are lying or being reticent ("*altro è la persona di confessore, altro è di giudice: il confessore crede tutto quello che li viene detto; il giudice ha sempre sospetto di reo*").[22] The Inquisition was yet another powerful weapon that the Church used to penetrate individual consciences. Whereas ordinary confessors did not have the power of granting absolution for sins of heresy, the inquisitor had the power to absolve the sinner of all sins, heresy included. The Inquisition could even summon at will believers who had already made their peace with the Church by way of confession. If they were

---

[18] See Lorenzo Polizzotto, *The Elect Nation: The Savonarolan Movement in Florence (1494–1545)*, Oxford: Clarendon Press, 1994.

[19] See Henry C. Lea, *A History of Auricular Confession and Indulgences in the Latin Church*, Philadelphia: Lea Bros. & Co., 1896.

[20] Carlo Delcorno, "Forme della predicazione cattolica fra Cinque e Seicento," *Cultura d'élite e cultura popolare nell'arco alpino fra Cinque e Seicento*, edited by Ottavio Besomi and Carlo Caruso, Basle, Boston, and Berlin: Birkhäuser, 1995, pp. 275–301.

[21] Adriano Prosperi, *Tribunali della coscienza*, Turin: Einaudi, 1996, p. 221; Lucien Febvre, "Un abuso e il suo clima sociale: la scomunica per debiti in Franca Contea," *Studi su Riforma e Rinascimento e altri scritti su problemi di metodo e geografia storica*, translated by Corrado Vivanti, edited by Delio Cantimori, Turin: Einaudi, 1966, pp. 205–231.

[22] Adriano Prosperi, *Tribunali della coscienza*, p. 223.

guilty of heresy or knew heretics, believers were invited by their confessors to present themselves before the Inquisition.[23] Italian believers were therefore subject to two authorities who could grant or deny the salvation of their souls: the confessor and the inquisitor.

The effect of the systematic efforts of confessors and inquisitors was to instill constant fear and submission in the hearts of the believers. An eloquent example is that of Zuane di Nicolò, an apprentice working in the workshop of the jeweler Battista Ferrari in Venice. Pressed by his confessor in the Dominican convent of San Zanipolo, the imprudent Zuane revealed that he did not believe in the value of confession because Jesus had never instituted such a sacrament. The confessor immediately suspended the confession and dispatched poor Zuane to the inquisitor; the inquisitor then sent Zuane back to the confessor and ordered the confessor to interrogate Zuane in the presence of his father and to write a detailed record of the examination. Since the stubborn Zuane reiterated his beliefs, the confessor reprimanded him with terrible and threatening words (*"verbis terribilibus et cominatoriis"*) and sent him back to the inquisitor.[24] The story ends with Zuane formally abjuring before the inquisitor Giovanni Paolo. As this example indicates, it was almost impossible for Italians to conceal their thoughts and beliefs. To clear their conscience, and to avoid serious punishments and even the risk of losing their lives, Italians had to accept humiliating practices that amounted to a complete surrender of their moral liberty: the liberty of believing what they personally regarded as right and true.

Believers learned how to conceal the truth in order to avoid the control of confessors and inquisitors. In the hopes of clearing their conscience, they designed techniques of taking a silent oath before God not to reveal the truth to the confessor and the inquisitor. Of course, they were aware that all these protective techniques were reprehensible. They also knew, however, that the Church would have sooner or later announced a Jubilee Year and, per the custom, grant plenary or partial indulgence for all sins, including heresy. A Modenese woman summarized very nicely the different techniques apt to shield one's inner conscience. If you are summoned by the inquisitor, she recommended, take a secret oath with your conscience not to tell him the truth; in this way, you shall not sin when you are lying. Be sure to tell him what he wants to hear and then wait for the next Jubilee Year when all sins shall be absolved.

Simulation was another less refined but surely effective technique to protect one's conscience. In Imola, Leone Dozza entertained heretic beliefs but still regularly attended the holy mass. Fabio Cioni, from Siena, did not believe in confession and the Eucharist, yet he confessed and took the holy Eucharist

---

[23] See Giovanni Romeo, *Inquisitori, esorcisti e streghe nell'Italia della Controriforma*, Florence: Sansoni, 2003.

[24] Adriano Prosperi, *Tribunali della coscienza*, p. 248.

regularly to show the world that he was a good Christian.[25] Italians became masters of the art of simulating and dissimulating their religious beliefs, an art called "nicodemismo."[26] Carlo Ginzburg has noted that around 1550 religious simulation was no longer connected to visions or hopes for moral and political regeneration of Christianity. Instead, religious simulation had become just a way of surviving. The noblemen, merchants, and artisans who were attending religious rites they did not believe in became indifferent to religious worship. Their indifference slowly evolved into a "cynicism of the defeated" (*"il cinismo degli sconfitti"*) that culminated in full deference to the dominant Catholic religion.[27] The works of the Bolognese humanist Achille Bocchi provide an eloquent example of how distant the mentality of the time was from prophetic spirit. A historian, poet, and founder of the Accademia Bocchiana, Bocchi was the author of a collection of emblems, the *Symbolicarum quaestionum*, published for the first time in 1555. In this highly ambiguous work, Bocchi roundly condemns the curiosity for divine mysteries and invites his readers to conceal religious faith. Truth does not need to be revealed. Even when it is concealed, it shines like a flame. He denounces the hypocrisy and the insincerity that dominates his times, but his bitter words are the words of a man who has given up all hopes for moral and political regeneration.[28]

No longer blamed but rather praised – or at least justified – simulation and dissimulation became pervasive practices of Italian social life. As Torquato Accetto remarked in *Della dissimulazione onesta* (1641), hiding our thoughts and feelings within the safe refuge of our hearts where nobody can see them is an art particularly useful to those who live under oppressive regimes.[29] While he praises simulation and dissimulation, Accetto reprimands prophets for their pretension to penetrate the fathoms of God's mind, and strongly urges his readers to accept God's will always with infinite reverence.[30] In addition to

[25] "Quando si fosse ricercata dall'Inquisitore di queste cose, che bisognava, quando si piglia il giuramento, giurare dentro di se stessa di non dire la verità, dicendo poi ch'alhora non è peccato. M'ha detto anchora che, quando si va inanzi al confessore, che non bisogna dire se non quello che si vuole che sappiano e che bisogna poi aspettare un Giubileo perch'allhora poi sono perdonati i peccati"; ibid., pp. 252–254.

[26] Carlo Ginzburg, *Il nicodemismo. Simulazione e dissimulazione religiosa nell'Europa del '500*, Turin: Einaudi, 1970.

[27] Ibid., p. 179.

[28] Achillis Bocchii Bonon, *Symbolicarum Quaestionum, De universo genere, quas serio ludebat*, Bologna: Apud Societatem Tipographiæ Bononiensis, 1574, pp. lxix–lxx; see Carlo Ginzburg, *Il nicodemismo. Simulazione e dissimulazione religiosa nell'Europa del '500*, pp. 179–181.

[29] "Sotto Domiziano, la miseria maggiore era vedere ed essere veduti, mentre si registravano i nostri sospiri, e a prendere nota di quanti impallidivano bastava che su di essi si fissasse quel suo terribile volto dal colorito acceso, onde nascondeva la vergogna"; Torquato Accetto, *Della dissimulazione onesta*, edited by Salvatore Nigro, Turin: Einaudi, 1997, p. 54, n.3.

[30] In chapter XVII ("The Divine mind is inscrutable"), Accetto writes: "L'ordine è forma che fa il tutto somigliante a Dio, che lo creò e lo serba col dono della sua providenza, la qual per lo gran mar dell'essere ogni cosa conduce con prospero viaggio, e, disponendo la medesima regola sopra

being a fine shelter against human beings, dissimulation is an honest guile that assures us a measure of consolation, a "sleep of tired thoughts" (*"sonno de' pensieri stanchi"*) that must not last too long, however, and turn into lethargy.[31]

Another work that documents the widespread disrespect for moral and intellectual integrity is Giuseppe Battista's *Apologia della menzogna* (1673). "If Truth is the mother of hatred, he asserts, lying is the mother of affection."[32] We may dislike this truth, but lies are our inseparable legacy (*"nostro retaggio inseparabile"*), particularly in courts, where "one hears nothing but the chatter of lies, praises of vice" (*"non s'ode altro che cicalecci bugiardi, encomi al vizio"*) and where "excessive flattery overflows with honey and accusations vomit forth poison" (*"le adulazioni grondano miele e vomitano veleno le accuse"*).[33] Therefore "a lie is neither to be muttered with bitter vehemence, nor denounced with heated words, when it seems to be a necessary seasoning of highly advantageous professions. [...] Whoever wants to speak the truth is censored as arrogant in character and loose-tongued. We willingly admit a flattering lie, and, although we confess to be undeserving of such an exaggerated honor, and our faces become red, pleasure nevertheless enters our heart and we content ourselves with those false words that are heard."[34] Accustomed to simulate and dissimulate their beliefs, Italians with few exceptions became deaf to voices calling for open and courageous moral choices. They became incapable of moral liberty.

3.2 PROPHETS OF SELF-DENIAL

Whereas Savonarola had announced the renovation of the Church in conjunction with the reform of mores and political institutions, the prophets of the Counterreformation encouraged the pursuit of spiritual perfection through self-annihilation. They maintained that God wants us to work hard to purify ourselves through a restless war against our passions and lusts.

---

il merito o demerito delle opere umane, si vieta nondimeno alla debolezza de' nostri pensieri il passar negli abissi de' consigli divini, alli quali si dee infinita riverenza, avendosi da ricever per giusto quanto consòna alla volontà di Dio," p. 49.

[31] Torquato Accetto, *Della dissimulazione onesta*, p. 52, and pp. 35–36.

[32] "Se la Verità [...] è madre dell'odio genitrice dell'affetto sarà la menzogna"; Giuseppe Battista, "L'apologia della menzogna,"*Delle giornate accademiche. Dedicate all'Illustriss.e Eccell. Sig. Francesco Marino Caracciolo, Principe d'Avellino*, Venice: Presso Combi, e LaNoù, 1673, p. 74.

[33] Ibid., p. 84.

[34] "Non si brontoli con agra veemenza, né si biasimi con parole riscaldate la bugia, quando parmi un necessario condimento delle professioni di gran vantaggio pregiate. [...] Chi vuol dire la verità è censurato per uomo superbo di genio e libero di lingua. Ammettiamo volentieri la bugia adulatrice, e quantunque confessiamo d'esse immeritevoli d'onore esagerato, e caldo rossore ci tinga il volto, pur non di meno entra nel nostro cuore il piacimento, e ci contentiamo di quelle insidie che si fanno all'udito"; ibid., pp. 86–88.

Battista da Crema (1460–1534) was the most eloquent example of the shift from a prophetic language of moral and social redemption to a prophetic language of purely inward renovation. The abbot of the convent of Santa Maria delle Grazie in Milan in 1497, and later the spiritual mentor of Ludovica Torelli, countess of Guastalla, Battista was suspected of holding heterodox ideas by the Church of Rome.[35] While an affirmed admirer of Savonarola, he advocated only for the renewal of one's inner life and taught a message of complete indifference to even the most tragic affairs of the world.[36] His model was Abraham, who was prepared to kill his own son to obey God's command.[37] The goal that Battista urged his followers to pursue was the complete victory over oneself: that is, the absolute removal of all suspects (*"suspitioni"*) and fantasies (*"fantasie"*) that render our soul "corrupt and lacerated," and prevent us from becoming "truly similar to God" (*"ben simili a Dio"*).[38]

In his vision, perfect Christians are like warriors and captains (*"very combattenti et capitanei"*)[39] who know how to do violence against their own bodies and minds (*"violentare il corpo et la mente"*),[40] to the point of coming to deeply hate oneself (*"perfetto odio di se stesso"*). In his *Philosophia divina*, Battista stressed that Christ's sacrifice on the cross has taught us the blessed lesson that true love of oneself is hatred of oneself, and that true salvation is mortification (*"il vero amar se stesso è ad odiarse, et il vero salvar se stesso è ad mortificarse"*).[41] Those Christians who achieve this goal through painful efforts become God and true children of the Omnipotent (*"tu sei fatto Dio e vero figliuolo del Onipotente"*).[42] Battista admonished against prophets' pretension – and doubted the possibility – of attaining direct communication with God (*"solo gli spirituali conoscono i segreti di Dio"*). Prophets work hard to

[35] Elena Bonora, *I conflitti della Controriforma. Santità e obbedienza nell'esperienza religiosa dei primi barnabiti*, Florence: Casa Editrice Le Lettere, 1998, p. 126.

[36] Battista da Crema, *Via de aperta verità*, Venice: Bastiano Vicentino, 1532, p. 152r.

[37] Battista da Crema, *Via de aperta verità*, p. 151r.

[38] Battista da Crema, *Specchio interiore opera divina, per la cui lettione ciascuno devoto potrà facilmente ascendere al colmo della perfettione*, Milan: Dal Calvo, 1540, p. 41v.

[39] Battista da Crema, *Opera utilissima de la cognitione et vittoria di sé stesso [...] componuta per il reverendissimo Battista da Crema maestro di scientia spirituale pratica et perfettione, christiano rarissimo*, Milan: Gottardo da Ponte, 1531, p. 221r.

[40] Ibid., p. 147. The work had a wide circulation, attested by the numerous reprints (Venice, 1545 and 1548), excerpts and translations. See Bonora, *I conflitti della Controriforma*, p. 147, n.64.

[41] Battista da Crema, *Philosophia divina di quello solo vero maestro iesu Christo crucifixo [...] donata a quelli che (de fatti et non di solo nome) desiderano di esser veri discipuli suoi et imitatori*, Milan: Gottardo da Ponte, 1531; I am quoting from Bonora, *I conflitti della Controriforma*, p. 160.

[42] Battista da Crema, *Opera utilissima de la cognitione et vittoria di se stesso [...] componuta per il reverendissimo Battista da Crema maestro di scientia spirituale pratica et perfettione, christiano rarissimo*, p. 222r.

decipher the text of the scriptures, but they forget that divine wisdom is all in Christ's sacrifice on the cross. If believers want to attain perfection but do not prepare themselves through contrition and tender tears (*"compunzione e suave lacrime"*), reading and meditating on scripture is of little help. The true way of learning God's secrets is simply to accomplish God's will. Perfect Christians may attain a much stronger and intimate union with God than the union that prophets claim to achieve. Prophets only receive God's light; perfect Christians who follow Battista's rules share God's essence: they think and feel like God.[43] Christian perfection is complete freedom from fear attained through indifference about world affairs, and through total conformity and obedience to God's will.[44] True Christians must regard defeats, setbacks, and humiliations not as occasions to redeem themselves, but as eloquent lessons about their worthlessness. They must learn that they cannot achieve anything if God's grace does not assist them.[45] Ancient prophets, and Savonarola, were speaking to all their fellow compatriots; for Battista, Christ's true teaching is accessible only to those select individuals who do not care if their fellow believers regard them as fools.[46]

During the same years, a large body of pious literature emerged to teach nuns and laypeople how to attain holy liberty (*"santa libertà"*) through a process of self-examination so severe that it required not only acceptance of one's own complete spiritual death, but also total and unquestioned submission to God's decrees. Early visionaries of the 1500s, like Maria Caterina Brugora, revealed prophecies of political calamities, wars, and invasions. Their prophetic visions were always mystical and spiritual and had union with God as their exclusive goal.[47] We do not become like God by serving the common good, as

---

[43] Battista da Crema, *Via de aperta verità*, p. 93*v*.

[44] "Non habbia paura di soldati o turchi, di vivi, né di morti, di foco né di acqua, di pestilentia o fame, di fulgori o terremoti, de spiriti né di demoni, di morte né de inferno, del giorno del giudicio né dell'ultima sententia né maledittione"; Battista da Crema, *Specchio interiore opera divina*, pp. 48*v*–49*r*. "Uno bono et santo mai si scandalizza o maraviglia per cosa alcuna"; *Specchio interiore opera divina*, p. 45*v*. "Gli è fatto così conforme al voler di Dio che esso non sente alcuna resistentia nè per sè per altri in cosa alcuna la qual possi accadere [...] Tal è così conforme al voler di Dio che, conoscendolo provvisore del tutto, ogni cosa gli dà contento"; *Opera utilissima de la cognitione et vittoria di se stesso [...] componuta per il reverendissimo Battista da Crema maestro di scientia spirituale pratica et perfettione, christiano rarissimo*, pp. 218*r*–218*v*.

[45] "Certo, Dio permette alli soi servi che caschino, anzi che spesso caschino, non perché si disperino, né che siano di poco animo, ma acciocché niente si confidino nelle proprie forze et opera, ma in la sola gratia de Dio"; Battista da Crema, *Specchio interiore opera divina, per la cui lettione ciascuno devoto potrà facilmente ascendere al colmo della perfettione*, p. 4*r*.

[46] Battista da Crema, *Opera utilissima de la cognitione et vittoria di se stesso [...] componuta per il reverendissimo Battista da Crema maestro di scientia spirituale pratica et perfettione, christiano rarissimo*, p. 199*v*.

[47] "Le rivelazioni della Brugora avevano deposto ogni interesse di tipo politico, avevano rinunciato a collegare le speranze di rinnovamento a una realtà concreta. Propaganda e profezie politiche, al di là delle generiche previsioni di imminenti flagelli o degli echi inevitabili di eventi terribili che si

old republican thinkers taught, but by governing our own body and soul with the utmost discipline. God shall call true Christians who have mortified their bodies and souls to sit in the highest rank on earth and later in the celestial Jerusalem.[48] This was the new ideal of sainthood: to live and, at the same time, to annihilate oneself (*"vivo io non già io"*).[49]

Antonio Pagani (1526–1589) was another influential champion of attaining complete acceptance of God's will through the repression of passions, imagination, and desires. He was member of the Barnabite order who attended the Council of Trento as a theologian and devoted the last years of his life to preaching and meditation. In his *Lettere spirituali*, Pagani stressed that we attain holy liberty (*"santa libertà"*) by constantly examining ourself and extinguishing one's being (*"morire a sé ed a tutto l'essere suo"*), as well as by yielding entirely to divine will. Complete emancipation from all sorts of fears is the perfect liberty of a will at last united with God.[50] Only a painful imitation of Christ permits us to reach a perfect and total victory over the self (*"perfetta vittoria di se stessi"*).[51] He prescribed a detailed ritual to help nuns attain simplicity of mind, inner peace, stillness of soul, and liberation from all

stavano compiendo, erano ormai scomparse dall'orizzonte dei frequentatori del chiostro benedettino"; Elena Bonora, *I conflitti della Controriforma*, p. 95. See also Anna Morisi Guerra, *Apocalypsis nova. Ricerche sull'origine e la formazione del testo dello pseudo-Amadeo*, Rome: Istituto Storico Italiano per il Medioevo, 1970.

[48] "Como l'anima era giunta a queta perfectione, che l'era trata dal Signore al più alto grado che la possese cingere in terra et che altro più non li ristava poi a fare, salvo che strugerse et consumarse el corpo et el sangue per salvezza de le anime per continuo desiderio et operatione. Et como alora tal anima era dal Signore chiamata uno altro Dio, operante nel mistero de la redemptione"; I am quoting from Elena Bonora, *I conflitti della Controriforma*, p. 101.

[49] Gian Pietro Besozzi, *Discorsi intorno alla vita di san Paolo apostolo*, Milan: Paolo Gottardo Pontio, 1573, pp. 122*v*–123*v*.

[50] "Quando nuovamente noi nasciamo dallo spirito di Dio et la volontà nostra unita alla volontà di Dio diventa libera, alhora il nostro spirito vien sollevato, assonto et unito in un spirito, in una qual divina libertà istessa con esso Iddio. Nella qual divina libertà certamente lo spirito dell' huomo sta superiore et per amor sempre inalzato sopra la sua propria natura, cioè sopra ogni cruciato e pena e fatica et sopra ogni cosa ch'ella abhorrisce, et sopra ogni cura, solecitudine et ansietà della morte, et sopra ogni timor dell'inferno e del purgatorio, et oltra tutte le molestie et afflitioni che al corpo overo all' anima possano in alcun tempo o per qualunque lunghezza o perseveranza con inovata intravenire. Perciochè le consolationi et i discontenti, la penuria et l'abbondanza, il vivere e'l morire et ciò che possa occorrer di prosperità o d'aversità o d'allegrezza o di tristezza, tutto resta sottoposto a questa libertà dei figliuoli di Dio, nella quale lo spirito dell'huomo è unito con lo spirito di esso Iddio, Laonde tali figliuoli di Dio carissimi etiandio in questa vita gustano alcuna caparra della futura felicità [...], dentro di sé godono una perpetua pace del cuore, et dello spinto"; Antonio Pagani, *La tromba della militia christiana*, Venice: Francesco Ziletti, 1585, p. 202*r*. I am quoting from Elena Bonora, *I conflitti della Controriforma*, p. 595.

[51] Elena Bonora, *I conflitti della Controriforma*, p. 588; see also Gabriella Zarri, "Disciplina regolare e pratiche di coscienza: le virtù e i comportamenti sociali in comunità femminili," *Disciplina dell'anima, disciplina del corpo, e disciplina della società tra medioevo ed età moderna*, edited by Paolo Prodi, Bologna: Il Mulino, 1994, pp. 257–278.

disquieting images.[52] We must be dead to ourselves, he proclaimed, and alive for God.[53] Thanks to union with God, true Christians elevate themselves above all the miseries, fears, and concerns of the human condition; they thereby enjoy on earth a perfect peace and happiness that foreshadows eternal beatitude in heaven.[54] Some seventy years earlier, Machiavelli had revealed in his letter of December 10, 1513 that he was liberating himself from life's anxieties – including the fear of death – by elevating his thoughts to the grand themes of political emancipation. The new prophets urge us to pursue liberation from life's anxieties and to attain inner peace through the complete mortification of oneself. Their God was no longer the friend of redeemers of peoples, like Machiavelli's God, but now the protector of Christians capable of self-denial.

Yet another religious trend utterly inimical to prophecy was the doctrine of Quietism that spread in the 1600s. This doctrine openly attacked the principle of free will that prophets regarded as the true cornerstone of moral and social emancipation. According to Quietists, true Christians must annihilate the powers of their soul and give back to God the very free will he has bestowed upon them. They must give up all worries about the afterlife, and renounce all ideas of self-improvement, of virtue, of salvation. They must not seek to aid their souls with prayers or meditation. If they are attacked by temptations, all they can do is surrender. In his *Vie della contemplatione*, Sisto De Cucchi from Bergamo explains that true contemplation consists in keeping our soul quiet, enjoying peace with few intellectual speculations, and cultivating visions of charity (*stare con animo quieto, e con silentio, e goderselo non con molti discorsi, e speculazioni dell'intelletto, ma con una semplice vista di carità*").[55] Mental prayer, not redemptive political action, makes us similar to God.[56] Humble Christians find consolation in the belief that they can accomplish nothing by themselves; that all their victories and all their virtues are owed only to God. They would be happier to suffer the greatest pains rather than to be capable of even the smallest virtue. The Quietists detested political and social life. In his *Paradiso interiore*, Paolo Manassei of Terni wrote that he was happy to offer up all the principalities and all the monarchies of the world for the

---

[52] Antonio Pagani, *Gli ordini della compagnia delle dimesse*, ms., Vicenza, Biblioteca Civica Bertoliana di Vicenza, n.190. I am quoting from Bonora, *I conflitti della Controriforma*, p. 590.

[53] "Semplici di mente, quieti, snudati delle immagini, immobili, liberi, morti a noi stessi et vivi a Dio"; Antonio Pagani, *Prima particella de i trionfi de combattenti per la perfetta riforma dell'huomo interiore*, ms., Vicenza, Biblioteca Civica Bertoliana di Vicenza, n.198; I am quoting from Bonora, *I conflitti della Controriforma*, p. 592.

[54] "Tali figliuoli di Dio carissimi etiandio in questa vita gustano alcuna caparra della futura felicità [...], dentro di sé godono una perpetua pace del cuore, et dello spirito"; Antonio Pagani, *La tromba della militia christiana*, Venice: Francesco Ziletti, 1585, p. 202r.

[55] I am quoting from Massimo Petrocchi, *Storia della spiritualità italiana*, vol. I, Rome: Edizioni di Storia e Letteratura, 1978, pp. 184–185 and p. 187.

[56] Ibid., pp. 186–187.

satisfaction of God. They stressed that we must love God with no pleasure and no consolation, at the cost of our own damnation.

An even more eloquent attack against the active life came from the pen of Pier Matteo Petrucci (1636–1701). Petrucci was the intellectual leader of the Quietists, a very learned bishop of Jesi, and later the chamberlain of the Sacred College of Cardinals in Rome. He confidently asserted that our soul desires nothing, seeks nothing, asks for nothing. It no longer yearns to produce acts of faith, hope, and charity. It remains arid, gloomy, unable of acting. Our will is powerless in the face of evil as well as before good. The rule of true Christians must therefore be total detachment from all affections, fantasies, and imaginations.[57] According to Petrucci, our will is unable to love God, incapable of willing and performing virtuous acts. Day after day, our soul plunges deeper and deeper into darkness.[58] The intellect itself becomes fully aware of its radical powerlessness. The soul is completely submissive and unknown to itself. Complete self-annihilation, Petrucci reassures, is the necessary preparation for complete abandonment and surrender to God.

Like other members of the "Quietist" movement, he had to retract his views on self-annihilation under the pressure of ecclesiastical authority. Nevertheless, the movement was able to count on other militants who forcefully asserted the principle of complete detachment from affections, sentiments, passions, and self-consciousness. To attain perfection, one should humiliate oneself without feeling the good feeling of humiliation; love without feeling the good feeling of love; and submit to God without feeling the good feeling of submission. In sum, the soul must strip itself of every pleasure so that it might feel pleasure only for God. In his *Passi dell'anima per il cammino di pura fede*, Giovanni Paolo Rocchi remarks that we can attain perfect contemplation of God through three steps. The first requires a complete undressing and resignation of ourselves. The second step involves a radical disregard for all images, figures, and symbols, including those that we use to meditate Christ. With no need for meditations, confessions, or discourses, all we must do is "attend to God" (*"attendere a Dio"*) with the pure gaze of our intellect. In the third step, the soul enters such darkness that it is unable to see anything that pertains at all to God. In this stage, now detached from all senses, the soul reaches its center and is at last able to enjoy a sweet and suave repose with God.[59]

Quietists wrote prophetic pages to invoke the return to moral innocence.[60] They announced that human beings shall no longer have free will (*"anzi che allora non haverà più l'huomo il libero arbitrio di morire nel peccato né di sepellirsi nell'inferno"*). All the faithful shall reunite as saints under the same pastor. Confessions shall no longer be necessary. There will no longer be any sacraments, except for baptism, for the sole purpose of preserving the memory

---

[57] Ibid., p. 199.   [58] Ibid., p. 200.   [59] Ibid., p. 205.
[60] "Non vi sarà più né disgratia, né peccato proprio perché tutta la malitia sarà resa al Demonio"; ibid., pp. 191–192.

of the past. All the faithful shall live in truth and grace.[61] The only difference between the saints living on earth and the blessed living in Paradise is that the former benefit from the vision of God while the latter are one with God. While humanist moral philosophers interpreted Christian life as a life of active commitment guided by *caritas*, the Quietists preached inactivity. God alone operates. True Christians must repel temptations by remaining indifferent. Salvation is found in the silence in which all human actions end.[62]

Mortification was yet another idea of seventeenth-century religious literature that was deeply inimical to political emancipation. The goal of our actions must be only God's glory, not God's *and* our glory.[63] Being happy means enduring suffering and completely submitting our will to God's. God does not want to help us to reform the world; he wants to help us find our tranquility in our souls. A good example of this line of thinking was Virgilio Cepàri (1564–1631), a professor of theology in Parma and Padova, and the spiritual assistant to Luigi Gonzaga and Maria Maddalena de' Pazzi. Cepàri explained that the presence of God translates into the control of our passions and senses, excites our desire for eternal life, gives us the strength to endure adversities, helps us to defeat temptations, comforts us in tribulations, unites our soul in pure and perfect love, and grants us the perfect cognition of our nothingness (*"perfetta cognitione del suo niente"*).[64] The light we receive from God gives to the soul the truth in which the soul itself reposes. Overwhelmed by the infinite object it perceives – happy even to rest in darkness – our spirit loves and delights in the complete liquefaction of our body. True mortification, explained Simone di San Paolo, must be above all mortification of the love of honor. Honor and glory are due only to God (*"e la gloria si deve solo a Dio"*). Instead of seeking honor and glory, we should be happy when people humiliate us and consider us worthless.[65] Carlo Ossola has wisely written that, after the Council of Trent, religious writers intended to purify souls for the benefit of individual salvation, not for the overarching purification of the world. Savonarola's exhortations to establish a New Jerusalem in obedience with God's will, as well as Machiavelli's appeal to liberate Italy, were but visions of a distant past.[66]

---

[61] "Non regnerà più l'huomo nel huomo, ma Dio nell'huomo e [...] si farà dell'huomo e di Dio un sol essere"; ibid., p. 192.

[62] Ibid., pp. 190–191.   [63] Ibid., p. 174.

[64] Virgilio Cepàri, *Essercitio della presenza di Dio*, Rome: Alessandro Zannetti, 1621, p. 208. See also Carlo da Sezze, *Trattato delle tre vie della meditazione e stati della santa contemplazione*, Rome: Ottavio Puccinelli, 1654, in *Opere complete*, vol. III, edited by Raimondo Sbardella, Rome: Isola del Liri, Tip. M. Pisani, 1967, p. 159.

[65] F. Simone di S. Paolo, *Riforma dell'huomo*, Florence: Stamperia di Piero Martini, all'insegna del lion d'oro, 1695, p. 258 and p. 261.

[66] "La mistica moderna, in specie dopo il Tridentino, ha cercato non già di purificare il mondo, ma sè, il proprio vedere, il proprio nutrirsi di forme; di spogliarsi, di denudarsi, lasciandosi polire come *tabula rasa*"; Carlo Ossola, "La parola mistica," *Mistici italiani dell'età moderna*, Turin: Einaudi, p. xiii.

3.3 PROPHECY, REASON OF STATE, AND UTOPIA

The language of reason of state that spread in Europe by the end of the sixteenth century was also radically hostile to prophecy and political emancipation. Even if the *Dialogo del reggimento di Firenze* (1521), in which the concept appears for the first time, was not printed until the nineteenth century, the father of reason of state was Francesco Guicciardini. The page in which Guicciardini presents the concept that would mark a watershed in the history of political ideas deserves full quotation:

The last defeat the Pisans suffered at the hands of the Genoese at Meloria affected them so badly that Pisa never recovered its vigor. The reason for this was that the Genoese never released any of their prisoners, who were extremely numerous. As a result, Pisa not only could never benefit again from the prisoners who died in prison, but it also lost their progeny, who would have been born had they been in Pisa. If it were said that by doing this one would acquire a name for cruelty and also lack of conscience, I would admit to both; but I would go on to say that anyone who wants to hold dominions and states in this day and age should show mercy and kindness where possible, and where there is no other alternative, one must use cruelty and unscrupulousness. For this reason, your great-uncle Gino wrote in those last memoirs of his, that it was necessary to appoint as members of the Ten of War people who loved their country more than their soul because it is impossible to control governments and states, if one wants to hold them as they are held today, according to the precepts of Christian law. [...] You see the position to which someone who wanted to govern states strictly according to conscience would be reduced. Therefore, when I talked of murdering or keeping the Pisans imprisoned, I didn't perhaps talk as a Christian: I talked according to the reason and practice of states. Nor will anyone be more of a Christian who rejects such cruelty but recommends doing everything possible to take Pisa, since this means in effect being the cause of infinite evils to occupy something that doesn't according to conscience belong to you. Anyone who doesn't acknowledge this has no excuse before God, because – as the friars like to say – it shows "crass ignorance." Anyone who does recognize it cannot say it is reasonable to listen to one's conscience in one case and to disregard it in the other.[67]

As Guicciardini explains with his typical sharpness, reason of state is a rule of conduct that authorizes princes to transgress Christian religion to preserve their states. He also underscores a very important consideration: namely, princes and governors who do not acknowledge the necessity of transgressing

---

[67] Francesco Guicciardini, *Dialogo del reggimento di Firenze*, in *Opere*, edited by Emanuella Lugnani Scarano, vol. I, Turin: UTET, 2010, pp. 463–464; English translation, *Dialogue on the Government of Florence*, edited and translated by Alison Brown, Cambridge: Cambridge University Press, 1994, pp. 157–158. In his *Ricordi*, Guicciardini writes: "Non si può tenere stati secondo coscienzia; perché chi considera la origine loro, tutti sono violenti; da quelli delle repubbliche nella patria propria in fuora, e non altrove: e da questa regola non eccettuo lo imperadore e manco e' preti, la violenzia de' quali è doppia, perché ci sforzano con le armi temporale e con le spirituale"; *Ricordi*, in *Opere*, p. 742; English translation, *Maxims and Reflections of a Renaissance Statesman (Ricordi)*, edited and translated by Mario Domandi, Gloucester, MA: Peter Smith, 1970, p. 54.

Christian religion for the sake of preserving their states show a crass ignorance and have no defense before God. If princes do instead recognize the necessity to use reason of state, we infer from Guicciardini's text, they can count on God's understanding and comprehension.

The same realist thinking that guided Guicciardini to identify the concept of reason of state also made him skeptical about prophecy and prophets. In the first place, he condemns prophets' pretension of predicting future specific events: "How wisely the philosopher spoke when he said: 'Of future contingencies there can be no determined truth'. Go where you will: the farther you go, the more you will find this saying to be absolutely true."[68] Like all reflections and investigations on matters that cannot be tested with the senses, predictions of future events are otiose intellectual exercises. Instead of trusting predictions of future events, a wise person must ground actions only on contingent facts:

Some men write discourses on the future, basing themselves on current events. And if they are informed men, their writings will seem very plausible to the reader. Nevertheless, they are completely misleading. For since one conclusion depends upon the other, if one is wrong, all that are deduced from it will be mistaken. But every tiny, particular, circumstance that changes is apt to alter a conclusion. The affairs of this world, therefore, cannot be judged from afar but must be judged and resolved day by day.[69]

Guicciardini asserts that it is utterly wrong to consult prophets and astrologers. The only available and reliable light comes from history. Past events "shed light on the future. For the world has always been the same, and everything that is and will be, once was; and the same things recur, but with different names and colors. And for that reason, not everyone recognizes them – only those who are wise and observe and consider them diligently."[70] Against prophets Guicciardini writes:

It is a mistake to think that the victory of a cause depends upon its justice, for we see the contrary every day. Not right, but prudence, strength, and good fortune bring victory. It is very true that right gives birth to a certain confidence, founded in the belief that God gives victory to the just cause; and that belief makes men ardent and obstinate, which

[68] "Quanto disse bene el Filosofo: *de futuris contingentibus non est determinata veritas!* Aggirati quanto tu vuoi, che quanto piú ti aggiri, tanto piú truovi questo detto verissimo"; *Ricordi,* in *Opere,* p. 745; English translation, *Maxims and Reflections of a Renaissance Statesman (Ricordi),* p. 56.

[69] Francesco Guicciardini, *Ricordi,* in *Opere,* p. 761; English translation, *Maxims and Reflections of a Renaissance Statesman (Ricordi),* p. 70.

[70] Francesco Guicciardini, *Ricordi,* in *Opere,* p. 826; English translation, *Maxims and Reflections of a Renaissance Statesman (Ricordi),* p. 123.

qualities sometimes bring victory. Thus, having a just cause may be indirectly useful, but it is wrong to believe it can be of direct use.[71]

Even more devastating to prophecy are Guicciardini's claims that it is wrong to believe that God always intervenes in history to help those who fight for justice: "Never say 'God helped so and so because he is good, and that so and so was unsuccessful because he is evil'. For we often see that the opposite is true. But neither must we say God is not just. His ways are so past finding out, that they are rightly called *abyssus multa*."[72]

Yet, like Machiavelli, Guicciardini concedes that invisible spirits that reveal the future to us might exist. What their nature is and how they communicate with human beings are mysteries that we are unable to unveil:

I think I can affirm the existence of spirits – I mean those things we call spirits, those airy ones who converse familiarly with people. I have had the sort of experience with them that makes me think I can be quite sure. But I believe that their nature, what they are, is just as obscure to those who profess to know as to those who never give it a thought. This knowledge of spirits and the prediction of the future, which we sometimes see people make either through their art or in a frenzy, are occult potencies of nature – or rather, of that higher agent who sets everything in motion. They are known to him, secret from us; the minds of men cannot reach them.[73]

Guicciardini did not rule out the possibility of prophetic inspiration. Indeed, he recognized its power. In the *Storie fiorentine* (1508–1509), he does not dispute Savonarola's claims that he had received knowledge of future events from God; that God, not men, had liberated Florence from the French army; and that God wanted the Florentines to institute a popular government like that of Venice. Guicciardini alludes that Savonarola's sermons were extraordinarily powerful due to divine inspiration ("*per virtù divina*"). Although powerful and eminent members of the Florentine ruling class opposed him, Savonarola's institutional reforms were enacted because the large majority of the Great Council believed

---

[71] Francesco Guicciardini, *Ricordi*, in *Opere*, p. 770; English translation, *Maxims and Reflections of a Renaissance Statesman (Ricordi)*, p. 78.

[72] "Non dire: Dio ha aiutato el tale perché era buono: el tale è capitato male perché era cattivo; perché spesso si vede el contrario. Né per questo dobbiamo dire che manchi la giustizia di Dio, essendo e' consigli suoi sí profondi che meritamente sono detti *abyssus multa*"; *Ricordi*, in *Opere*, p. 754; English translation, *Maxims and Reflections of a Renaissance Statesman (Ricordi)*, p. 78.

[73] "Io credo potere affermare che gli spiriti siano; dico quella cosa che noi chiamiamo spiriti, cioè di quelli aerei che dimesticamente parlano con le persone, perché n'ho visto esperienzia tale che mi pare esserne certissimo; ma quello che siano e quali, credo lo sappia sí poco chi si persuade saperlo, quanto chi non vi ha punto di pensiero. Questo, ed el predire el futuro, come si vede fare talvolta a qualcuno o per arte o per furore, sono potenzie occulte della natura, overo di quella virtú superiore che muove tutto; palesi a lui, segreti a noi, e talmente, che e' cervelli degli uomini non vi aggiungono"; *Ricordi*, in *Opere*, p. 790; English translation, *Maxims and Reflections of a Renaissance Statesman (Ricordi)*, p. 95.

God was behind him.[74] As I have remarked, Guicciardini acknowledged the power of prophetic language thirty years later in his monumental *Storia d'Italia* (1537–1540). He stressed that the supporters of the Last Florentine Republic believed that God would have helped them to defend their liberty even against the most powerful of enemies.[75]

The texts that best document Guicciardini's belief in the power of prophecy are the large excerpts from Savonarola's sermons that he transcribed for himself after the Sack of Rome. Why did Guicciardini decide to read Savonarola's old sermons and then transcribe the lines with the strongest prophetic content? After 1527, Guicciardini was a beaten man. He had failed to achieve all his political ideals: "a well-ordered republican government in Florence; Italy free from the barbarians; the entire world free from the tyranny of these wicked priests."[76] In the remote words of Savonarola, he was probably searching for some light that might help him understand why he failed to achieve his ideals. In fact, a large portion of Guicciardini's selection from Savonarola's sermons focuses on the nature and the power of prophecy. He remarks, for instance, that in the sermon of January 13, 1495, Savonarola asserted that his prophecies were true because they were coming from divine inspiration.[77] God himself opens the mouth of prophets.[78] Thanks to the light that God bestows on them, Savonarola had proclaimed, prophets are able to read the signs of the times. Over his long political career, Guicciardini too had endeavored to read the signs of the times, albeit with the help of natural reason. But natural reason was not a completely reliable guide.[79]

The power of Savonarola's prophetic language to provide hope even in the most hopeless situations attracted the politically defeated Guicciardini.[80]

---

[74] Francesco Guicciardini, *Storie fiorentine*, in *Opere*, pp. 134–135.

[75] See also Francesco Guicciardini, *Storia d'Italia*, edited by Emanuella Lugnani Scarano, Turin: UTET, 1981, p. 448; English translation, F. Guicciardini, *The History of Italy*, edited by Sidney Alexander, Princeton: Princeton University Press, 1969, p. 430.

[76] "Uno vivere di repubblica bene ordinato nella città nostra, Italia liberata da tutti e' Barbari, e liberato el mondo dalla tirannide di questi scelerati preti"; Francesco Guicciardini, *Ricordi*, in *Opere*, p. 800; English translation, *Maxims and Reflections of a Renaissance Statesman (Ricordi)*, p. 101.

[77] "Io sono certo di quello ho predetto, più che io non sono che io tocco questo legno; perché questo lume è più certo che non è el senso del tatto, ed è già 15 anni e forse 20 che io cominciai a vedere queste cose; ma ho cominciato a dirle da 10 anni in qua; e prima dissi qualcosa a Brescia dove io predicai [...]. Erano vere perché nascevano da ispirazione divina: tutto quello che t'ho detto, l'ha detto Dio; se Dio è bugiardo, io sarò bugiardo ancora io"; Francesco Guicciardini, "Estratti savonaroliani," *Scritti autobiografici e rari*, edited by Roberto Palmarocchi, Bari: Laterza, 1936, p. 285.

[78] Ibid., p. 291.

[79] "È Dio stesso che apre la bocca del profeta: "se verrà mai tempo che io possa aprire la bocca, io dirò cose che io vi farò maravigliare; pregate Dio che m'apra la bocca, che io dirò cose che farò stupire tutto el mondo"; ibid., p. 303.

[80] "Non v'ho io detto tante volte, quando questa cosa vi parrà spenta risurgerà più gloriosa che mai? Vedi che ognuno diceva: – egli è spacciato questa cosa è per terra, – pure noi siamo ancora

Savonarola had announced that prophetic voices cannot die because they come from God. A prophet may be killed, but others shall come to inspire the people to continue his struggle with the help of supernatural light.[81] Italy and Florence were facing a tragic destiny because the Florentines and the Italians did not listen to Savonarola's voice.[82] Yet, Savonarola had himself said many times that God would destroy Florence and Italy just as he had destroyed Jerusalem because its citizens were ungrateful to God and had derided the prophets.[83] Had Florence and Italy listened to the prophet that God had sent – that is, Savonarola – they would be free and glorious.[84] Guicciardini also turned his attention to Savonarola's prophecies in order to understand the fate of the popular government instituted in Florence in 1527. Although he thought that it had no chance of lasting, Guicciardini transcribed the lines where Savonarola asserted that the popular government was under God's protection and would triumph over all its enemies.[85] For the realist Guicciardini, the republicans were fools. However, he admitted that they accomplished remarkable examples of valor in defense of their fatherland, feats indeed sustained by the force of prophecy.

Much more hostile to prophecy was Giovanni Botero, the founder of the intellectual tradition of reason of state. In *Della Ragion di Stato* (1586), Botero made clear that reason of state and prophecy are mutually exclusive. The purpose of reason of state is to preserve existing political orders; the purpose of prophecy is to create new political orders or to reform radically the existing ones.[86] Consistently, *Della Ragion di Stato* is silent on prophecy. Botero's

---

qua, e vogliamo combattere e vincere a ogni modo; e dicoti che non fu mai el più glorioso tempo né el più felice di questo, e vogliamo fare cose gloriose e grandi, e Dio sarà quello che le farà a consolazione de'buoni"; ibid., p. 311.

[81] "Se io fussi bene morto o cacciato, non si spegnerà questo lume, perché è attaccato in molti luoghi ed in tutte le religione, e tu lo vedrai suscitare in molta gente, è leverannosi su molti contra e' loro medesimi e del loro ordine, e susciterassene per tutta Italia ed a Roma; e già vi è acceso di questo fuoco in vescovi, prelati e cardinali; e se tu ne spegnerai uno, ne verranno degli altri e più forti; ed io sono per difendere questa verità, o voglinla fare con ragione, o per altri mezzi che non ti voglio dire adesso, o per via naturale o sopranaturale"; ibid., pp. 293–294.

[82] "Italia Italia, Firenze Firenze, *quae occidis prophetas et lapidas eos, qui ad te missi sunt*; tu cerchi di uccidere e' profeti, Italia, tu cerchi, Firenze, di ammazzare coloro che ti sono mandati da Dio; tu ti fai beffe de' profeti"; ibid., p. 330.

[83] Ibid., pp. 297–298.

[84] "Fate quattro cose: prima, el timore di Dio; secondo, el bene commune; terzio, la pace universale; quarto, la riforma; e se fate questo; Firenze, sarà più gloriosa e più ricca che mai; e se avessi fatto quanto t'ho detto, aresti ora riavuta Pisa, e si saria dilatato lo imperio tuo ed io arei detto, a quelli che governano, el modo che avevano a tenere e dove si sarebbe dilatato"; ibid., p. 285.

[85] "Questa opera andrà innanzi a dispetto di tutto el mondo"; ibid., p. 287 and p. 295.

[86] Reason of state is "notitia di mezzi atti a fondare, conservare et ampliare un dominio." To preserve, he stresses, is more important than founding and expanding: "egli è vero che se bene, assolutamente parlando, ella [la ragion di stato] si stende alle tre parti sudette, nondimeno pare che più strettamente abbracci la conservatione che l'altre, e dell'altre due più l'ampliatione che la fondazione"; Giovanni Botero, *Della Ragion di Stato Libri Dieci, con Tre Libri delle Cause della Grandezza, e Magnificenza delle Città*, Venice: I Gioliti, 1589, pp. 1–2; English translation,

silence is even more telling if we consider that, ten years earlier, he had himself utilized prophetic language to admonish governors and peoples to respect the principles and the rituals of Christian religion in the *De Regia Sapientia*. In the long appendix dedicated to the Turkish heresy *(Turcae Haeretici)*, he explained that the ascent of the Ottoman Empire was a clear sign that God intended to punish Christian nations for their moral and religious corruption. Botero claims that God unchained the Turkish fury because the sins of the Christians were worse than the Turks' sins. To make His punishment even harsher, God deprived Christian princes of His wisdom and grace. Christian peoples shall be able to free themselves from the Ottoman threat, Botero concludes, only when they shall redeem themselves from sin.[87] Whereas prophets like Savonarola had severely chastised the Church's corruption, Botero absolved it. He rejects the distinction between religion, priests, and monks that all reformers had upheld. Instead, he points to the early Christians' humility and obedience as models of behavior.[88] He praises the most ceremonial and super-stitious aspects of the Catholic religion, including the cult of relics, for human beings ultimately long to see God. But because God is invisible, humans need some visible, though indirect, signs of his presence, such as relics.[89] While prophets had taught to be strong before the powerful, Botero championed docility. The very social peace that the prophets did not hesitate to upset on behalf of justice became for Botero the highest good that had priority over any other consideration, including justice.[90]

On the contrary, critics of reason of state were sympathetic to prophecy. An example is the eminent historian and churchman Scipione Ammirato (1531–1601), author of the *Discorsi sopra Cornelio Tacito*.[91] He interpreted reason of state as derogation of civil laws that sought to secure a more universal good.[92] Religion is highly beneficial for the stability of the state, and princes

---

Giovanni Botero, *The Reason of State*, edited by Robert Bireley, Cambridge: Cambridge University Press, 2017. On reason of state see *Botero e la ragion di Stato: atti del Convegno in memoria di Luigi Firpo*, edited by A. Enzo Baldini, Florence: Olschki, 1992. See also Federico Bonaventura, *Della ragion di stato et della prudenza politica*, edited by Nicola Panichi, Rome: Edizioni di Storia e Letteratura, 2007, p. 2.

[87] Ioannis Boteris Benensis, *De regia sapientia libri tres*, Milan: Apud Pacificum Pontium, 1583, pp. 112–115. Cfr. Cesare Vasoli, "A proposito della 'Digressio in Nicolaum Machiavellum': la religione come 'forza' politica nel pensiero di Botero,"*Botero e la ragion di Stato: atti del Convegno in memoria di Luigi Firpo*, pp. 41–58.

[88] "È impossibile che stimi la religione chi non fa conto dei religiosi"; *Della Ragion di Stato Libri Dieci, con Tre Libri delle Cause della Grandezza, e Magnificenza delle Città*, p. 95.

[89] Ibid., p. 91.

[90] "La legge cristiana: 'vuole che si obedisca a' Principi discoli, non che a' moderati; e che si patisca ogni cosa, per non perturbar la pace'"; ibid., p. 94.

[91] Scipione Ammirato, *Discorsi sopra Cornelio Tacito*, Florence: Filippo Giunti, 1594.

[92] "Ragione di stato altro non essere che contraventione di ragione ordinaria per rispetto di publico beneficio, overo per rispetto di maggiore e più universal ragione"; Scipione Ammirato, *Discorsi sopra Cornelio Tacito*, pp. 226 and 233.

must obey the principles of Christian religion even at the cost of losing their
kingdoms and lives.[93] To believe otherwise is like pretending that seasons
adjust themselves to human beings rather than vice versa.[94] For Ammirato,
the widespread belief that princes can ignore religion for reason of state is
unacceptable. Sovereign power is safe when it obeys the precepts of divine
wisdom.[95] As Livy's history shows, the Romans were able to expand their
empire when they respected religion and refused to follow reason of state.[96]
Princes must adjust reason of state to religion and must hold prophets in the
highest respect.[97] Prophets must, in turn, have the courage to speak truth to
princes. Ammirato notes how Micaiah told King Ahab unpleasant truths, and
ridiculed princes who preferred to hear lies and accuse God of their failures.[98]

Another critic of reason of state who supported prophecy was the theologian
and historian Giovanni Maria Bonini (1612–1680). In the *Ciro politico*, published for the first time in Genoa in 1647, he defined reason of state as the art of
tyrants. Along with his attacks against reason of state, Bonini also launched
several critiques against astrologers and diviners who pretended to penetrate
the "immense abyss of God's inscrutabilities" ("*immenso abisso de' suoi pro-
fondissimi arcani*"). He maintained that astrology was an entirely deceitful art
that caused innumerable quarrels, enmities, and wars. God created the heavens
like an open book to allow human beings to contemplate His wisdom, not to
invite them to investigate His secrets. If they do not want to become blind,
Bonini states, humans must give up their foolish ambition to read God's
mind.[99] Yet, his attacks against astrology and divination accompany an explicit
recognition of the legitimacy and value of prophecy. For Bonini, Aristotle's
celebrated sentence that we cannot have true knowledge of future contingent
events is wrong. God has that knowledge, and He communicates it to the
prophets; he likes to talk to man in man's language ("*si compiace di parlare
all'huomo con la lingua dell'huomo*"). Satan too wants his prophets in the
world, but they are false prophets who cause innumerable calamities that have

---

[93] "Hora a te principe è così ben palese che ti convien morir prima che rinegar Christo, e se ti
converrà morire, viene per conseguenza la perdita del regno"; Scipione Ammirato, *Discorsi
sopra Cornelio Tacito*, pp. 228–229 and p. 232: "perché la religione è cosa maggiore, come
abbiamo detto, della ragione di stato, e fa i conti suoi diversamente da quelli degli uomini, e non
si dà proportione delle cose temporali all'eterne, conviene, che in tali accidenti tu ricorra
primieramente alla religione, e vedi se ella ti si oppone perché in tal caso bisogna accomodar
la ragione di stato alla religione, e non la religione alla ragione di stato."

[94] Ibid., p. 184.   [95] Ibid., p. 229.   [96] Ibid., p. 231.

[97] "Et se alcuno mi dicesse che noi non siamo in tempo di Profeti per bocca de quali Iddio favelli
agli huomini, ti rispondo che le buone leggi sono oracoli di Dio, e quando il re secondo quelle si
governa, secondo il voler di Dio si governa"; ibid., p. 290.

[98] Ibid., p. 473.

[99] Filippo Maria Bonini, *Il Ciro politico*, Venice: Niccolò Pezzana, 1658, pp. 175–176. See also
Rodolfo De Mattei, *Il pensiero politico italiano nell'età della Controriforma*, Milan-Naples:
Ricciardi, 1982.

afflicted and still afflict human life.[100] True Christians must entirely commit their destiny to God, the absolute ruler of this universe.[101]

Nevertheless, the prevailing intellectual trend in Counterreformation Italy was hostile to prophecy. A particularly eloquent example is the Bolognese jurist and moralist Fabio Albergati (1538–1606). In *La republica regia* (1627), Albergati roundly dismisses prophecy with the argument that human beings can attain knowledge of God's will by natural reason alone (*"luce naturale"*). Since natural reason, together with the assistance of God's grace, gives us both the true knowledge of God and the knowledge of the right principles of politics, prophetic light is useless.[102] He ignores Savonarola with a resounding silence. Republics find their guidance in the Catholic Church. Virgilio Malvezzi (1595–1654), another representative political writer of the Counterreformation, also disparaged the role of prophecy albeit for different but concurring reasons. In his *Davide perseguitato*, Malvezzi stresses that God does indeed speak to men, but they are deaf and blind. They do not listen to God's words and do not read the scriptures.[103] In scripture, God has revealed the reasons for political revolutions, the rise and decline of nations, famines, wars, plagues. If we do not grasp God's warning, it is entirely our fault.[104] It is to God that we should turn, not to the works of pagan philosophers.[105] Malvezzi admits the possibility of knowing the future only with the help of the devil, thanks to God's permissive will (*"volontà permissiva di Dio"*).[106] But he altogether denies the legitimacy of astrologers' efforts to perceive the future from the stars. Only God has the power of knowing the future, and his reasonings remain inscrutable to humans.[107] When we see that he decimates princes and elevates the poor and the oppressed, we can assume that He does so

---

[100] Filippo Maria Bonini, *Il Ciro politico*, pp. 175–176.   [101] Ibid., p. 177.

[102] Fabio Albergati, *La repubblica regia*, Bologna: Vittorio Benacci, 1627, p. 17.

[103] "Credino fermamente, che egli parla, ma troppo sono sordi quelli, che non odono il linguaggio. Credino fermamente, che egli scrive, ma troppo sono ciechi, quelli, che non vedono il carattere. Chi vuole intendere la sua voce, ò leggere la sua lettera, ricorra alla sacratissima Storia; Ella è un Vocabulario, che ci ha lasciato lo Spirito di Dio per dichiarare gli altissimi suoi linguaggi. Ella è una chiave, che apre tutte le cifrare che si dispacciano dal Paradiso"; Virgilio Malvezzi, *Davide perseguitato*, Venice: Filippo Alberto, 1636, pp. 5–6.

[104] "Quei misteri Divini, che essi viddero solamente ombreggiati frà le caligini, hora limpidissimi si scorgono à Ciel sereno; ma le cagioni de le rivolte degli Stati, dell'accrescimento dell'uno, della diminutione dell' altro, delle cadute de' Principi, della fame, della peste, della guerra, furono loro chiarissimamente spiegate, e noi sotto l'oscurità di mille ambagi le rivolgiamo, quasi che non sia vero quello, che disse il maggiore de' Teologi, che i gastighi, che avvennero à gl'Israeliti, avvennero loro in figura per noi"; ibid., p. 7.

[105] Ibid., p. 8.

[106] "Ma perché Iddio voglia le destruttioni di i Re, e de' Regni, sarebbe anche facile ad insegnare se non fosse, che la volontà di lui non è sempre fattiva, ma tal volta anche permissiva. Ei vuole, che perdano i Regni coloro, che l'abbandonano e che gli acquistino coloro che lo seguono. Donde avvenga poscia che tal volta permetta, che coloro che lo seguitano, siano abbassati, e coloro, che l'abbandonano, siano inalzati, io non lo so, e forse ne sanno anche poco gli altri"; ibid., p. 208.

[107] Ibid., p. 180.

to teach that those princes who follow his will prosper and those who disobey him fall. We must be aware, however, that we are only guessing, and that prophets cannot help us.

One of the most refined philosophers of reason of state, Ludovico Zuccolo (1568–1630), was also quite distant from prophetic sentiments and hopes. While totally absent in his essays on reason of state, prophetic language surfaces in his *Discourse on Love of Country (Discorso dello amore verso la patria)*, published posthumously in Venice in 1631. He asserts that Italy will be "the house of the Italians and not of foreigners" only when love of country shall unite the Italians' will.[108] He then disconsolately remarks that conflicting interests among Italian princes – along with Italy's intellectual and political subjugation to foreign peoples – have cooled love of country and effectively rendered Italy's political emancipation utterly impossible. As a result, Italy's condition is the same as Petrarch had depicted it in the fourteenth century: "Now in one pen / sleep wild beasts and meek flocks / and the gentler now always groans."[109]

These verses are from Petrarch's canzone *Italia mia benché el parlar sia indarno*, the same canzone from which Machiavelli extracted the words that conclude *The Prince*: "Virtue will take up arms against fury / and cut short the warring because / ancient courage is not yet dead in Italian hearts." Machiavelli had selected from Petrarch's poem a prophecy of emancipation. Zuccolo cites the verses that describe the sad and humiliating condition of an Italy unable and unwilling to fight for its redemption. Zuccolo's use of Petrarch's poem is an eloquent sign of the decline of prophetic visions of emancipation under the intellectual hegemony of reason of state. No theorist of reason of state ever delivered prophetic messages; reprimanded the princes and mores of his times; denounced injustice and corruption; announced a religious and moral reformation; invoked a redeemer of Italy.

Along with the tracts on reason of state, several utopian works were circulating in seventeenth-century Italy. While some of them took inspiration from Thomas More's *De optimo statu reipublicae deque nova insula utopia* (the text that inaugurated the tradition of modern utopian political thought), others were openly polemical against More.[110] Although they are apparently similar, prophecy and utopia are in fact different types of moral and political language.

---

[108] Ludovico Zuccolo, *Discorso dello amore verso la patria*, Venice: Evangelista Deuchino, 1631, p. 3.

[109] "Hor dentro ad una gabbia / fiere selvagge et mansuete gregge / si annidan sí, che sempre il miglior geme"; ibid., p. 3.

[110] As Quentin Skinner has written, the model text of modern utopian literature, Thomas More's *De optimo statu reipublicae deque nova insula utopia*, is unquestionably a radical critique of corrupt mores and unjust social order. See Quentin Skinner, "Thomas More's *Utopia* and the Virtue of True Nobility," *Visions of Politics*, Vol. 2. *Renaissance Virtues*, Cambridge: Cambridge University Press, 2002, pp. 213–244. See also *Utopias and Utopian Thought*, edited by Frank E. Manuel, Boston: Houghton Mifflin, 1996. On utopia as a language of social

With concise and clear words, prophets urge their compatriots to make moral choices and to work together for a radical transformation of the social and political order. Utopian narrations' authors do not call for a moral choice and do not intend to mobilize consciences. The perfect republics that they describe do not need to be founded or reformed. All one must do is go there. The only problem is that they exist nowhere. When these authors criticize existing social and political orders, they do so in the veiled and oblique form of a dialogue to provide consolation or intellectual distraction.

A good example is Ludovico Agostini, a pious jurist and a very poor writer who spent most of his long life (1536–1609) withdrawn in his villa near Pesaro. Between 1583 and 1584, he composed the *Dialoghi dell'infinito*.[111] He filled his pages with long extracts from scripture, citations from classical authors (notably Aristotle), and long digressions. This obscure and tedious prose notwithstanding, a timid and vague critique of his times emerges (*"infernale confusione"*) from his work. Agostini recognized some rights of the lower classes, urged practices of charity, and praised the pursuit of mundane achievements (so long as said pursuit respected religious duties). With the strictest adherence to the dogmas of the Roman Catholic Church, religion inspires and controls all aspects of the citizens' life in his ideal republic. Each morning, everyone must attend mass before going to work. At lunchtime, everyone must genuflect when bells sound to remember the dead. Next to the prince sits the bishop, who supervises the conduct of priests, organizes charitable functions, helps to redeem sinners, pacifies enmities, reunites families, and chastises gamblers and blasphemers.[112] Agostini's utopia is a social theocracy with an explicit injunction to obey religious and secular authorities. No emancipatory intent is found therein.

Other examples are Ludovico Zuccolo's utopian works, *Della Repubblica d'Utopia* and the *Repubblica d'Evandria*.[113] The first is a direct attack against More's *Utopia*. Given the malignancy and corruption of men, Zuccolo asserted, it is utterly impossible to establish a community like the one depicted by More. For him, all the institutions of the Commonwealth of Utopia are seriously flawed (*"leggi e istituti quale pravo, quale poco retto, quale su debil base appoggiato"*). The laws compelling citizens to alternate between agriculture and manual arts, for instance, prevent citizens from attaining the moral excellence that must be the true purpose of good republics. Manual labor weakens intellectual capabilities and makes citizens unfit to participate in the

emancipation, see also I. Calvino, "Introduzione to Ch. Fourier," *Teoria dei quattro movimenti. Il nuovo mondo amoroso*, Turin: Einaudi, 1971.

[111] Carlo Curcio, *Utopisti e riformatori sociali del Cinquecento*, Bologna: Zanichelli, 1941, and ibid., *Utopisti italiani del Cinquecento*, Rome: Colombo, 1944.

[112] See Luigi Firpo, "L'utopia politica nella Controriforma," *Contributi alla storia del Concilio di Trento e della Controriforma*, edited by Eugenio Garin, Florence: Vallecchi, 1948, p. 94.

[113] Both works are published in Ludovico Zuccolo, *Dialoghi*, Venice: Marco Ginammi, 1625.

government of the polity. Equally wrong was the utopian practice of tolerating different religions. Religious unity is the strongest bond of political communities. The most blameworthy of More's views, Zuccolo remarks, are his communist social ideas.[114] Communism might perhaps work for communities of monks, not for citizens. With his critique of visions of emancipation, Zuccolo's utopia was an intellectual divertissement completely alien to the prophetic tradition.

Zuccolo issues another forceful warning against social and political change in another utopian work, *Il porto, overo della Republica d'Evandria*. The narrator is Lodovico da Porto, a man who dedicated all his life to defending Italy's liberty. When he realized that his fatherland was doomed, he resolved to travel all over the globe. He returned to his country happy to share his wisdom in his old age.[115] After an enthusiastic description of the landscape's beauty, he asserts that the Evandrians (their island was close to that of Utopia) are much happier than any other people, above all the Italians, due to the excellence of their laws and mores.[116] While the Italians are consumed by fraud and vices ("*pieni di frodi e colmi di vitij*"), the Evandrians dress soberly, do not indulge in luxury, and do not practice the shameful habit of dueling.[117] Although he praises civic virtue and courage, Lodovico da Porto does not exhort Italians to fight their corruption and their servitude. The spirit of the Italians is so corrupt that there is no courage left in them. "Better to go to sleep," he gloomily said. And it is on this most somber note that he ends his speech.[118]

A similar message is also found in the *Città Felice*, a discussion on the best form of the republic ("*ragionamento della ottima forma di Republica*") based on a report on the institutions and mores of the small republic of San Marino situated on top of Monte Titano.[119] Through the words of Captain Giovanni Andrea Belluzzi, Zuccolo propounds straight republican beliefs. He maintains that those peoples that fight to defend their liberty are more courageous than peoples who fight on behalf of a lord. Republics are stable if they preserve moderate equality among their citizens so that no one is so poor to be forced to beg, and so that no one is so wealthy as to be able to impose his will and his

---

[114] Ibid., p. 258.
[115] "Gli Evandrij erano i più da bene huomini del Mondo, e che la Città loro era più d'ogni altra felice"; "Della repubblica d'Evandria," ibid., p. 212.
[116] Ludovico Zuccolo, 'Della repubblica d'Evandria," ibid., p. 213.
[117] Ludovico Zuccolo, "Della repubblica d'Evandria," ibid., pp. 215–221.
[118] Ludovico Zuccolo, "Della repubblica d'Evandria," ibid., pp. 237–238.
[119] "Stelle, disse egli più delle altre felici ò fortuna contra il proprio genio stabile, e costante, ò sopra humana prudenza hà quefla patria libera conservata per tanti secoli, mentre gli altri popoli d'intorno, più ricchi, e più potenti hanno ben mille volte portato il giogo, e strascinate le catene, quando degli Italiani medesimi, quando de 'Barbari'! Se rimane reliquia dell'antico secolo dell'oro in quello solo giogo di monte, perché invidia a disturbarlo, ò zelo a goderlo non move anco i più remoti popoli d'Europa!"; "Della città felice," ibid., p. 161.

interests ("*habbia potenza da soprafar gli altri*").[120] For Zuccolo, both extreme poverty and excessive wealth are a lethal threat to the stability and the liberty of republics. Excessively wealthy citizens are insolent, ambitious, slothful, avaricious; inordinately poor citizens have no attachment to the republic and, moved by hatred and envy, are keen to favor political changes.[121] Moreover, poverty makes citizens robbers, unfaithful, liars – all vices that destroy civil happiness. In sum, inequality is the main cause of seditions and revolutions, while moderate equality produces loyalty and unity. Despite its praise of San Marino as a perfect republic, the dialogue does not encourage social and political reforms at all. San Marino is an exceptional case due to the felicitous influence of the stars and its special geographic position.[122] It is a republic worth studying, but it is most certainly not the New Jerusalem of the prophets.[123] Reason of state and utopian theories were de facto allied in the effort of burying both prophecy and social emancipation. Reason of state dispatched prophecies as vain dreams and visions of emancipation as seditious ideas; utopian theories replaced prophets with narrators of imaginary journeys to perfect cities that existed nowhere. Their alliance powerfully contributed to make the intellectual context of Counterreformation Italy utterly inimical to prophets of emancipation.

3.4 REVERBERATIONS OF BYGONE PROPHETIC TIMES

Some interest in prophecy survived even within the hostile political and intellectual context of the Counterreformation.[124] A relevant example is Antonio Brucioli (1498–1566). A pupil of the Neoplatonist philosopher Francesco da Diacceto, Brucioli fled Florence for Venice in 1522 after a failed anti-Medicean conspiracy. He later traveled to Lyon where he completed his major work, the *Dialogi della morale filosofia*, published for the first time in Venice in 1526. He returned to Florence in 1527 when his fellow citizens established a new popular government. The new regime looked on him suspiciously because of his connections with the Alamanni family, the leaders of the oligarchic opposition. After the fall of the moderate gonfalonier Niccolò Capponi, the new Savonarolan regime sent Brucioli into exile because of his sympathies for the Reformation. He spent the rest of his life in Venice translating and editing works of classical philosophy and the scriptures.

---

[120] "Della città felice," in *Dialoghi*, p. 165.   [121] Ibid., p. 166.

[122] "Forse altresì buon genio di questa terra, ò pur felici felle, che la mirarono propitie al nascer suo, l'aiutano a conservarsi tanto tempo libera e in tranquillo stato"; ibid., p. 172.

[123] Ibid., pp. 172–173.

[124] On the persistence of prophecy, see Adriano Prosperi, *L'eresia del Libro Grande: storia di Giorgio Siculo e della sua setta*, Milan: Feltrinelli, 2011, p. 234. Prosperi also claims that Ottavia Niccoli is wrong to maintain that prophetic spirit and hopes died around 1530; ibid., p. 440, n.33.

In the *Dialogi*, Brucioli discusses the fundamental concepts of republican political theory in depth. As he explains in the dedicatory epistle, the art of instituting and preserving good customs and inviolably sacred laws is a division of philosophy, itself the only discipline that can instill love of virtue in our hearts.[125] Good government encourages human beings to live according to reason. Since reason is the divine component of men's souls, we become like God – and then later attain eternal beatitude in the afterlife – when we live according to reason. For Brucioli, religion is a necessary foundation of republican life. It is difficult to govern cities in the absence of the fear of God, "for many who care little for the laws of man yet fear those of God." "Our religion" instills "hopes of immortality" in men. And because of that hope, men achieve great things and are willing to face "the danger of dying for their fatherland." Republics are powerful and flourish only if their citizens are "learned, wise, good, upright, justly educated, and behave in a way that pleases God." True lawgivers who wish to establish the best republic must ensure that "everyone piously understands all of God's matters." Man "cannot be good, nor can anything good happen to them unless they live with the love and the fear of God."[126]

In the *Dialogi*, Brucioli's restatement of the social and political utility of religion accompanies a strong warning against false prophets.[127] However, in another set of Brucioli's dialogues composed around the same time and published in Venice in 1528, we find detailed and learned reflections that show his deep interest in prophecy. The overarching premise of his argument is that human intellect can connect to angelic intellect and can therefore attain knowledge of future events (*"a quello si congiunge"*).[128] The connection happens

---

[125] Antonio Brucioli, *Dialogi*, Venice: Gregorio de Gregori, 1526.

[126] Antonio Brucioli, "Della Republica dialogo quinto," in *Dialogi*, p. xxixv.

[127] "Et se per sorte surge nella Republica uno falso Propheta, che predica alcuno segno futuro, o gran portento, e ch'egli avenga secondo che disse, e poi voglia ritrarre i popoli dal vero divino culto, tirandoli a nuove, o ad altre vecchie leggi, o culti divini persuadendo il servire a quelle, si dee per leggi ordinare, che non si odino le parole di quel Propheta, o sognatore. Perché alcuna volta aviene, che Idio tenta tutto uno popolo, perché si faccia manifesto se l'ama, o no, con tutto il core, e con tutta l'anima sua: e quel Propheta o fingitore di sogni sia morto, havendo parlato per divertire gli huomini dal vero culto divino: e sia lecito a ciascuno (se non si potrà co' buoni ammonimenti ritrarre il persuasore a migliore opinione) di mettergli le mani sopra, e menarlo al giudicio de' più vecchi, essendo ciascuno tenuto, e obligato aiutarvelo a menare: e quivi dee essere lapidato." "Della legge della republica dialogo sesto," in *Dialogi*, p. xlviir; see also Aldo Landi, "Nota critica," in Antonio Brucioli, *Dialogi*, edited by Aldo Landi, Naples and Chicago: Prismi Editrice and The Newberry Library, 1982, p. 563. See also Carlo Dionisotti, "La testimonianza del Brucioli,"*Machiavellerie*, Turin: Einaudi, 1980, p. 204.

[128] Antonio Brucioli, "Dialogo IX dello intelletto," in *Dialogi*, vol. I, Venice: Giovannantonio e i fratelli da Sabbio, 1528, p. 85r. On angels, see *Gli angeli custodi: storia e figure dell'amico vero*, edited by Carlo Ossola, Silvia Ciliberti, and Giacomo Jori, Turin: Einaudi, 2004.

because human intellect transcends into the angelic realm, in a manner similar to how persons who study a discipline well can equal their teachers. The crucial difference between human and angelic intelligences is that, while all things are present in angelic intellect, all things are future in human intellect (*"tutte le cose sono presenti nell'intelletto angelico, tutte le cose sono future nell'intelletto umano"*).[129] Angelic intellect is purely contemplative; human intellect is eminently active. In the pursuit of knowledge, though, human intellect is like the angelic in that it becomes quiet and contemplative (*"quieto e contemplativo diviene"*).[130] Both the angelic and the human intellects are close to God, and, for this, they receive His beneficial light (*"vero e naturale speculo della divina luce"*). Even if good and wicked men alike display prophetic powers, we can continue to believe that those powers come from God.[131]

Prophecy is the result of prophets' capacity to penetrate God's secret designs. The power of their mind is far superior to human beings' ordinary powers. They foresee future events because God has infused that knowledge in them through the angels, either directly or indirectly.[132] For this reason, prophets do not know all future contingent events that prophetic power could possibly know, but only the portion of events that the divine has revealed to them. Prophetic power is not permanent but discontinuous (*"nè quella cosa, che conosce, sempre la conosce, se non mentre che partecipa di tale numine"*).[133] Because it requires an outstanding ability of the mind to connect to "intelligible essences" (*"sustantie intelligibili"*), prophetic intelligence works best when prophets are detached from the senses, such as when they are asleep or melancholic, when they are in a state of ecstatic disposition (*"il propheta è tutto acceso di mente"*) and have visions through the eyes, or when they are dreaming. Prophets may also perceive God's mind through signs or voices sent by the heavens. In general, prophets prophesy in a state of alienation (*"così il profeta divinando da una certa alienatione, è in un certo modo oppresso"*). Prophecy is then "a mood of passion" (*"un modo di passione"*) in which prophets' minds become the mirror of eternity. God bestows upon them a special grace beyond and above the order of nature.[134] For Brucioli, the celestial ray that God in His infinite goodness instills in human beings transforms them into a kind of divinity. But to be able to receive the celestial ray, the human soul must be purged. In full agreement with the conventional understanding of prophecy, Brucioli asserts that only persons who live an impeccable life can be true

---

[129] Antonio Brucioli, "Dialogo IX dello intelletto," in *Dialogi*, p. 86*v*.
[130] Antonio Brucioli, "Dialogo IX dello intelletto," in *Dialogi*, p. 89*v*.
[131] Antonio Brucioli, "Dialogo XIX della divinatione per i sogni," in Antonio Brucioli, *Dialogi*, pp. 156*v*–157*r*.
[132] Ibid., p. 163*r*.   [133] Ibid., p. 63*v*.   [134] Ibid., pp. 164*r*–165*v*.

prophets.[135] The certainty of prophecy comes from the authenticity of the inspiration and dignity of prophets.[136]

About ten years later, around 1539, Brucioli completed a new translation of and massive commentary on the *Old Testament*. In the dedicatory letter to Francis I, king of France, Brucioli stresses that the Bible is full of the prophetic wisdom of God's Holy Spirit. God makes the princes and peoples who love him and obey his holy laws victorious and prosperous; he punishes those who disobey him with subjugation and defeat.[137] Similar prophetic language appears in the dialogue *Del governo dello ottimo principe et capitano dello esercito*, composed in 1539–1540 and addressed to Cosimo I de' Medici. Here Brucioli states that God does not immediately punish princes for their sins. Should they wish to live securely and enjoy the blessings of their exalted status, those who govern the earth must exercise their power with a meek spirit.[138] In another dedicatory letter also addressed to Francis I, Brucioli quotes 1 Corinthians 14:3 to reaffirm his high opinion of prophecy as a special language that has the power to edify, to exhort, and to console: "he who speaks

---

[135] "E si fa uno con Iddio per una certa deiformità, e connessione, e unione sopradivina, per la quale le pie menti, illuminate da quel supremo razo, sono inserte con Iddio, e vivacemente e singularmente se gli congiungono, perché come il ferro affocato in un certo modo si fa una cosa medesima con il fuoco, che lo accende e include in modo che di già non appare più ferro, advegna che secondo la sustantia ferro resti, [...], così le sincere Menti, le quali degna Iddio fare partecipi della sua illustratione, per esso divino Lume trapassano in Dio, per una certa conformità et assimigliatione, accioche strettissimamente se gli congiunghino, e diventino uno con quello non per sustantia, ma per ispecie. Ma come nel ricevimento del Lume sensibile debbe essere l'Occhio purgato dalle lippitudini e nocevoli brutture, e debbe essere ferma la vista di quello, la quale non trepidi, et vadia vagando." "Dialogo undecimo della luce divina, interlocutori Luigi Alamanni, et Bernardo Altoviti," in *Dialogi*, p. 57r.

[136] "Et tanto in quello propheta quanto negli altri troverai diligentissimamente havere osservato, che i loro parlari affermano essere da Iddio, perché i falsi propheti sono quegli che parlono da loro, i quali non pronunziano mai sincerantente il verbo di Iddio per la quale cosa i santi episcopi, certamente veri evangelisti, per tutti i modi fuggano di parlare alcuna cosa da loro proprii, sapendo che la sia menzogna. Et dice la parola del Signore, quasi dica queste non sono parole di Osea, ma del Signore Iddio, il quale ha usato Osea come strumento suo, a manifestare la sua verità e al quale non è lecito a alcuno a contradire, descrive dipoi i varii tempi, ne' quali prophetasse, perché non picciola utilità apporta sapere sotto quale Re si prophetasse perché si rende la certezza della cosa maggiore, e veggiamo in che tempo prophetassi"; Antonio Brucioli, "Libro di Osea Propheta," *Tomo terzo de' sacrosanti libri del Vecchio Testamento tradotti dalla Ebraica verità in Lingua Italiana & con breve & catholico commento dichiarati per Antonio Brucioli*, Venice: Alessandro Brucioli e frategli, 1546, p. 172v.

[137] Antonio Brucioli, *La Biblia quale contiene i sacri libri del vecchio testamento, tradotti da la hebraica verità in lingua toscana per Antonio Brucioli*, Venetia: Lucantonio Giunti fiorentino, 1532, p. 2.

[138] Antonio Brucioli, *Del governo dello ottimo principe et capitano dello esercito di Antonio Brucioli Allo illustrissimo et eccellentissimo Duca Cosimo de medici Duca di Firenze*, ms., BNCF, Magl. XXX 19, ff. 11r–12r. Cfr. Chiara Lastraioli, "Utopies célestes et terrestres dans la production d'Antonio Brucioli," *MORUS – Utopia e Renascimento* 8 (2012): pp. 231–245.

the languages of the world edifies himself: he who prophesies edifies the church."[139] The gift of prophecy passes from one generation to the next, and, as a result, the spiritual wealth of the early apostles does not perish with the passing of time.[140]

Prophets have the duty to reprehend princes and those with power when they oppress poor subjects and when they lack compassion. These leaders, who should set the right example for their people, are often ungrateful to God and greedy. They display only an external respect for God. Brucioli points to Amos as an example of a good prophet. Amos spoke against the moral corruption of his own people and called for their spiritual regeneration.[141] Prophets are severe critics of corruption and exhort their fellow citizens to commit themselves to the hard task of spiritual and social renovation. It is for this reason, Brucioli gloomily concludes, that prophets are despised and shunned. The most eloquent documentation of Brucioli's reverence for prophecy is the collection of Savonarola's sermons that he edited and published in Venice in 1540 and in 1544.[142] In the dedicatory epistle, he calls Savonarola a "great preacher of God's word." Moreover, he presents Savonarola's sermons as works replete with eloquent signs of authentic Christian faith.[143] In the spirit of Savonarola, Brucioli announces the imminent renovation of the Church. He wrote the same words that Savonarola had thundered forth from the pulpit. But now those words had no redemptive pathos. No one was willing to listen. His aspirations for moral and religious regeneration were reverberations of bygone times.

Other documents that attest to the survival of prophetic language are Francesco d'Antonio de' Ricci's works and letters. Ricci was a prosperous Florentine citizen who remained distant from political life, and who

---

[139] Antonio Brucioli, "Al Christianissimo Re Francesco, Primo Re di Francia, Antonio Brucioli Salute, et Pace in Christo Giesu Signore, et Salvatore Nostro," *La Biblia la quale in sè contiene i sacrosanti libri del Vecio e Nuovo Testamento, i quali ti apporto Christianissimo Lettore, nuovamente tradotti de la Hebraica e Greca verità in Lingua Toscana*, Venice, 1541, no publisher, no page number.

[140] Antonio Brucioli, "Allo Illustrissimo et Reverendissimo Signore Hipolito Estense, Cardinale di Ferrara," *Tomo terzo de' sacrosanti libri del Vecchio Testamento tradotti dalla Ebraica verità in Lingua Italiana & con breve & catholico commento dichiarati per Antonio Brucioli*, no page number.

[141] Antonio Brucioli, "Il Libro di Amos Propheta," ch. I, *Tomo terzo de' sacrosanti libri del Vecchio Testamento tradotti dalla Ebraica verità in Lingua Italiana & con breve & catholico commento dichiarati per Antonio Brucioli*.

[142] Antonio Brucioli, *Prediche del reverendo padre fra Gieronimo da Ferrara per tutto l'anno nuovamente con somma diligentia ricorrette*, Venice: no publisher, 1540.

[143] "Tantissimi documenti cristiani per i quali leggendo consolerete la christianissima anima vostra, veggendo in questo christianissimo scrittore con grandissima efficaccia profertarse [sic] la universali [sic] renovatione della chiesa, la quale hora soprasta al mondo, e già è in su le porte e la quale Iddio tosto conduca alla sua perfettione accioche tutti gli universi popoli diano laude al creatore dell'universo, e al suo figliuolo Christo Giesu Signore e Salvator nostro, al quale honore e gloria nel secolo di secoli"; "Al reverendissimo Monsignor Gieronimo Arsago," *Prediche del reverendo padre fra Gieronimo da Ferrara*, p. 2.

distinguished himself for his exemplary religious and moral conduct. He began to write prophetic letters around 1520 and persisted in his effort until the early 1530s. In the conversations held with Cardinal Giulio de' Medici at the time when a constitutional reform for Florence was being considered, Ricci harped on the familiar theme that great scandals and suffering would surely befall Florence if a religious and moral reformation was not carried out.[144] If the reforms were initiated, Ricci reassured Cardinal Giulio, God would raise him to heaven and appoint him as his minister. As his words reveal, Ricci was rephrasing the classical prophetic myth of Scipio's Dream that had long been a part of Christian prophetic language. In later letters composed after the Last Florentine Republic's defeat in 1530, Francesco expanded and refined his prophetic ideas. Here his addressee is again Cardinal Giulio de' Medici, by that time Pope Clement VII. Ricci begins his exhortation with typical prophetic counsel warning that Rome and Florence will be soon visited by God's wrath if they do not repent. He then proceeds to outline a reinterpretation of Florence's history. Therein, he assigns Clement VII the formidable task of carrying out the plan that God had entrusted to the Medici since the times of Cosimo the Elder in 1434.[145] Florence's prophetic history clearly indicates that God has entrusted the Church's governance to Clement VII to immediately remedy the disorders afflicting God's city. This, Francesco remarks, is the prophecy (*"hoc illud propheticum"*).[146]

In another letter written on the occasion of Clement VII's meeting with the king of France in Marseille, Ricci warned the pope of the prophetic reprobation (*"exprobatione prophetica"*) that would befall him and the king of France should they neglect God's derelict flock. To reinforce his prophetic warning, Ricci cites *Psalm* 2:1–5 and comments that God himself will initiate the moral and religious reform that will bring peace and glory to his elect people.[147] He also prophesied that tribulations would be over by September 1534, one hundred years since the beginning of the Medici's regime in Florence. Ricci claimed that God would set the foundations for the religious reform in his beloved city, and, like Savonarola, he announced that the light of Christian faith and charity would spread over the whole world from a reformed Florence.[148] As a just reward for her just undertakings on God's behalf, Florence would attain unprecedented greatness. Redemption will come after great suffering. Those who remain alive will become divine individuals with a

---

[144] See Lorenzo Polizzotto, "Prophecy, Politics and History in Early Sixteenth-Century Florence: the Admonitory Letters of Francesco d'Antonio de' Ricci," *Florence and Italy. Renaissance Studies in Honour of Nicolai Rubinstein*, edited by Peter Denley and Caroline Elam, London: Westfield College-University of London Committee for Medieval Studies, 1988, pp. 107–131.
[145] Ibid., p. 126.   [146] Ibid., p. 127.   [147] Ibid., p. 129.
[148] "Dal quale lume del popolo Sancto sarà diffuso la fede et carità christiane in tutto il mondo in stato e stato"; ibid., p. 129.

status higher than that of lords, kings, and emperors.[149] As Lorenzo Polizzotto has magnificently remarked, Francesco de' Ricci's language reveals that he was aware his prophecies would not translate into a political and social reform that followed Savonarola's prophecies. The dream of Florence as the New Jerusalem had lost the persuasive power to move Florentine minds and hearts.[150]

Francesco Pucci (1543–1597) is another example of the tenacity and sacrificial spirit of the prophets of the Counterreformation. A Florentine educated in humanism, Pucci lists Savonarola among the prophets who were influential to his formation, and he also goes on to describe his parents as spiritual guides:

The first reason and demonstration is the inclination and the more than ordinary ability that I have had since childhood to listen attentively to sacred offices, and to study those authors who deal with divine matters, according to the opinion and custom of my parents, who always had Holy scripture in their hands and on their tongues: the writings of Savonarola and of similar excellent preachers, Dante's *Divine Comedy*, the most spiritual works of Petrarch. They instilled in me the necessity to imitate these great figures of my language and homeland, thus inciting within me not only the desire to see Christianity re-united, but also grief in seeing it in decline in Europe and finding modern schools full of vanity and folly. Hence, often the most learned know how to live in accordance with God's wisdom less than others do.[151]

In a letter dated July 12, 1579, Pucci confides to his mother that he considers the spiritual goods that come from studying the scriptures more precious than any external good. In order to interpret scripture correctly, a true Christian must abandon the self and place himself in God's hands. Like Savonarola, Pucci claims to have received the gift of God that allows him to understand scripture better than many prelates and writers. Encouraged by his prophetic visions, he reveals that God would use him for grand designs. Pucci proudly defends his right and his duty to criticize the erroneous beliefs of his compatriots, just as the prophets, Christ, the Apostles, and the great men of Athens and Rome had done.[152] He announces that new prophets will come and will demonstrate the inspiration's truth with doctrine and acts. They will guide the "reform of religion and of the republic" with their divine authority.[153] If Machiavelli had known Pucci, writes Giorgio Caravale, it is easy to imagine that he would have recognized in Pucci the same traits of an unarmed prophet that he had seen in

---

[149] Ibid., p. 120.   [150] Ibid., p. 111.

[151] Letter to Pope Clement VIII, Amsterdam, August 5, 1592, in Francesco Pucci, *Lettere, documenti e testimonianze*, edited by Luigi Firpo and Renato Piattoli, Florence: Olschki, 1955, vol. I, p. 142.

[152] Ibid., p. 120.

[153] "As for the rest, I don't mind telling you that I have taken my hand away from writing about sacred things, for the Lord has revealed to me that true reform must take place not by way of writing, but through living witnesses sent by him for this purpose, according to the promise made in Chapter XI of the Book of Revelation." Francesco Pucci to his brother Giovanni, Krakow, March 15, 1584; ibid., p. 64.

Savonarola. Pucci wanted to revive the ideals of republican freedom. From Florence, he wandered to Lyon and Paris, London, Oxford, Basle, Cracow, and Prague before returning to France. It was from there that he took a final trip to Rome, where the Inquisition sentenced him to the stake (July 5, 1597). Wherever he went, he showed his "ardent affection" for "citizens who love the common good and their homeland" and his "mortal hatred of all tyranny and lack of justice," as he wrote in the letter he sent to Clement VIII in 1592.[154]

Pucci considered himself the depositary for the prophetic mission of Christianity's religious and political renewal. In his heart, he was convinced that the pope and rulers would understand that his was a sincere, prophetic voice, and that they would eventually agree to work for the ideals he outlined. He wrote to the king of France, Henry IV, and asked him to convene a holy council that would bring the Israelites back into the flock and thus open the way for the coming advent of the "kingdom of Christ." Not only the Jews, but the Indians and the Chinese would also be gathered together "in the wondrous kingdom that God wants to establish on earth." Pucci's prophetic vision welcomed the myth of the millennium: "Those golden years and divine century [...] this most happy kingdom [...] will last a thousand years, at the end of which Satan will be again unleashed for a short time. And when Satan's last efforts are finished, he and all those who follow him – all adversaries of God – will be miraculously defeated and overthrown."[155]

In *Forma d'una republica catholica*, written in England in 1581, Pucci also resorted to the models and themes of the utopian tradition. His "republic" was to be an association of "men of good will," a secret society governed by precise rules and that had to meet periodically as a general group in the court of a nobleman or friendly sovereign.[156] His mission was to prepare a holy and free council of princes that would be able to bring peace to and unite Christendom. Pucci assures that the "republic" would triumph over its powerful enemies with God's help:

Moreover, it is necessary to trust in God with firm faith, and to strive to overcome vices with virtue. Do not doubt this victory, for, even if it seems that we are just a small number at the start, God's hand will support us and shall be able to do more than the opposing forces. And it will be seen in time that our strength is greater than that of the enemies: we are much better accompanied than them, because this favor from above is so great that all difficulties are easily overcome with it. We, who have placed our trust in God most high, cannot but prosper by his hand.[157]

[154] Giorgio Caravale, *Il profeta disarmato: L'eresia di Francesco Pucci nell'Europa del Cinquecento*, Bologna: Il Mulino, 2011, p. 85.

[155] Ibid., p. 116.

[156] Francesco Pucci, "Forma d'una republica catholica,"*Per la storia degli eretici italiani del secolo XVI in Europa*, edited by Delio Cantimori and Elisabeth Feis, Rome: Reale Accademia d'Italia, 1937, p. 171.

[157] Ibid., pp. 173–174.

In order to persuade people of his proposition's worth, Pucci does not resort to magical, astrological, or alchemical allusions. He does not even mention visions or revelations, as he does in other writings. His language, though, is that of the prophet. He promises God's help and provides reassurance that divine inspiration will illuminate the council. In a fashion that remains closer to utopian models than to the prophetic tradition, Pucci delays in outlining the organizational details of the "republic." Each "college" must elect a provost, or consul, a censor, and a chancellor. Male citizens who have reached the age of twenty-five have the right to vote. The censor is to monitor the moral life of the citizens and of the other two magistrates. Pucci warns that the "republic" will be able to count on God's help only if citizens respect the laws of Christian morality with the utmost discipline. He also explains that "citizens" must obey the civil authorities and practice religious worship within their families, and he underscores the importance of education.[158] To accomplish this formation of citizens, Pucci recommends family prayer, physical activity, providing assistance and comfort to the sick and prisoners, and burying the dead.

The text does not clarify whether the "republic" will be a transitional institution destined to be dissolved when the council of princes is established, or whether it prefigures the ideal Christian society that Pucci would like to see born. I think the second hypothesis is more convincing than the first. If the "republic" prefigures new times, Pucci's message of social emancipation is lacking. It does not indicate any institutional change; it does not open new horizons of freedom and justice. There is not a word devoted to the emancipation of the poor and dispossessed. The peaceful future that Pucci hopes for will be the work of princes and the pope, together with God's assistance, not an undertaking made by the people. The "*republica catholica*" must exert pressure from below in order to favor the work of the princes and the pope.[159] But what pressure can a secret association of citizens exert if they do not stand out in any way – in their worship practices and in public life – from other subjects and the other faithful of the Catholic Church? Despite appeals to Henry IV and Clement VIII, the "*republica catholica*" and the universal council remained ingenuous wishes.

Yet, Pucci was certain that reform was imminent because he had received a revelation from God and an angel: "God has spoken to me by name with much clarity, effectiveness, seriousness, and discretion about the Church and of the

[158] Ibid., pp. 194–195.
[159] On this matter, see M. Eliav-Feldon, "Secret Societies, Utopias, and Peace Plans: The Case of Francesco Pucci," *Journal of Medieval and Renaissance Studies* 14 (1984): p. 151. See also E. Barnavi and M. Eliav-Feldon, *Le périple de Francesco Pucci: Utopie, hérésie et vérité religieuse dans la Renaissance tardive*, Paris: Hachette, 1988; Silvia Ferretto, "'Una chiesa rinnovata' e 'un popolo fatto tutto santo': la visione del Cristianesimo tra riflessione teologica e millenarismo in Francesco Pucci,"*Archivio Storico Italiano* 165 (2007): pp. 77–120; Neil Tarrant, "Concord and Toleration in the Thought of Francesco Pucci, 1578–81," *The Sixteenth Century Journal* 46 (2015): pp. 983–1003.

Apostolic See of Rome [...]. Then this angel told me very serious matters about how the Antichrist is to come soon. I had a great confirmation of my hope regarding the next renewal: God is to accomplish it quickly through persons authorized by him to do so and who are sufficient for such an undertaking."[160] True prophets, Pucci adds, are examples of holiness. Posterity recognizes great honor and fame in them. Pucci's fate, however, was quite different. The Church had him beheaded as a heretic and burned his body. No remembrance remains of his life and his writings. His sincere faith and prophetic undertakings notwithstanding, Pucci was an isolated heretic and agitator who left no marks on religious and political history.[161] His defeat was another eloquent sign demonstrating the exhaustion of the "vital thrust of the Italian Reform."[162]

Though he interpreted prophecy from a radically naturalistic perspective, Giordano Bruno (1548–1600) also contributed to keeping alive prophetic ideas in Counterreformation Italy. He regarded Moses as a capable magician who knew the secrets of the Egyptian priests. According to some witnesses, at the time when he was tried for heresy (and sentenced to death), he used words like imagination, deception, imposture, fake miracles, shrewdness, melancholy, intervention of aerial spirits, and so on to describe Moses' and Christ's acts. Of Moses, again according to witnesses, he asserted that he had merely simulated that he was talking to God. Bruno believed that the main cause of prophecies is the power of shrinking one's spirit through meditation in solitude. Alleged revelations come from purely natural causes. They come from the prophets' extraordinary imagination, reinforced through study and meditation, and from their physical complexion, character, and culture. God and human

---

[160] Francesco Pucci from Prague to his mother Lisabetta Giambonelli in Florence, August 13, 1585, in *Lettere, documenti e testimonianze*, p. 68.

[161] Francesco Pucci, "Premessa," *Lettere, documenti e testimonianze*, pp. 5–57. A similar fate befell Jacopo Brocardo who published in 1581 *Mystica et prophetica libri Geneseos interpretatio*, in which he reproposed Joachim of Fiore's eschatological vision. He announced that Christ would inspire and help the Huguenots in the Netherlands and France join with the true believers of Germany in the formation of a league that could militarily defeat the papists in Germany, France, and Italy. With the papists defeated, true believers would hold a first general council in Venice to decree the end of the papacy and the abolition of imperial law, and thus inaugurate the kingdom of Christ on earth. A second general council, also held in Venice, would bring all Christian people together and establish the "heavenly Jerusalem" on earth. Finally united, Christianity would then defeat the Turks, convert the Jews, exterminate the lineage of Charles V, and lay the foundations of the "novus status mundi." On Brocardo, see Antonio Rotondò, "Jacopo Brocardo," *Dizionario Biografico degli Italiani*, vol. XIV, pp. 384–389; Delio Cantimori, "Visioni e speranze di un ugonotto italiano," *Rivista Storica Italiana* 62 (1950): pp. 199–217; Rodney L. Petersen, *Preaching in the Last Days: The Themes of the 'Two Witnesses' in the Sixteenth and Seventeenth Centuries*, New York and Oxford: Oxford University Press, 1993, pp. 162–165; Marion L. Kuntz, *The Anointment of Dionisio: Prophecy and Politics in Renaissance Italy*, University Park, PA: The Pennsylvania State University Press, 2001, pp. 119–126; Federica Ambrosini, *L'eresia di Isabella: Vita di Isabella da Passano, signora della Frattina (1542–1601)*, Milan: Franco Angeli, 2005.

[162] Giorgio Caravale, *Il profeta disarmato*, pp. 28–29.

beings cannot possibly communicate. They speak completely different languages.[163]

If God does not speak to human beings, there is no prophecy. Nonetheless, Bruno believed that God is infinite cause, impersonal power, a greatest artist with no face. He is *in rebus*, pervades nature, reveals himself and acts on human beings. He can inspire them. Through the medium of nature prophecy is therefore possible. His words evoke the page of *The Prince* in which Machiavelli celebrates those rare and marvelous men (*"rari e maravigliosi"*) who deserved God's friendship, redeemed their peoples, and thereby attained immortality. However, Bruno's heroic and divine men do not aspire to emancipate peoples from political oppression. Their goal is to attain "the truth and universal good" (*"verità e bene universale"*). Their arms are truth and divine intelligence. They take up their arms not against the barbarians but against ignorance (*"contra la fosca ignoranza, montando su l'alta rocca et eminente torre della contemplazione"*). Any other enterprise is for them base and worthless.[164] Like Machiavelli's redeemers, they attain immortality in this world and become similar to the divinity. They attain immortality, for Bruno, even if they are defeated.[165]

Historians of political ideas discuss Tommaso Campanella (1568–1639) mainly as the author of the utopian work *La Città del Sole* (*The City of the Sun*)

---

[163] See Eugenio Canone, "Ispirati da quale Dio? Bruno e l'espressione della sapienza," *Bruniana & Campanelliana* 11 (2005): pp. 389–409, especially pp. 396–397. On Bruno's trial see Luigi Firpo, *Il processo di Giordano Bruno*, edited by Diego Quaglioni, Rome: Salerno Editrice, 1993; Ingrid D. Rowland, *Giordano Bruno: Philosopher and Heretic*, New York: Farrar, Straus and Giroux, 2008; Frances Yates, *Giordano Bruno and the Hermetic Tradition*, London: Routledge and Kegan Paul, 2004; Michele Cilberto, *L'occhio di Atteone: nuovi studi su Giordano Bruno*, Rome: Edizioni di Storia e Letteratura, 2002; Hilary Gatti, "The sense of an ending in Bruno's *Eroici furori*," *Essays on Giordano Bruno*, Princeton: Princeton University Press, 2011; Nicoletta Tirinnanzi, "Filosofia, politica e magia nel Rinascimento: l'esperienza di Giordano Bruno," *Giordano Bruno nolano e cittadino europeo*, Grottaglie: CRSEC e Scorpione editrice, pp. 31–59.

[164] Giordano Bruno, *Des fureurs héroïques*, in *Oeuvres complètes de Giordano Bruno*, vol. VII, edited by Miguel Angel Granada, Paris: Les Belles Lettres, 1999, p. 377.

[165] "Gli uomini rari, eroichi e divini passano per questo camino de la difficoltà, a fine che sii costretta la necessità a concedergli la palma de la immortalità. Giungesi a questo che, quantumque non sia possibile arrivar al termine di guadagnar il palio: correte pure, e fate il vostro sforzo in una cosa de sì fatta importanza, e resistete sin a l'ultimo spirto. Non sol chi vence vien lodato, ma anco chi non muore da codardo e poltrone: questo rigetta la colpa de la sua perdita e morte in dosso de la sorte, e mostra al mondo che non per suo difetto, ma per torto di fortuna è gionto a termine tale"; Giordano Bruno, "Le souper des Cendres," *Oeuvres complètes de Giordano Bruno*, vol. II, preface by A. Ophir, notes by G. Aquilecchia, translation by Y. Hersant, Paris: Les Belles lettres, 1994, p. 93. On Machiavelli and Bruno see Michele Cilberto, *Niccolò Machiavelli. Ragione e pazzia*, Rome and Bari: Laterza, 2019, in particular ch. VIII, "Nel labirinto della fortuna: Machiavelli, Bruno, Spinoza."

composed in 1602 and published in 1623.[166] Though written according to the canonical rules of the utopian genre, the Città del Sole contains a visible prophetic message.[167] The text subsists as a dialogue between a Genoese sailor who had traveled with Christopher Columbus, and a knight from Malta whose only role in the dialogue is to ask for explanations and clarifications. Situated somewhere in the sea of Sonda near Sumatra, the blessed City of the Sun

[166] On Tommaso Campanella see Germana Ernst, *Il carcere, il politico, il profeta. Saggi su Tommaso Campanella*, Pisa and Rome: Istituti editoriali e poligrafici internazionali, 2002; Luigi Firpo, "Il Campanella astrologo e i suoi persecutori romani,"*Rivista di filosofia* 30 (1939): pp. 200–215; and *Ricerche campanelliane*, Florence: Sansoni, 1947, pp. 134–173; Daniel P. Walker, *Spiritual and Demonic Magic from Ficino to Campanella*, London: Warburg Institute, University of London, 1958, pp. 203–236; Germana Ernst, "Aspetti dell'astrologia e della profezia in Galileo e Campanella," *Novità celesti e crisi del sapere*, edited by Paolo Galluzzi, Florence: Giunti, 1983, pp. 255–266; Gianfranco Formichetti, "Il de siderali fato vitando di Tommaso Campanella," *Il mago, il cosmo, il teatro degli astri: saggi sulla letteratura esoterica del Rinascimento*, edited by Gianfranco Formichetti, Rome: Bulzoni, 1985, pp. 199–217; Germana Ernst, "Vocazione profetica e astrologica in Tommaso Campanella," *La città dei segreti. Magia, astrologia e cultura esoterica a Roma*, edited by Fabio Troncarelli, Milan: Franco Angeli, 1985, pp. 136–155; Germana Ernst, "'L'alba colomba scaccia i corbi neri': Profezia e riforma in Campanella," *Storia e figure dell'Apocalisse fra'500 e'600*, edited by Roberto Rusconi, Rome: Viella, 1996, pp. 107–125; Lina Bolzoni, "Una pretesa di libertà. Poesia, magia, profezia in Tommaso Campanella," *Storia della letteratura italiana*, vol. V, edited by Enrico Malato, *La fine del Cinquecento e il Seicento*, Rome: Salerno Editrice, 1997, pp. 869–903; Germana Ernst, "'L'aurea età felice': Profezia, natura e politica in Tommaso Campanella," *Tommaso Campanella e l'attesa del secolo aureo. Atti della III Giornata Luigi Firpo*, Florence: Olschki, 1998, pp. 61–88; Lina Bolzoni, "Prophétie littéraire et prophétie politique chez Tommaso Campanella," *La prophétie comme arme de guerre des pouvoirs (XV–XVII siècles)*, Paris: Presses de la Sorbonne Nouvelle, 2000, pp. 251–263; Pasquale Tuscano, *Del parlare onesto. Scienza, profezia e magia nella scrittura di Tommaso Campanella*, Naples: Edizioni Scientifiche Italiane, 2001; Germana Ernst, "'Redeunt Saturnia regna': Profezia e poesia in Tommaso Campanella,"*Bruniana & Campanelliana* 11, no. 2 (2005): pp. 429–449; Alessio Panichi, *Il volto fragile del potere. Religione e politica nel pensiero di Tommaso Campanella*, Pisa: ETS, 2015.

[167] In his *Ateismo trionfato* Campanella claimed he saw no relevant differences between the visions of ideal cities of the philosophers and the visions of prophets. And later he cites his own *Città del Sole* to restate a clearly prophetic message: "O veramente le tre misure son la potenza, la sapienza e l'amore, delle quali costa ogni ente et ogni ragunanza e republica, li quali son ancora farina naturale, o guasta, fatta tirannide, sofistica et hippocrisia: ma questo fermento di Christo li riducerà a fratellanza, senno e charità. E che sia possibile lo dimostrai nel libro della *Monarchia christiana* e nella propria republica detta la *Città del sole*, e che solo in quel tempo li profeti promettono republica al mondo stabile, felice, senza guerra, senza carestia e senza heresia e senza pestilenza, e secolo aureo. Perché, come pregano nell'oratione di Christo, si farà la voluntà di Dio in terra come si fa in cielo; e questo sia nella cascata dell'antichristo, e dopo molto tempo sorgerà Gog e Magog per occasion di vittoria alli santi, e poi questo regno fia trasferito in cielo, evacuati li principati e potestati inferiori e superiori: del che alrrove"; Tommaso Campanella, *L'ateismo trionfato*, vol. 1, edited by Germana Ernst, Pisa: Edizioni della Normale, 2004, pp. 106–107. Germana Ernst has remarked that in Campanella's philosophical and political thought, prophecy and utopia are hardly distinguishable. See Germana Ernst, *Il carcere, il politico, il profeta. Saggi su Tommaso Campanella*, p. 66.

imitates the urban design of a Greek polis. Its political order, however, is hierarchical and authoritarian. The chief mission of the City of the Sun is to eradicate egotism from human hearts and to wipe out all occasions for sin. To this effect, its founders abolished private property and family, and organized all social and private activities in a communal manner. Despite its theocratic and authoritarian content, the *Città del Sole* conveys aspirations of social justice like those that prophets had sustained, albeit with a different language.[168]

As early as 1598, Campanella wrote to his brother that he was one of the many prophets persecuted by princes, tyrants, flatterers, and corrupt priests.[169] He also asserted he had a special talent for uncovering the veiled meanings of the scriptures. Like the humanist scholars and Savonarola, Campanella interpreted the Bible *per figuras*, that is, allegorically. He looked for meanings concealed under the literary sense of the sacred text. When the Catholic Church tried him for heresy, he boldly confessed his allegiance to prophecy.[170] As he approached the end of his life, he declared his prophetic mission even more forcefully. In a letter of July 1638, he writes that he has "been sent by God" ("*Dio m'ha mandato*") to teach divine wisdom ("*senno divino*") and to reform all sciences according to nature and the scriptures.[171] Against the conventional view that considered prophets as defeated dreamers, he proclaimed that their failures were not the consequence of their errors, even less of their vices. Rather, they were instead authentic marks of the truths that they

---

[168] As Luigi Firpo has written, Renaissance utopia was not advocating deism or heresy, but a religious reform in the sense of return and rediscovery of founding principles. See Luigi Firpo, "L'utopia politica nella Controriforma," in *Contributi alla storia del Concilio di Trento e della Controriforma*, edited by Eugenio Garin, Florence: Vallecchi, 1948, p. 84. See also Luigi Firpo, "Introduzione," Tommaso Campanella, *La Città del Sole*, edited by Germana Ernst and Laura Salvetti Firpo, postfazione di Norberto Bobbio, Bari: Laterza, 1997, pp. xxx–xxxv. See also Elisa Tinelli, "Le utopie del secondo Cinquecento e del primo Seicento, come *renovatio* laica dell'ideale della *fuga mundi*,"*Quaderni di Storia* 90 (2019): pp. 157–175.

[169] "Ma non è forse vero che tutti i profeti e i sapienti sono stati colpiti da queste stesse accuse nei grandi articoli dei tempi, ed io con loro? I satrapi e i farisei, adulatori dei principi grazie ai quali si ingrassano, vedendo che dalla novità del secolo e dall'onestà dei costumi, che i sapienti annunciano e persuadono, i loro inganni vengono svelati, e vengono illuminate le tenebre nelle quali stanno acquattati per fare del male, e che verrà a loro mancare il pane della menzogna e dell'inganno, insorgono immediatamente, e perché non possono dir nulla contro i loro costumi santi, ricorrono all'accusa di ribellione ed eresia, e aggrediscono gli uomini in quello che hanno detto, perché non si accorda con quanto dicono loro. Ecco che insorgono contro Geremia [...] e contro Isaia ed altri [...], e insorsero contro gli apostoli, come se fossero pseudoprofeti ingannatori, seduttori e avidi del regno, e Cristo sia la figura esemplare di tutto ciò"; Tommaso Campanella, *Lettere*, edited by G. Ernst, Florence: Olschki, 2010, p. 540. See G. Ernst, *Il carcere, il politico, il profeta. Saggi su Tommaso Campanella*, p. 68.

[170] See Germana Ernst, "Profezia (*prophetia*)," *Enciclopedia Bruniana e Campanelliana*, vol. 1, edited by Eugenio Canone and Germana Ernst, Pisa: Istituti editoriali e poligrafici internazionali, 2006, p. 303.

[171] "Tommaso Campanella al Granduca Ferdinando II de' Medici in Firenze," Paris, July 6, 1638, in Tommaso Campanella, *Lettere*, pp. 509–510.

announced. Because prophets teach people to follow the correct Christian pathway, they incur the hatred of bad princes (*"chi governa male"*) and are consequently put to death. The prophets' defeat, however, is only superficial. Their message survives after their death. Whereas their persecutors are detested, they are remembered and loved. The golden age shall come again, even if the peoples, immersed in the miseries of present times, do not understand or realize the imminent coming of new times.[172] For Campanella, to work to institute the republic envisioned by the prophets before him was a most glorious effort.

Over his long and tormented life, Campanella resorted to prophetic language many times to advocate projects and hopes for religious and social reform. Prophetic visions guided his failed conspiracy of 1598–1599. He had hoped to liberate his Calabria from corrupt Spanish domination and establish a communitarian and theocratic republic under his own direct leadership. Celestial signs and extraordinary events taking place in Southern Italy – floods, earthquakes, invasions of locusts – persuaded him that the times were ripe for radical reform and led him to conceive and attempt to execute his unrealistic plan. His goal was to carry out the prophetic vision of the Christian world's renovation that would finally satisfy people's aspirations for peace and justice. Campanella's fullest treatment of prophecy is his *Articuli prophetales*.[173] In this work, probably composed between 1600 and 1609, he stressed that the Bible contains all the notable events of the past and the future and is therefore a sufficient guide for the legislators of the Church of God (*"in sacris Bibliis contineri omnes notabiles eventus praeteritos ac futuros"*). He also restated the conventional prophetic idea that before the end of the world – which he asserted was imminent – a Christian republic shall encompass the whole of humanity and provide human beings with the greatest happiness. Shattered by the devil into the multiplicity of present religions and kingdoms, the primeval unity of the world shall return, and the earthly republic shall be the prelude of the heavenly one. Christ's authentic spirit shall reign. This prophecy, Campanella proclaimed, comes not just from the predictions of the poets, the philosophers, and the prophets of all nations, but also from humanity's natural desire.[174]

In Campanella's view, successful political action needs the help of prophecy. Political events are governed by three main causes: God, prudence, and occasion. God is the most important for He rules everything, even when his power is not visible. This means that a wise prince must consider human causes as well as chance and God's plan. Whereas prudence can help a prince understand human causes, only astrology can unveil how our fate is written in the heavens, and only prophecy can penetrate God's light. In this spirit Campanella ventured

[172] "Se fu nel mondo l'aurea età felice, / ben essere potrà più ch'una volta, / ché si ravviva ogni cosa sepolta, / tornando 'giro ov'ebbe la radice"; ibid., p. 236.

[173] Germana Ernst, "Nota critica," Tommaso Campanella, *Articuli prophetales*, edited by Germana Ernst, Florence: La Nuova Italia, 1977, pp. xlii–xlv.

[174] Tommaso Campanella, *Articuli prophetales*, p. 80.

all his prophecies addressed to monarchs. Composed in 1600, his *Monarchia di Spagna* announces that the king of Spain will unify peoples and establish a universal Christian monarchy. With the argument that the Spanish had failed in their mission and had behaved like squanderers and henchmen of humanity, Campanella assigned a similar task to the king of France in the 1630s.[175] At the end of his life, he spoke prophetically yet again and integrated his visions with a good deal of pragmatic considerations. In his letters to princes of 1635–1638, he claimed that the golden age would come only if Venice struck an alliance with Rome, for the alliance in question would ensure the greatest advantages to both powers.[176] If Venice rediscovers and appreciates religion – Campanella stresses – her future will be bright, and her power will ensure liberty and security to all Italians.

In complete agreement with the ideas of prophetic poetry, Campanella asserts that true poets are prophets. Inspired by the divine, poets have access to the highest truths that ordinary human beings are unable to see. With their words' power and beauty, they inspire a warm love of virtue and reason in their fellow human beings (*"il caldo amore della virtù e della ragione"*). For this reason, prophetic poets are indispensable agents of moral and political redemption. Their mission is to decry tyrants and reawaken virtue. On the other hand, false poets, such as the Greeks, invent myths and fables to mock religion, corrupt the mores, and ridicule virtue. They are well regarded only in tyrannies where lies serve the purpose of keeping subjects ignorant and docile. True poets are teachers of moral and political liberty; false poets are teachers of servitude.

If philosophers thought correctly, they would understand that planets and stars have power not over God who sits above them, but over the creatures that stand below them. In full agreement with the Renaissance prophetic tradition, Campanella claims that we must take celestial signs seriously should we want to avoid unpleasant surprises and suffer tragic consequences. Signs from the heavens announce the familiar vision of redemption after suffering. The angelic pope prophesied by Gioachino da Fiore will sit on the throne of Saint Peter to unite peoples and carry out a universal renewal (*"saeculi renovationem, ex prophetia divina et naturali"*). Before his arrival, however, God will harshly punish all Christians and, more severely so, the pope and clergy for their corruption, avarice, and lust for power.[177] In a text that Germana Ernst has dated to 1627, Campanella claimed that wicked men and princes are

---

[175] Germana Ernst, "Ancora sugli ultimi scritti politici di Tommaso Campanella," *Bruniana & Campanelliana* 5 (1999): p. 140.

[176] "Né mai si gusterà il secol d'oro, se non si arriva a questa libertà commune a Venezia e a Roma, però m'ammiro [che] per un passo di terra e per bagatella i prudenti Veneziani tengon discordie con il papa, e non vogliono la sua grandezza, cosa che nel secreto dell'animo loro è altrimenti intesa, perché sanno assai, sono scola e orologio di principi, e bene intendono che i cristiani e l'inimici loro non desirano altro che questa discordia"; quotation in Germana Ernst, "Ancora sugli ultimi scritti politici di Tommaso Campanella," pp. 152–153.

[177] Tommaso Campanella, *Articuli prophetales*, p. 184.

teachings through which God compels us to appreciate the virtues He has bequeathed on us. Although they are not aware of it, they too are obeying God's will (*"eseguiscono quel che Dio vole"*).[178]

While he forcefully exalts the value of prophecy, Campanella severely chastises Machiavelli's vindication of armed prophets. He takes issue with Machiavelli's (alleged) claim that Moses' accomplishments – even with God's guidance – were no greater than those of Cyrus. Campanella rebuts that Moses' deeds are by far more glorious than those of Cyrus because he enacted a law that the whole world today believes to be the law of God. All peoples revere him as a pupil and messenger of God (*"discepolo e messagier di Dio"*); they are ready to die in order to defend his law and regard him as a prophet, like Christ (*"Mosè e Christo son tenuti per profeti"*). Campanella fails to note, or deliberately ignores, that Moses was Machiavelli's example of the armed prophet par excellence. As a critique of Machiavelli's views on the weakness of unarmed prophets, Campanella's argument misses the mark. What Campanella had intended to vindicate was the power of unarmed prophecy as a force capable of conquering the souls of human beings – for him, a victory more glorious than any military or political achievement.[179] Moses, and even more so Christ, were therefore more victorious than the great conquerors. In Campanella's conception, only if we were immortal would Machiavelli's argument have some value. Since we are mortal, it is wise and noble to give one's life to defend the divine law that through grace makes us immortal. Peter and Paul were both unarmed and were later killed. Yet, they rule present-day Rome and have many churches dedicated to them. On the other hand, Romulus and Nero – who were both armed and killed many people – are completely forgotten and have neither temples nor monuments erected in their honor.[180] For Campanella, it is a very imprudent idea to believe that human prudence is sufficient to found and preserve states without the help of prophecy. He thus exhorted princes to uphold Christian life and announced the coming of the golden age with great eloquence and pathos. Like the other prophetic voices that spoke in late sixteenth- and seventeenth-century Italy, Campanella found no followers. His great yearning notwithstanding, he too could not be the herald of a new history of moral and political redemption.

The corruption of consciences was so deep and so widespread in Counterreformation Italy that no moral or political reform was possible. The

---

[178] Germana Ernst, *Il carcere, il politico, il profeta. Saggi su Tommaso Campanella*, p. 171.

[179] Tommaso Campanella, *Atheismus triumphatus*, X.2–4, edited by Germana Ernst, Pisa and Rome: Fabrizio Serra, 2013, pp. 93–94 (reprint of the Rome edition of 1631). See also Luigi Firpo, "Risposte alle censure dell' 'Ateismo triunfato' (1631)," T. Campanella, *Opuscoli inediti*, Florence: Olschki, 1951, pp. 9–54; Luigi Firpo, "Appunti campanelliani, XXI. Le censure all' 'Atheismus trionfato,'" *Giornale Critico della Filosofia Italiana* 30 (1951): pp. 509–524.

[180] Tommaso Campanella, *Atheismus triumphatus*, X.8, p. 106. Campanella strongly defended Savonarola against Machiavelli's allegation that unarmed philosophers are bound to be defeated. See also XIX, p. 185.

literature of the seventeenth century provides eloquent examples of the persuasion that times of reform were over. A particularly illuminating document is Trajano Boccalini's (1556–1613) hilarious description of the failed attempt to reform their century from its vices and corruption in his *Ragguagli di Parnaso* (1612–1613). Apollo, the wise ruler of Parnassus, summons the greatest men of antiquity to find a cure for the moral corruption of the "Age" ("*Secolo*"). Once assembled, they ask "the Century" to describe his diseases. He replies:

Soon after I was born, Gentlemen, I fell into these maladies which I now labour under. My face is now so fresh and ruddy because people have colored it. [. . .] My sickness resembles the ebbing and flowing of the sea, which always contains the same water, though it rises and falls. With this vicissitude notwithstanding, as when my looks are outwardly good, my malady (as at this present) is more grievous inwardly. When my face looks ill, I am best within. For what my infirmities are, which do so torment me at the present, do but take off this gay jacket, wherewith some good people have covered a rotten carcass, that notwithstanding breathes, and view me naked, as I was made by Nature, and you will plainly see I am but a living carcass.

Boccalini tells us that all the philosophers "hasted, and having stripped the Age naked, they saw that the wretch pargeted with appearances four inches thick, all over his body." Then:

the Reformers caused ten razors to be forthwith brought unto them, and every one of them taking one, they fell all to scrape away the pargeting aforesaid; but they found them so far eaten into his very bones, as in all that huge Colossus, they could not find one ounce of good live flesh. At which they were much amazed, then put on the Age's jacket again and dismissed him. Finding that the cure was altogether desperate, they assembled themselves close together, and forsaking the thought of all public affairs, they resolved to worry about their private reputation.

After a long and learned debate, the wise men of antiquity concluded with Tacitus that, "as long as there be men, there will be vices" ("*Vitia erunt, donec Homines*"; *Historiae*, Book 4). Men live on earth, and they do so by tolerating as little ill as possible rather than seeking for an ultimately irretrievable good. The height of human wisdom, they agreed, consists in being so discreet as to be content to leave the world as we find it.[181]

To listen to prophets' calls to fight for political and social redemption, a people (or at least the best citizens) must have the moral strength to create new and higher forms of ethical life. But Italians had almost completely lost their creative moral energy. As Benedetto Croce eloquently stressed in his *Storia dell'età barocca in Italia: Pensiero, poesia e letteratura vita morale*, Italians were not just politically enslaved, but also morally dead.[182] In this work,

---

[181] Traiano Boccalini, *Ragguagli di Parnaso e pietra del paragone politico*, vol. 1, Ragguaglio LXXVII, edited by Giuseppe Rua, Bari: Laterza, 1910, pp. 258–285.

[182] Benedetto Croce, *Storia della età barocca in Italia: Pensiero. Poesia e letteratura. Vita morale*, Bari: Laterza, fourth edition, 1957, p. 7 (first print 1929 [but written in 1924–1925]). On this

written between 1924 and 1925 but not printed until 1929, Croce underscored that the Counterreformation did not have a "human and eternal character," and hence is not on the same level as the Renaissance and the Reformation. It was instead the mere defense of the Catholic Church, a great institution but not an eternal, spiritual, and moral ideal.[183] While the Counterreformation did indeed bring forth austere men, heroic missionaries, spotless and generous souls, these virtuous figures lacked moral inventiveness – that is, the faculty of creating new and progressive forms of ethical life.[184] Moral enthusiasm withered away, and Italy fell into decline with respect to the other countries. Counterreformation, Jesuitism, pomposity, fetish about titles, races in cere-monies, duellism, bad taste, baroquism, empty virtuosity, scientific hair-splitting – all these became specific characters of the Italian way of life, so much so that one said that Italy was now taking a rest. Italy "was amusing itself

subject see Giorgio Spini, *Ricerca dei libertini. La teoria dell'impostura delle religioni nel Seicento italiano*, Florence: La Nuova Italia, 1983 (first edition, Rome: Editrice Universale, 1950). "E perciò non è un paradosso nemmeno affermare che il Seicento Italiano, pure così affollato di chiese e di monasteri, pure così occhiutamente vigilato da teologi e da inquisitori, è privo di un fondamentale connotato cristiano, in ragione appunto della sua natura di età immobile, di età senza speranza ed insoddisfazione, di età prosternata davanti a ciò che è storico e contingente, invece che davanti a ciò che è eterno ed eternamente sollecitante," pp. 43–44; and "Il Seicento italiano è in parte enorme prigionia dell'uomo nel presente, nel dato naturale od in quello istituzionale, rinunzia a guardare avanti, dominio di legisti o di dommatici, piutosto che di profeti; età profondamente immanentistica, neopagana, non cristi-ana," pp. 45–46.

[183] Benedetto Croce, *Storia della età barocca in Italia. Pensiero. Poesia e letteratura. Vita morale*, p. 10.

[184] In a seminal essay, Delio Cantimori (1904–1966) has written that, around 1550, Italian reformers reached the conclusion that in Italy there was no chance of religious reform and that there was no true church ("non vi è forma alcuna di chiesa"). The few reformers who resolved to stay in Italy became utterly impious and corrupt: without God and without religion ("senza Dio e senza alcuna religione"). Preaching became meager and cold. The only available alterna-tives were to go into exile or to adapt to the Catholic religion and its corrupt mores. Italian Calvinists listened to their preachers coming from Geneva and devoutly read the Bible with them. But their faith was lacking the fanatical engagement of their northern brothers. See Delio Cantimori, *Prospettive di storia ereticale*, Bari: Laterza, 1960, pp. 445–452. Federico Chabod (1901–1960) too has written a very fine page on the failure of the hopes for political and religious reform in Italy: "during the crisis of the sixteenth century, political protest and religious protest came into the world at a single birth pang: exceedingly different, indeed, antithetical as to objective and in terms of means and tone, and therefore not nourished on the same spirit of reaction against the immediate past, but germinating in the same climate of general anguish, doubt, and unease; destined, both one and the other, to failure, at least in practical and immediate terms, and to be followed, rather than by the redemption of Italy at the hands of a prince of great virtue, by the definitive establishment of Spanish dominion. [. . .] The 'return to principles' took place in neither of the two fields: Machiavelli was succeeded by Ammirato and Botero, well content that so much of Italy had come under the domination of His Catholic Majesty; while Valdés and Ochino and the other reformers were succeeded by the diocesan synods of the Counter Reformation"; Federico Chabod, *Per la storia religiosa dello Stato di Milano durante il dominio di Carlo V*, Bologna: Zanichelli, 1938, p. 85.

and was laughing, laughing at everything and everyone, and even at itself."[185] Amid all the laughing, the Catholic Church taught a religiosity that pushed towards civil decadence. Closed to any attempt to lead souls back to that realm where they find themselves alone before God and humbled before divine grace, the Catholic Church vehemently refuted what had been the best elements of the Reformation. Croce concluded that the religiosity of the Counterreformation curbed bad passions but did not become a foundation for civil and ethical life. It remained a legalistic and outward religiosity, a spirit completely opposed to prophecy.[186]

No prophet, however inspired and eloquent, was able to infuse aspirations of liberty in the hearts and minds of a people that did not have faith in its own power and that had even lost the desire to redeem itself from religious and political servitude. A Catholic Church capable of controlling individual consciences; prophets preaching self-denial and self-annihilation; reason of state advocating for the conservation of existing governments, both good and bad; utopists designing perfect republics that existed nowhere: all these intellectual trends contributed to make the Italians deaf to prophets of emancipation. Only one additional step was necessary to complete the process of closing Italian hearts and minds to visions of emancipation: to proclaim that prophets are impostors or fools.

3.5 PROPHETS ARE IMPOSTORS OR FOOLS

The most direct attack against prophets came from the quarters of philosophers who proclaimed that Moses, Jesus, and Muhammad were nothing but astute impostors. The earliest document reporting this allegation was the long and violent encyclical letter of July 1, 1239, in which Pope Gregory IX accused Frederick II of saying that Christ, Moses, and Muhammad had deceived the whole word ("*totum mundum fuisse deceptum*"). The *Vita Gregorii IX*, a text from 1240 most probably authored by Iohannes de Ferentino, confirms the same accusation against Frederick II. Around 1252, Alberico of Trois-Fontaines wrote in his *Chronica* that the emperor impiously declared that Moses, Christ, and Muhammad were "baratores sive guillatores."[187] This school of thought continued into the fourteenth and fifteenth centuries. In his commentary on Dante's *Divine Comedy*, Benvenuto of Imola attributed the blasphemous belief of the three impostors to Averroes. A noteworthy variation in the tradition is found in a letter of Pope Pius II (Enea Silvio Piccolomini) dated November 14, 1459, that denounces a priest from Bergamo who claimed that Christ did not die to redeem mankind. The priest instead proclaimed not

---

[185] Benedetto Croce, *Storia della età barocca in Italia*, p. 51.   [186] Ibid., p. 498.

[187] See Mario Esposito, "Una manifestazione d'incredulità religiosa nel medioevo: il detto dei 'Tre Impostori' e la sua trasmissione da Federico II a Pomponazzi,"*Archivio Storico Italiano* 89 (1931): pp. 3–48.

only that Christ died because of the inescapable influence of stars (*"stellarum necessitate"*), but also that Christ himself, as well as Moses and Muhammad, governed the world to satisfy their desire for power. According to this line of thinking, either all their laws are false and therefore they have deceived the whole world, or at least two of them are false and therefore they have deceived the greatest part of the world.[188]

The theory of the three impostors gained popularity, and took up new and more radical contents, in the age of the Counterreformation. A vociferous proponent of the theory was Giulio Cesare Vanini (1585–1619), an Italian libertine, eventually condemned to a horrible death by the Parliament of Toulouse. To begin with, he claimed that the fundamental tenet of prophecy, divine inspiration, is clearly false. Divine inspiration plays no role whatsoever for prophets.[189] Aware rather that human beings would not believe new prophets unless they saw them perform miracles, the heavens concentrated in the prophet all the natural qualities and powers that they normally distribute to animals, plants, and rocks. Endowed by so many natural powers (*"naturali impetu"*), the prophet accomplishes extraordinary things and persuades people. To stress the purely natural cause of prophecies, Vanini remarked that prophets and sibyls are under the influence of melancholic humors (*"humori melancholico"*). He also asserted that prophets do not appear in all parts of the world, and that it is utterly impossible to have prophets near the poles because the climate there prevents the mind from obtaining the purity that prophecy requires.[190]

Vanini reinforced the theory of the impostors with the argument that Christ, "the wisest among the prophets" (*"Prophetarum Sapientissimus"*), invented the theory of the antichrist to ensure that his law would last forever. Not only does he maintain that Christ wanted to be sacrificed (*"Oblatus est Christus quia ipse voluit"*), he also writes that Moses wanted that his people venerated him above all the prophets and believed that he was not subject to death.[191] Fear was the origin of religious sentiments. Easy to be deceived, the populace

---

[188] "Non est peccatum illud concedere, immo necesse est concedere aut quod totus mundus decipitur aut saltemmaior pars. Nam supposito quod tantum sint tres leges, Christi scilicet, Moysis et Mahumethi, aut igitur omnes sunt falsae, et sic totus mundus est deceptus; aut saltem duae earum, et sic maior pars est decepta"; see ibid., p. 57.

[189] "Caesaris Vanini Neapolitani Theologi, Philosophi, et Iuris utriusque Doctoris," *De Admirandis Naturae Regina Deaque Mortalium Arcanis Libri quatuor*, Paris: Apud Adrianum Perier, 1616, in Giulio Cesare Vanini, *Tutte opere*, edited by Francesco Paolo Raimondi and Mario Carparelli, Milan: Bompiani, 2010, p. 1404-1408. The philosopher and astrologer Giovan Battista Della Porta, a contemporary of Vanini, attributed prophecy to the influx of the planet Mercury. Under the influx of Mercury are also the fraudulent. The "Mercuriali," he writes, are "amici fedeli, indovini, sortilegi, auguri, e adorni d'interpretazion divina, ancora mercantia, ambasciatori, oratori, & huomini, che spesso ingannano con astutia fraudolente"; Giovan Battista Della Porta, *La fisionomia dell'huomo et la celeste. Libri sei*, Venice: Nicolò Pezzana, 1668, p. 445.

[190] Ibid., p. 1354.   [191] Ibid., p. 1356.

believed in religion for it promised life after death.[192] On the contrary, philosophers could not be fooled, and rightly considered religion as a means to preserve and expand the state. However useful, religions remain hoaxes invented by priests.[193] God operates in the world, by way of the heavens. When He wants to warn human beings, He connects to them in dreams.[194] Miracles too are the effects of natural causes. The stars concentrate in a single individual all the natural powers that are normally dispersed in many individuals.[195] Celestial bodies operate by divine mandate (*"ex Dei mandato"*). However, they have the power of governing religions' growth and decline, and of empowering those founders of religions who are called sons of God. Special astrological conjunctions produce the birth of new religions that replace the ancient ones (*"Religiones opus esse stellarum"*).[196] For Vanini, prophets are simply wise men longing for holy honors and eternal fame. Wishing to be considered omnipotent, they do nothing more than take credit for miracles that are simply the outcome of celestial bodies' natural powers.[197]

Most probably composed around 1659, the anonymous *Theophrastus redivivus* is another work that continued and refined the belief that prophets are impostors.[198] According to the *Theophrastus*, all religions are fraudulent artifices and deceptions that serve the purpose of sustaining political institutions by teaching the plebs that God presides over the work of founders and legislators.[199] Moses was the greatest example of an impostor. To begin with, he was not the author of *Deuteronomy*, and his alleged miracles were nothing but clever tricks. He was surely a very able politician and governor (*"artis politicae et regnandi scientiae peritissimus"*). Even if he astutely took advantage of the ignorance and stupidity of his people, he succeeded in the hard task of imposing new and fair laws on them. For this achievement, Moses deserves to be admired as the most glorious man of all times. As for Christian religion, the author of the *Theophrastus* denounces dogmas, traditions, and rituals as contrary to natural reason (*"ratio naturalis"*). Moreover, they are but inventions of priests that distract from Christ's true teaching. While the author recognizes Christ as a very wise and excellent man (*"sapientem et preclarum hominem"*), he flatly denies Christ's divinity. Like all human beings, Christ was under the power of

---

[192] Ibid., p. 1362.   [193] "Nihil aliud quam sacerdotum imposturas fuisse"; ibid., p. 1364.

[194] Ibid., p. 1386.   [195] Ibid., p. 1392.   [196] Ibid., pp. 1392 and 1394.

[197] "Quare vir sapiens, sacros aeterni nominis honores appetens, cum haec futura praevided, Prophetam a Deo missum se praedicat, quaeque necessaria coelestium corporum vi miracula fiunt, confictae sui ipsius omnipotentiae adscribit atque ita delusa plebecula illum admiratur et adorat"; ibid., p. 1398.

[198] See Eugenio Garin, "Da Campanella a Vico," *Dal Rinascimento all'Illuminismo. Studi e ricerche*, Pisa: Nistri-Lischi, 1970, pp. 79–117, in particular p. 87, n.9. See also *Theophrastus redivivus*, edited by Guido Canziani and Gianni Paganini, vol. I, Florence: La Nuova Italia Editrice, 1981, pp. xv–lxviii.

[199] Tullio Gregory, *Theophrastus redivivus. Erudizione e ateismo nel Seicento*, Naples: Morano, 1970, pp. 156–195.

the stars and subject to the natural laws of generation, growth, and death. He was not fulfilling a divine design or having a divine nature. Christ did nothing more than carry out the mission which a special conjunction of stars (*"concursus caelorum"*) conferred upon him. As the Gospels clearly show, he had human passions like fear, hope, and love. His miracles are like those that Moses and Numa performed. If we accept alleged miracles as evidence of a divine nature, Moses and Numa too – along with many others – were gods. Like Moses, Christ too was an impostor who was eager to attain glory and fame (*"ex imposture excogitate, sive ad famam et gloriam consequendam"*) by founding a new religion: a religion that, like all other religions, was a very useful political art.[200] Unlike his ambitiously vain and avaricious successors and vicars, though, Christ did not long for political power. Leaving Christ's moral dignity aside, priests and popes of later centuries inculcated superstitions and false beliefs into people's minds by preying on their fears and hopes. Indeed, this exploitation rendered the people but threads in the institutional Church's hegemonic fabric. The author of the *Theophrastus* concludes that wise men must remain distant from the world, for it is only by doing such that they can cultivate their moral liberty and enjoy the happiness of a mind free from the errors that prophets spread among the plebs.

Le Traité des trois imposteurs ou Esprit de Mr. Spinosa was another anonymous text written around the end of the seventeenth century. Published in 1719, it forcefully denounced the prophets Moses, Christ, and Muhammad as impostors. The author claimed that prophets do not have any special wisdom on religious matters.[201] With harsh words, he then directly attacked prophets' pretentions of being inspired God.[202] The author claims that people

---

[200] "Atque haec sunt quae de Christo eiusque religionis fide dicuntur, ut ostendatur hanc non esse ab aliis diversam et eodem quo caeteras inniti fundamentum, fabulis videlicet ex arte politica ad commodum et utilitatem publicam confictis"; ibid., p. 166.

[201] "En effet il n'est besoin ni de hautes spéculations, ni de pénétrer fort avant dans les Secrets de la Nature, il ne faut qu'un peu de bon sens, pour voir que DIEU n'est ni *colére*, ni *jaloux*, que la *Justice* & la *Miséricorde* sont de faux tîtres qu'on lui attribüe, & qu'enfin rien de ce que les *Prophétes* & les *Apôtres* en ont dit, ne constitüe ni sa Nature, ni son Essence. A parler sans fard, & à dire la chose comme elle est, il est certain que ces Gens-là [les prophètes et les apôtres] n'étoient ni plus habiles, ni mieux instruits que le reste des Hommes sur ces Articles. Bien loin de cela, ce qu'ils en disent est si grossier, qu'il faut être Peuple pour le croire": *Le Traité des trois imposteurs ou Esprit de Mr. Spinosa*. I.4. I am citing from *Trattato dei tre impostori. La vita e lo spirito del Signor Benedetto de Spinoza*, edited by Sivia Berti, Turin: Einaudi, 1984, p. 68.

[202] "Mais pour leur Esprit, on prétend que DIEU le dirigeoit par une *Inspiration* immédiate, & que leur Entendement étoit bien plus éclairé que le nôtre. Il faut avoüer que le Peuple a bien du penchant à s'aveugler. On lui a dit que DIEU aimoit mieux les *Prophétes* que le reste des Hommes; qu'il se communiquoit à eux particuliérement, & il en est aussi fermement persuadé que si la chose lui étoit démontrée. Et sans considérer que tous les ont tous un même il croit que ces Gens-là étoient d'une trempe extraordinaire, & faits exprès pour débiter les *Oracles* de DIEU"; ibid., I. 5, p. 68.

were wiser in ancient times. For this reason, they did not hold prophets in great admiration, but even put them to death when they disrupted the obedience that peoples owed to their legitimate kings. While Christ was executed, Moses escaped punishment only because he had an army under his command.[203] The true goal of prophets and legislators was to attain perennial fame (*"éterniser leur mémoire"*) by making people believe that they were secretly talking with the divine. As Moses did, however, they had often to resort to force in order to succeed. If we read the scriptures carefully, we can easily notice how often prophets contradict themselves. They assert that God is invisible, but then they assure us that they have seen him in one form or another; they say that God is good, sweet, benign, merciful, patient, but then they say that he is severe, terrible, fearsome, and takes pleasure in punishing sinners.[204] To believe the contradictory assertions of prophets, one must be as coarse and stupid as the people who believed that a golden calf was the God who delivered them from slavery in Egypt. All religions are distant from common sense and ordinary human intelligence. Yet, people have faith in the prophets because they think prophets are rare and excellent souls who have received an extraordinary and celestial revelation (*"revelation extraordinaire & celeste"*).[205] The author states that religions are born and prosper by way of exclusively human means. If it were true that religions come from a direct intervention of God, everyone would hold the same faith and there would be no dissensions and no conflicts over religious matters.

Following Machiavelli's steps, the author then declares that all ancient and modern legislators persuaded their peoples that they had received their laws from a divinity. To achieve their goal, these legislators spread revelations and prophecies to scare, astound, shake, encourage, and harden the people as circumstances required. Prophets like Moses, Numa Pompilius, Jesus Christ, and Muhammad do not give us a true idea of God. They are impostors (*"sont des impostures"*) who deserve to be rejected by all those who love truth. To deceive peoples, prophets proclaim that direct communication with God allows them to predict future events.[206] The best impostors have been the great legislators, for they astutely took advantage of people's desire to know their fate. Moses, Numa Pompilius, Jesus Christ, and Muhammad were all ambitious men who persuaded ignorant peoples that they had received their laws from a God or Goddess.[207] The author claims that Moses was the cleverest of

---

[203] "Aussi voyons nous, que dans l'ancienne Loy, on n'avoit pas pour les *Prophétes* autant d'estime qu'on en a aujourd'huy. Lorsqu'on étoit las de leur *babil*, qui ne tendoit le plus souvent qu'à détourner le Peuple de l'obéissance qu'il devoit à ses Roys légitimes, on les faisoit taire par divers Supplices; jusques là, que JÉSUS CHRIST succomba, parce qu'il n'avoit pas, comme MOYSE, une Armée à sa suite pour deffendre ses Opinions"; ibid., I.5, p. 70.

[204] Ibid., I.6, pp. 72–74.   [205] Ibid., XIII.7, p. 168.   [206] Ibid., IV.8, p. 106.

[207] "Ils les avoient reçûes d'un Dieu, ou d'une Déesse"; ibid., V.1, p. 111.

them. After all, he was able to convince the Jews (who had been expelled from Egypt because they carried a horrible disease) that he was their commander by God's order, and that God himself had declared that the Jews would be His chosen people so long as they obeyed his commands.

To reinforce his authority over the people, Moses feigned miracles and withdrew in solitude under the pretext that he needed to confer secretly with God. When a few enlightened men discovered his ruses, Moses showed he was more a tyrant than a father figure, and, like a true politician, he did not hesitate to resort to unleashing most unjust and cruel violence upon his own people. Staging even his death in a way that did not allow the people to find his body, he convinced them that God had assumed him into heaven.[208] Numa Pompilius resorted to similar tricks to inspire the fear of God in the ignorant, ferocious, and superstitious Romans. Wanting to equal Moses' fame, Jesus Christ succeeded in amassing many followers by persuading them that the Holy Spirit was his father and that his mother was a virgin. Used to hearing and trusting in dreams and fantasies, the poor Jews believed everything he wanted them to believe (*"crurent tout ce qu'il voulut"*).[209] Christ was just as astute as the other legislators, but, unlike Moses and Muhammad, he made the great political mistake of failing to take the right measures to protect himself (*"le plus grand défaut de sa Politique a été de navoir pas pourvu assez à sa sûreté"*).[210]

Such libertine critiques of religious imposture had a significant impact on the works of the leading Italian freethinker Alberto Radicati di Passarano (1698–1737). In his *Parallel between Muhamed and Sosem* (1732), he called Moses (Sosem, in the text) a tyrant and an impostor who "established religious Ordinances altogether new, and opposite to those of all other men and Countries," in order to "ensure the Subjection of the Nation to himself forever."[211] In his *Discourses concerning Religion and Government* (1734), Radicati claimed that Moses was not "really inspired and chosen by God to declare his Will to Men," but a man who "only persuaded himself that he was, and had a mind to persuade the Jews of it too."[212] Legislators, not God, introduced religion in civil societies to provide solid foundations for their states. Religions are "no more than the product of human mind." If God is perfect, eternal, and immutable, his laws too must be perfect, eternal, and immutable – as is the case with the true divine law, the law of nature. On the

---

[208] Ibid., V.3, p. 112.   [209] Ibid., VII.1, p. 121.   [210] Ibid., VII.1, p. 122.

[211] Alberto Radicati di Passerano, *A Parallel between Muhamed and Sosem, the Great Deliverer of the Jews by Zelim Musulman: in a Letter to Nathan Rabby*, London: J. Harbert, 1732, p. 23. On Alberto Radicati di Passerano, see Franco Venturi, *Saggi sull'Europa illuminista. I. Alberti Radicati di Passerano*, Turin: Einaudi, 1954.

[212] Alberto Radicati di Passerano, *Twelve Discourses concerning Religion and Government Inscribed to all Lovers of Truth and Liberty*, Second Edition, London (no publisher given), 1734, pp. 229–230.

other hand, the laws that all religions have spread throughout the world "confound the notions of Moral good and evil," and "deprive men of their natural right and then erect a Tyranny in the world."[213] Radicati wanted to emancipate his fellow human beings from the errors that religious impostors had instilled in their minds. He wished to inspire them "with Virtue and Courage enough to shake off the yoke that galls them." Yet, Radicati dismally acknowledged that the moral and political emancipation he hoped for was "almost impossible" because tyrants are too strong, and because oppressed peoples have neither the strength nor the resolution to extricate themselves out of their misery. Only princes – not prophets – could emancipate peoples from "the Tyranny of priests," if they are willing and able to unite in their hands both political and religious power. Since religions owe their rise to princes or legislators, they must be subject to the prince, not vice versa, and both princes and peoples must not listen to prophets.

The eminent historian Pietro Giannone (1676–1748) also contributed on philosophy's behalf to the assault against prophecy. Vehemently attacked by the Church, Giannone's *Istoria civile del Regno di Napoli* (1723) states that Campanella was a man with a turbid and restless mind who attempted social upheavals because he resented the punishments he suffered from the Church of Rome.[214] Asserting that he was inspired by God and that God had sent him to liberate the peoples oppressed by the king of Spain and his dignitaries, Campanella promised to institute a free republic. As Giannone dissects these vicissitudes, he labels Campanella an ambitious impostor who allowed followers to greet him as the new messiah.[215] In his *Discorsi sopra gli Annali di Tito Livio* (1738), Giannone presents Livy as a wise historian who ridiculed the people's superstitions and who explained omens, dreams, and visions in purely natural terms (*"secondo il corso di natura"*).[216] He also praises Livy's condemnation of the priests' and augurs' shrewdness and cunning (*"l'accortezza e la furberia de' sacerdoti e degli àuguri"*) when they deceive the people with their prophecies.[217] In full agreement with Livy, he regarded the Roman religion as the main cause of civic peace and military prowess. Romulus deserves special commendation because he instilled fear of the divinities in the Roman plebs with simulations and lies. In the centuries that followed and in diverse cultural contexts, many valiant captains encouraged their soldiers by making them

---

[213] Ibid., pp. 225.

[214] Pietro Giannone, *Istoria civile del Regno di Napoli*, vol. X, Milan: Società Tipografica de' Classici Italiani, 1823, pp. 352–353.

[215] Ibid., p. 354.

[216] Pietro Giannone, *Discorsi sopra gli annali di Tito Livio*, in *Opere di Pietro Giannone*, edited by Sergio Bertelli and Giuseppe Ricuperati, vol. 1, Milan-Naples: Riccardo Ricciardi, 1972, p. 748.

[217] Ibid., pp. 754–755.

believe that they could count on God's help. Whereas prophets had lost the respect of enlightened scholars, religious simulation was held in high esteem.

3.6 THE REVOLUTION OF THE PHILOSOPHERS AND THE COUNTERREVOLUTION OF THE PROPHETS

Vilified as impostors, derided as fools, and denounced as supporters of tyranny, prophets were no longer credible in eighteenth-century Italy.[218] The prevailing persuasion was that the philosophers, immune from popular illusions and prejudices, ought to take the prophets' place. This line of thinking marked a radical change in the history of political and social emancipation. To put philosophers in place of prophets meant to present emancipation as a conquest of reason, not as the triumph of God's will. Philosophers teach; prophets inspire. If the task of moral and political emancipation was to transform consciences, to instill the determination to fight and suffer, to give hope – as was the case in Italy – then teaching with reason was not enough. To accomplish such a task, the inspiration that only prophets have and can offer their fellow citizens is required.

Gaetano Filangieri (1752–1788) was the most prominent and respected advocate of the idea that enlightened philosophers must be the leaders of political emancipation. Published for the first time in 1791, his *Scienza della legislazione* claimed that religious experience was not a superstitious fraud but a powerful force for social unification that responded to the demands of the multitudes. From these premises, Filangieri derived the idea of a civil religion that would proceed from the lodges of the Freemasons to the elites and then to the populace at large. Such a civil religion ought to fight against fanaticism and irreligiosity. Through legislative measures, it should put an end to the privileges enjoyed by the clergy, as well as to the existence of a Church that was separate from and hostile to the civil power.[219] Filangieri theorized a gradual transition from the old superstitious religion to the new civil religion. In his project, reform did not mean a return to the original principles of the Christian faith,

---

[218] The text that best represents the rational critique of prophecy is Voltaire's *Dictionnaire philosophique*, published in 1764, where we read: "il faut convenir que c'est un méchant métier que celui de prophète. Pour un seul qui, comme Élie, va se promener de planètes en planètes dans un beau carrosse de lumière, traîné par quatre chevaux blancs, il y en a cent qui vont à pied, et qui sont obligés d'aller demander leur dîner de porte en porte." Since prophecies are a mass of contradictory and often absurd assertions, Voltaire sarcastically remarks, we need the power of the Church to distinguish true from false prophets, and in this way we contribute to reinforce the secular powers of bishops and abbots. Voltaire, *Dictionnaire philosophique*, vol. 20, Paris: Garnier, 1878, pp. 280–294.

[219] Gaetano Filangieri, *Scienza della legislazione*, I, Milan: Giuseppe Galeazzi Regio Stampatore, 1791, pp. 57–58. I am quoting from Vincenzo Ferrone, *La società giusta ed equa: Repubblicanesimo e diritti dell'uomo in Gaetano Filangieri*, Bari and Rome: Laterza, 2003, p. 154.

but rather the construction of a new theological and moral edifice. Once the civil power has discredited the old religion and its superstitions, it could establish new rites and ceremonies "controlled by the concealed hand of the legislator" that would constitute the new religion of the state and of the government.[220]

According to Filangieri, philosophers ought to define the dogmas of the new religion. In turn, the legislator should translate these dogmas into civil laws and then outline sanctions that would persuade citizens to obey the principles of the civil religion.[221] After providing a detailed indication of the new religion's educational and social purposes, the essay ends with the exhortation to the legislator to avoid the two extremes of fanaticism and irreligion.[222] Death prevented Filangieri from completing his essay. From the table of contents that he had drafted, however, we have a clear idea that he intended to complete his project with a precise set of rules designed to select and instruct a new clergy capable of implementing the new civil religion. In the entire essay, there is not even a single word on the need to have prophets to inspire the new religion in the hearts of the people. Filangieri only needed philosophers to specify the dogmas, and the legislator to implement these dogmas with the force of law. His new civil religion was the product of a rational vision. It had the strength of rational principles but lacked prophetic pathos.[223]

In the "Jacobin years" (1796–1799), visions and projects of political emancipation flourished in the republics born under the shadow of the French armies. With greater or lesser conviction and wisdom, they tried to corroborate new political institutions with a republican religion founded on reason. A fierce proponent of a new philosophical republican religion was Girolamo Bocalosi, author of *Dell'educazione democratica da darsi al popolo italiano* (1797). Following in the footsteps of Rousseau, Bocalosi's book theorizes a full-fledged religious revolution: not just a new interpretation of Christianity, but an entirely new religion that was supposed to destroy Christianity's dogmas, language, and rites. Since the Christian religion was incapable of regenerating the people, it was necessary to elaborate new principles that could effectively educate good citizens.[224] A radical political revolution needed the support of an equally radical religious and moral revolution.[225]

---

[220] Vincenzo Ferrone, *La società giusta ed equa*, p. 153. See also Luigi Salvatorelli, "Il problema religioso nel Risorgimento," *Atti del XXXIII Congresso di Storia del Risorgimento Italiano*, Rome: Istituto per la Storia del Risorgimento Italiano, 1958, p. 9.

[221] "Le sue sanzioni dovrebbero partire dal dogma dell'altra vita, ma questo dogma non dovrebbe contenere alcuno di que' principi, che possono eluderne i preziosi effetti"; Vincenzo Ferrone, *La società giusta ed equa*, p. 99.

[222] Ibid., p. 100.   [223] Ibid., pp. 354–355.

[224] Girolamo Bocalosi, "Dell'educazione democratica da darsi al popolo italiano," *Giacobini italiani*, vol. II, edited by Delio Cantimori and Renzo De Felice, Bari: Laterza, 1964, pp. 144–145.

[225] Ibid., p. 147.

Enrico Michele L'Aurora (1760–1803?), another Jacobin militant, offered in lieu of prophecy a new theology of the Supreme Being. In *All'Italia nelle tenebre l'aurora porta la luce* (1796), he denounced "the wickedness and ignorance of the ecclesiastics," who were guilty of having for centuries deceived the people with countless falsehoods and of having preached a gospel of resignation.[226] In contrast to the temporal power and corruption of the Church, L'Aurora exalted the figure of Christ.[227] Yet, he did not want to set in motion a reformation that might call religious practice back to its first principles. From his praise of Christ, L'Aurora derived the dream of a rational religion founded upon the belief that God is the Supreme Being who is good in the highest degree and the creator of heaven and earth. In L'Aurora's fervid imagination, the new rational religion would replace an old, superstitious Catholicism, and would educate the people in the ways of peace, tolerance, and respect for republican values.

Matteo Galdi (1765–1821) also invoked a new civil religion. A friend of the great conspirator Filippo Buonarroti, Galdi attained high public honors in the Cisalpine Republic, and then under Gioacchino Murat in Naples, where he died in 1821. Rallying against the central tenets of prophetic visions of emancipation, he claimed that Christianity cannot be reformed: "However pure and innocent this cult may have been in its beginnings, it is now too corrupt to be drawn back to its proper boundaries; too many factions and religious wars would be ignited between the reformed and the reformers; too insolent, avaricious, and ignorant are its ministers to be able to be summoned back to the right way."[228] From this observation, Galdi draws the conclusion that it was necessary to establish a completely new religion that he called "*teofilantropismo*" (theophilanthropism), founded upon the principle of the love of God and our neighbor. For Galdi, only such a theophilanthropic cult could eradicate superstitions and terminate Christianity's political influence. A product of the republican revolution, the new religion was in his view the only creed consistent with the progress of the human spirit.[229]

A man of great moral and civic virtue, and a martyr of the Neapolitan republic, Vincenzo Russo (1770–1799) advocated most passionately for the project of political emancipation without prophecy. He theorized the possibility of uprooting superstition through the work of a censor who, with unequivocal facts and luminous words, would demonstrate to the people that a morality independent from theology was possible. Russo believed that oppressed people would love the new morality from the moment enlightened philosophers

---

[226] Enrico Michele l'Aurora, "All'Italia nelle tenebre l'aurora porta la luce," *Giacobini italiani*, vol. I, p. 173.

[227] Ibid.

[228] Matteo Galdi, "Saggio d'istruzione pubblica rivoluzionaria," *Giacobini italiani*, vol. I, pp. 242–243.

[229] Ibid., p. 242.

announced it.[230] For him, a civil religion was the only religion that ought to exist in a republic.[231] Russo had nothing against those who in good faith adore "a God of peace," that is, a God who teaches the faithful to love their neighbors.[232] He also conceded that religion can stimulate men to act in ways that remain beneficial to civil life. He forcefully emphasized, however, that good republican institutions can obtain the same results – with notably lesser dangers – by leaving religion aside: indeed, by trying to extinguish religion and replace it with a rational ethics defined by philosophers.[233]

The founder of the Republic of Alba in April 1796, Giovanni Antonio Ranza (1741–1801) championed a religious reform over the foundation of completely new religion. The reform he envisioned would amount to a return to the ethos of equality and democratic liberty present during the earliest times of the Christian Church. In *For the republican Lombardy* (*Per la Lombardia repubblicana*), he announced a "religious reform" that would correspond "to the simplicity and dignity of the democratic government." The reformed religion should set itself the task of "reforming abuses, uprooting errors, banishing superstition, and preserving only truly Catholic and apostolic dogmas." Replacing casuistical morality with evangelical morality, and simplifying the ridiculous mess of ceremonies endlessly multiplied over the course of sixteen centuries, this properly reformed Christianity would be of precious service to republican liberty.[234]

In the intellectual context of the Neapolitan Revolution, Eleonora de Fonseca Pimentel (1752–1799) deserves special attention for the purity of her religious sentiment, her devotion to the republican cause, and the strength with which she faced martyrdom. Imbued with charity, Pimentel was a woman of a true Christian faith that was far from dogmas and aimed at alleviating the human condition in the world. As long as the Neapolitan Republic was alive, Eleonora worked for the newspaper *Monitore Napoletano* and tirelessly explained how the Christian religion commands the defense of liberty. In one of its first issues on February 5, 1799, she stressed that the republican government must exhort the clergy to teach republican principles with the same zeal they had utilized to preach the word of Christ.[235] While Pimentel may have deceived herself about the civic consciousness of the Neapolitan clergy, she aptly identified that the religious and moral education of the people was urgently necessary, if the Republic was to be saved. Although the task was indeed urgent, it remained impossible because time was short and the number of priests willing to become preachers of liberty exiguous. In an article titled

---

[230] Vincenzio Russo, "Pensieri politici," *Giacobini italiani*, vol. I, pp. 321–322.

[231] Ibid., p. 371. [232] Ibid., p. 372. [233] Ibid., p. 373.

[234] Giovanni Antonio Ranza, "Della vera chiesa istituita da Gesù Cristo," *Giacobini italiani*, vol. I, p. 218.

[235] Giorgio Spini, *Una "testimone della verità". Eleonora de Fonseca Pimentel tra impegno civile e riflessione etico-religiosa*, Naples: La Città del Sole, 2007, p. 63.

"Gli ecclesiastici e la repubblica" (*"The clergy and the Republic"*), published in the *Monitore* on February 19, 1799, Pimentel argued that a priest's duty was to provide an example of loyalty and obedience to the laws of the fatherland. The brotherhood that the Gospel teaches is the same brotherhood that the Republic promotes, that is, the brotherhood of true democracy.[236] The right foundation of the Republic was for her the Gospel.[237]

Pimentel was not alone in propounding Christian religion as a friend of democracy. Several Catholic sermons were adorned to greater or lesser degrees by historical arguments and biblical references. An example is the leaflet *La Religion cattolica amica della democrazia: Instruzione d'un teologo al clero e al popolo romano*, which was printed in Perugia in 1798. Its author wanted to instruct the people about the perfect agreement between religion, summoned back to its pure principles, and democratic government, rightly represented.[238] Since religion and politics share the principle of divine order, they must support each other and be loyal to republican institutions.[239] Proponents of despotism maintain that monarchy is the form of government most consistent with the Christian religion.[240] Yet, on the basis of sacred texts, the form of government that is more consistent with Christian religion is in fact democracy. Democratic government functions in a state where the people freely elect the magistrates, dictate the laws to themselves, and create their presidents and ministers. In sum, it is a regime in which the government depends on the absolute will of the nation.[241] The Christian religion precisely supports and elevates the fundamental republican principle of liberty.[242] Moreover, Christ taught liberty in its truest sense: liberty of the spirit and liberty from bad laws and customs. He also taught a love of virtue, which, together with liberty, constitutes the basis upon which republican government rests. Terror, force, violence, vile and shameful licentiousness all support despotism. Virtue alone creates and preserves democracy. Religion, furthermore, advocates a respect for laws. Wherever the people's customs are informed by the majestic and divine morality of the Gospel, there will certainly be a happy democracy.[243]

[236] Ibid., pp. 68–69.
[237] Ibid., pp. 30–31. See also Benedetto Croce, *La rivoluzione napoletana del 1799: biografie, racconti, ricerche*, Bari: Laterza, 1948.
[238] *La Religion cattolica amica della democrazia. Instruzione d'un teologo al clero e al popolo romano*, Perugia: Carlo Baduel e Figli stampatori nazionali, 1798, in Vittorio E. Giuntella, *La Religione amica della democrazia. I cattolici democratici del Triennio rivoluzionario (1796–1799)*, Rome: Studium, 1990, p. 166. See also *I preti della libertà*, edited by Alfonso Gargano, Naples: Magmata, 2000; Domenico Scarfoglio, *Lazzari e giacobini. Cultura popolare e rivoluzione a Napoli nel 1799*, Naples: L'ancora, 1999.
[239] *La Religion cattolica amica della democrazia. Instruzione d'un teologo al clero e al popolo romano*, in Vittorio E. Giuntella, *La Religione amica della democrazia. I cattolici democratici del Triennio rivoluzionario (1796–1799)*, p. 167.
[240] Ibid., p. 169.   [241] Ibid., pp. 172–174.   [242] Ibid., p. 175.   [243] Ibid., pp. 176–178.

The preachers of the new religion were confident in their ability to radically change the minds of their fellow compatriots and to convert them into fervent supporters of democracy. In *I Diritti dell'uomo. Catechismo Cattolico-democratico del cittadino*, the Catholic priest Riccardo Bartoli (1747–1806) wrote that a people corrupted by erroneous religious education can be transformed into "a people of excellent citizens."[244] He insisted that Christ was a perfect democrat who proposed an interpretation of Christianity as a religion that instills virtue. Charitable towards the humble and the suffering, Christ was uncompromising with the arrogant and the corrupt:

Easy to prove is his [Christ's] inflexibility in resisting, correcting and discrediting the insolence, haughtiness, shrewdness and detestable deceit of the Pharisees, the scribes, the pseudo-pontiffs and all the other proscribed race of the chiefs of the Sanhedrin and of the Synagogue, who were the most predominant and overbearing aristocrats of those days. They always kept separate from the people, conferred upon themselves a grand air of dominion, and thought they would have vilified themselves, had they familiarized with the people.[245]

In the pamphlet *La libertà e la legge considerate nella libertà delle opinioni e nella tolleranza de' culti religiosi* (Genoa, 1798), the Jansenist Vincenzo Palmieri (1753–1820) maintained that virtue and religion are inseparable:

Religion! Majestic virtue, which, starting from the inalterable foundation of every morality, and from the eternal rule of the honest and the just – which is God – fixes in men the true idea of every virtue, and renders it more sublime and more noble to the extent that more sublime and more noble is the principle from which it starts. Religion! Majestic virtue, which, speaking that noble language which is so worth of man – and of God – does not compel, but rather invites, entices, allures: religion that does not want violent, boastful and excessive actions, but teaches sweetness, charity, benevolence, the voluntary subjection to the laws; and not for the fear typical of slaves, but for the sweet pliability of a reasonable and free soul; religion that simply forbids to act through violence, and promises pure and sublime contentements, [*sic*] and the peace of the heart. I wonder if this Religion might be proposed, adopted, established as the foundation and wall of defense for the virtues that are so necessary to the State.[246]

---

[244] Riccardo Bartoli, *I Diritti dell'uomo. Catechismo Cattolico-democratico del cittadino. Riccardo Bartoli M[inore] O[sservante] sacerdote reggiano*, Reggio: Davolio, 1797, in Vittorio E. Giuntella, *La Religione amica della democrazia. I cattolici democratici del Triennio rivoluzionario (1796–1799)*, p. 209. See the corresponding entry edited by Fernando Manzotti, in *Dizionario Biografico degli Italiani*, vol. VI, Rome: Istituto della Enciclopedia Italiana, 1964, pp. 588–590.

[245] Riccardo Bartoli, *I Diritti dell'uomo*, pp. 217–219.

[246] Vincenzo Palmieri (Niceta Tirio), *La libertà e la legge considerate nella libertà delle opinioni e nella tolleranza de' culti religiosi*, Genoa: Olzati, 1798, in Giuntella, *La religione amica della democrazia*, pp. 255–256.

Though their intentions were laudable, republican militants did not know how to persuade the people to embrace the new civic religion that they were striving to institute. In his masterful account of the Neapolitan Revolution of 1799, Vincenzo Cuoco has remarked that in many cases these militants were contemptuous of the very people in whom they wanted to instill republican vigor. Some even carelessly offended "everything that the people had most sacred – their gods, their customs, their very name."[247] Others used totally ineffective declamatory language:

What could be hoped for from the language used in all the proclamations addressed to our people? *"Finally, you are free."* The people did not yet know what liberty was; it is a sentiment, not an idea; it is experienced with facts, not demonstrated with words. *"Your Claudius has fled; Messalina is trembling."* Did the people have to know Roman history to know happiness? *"Humanity wins back all its rights."* Which ones? *"You will have a free and just government, founded on principles of equality; positions will no longer be the exclusive privilege of the noble and wealthy, but the reward for talent and virtue."* A powerful motive for the people, this, who pride themselves on neither virtues nor talent, who want to be governed well and do not aspire to hold positions! *"Let a holy enthusiasm be manifested in all places, let tricolor flags be hoisted, let trees be planted, municipalities, civic guards be organized."* What a collection of ideas, which the people neither understood nor cared about! *"The destinies of Italy must be fulfilled. Scilicet id populo cordi est: ea cura quietos sollicitat animos"* [...] Gently, my dear orator! Up to this point you have been only useless; now you risk also doing some harm.[248]

The philosophers of the Neapolitan Revolution were eloquent, at best. Never were they prophetic. Their voices lacked the warmth that originates from prophetic inspiration. The prophets of the Counterrevolution were much more effective than the revolutionary philosophers. Years before the Neapolitan Revolution erupted in 1799, they began to mount a campaign to persuade the peoples of the southern provinces that God was on the side of the king. A revealing example of Counterrevolutionary use of prophetic discourse

[247] Vincenzo Cuoco, *Saggio storico sulla rivoluzione di Napoli*, edited by Antonino De Francesco, Rome and Bari: Laterza, 2014, p. 157; English translation, Vincenzo Cuoco, *A Historical Essay on the Neapolitan Revolution of 1799*, edited by Bruce Haddock and Filippo Sabetti, Toronto: University of Toronto Press, 2014, pp. 148–149.

[248] Vincenzo Cuoco, *Saggio storico sulla rivoluzione di Napoli*, p. 108; English translation, Vincenzo Cuoco, *A Historical Essay on the Neapolitan Revolution of 1799*, p. 106. Whereas the speeches of the lay militants of the revolution exhibit a philosophical and oratorical style, the sermons that the Catholic priests who supported the revolution delivered in churches abound in citations from the scripture. Their speeches show a consummate mastery of religious eloquence. See *Omelia del cittadino cardinal Chiaramonti vescovo d'Imola diretta al popolo della sua diocesi nella Repubblica cisalpina nel giorno del santissimo Natale l'anno MDCCXCVII* [*Homily by citizen Cardinal Chiaramonti, Bishop of Imola, directed to the people of his diocese within the Cisalpine Republic, on the day of holy Christmas, year 1797*], in Vittorio E. Giuntella, *La Religione amica della democrazia*, pp. 274–275. See also Giuseppe Maria Capece Zurlo, *Lettera pastorale dell'arcivescovo di Napoli card. Giuseppe Maria Capece Zurlo*, in Vittorio E. Giuntella, *La Religione amica della democrazia*, pp. 293–294.

is the *Storia generale della Chiesa cristiana dalla sua nascita all'ultimo stato di trionfo nel cielo tratta principalmente dall'Apocalisse di S. Giovanni Apostolo*, a translation of an English work published by Bishop Charles Walmesley (1722–1797) in 1794–1795 with the title *The General History of the Christian Church from her birth to her final triumphant state in heaven, chiefly deduced from the Apocalypse of St John the Apostle* (1771). In a typically prophetic style, the author states that evident signs were signaling the Church's last era on earth, a time marked by calamities, wars, apostasy, a decline in faith, and the corruption of mores.[249]

Count Alfonso Muzzarelli (1749–1813) was another enemy of revolutions and a fervent apologist of the alliance between the throne and the altar. Originally printed in 1792 and then subsequently reprinted many times in the following century, his *Delle cause dei mali presenti e del timore de'mali futuri e suoi rimedj: Avviso al popolo cristiano* insisted that the nations had declined from the truly Christian seventeenth century to a most impious eighteenth century.[250] Writing like an *Old Testament* prophet, Muzzarelli announced God's most terrifying scourge against the horrible sins perpetrated by the French and their Italian followers. Calling true Christians to atone themselves through penance, he urged them to return to the benevolent guidance of the Catholic Church. He claimed that the material prosperity of his times – and even the lack of great calamities – was a clear sign that God no longer loved His people. If God did in fact still love His people, he would correct them through devastating plagues, earthquakes, and famines, just as He did many times in the past. God's disapprobation is further evidenced by the "silence of consciences" (*"il silenzio delle coscienze"*), as is noted in *Isaiah* 29:10. For Muzzarelli, all

---

[249] *Storia generale della Chiesa cristiana dalla sua nascita all'ultimo stato di trionfo nel cielo tratta principalmente dall'Apocalisse di S. Giovanni Apostolo. Opera di Mr. Pastorini trasportata da un monaco benedettino della Congregazione di S. Mauro dall'idioma inglese al francese, e resa ora per la prima volta all'italiana favella*, Cesena: Eredi Biasini all'insegna di Pallade, 1794–1795, p. 35. The Jesuits also produced and circulated a large corpus of prophetic texts in response to the abolition of their order in 1773. The nun Maria Teresa del Cuore di Gesù and the peasant Bernardina Renzi, who resided in a small town of the Diocese of Montefiascone, announced prophecies in favor of the Jesuit Order. See Marina Caffiero, *La nuova era. Miti e profezie dell'Italia in rivoluzione*, Genoa: Agorà, 1991, pp. 21–20. As the French troops came closer and closer to Rome, Counterrevolutionary prophecies became more and more vibrant and resorted to the typical prophetic topos of interpreting calamities as a punishment that God inflicts on his peoples in order to prepare them for a future and better order. Even an enlightened abbot like Giovanni Cristofano Amaduzzi indulged in prophecies of imminent revolutions and regeneration. The Jansenist bishop, Scipione de' Ricci, kept Nostradamus' prophecies within his papers. See Marina Caffiero, *La nuova era. Miti e profezie dell'Italia in rivoluzione*, pp. 30–39.

[250] Alfonso Muzzarelli, *Delle cause dei mali presenti e del timore de'mali futuri e suoi rimedi. Avviso al popolo cristiano*, Foligno: G. Tomassini, 1792, in *Le dolci catene. Testi della controrivoluzione cattolica in Italia*, edited by Vittorio E. Giuntella, Rome: Istituto per la Storia del Risorgimento Italiano, 1988, pp. 160–161.

individuals, including the most learned persons, are acquiescent to the evils of the times when they claim that speaking and denouncing moral and political evils would only make things worse (*"produrrebbe un maggiore male"*). As a result, vices and abuses grow stronger and stronger. Yet another punishment is God's silence itself (*"il silenzio della parola di Dio"*). Deprived of the word of God, Christian communities languish in misery and despair, and many beautiful souls are miserable and lost. God has closed the fountains of His mercy to His people (*"ha chiuso con noi le fonti della misericordia"*) and no longer sends His prophets. Of all His punishments, this is the most dreadful.[251]

Why was God no longer manifesting His omnipotence? Muzzarelli knew God's mind: God no longer sends prophets and persons capable of performing miracles because He wants to punish the people's unwillingness to accept His grace. Despite having records of miracles, the people wish to see more and more of them. Irritated by such requests, God has decided to remain silent.[252] He hides in response to this disbelief. The consequences of God's silence are found in society's dreadful degeneration into sin and vice. Where is the sincere worship, a true love of God? God is right to remain silent. He will speak again and send new prophets only when He decides that it is time to help His creatures to resurrect. Should God speak again, would the people truly understand? Should He send prophets, would the people despise and reject them? Until God speaks again, Christian peoples must wait and dutifully prepare themselves to listen to His voice. No one knows when God will finally speak again and send new prophets. But, for Muzzarelli, the persuasion that God eventually will do so must encourage the work of emancipation from moral slothfulness.[253]

While Muzzarelli was invoking new prophets capable of reviving God's word, Francesco Gusta invoked more belligerent prophets capable of launching and leading a true crusade against the enemies of the Church and the Christian faith, by which he meant the French Jacobins and their Italian followers. Born in Barcelona in 1744, Gusta attended the novitiate with the Jesuits and then spent most of his life in Italy, where he died in 1816. He fiercely proclaimed that it was time to take up arms in defense of the throne and the altar (*"per la difesa del trono, non che della Religione"*) for "God wants it" (*"Dio lo vuole"*). Gusta too knows the mind of God and announces his edicts.[254] In the past, God has inspired Christians to sacrifice their lives against infidels and against heretics. He must similarly inspire eighteenth-century Christians to resist atheist republicans. If defenders of the throne and the altar will speak with sincere faith on behalf of God (*"a nome di Dio"*), they will surely provide Christian peoples with the moral strength that will permit the liberation from the false beliefs

---

[251] Ibid., pp. 162–164.   [252] Ibid., p. 167.   [253] Ibid., p. 167.

[254] Francesco Gusta, *Saggio critico sulle crociate*, second edition, Foligno: Giovanni Tomassini, 1794, in Vittorio E. Giuntella, *Le dolci catene*, pp. 218–219.

that confuse their minds.[255] A devout Catholic, Gusta wanted an army of saints that would fight under the cross and banners with the image of Christ. Inspired by the words of the prophets, these Christian soldiers must believe that they fight on Christ's behalf. These new soldiers of Christianity must believe that they will be saved, regardless of whether they win or die in battle (*"vincendo o morendo, vincono o muoiono per Cristo"*).[256] Priests and all God's ministers must encourage new soldiers, bless their swords, put the cross around their necks, counsel them, and reconcile them with God in the moment of death. With the presence of the priests in their ranks, marching under the banners with the image of Christ, and led into battle by the cross, the soldiers shall be persuaded that God is on their side and will give them victory (*"Dio ci darà la vittoria"*).[257]

Felice Antonio D'Alessandria, the bishop of Cariati e Gerenza, was another prophet of the Counterrevolution. In his *Istruzione pastorale sull'ordinata recluta, per gli occorrenti bisogni*, he claimed that God is a friend of monarchy. Thundering against the false ideas of atheistic philosophy, he invited the faithful to ask God to assist the supporters of the king in their struggle against atheist republicans.[258] A sonnet of the "most humble" servant of God Suor Maria Girolama C.S. (probably a member of the Convent of San Giacomo in Eboli) reports that Christ himself assured her that he would save the kingdom and crush the enemies of faith.[259] Inspired by God, the humble nun delivered a comforting prophecy that announced the Counterrevolutionary armies' complete and imminent victory.[260] In some cases, advocates of the Counterrevolution decided to respond word for word to the republican militants' poems and the manifestos. A truly outstanding example of this clash between philosophers and prophets is the hymn sung when the Holy Cross was erected in place of the trees of liberty that had been erected by republicans (*Inno da cantarsi nell'erezione della S. Croce ne' luoghi dove erasi alzato l'infame arbore della libertà*). The revolutionaries' hymn urged citizens to respond to the holy call (*"sacro invito"*), and to rally around the tree that announced the end

---

255 Ibid., p. 223.   256 Ibid., p. 230.

257 Ibid., p. 231. On the eve of the revolution, Giovanni Marchetti (1753–1829), who held many important offices in the Vatican hierarchy, repeated the conventional litany that the French Revolution and the institution of Jacobin republics under the protection of French armies were God's punishments intended to rekindle in the hearts of peoples the faith they had lost under the influence of atheist philosophers. See Giovanni Marchetti, "Che importa ai preti (1798)," in Vittorio E. Giuntella, *Le dolci catene*, pp. 336–338.

258 "A quel Dio, da cui può venire, e per cui sperar si deve ogni ajuto, piangenti si alzino gli occhi, e pure le mani"; Anna Lisa Sannino, *L'altro 1799. Cultura antidemocratica e pratica politica controrivoluzionaria nel tardo Settecento napoletano*, Naples: ESI, 2002, pp. 169–170.

259 "Mi rispose Gesù; la navicella / Al porto guiderò, e la mia voce, / frenerà l'onde, e la nazion ribella, / Perirà, finirà se tanto nuoce"; ibid., p. 210.

260 "Serena il ciglio ho, che il fier nemico / Abbattuto sarà, presto in catene, / Dal braccio forte del fedel mio amico. / Tosto sciolto il mio cor da tante pene / fu; e vidi trionfar già Lodovico [Lodovici], / che ha dato al re, e a noi, contento e bene"; ibid., p. 208.

of tyranny (*"dell'ignobile servaggio / L'empio laccio è già spezzato"*). It went on to declare that the monarchy and temporal power of the Church were no longer sacred names protected by God (*"Sacri nomi in ciel protetti"*). Nourishing an eternal hatred against monarchy and papacy, the revolutionaries proclaimed that only the law shall reign (*"sol la legge regnerà"*), that God was their only God sovereign. On the contrary, Counterrevolutionaries urged citizens to rally against the false tree of liberty, to be confident that their faith is protected by God, and to know the only God on earth is his majesty the king.[261] In another Counterrevolutionary text of May 1799, we read that "there is a God who exalts the humble and represses the proud," that is to say, the republicans who challenged the king's legitimate authority.[262] Consistent with their prophetic declamations, the Counterrevolutionaries attributed their victories to God's help.[263]

The prophets of the Counterrevolution took advantage of the lack of prophetic pathos of the leaders of the republican revolution, and astutely used prophetic language to invoke God in support of monarchy and of the Catholic Church. They spoke in the name of the God whom peoples had been venerating for centuries. Their prophetic eloquence was effective in mobilizing the urban and rural plebs against the republic of the philosophers. Many republicans made the mistake of believing that the institutions and laws of the republic – born out of revolutions that triumphed with the help of foreign armies – could have the power to uproot traditional religious and political beliefs from the people's minds. They did not take into consideration the fact that, while armies can create new republics, only prophets can change consciences and establish a new republican ethos. The republican militants made serious efforts to use Christian language to exhort their compatriots to embrace republican principles. But they failed to persuade the people that they were prophets inspired by God. As we shall see in the next chapter, the defeat of the Neapolitan Revolution taught the most perceptive Italian patriots that the cause of political emancipation needs prophets.

---

[261] Ibid., pp. 195–196.

[262] "Esiste un Dio: e no'l vedete o stolti / Esiste un Dio, che con virtù sublime / Gli umil esalta, ed i superbi opprime, / E tien gli occhi pietosi a noi rivolti. / Scesero già nel fanatismo avvolti / Gli Atei superbi dall'alpestri cime: / Ma chi gli urta, l'abbatte, e chi l'opprime? / Dio, che ne' loro aguati alfin gli ha colti. / Fu un uom sol, che sconcertò, che assalse / Che d'empietà sconfisse i rei Giganti, / Non di fulmini e tuon egli si avvalse. / Ecco ov'andar que' temerari vanti! / Come David contra Golia prevalse, / Così fu Ludovici incontro a tanti!"; ibid., p. 199.

[263] "Fidiamo in Dio, nè si disperi ancora. / Dio divise il Mar Rosso; e limpid'acque / Fe' scaturir da rupi aride, e dure / Per rinfrescare il Popol suo diletto: / Dio permise che Olia restasse ucciso / Dalle tenere mani / Di un debol Garzon: questo Dio stesso / Fe' che venisse a noi con forti squadrre /, qui Lodovici il difensore, e'l Padre"; ibid., p. 202.

4

The Prophetic Voices of the Risorgimento and the Anti-Fascist Resistance

The history of political ideas offers amazing surprises. A sentence or even a single word in a text can suggest suppositions that catalyze research. If our suppositions are keen, the texts that we study disclose pieces of evidence that fall into place one after the other, and reveal a story that we were not aware of. When this happens, a historian's work delivers a special intellectual felicity comparable, I imagine, to the awe and the excitement of a traveler who sees new lands and new seas, to paraphrase Machiavelli's well-known phrase.[1] I have enjoyed this sort of experience while elaborating the hypothesis that prophetic words and sentiments inspired and sustained the Italian Risorgimento. The earliest prophetic voices were those of poets, above all Vittorio Alfieri, Ugo Foscolo, and Alessandro Manzoni. The towering prophet of the Risorgimento, though, was Giuseppe Mazzini. His writings left a deep mark in the minds of Italian patriots. As the Risorgimento moved to its conclusion in 1870, a pragmatic and disillusioned intellectual mood dominated Italian culture. Prophetic voices survived only within small and marginal communities proclaiming radical egalitarian and republican ideas, and within the socialist movement. But they were all voices that had lost the warmth and faith of the Risorgimento's prophets. It appeared as if prophecy was dead. Yet, prophetic voices surprisingly resurfaced among the militants who committed

---

[1] "Ancora che, per la invida natura degli uomini, sia sempre suto non altrimenti periculoso trovare modi ed ordini nuovi, che si fusse cercare acque e terre incognite, per essere quelli più pronti a biasimare che a laudare le azioni d'altri; nondimanco, spinto da quel naturale desiderio che fu sempre in me di operare, sanza alcuno respetto, quelle cose che io creda rechino comune benefizio a ciascuno, ho deliberato entrare per una via, la quale, non essendo suta ancora da alcuno trita, se la mi arrecherà fastidio e difficultà, mi potrebbe ancora arrecare premio, mediante quelli che umanamente di queste mie fatiche il fine considerassino"; Niccolò Machiavelli, *Discorsi sulla prima deca di Tito Livio*, in *Tutte le opere*, p. 76; English translation, *Discourses on Livy*, p. 5.

themselves to resist and fight fascism's political religion. The purpose of this concluding chapter is to highlight this story.

4.1 THE TIMES OF PROPHETS

Since Benedetto Croce published the *Storia d'Europa nel secolo XIX* (*History of Europe in the Nineteenth Century*) in 1932, we know that the Italian Risorgimento was prepared and sustained by a religious sentiment. Calling it "a religion of liberty" (*"religione della libertà"*), Croce described it as a conception of reality to which an accompanying ethics respectively conforms. The religion of liberty does not need "personifications, myths, legends, dogmas, rites, propitiations, expiations, classes of clergymen, pontifical paludaments and the like." It condemns the literary man as well as the faint-hearted and dreamy philosopher. It denounces servile mentality and courtly flattery and does not accept any maneuvers that seek to "separate man from citizen, the individual from the society which forms him and which he forms." It champions the love of one's country; it infuses the sense of duty; it requires the search for truth; it demands commitment in action, or at least the desire for action; it instructs looking upon defeats as occasions for demonstrating and reaffirming the strength of liberty.[2] After Croce, scholars have continued to emphasize the religious dimension of the Risorgimento. They have not noticed, however, the rebirth of prophetic language therein.[3] That rebirth occurred within a European intellectual context marked by the appearance of prophetic voices

---

[2] Benedetto Croce, *Storia d'Europa nel secolo XIX*, Bari: Laterza, 1932, p. 356.

[3] A few years before Croce's *Storia d'Europa*, Adolfo Omodeo (1889–1946), one of the most distinguished Italian historians, had stressed – against Piero Gobetti's claim that the achievement of independence did not bring about a moral and religious reformation – the religious dimension of the Risorgimento: "Ma il Gobetti avrebbe dovuto notare come il Risorgimento abbia una vita religiosa sua interna, tale da ridurre e risospingere in ristretti limiti le esigenze del cattolicesimo gesuitico. Anche senza tentare un'organizzazione religiosa in senso stretto, quegli uomini vivevano una fede nuova, anche quelli che si credevano ancora cattolici. La riforma cattolica del Gioberti ha inizio prima di lui e consiste nel pregio sacro dato alla civiltà. Da ciò quel cattolicesimo dimezzato e limitato che era la bestia nera di Pio IX, il quale cercò di esorcizzarla col *Sillabo*. Questa era l'unica via da seguire, e per essa si procedè. Una nuova fede attiva apparentemente politica fu affiancata alla vecchia fede fossile e si andò dilatando. Per essa, per le idee liberali, fermenti purificati di protestantesimo calarono a disintossicare l'Italia dal virus gesuitico"; Adolfo Omodeo, "Risorgimento senza eroi," *Difesa del Risorgimento*, Turin: Einaudi, 1951, pp. 439–446. In 1938, Ettore Rota, another eminent historian, traced the origins of the new religious and moral spirit in the early 1700s and pointed to Giovanbattista Vico as its precursor; see *Le origini del Risorgimento*, vol. 2, Milan: Vallardi, p. 716. See also Maria Sticco, *La poesia religiosa del Risorgimento*, Milan: Vita e Pensiero, 1945, in particular pp. 68–72; Luigi Salvatorelli, *Il pensiero politico italiano dal 1700 al 1870*, Turin: Einaudi, 1935; Carlo Calcaterra, *Il nostro imminente Risorgimento: gli studi e la letteratura in Piemonte nel periodo della Sampaolina e della Filopatria*, Turin: Società Editrice Internazionale, 1935; Arturo Carlo Jemolo, *Il Giansenismo in Italia prima della rivoluzione*, Bari: Laterza, 1927; Francesco Olgiati, *La pietà cristiana. Esperienze ed indirizzi*, Milan: Vita e pensiero, 1935.

announcing a radical religious, moral, and political change in the history of humanity. The early nineteenth century truly was, as the historian Paul Bénichou has written, the times of prophets.[4]

Among the many works that attest the spread of prophetic ideas of social emancipation in the early nineteenth century, a place of honor must go to Henri de Saint-Simon's *Le Nouveau Christianisme*, published for the first time in 1825. The author declares that his ideas of religious and moral reformation came from divine inspiration and that his own mission on earth was to submit human institutions to God's will.[5] In the spirit of the prophets, Saint-Simon denounces the corruption of the Catholic Church and its false doctrines. The true principle of Christianity prescribes pursuing the hastiest improvement of the poorest social classes. This principle shall inspire a radical religious renovation: the triumph of a new and true Christianity at last based upon the authentic teaching of Christ.[6] In addition to his moral and religious message, Saint-Simon powerfully advocated social justice:[7] "Religion must guide society ever closer to the great aim of hastily improving the fate of the most destitute class." Sure of God's inspiration, Saint-Simon felt confident to exhort the princes to listen to God's voice speaking through his voice.[8]

Another chief work of the prophetic renaissance is Gotthold Ephraim Lessing's (1729–1781) *Die Erziehung des Menschengeschlechts* (*The Education of Humankind*). Published for the first time in Germany in 1780, it gained a much wider circulation when it was translated into French by Saint-Simon's disciples and published in a volume that also contained the *Nouveau Christianisme*.[9] In this text, Lessing explained that the Christian religion had demonstrated in history the superiority of its principles. For this reason, it can

[4] See Paul Bénichou, *Le temps des prophètes. Doctrines de l'âge romantique*, Paris: Gallimard, 1977; see also Adolfo Omodeo, *Studi sull'età della restaurazione*, Turin: Einaudi, 1970; Marjorie Reeves and Warwick Gould, *Joachim of Fiore and the Myth of the Eternal Evangel in the Nineteenth Century*, Oxford: Oxford University Press, 1987; Henry de Lubac, S.J., *La posterité spirituelle de Joachim de Flore*, Paris: Lethielleux, 1979–1981.

[5] "Oui, je crois que le christianisme est une institution divine, et je suis persuadé que Dieu accorde une protection spéciale à ceux qui font leurs efforts pour soumettre toutes les institutions humaines au principe fondamental de cette doctrine sublime; je suis convaincu que moi-même j'accomplis une mission divine en rappelant les peuples et les rois au véritable esprit du christianisme"; Henri de Saint-Simon, *Le Nouveau Christianisme*, Paris: Au Bureau du Globe, 1832, p. 100.

[6] Ibid., p. 15; see also p. 20.   [7] Ibid., p. 20; see also p. 18.

[8] "Princes, écoutez la voix de Dieu, qui vous parle par ma bouche, redevenez bons chrétiens, cessez de considérer les armées soldées, les nobles, les clergés hérétiques et les juges pervers comme vos soutiens principaux; unis au nom du christianisme, sachez accomplir tous les devoirs qu'il impose aux puissants; rappelez-vous qu'il leur commande d'employer toutes leurs forces à accroître le plus rapidement possible le bonheur social du pauvre"; ibid., p. 104.

[9] Gotthold Ephraim Lessing, "Die Erziehung des Menschengeschlechts," *Nouveau Christianisme. Lettres d'Eugène Rodrigues sur la religion et la politique. L'éducation du genre humain de Lessing traduit, pour la première fois de l'allemand par Eugène Rodriguez*, Paris: Au Bureau du Globe, 1832, pp. 299–300.

still lead humanity to rediscover the true ideas about the "divine Being," human nature, and our relationships with God. Summoned by a well-understood Christianity, the time shall come in which human beings will do good just for the sake of the good and will appreciate the inner recompenses for virtue as their most coveted reward. That shall be the time of the "new eternal Gospel" promised by the books of the new alliance and guaranteed by Providence.[10] The core of Lessing's prophetic message was the belief that God reveals His will to the whole of humanity according to a precise order and measure.[11] The chosen ones whom He unveils his will have the duty of educating their own people and all the peoples of the earth.[12] Thanks to the efforts of the prophets, humanity shall be composed of individuals who live their lives by the principle of duty. They will accomplish an *"avenir séduisant,"* "seductive future," a new alliance between God and humanity. This "future," Lessing proclaimed, shall come for sure.[13] But one must not rush to it; one must have patience.[14] Even if God's providence proceeds slowly and tortuously, we must have faith in it. Lessing's message, in tune with the prophetic sentiment of the times, was a message of hope.

Within the same intellectual context, Lamennais (Hugues-Félicité-Robert de Lamennais (1782–1854) emerges as a prophet of a religious and moral reform.[15] He had no doubt that prophets are able to penetrate and read God's mind and see the coming of a time in which liberty and civility will triumph over oppression and barbarism:

As it develops, the human spirit penetrates ever deeper into the infinite depths of unchanging, divine truths. Through a comparable process, human society tends to grow increasingly spiritual and draw ever closer to the Church, which itself transforms its visible outlines and its relational modes with society according to this progress [...]. The spirit of persecution, which has been relegated to a small number of men, is extinguished and will soon yield fully to those righteous ideas of liberty which propagate rapidly and are already prevailing in the public opinion. The final remnants of barbarism are

---

[10] Ibid., pp. 341–344.   [11] Ibid., p. 315.   [12] Ibid., pp. 313 and 315.

[13] "Non il viendra, il viendra certainement le jour de l' *accomplissement*, où plus l'intelligence de l'homme se sentira persuadée d'un avenir toujours meilleur, moins l'homme aura besoin d'emprunter à cet avenir des motifs pour ses actes, où il fera le bien parce que c'est le bien, et non parce qu'il s'y rattache des récompenses arbitraires qui n'avaient pour but auparavant que de fixer avec plus de force son regard volage, pour lui faire reconnaître les récompenses intérieures et plus élevées qui attendent la vertu"; ibid., pp. 341–342.

[14] "Marche à pas insensibles, Providence éternelle! laisse-moi seulement ne pas désespérer de toi, à cause de l'insensibilité de ton mouvement. Laisse-moi ne pas désespérer de toi, alors même que ta marche me semblerait rétrograde! Il n'est pas vrai que la ligne la plus courte soit toujours la ligne droite"; ibid., pp. 343–344.

[15] "J'y trouve [dans mon âme]," he writes in 1834, "une foi immense dans l'avenir de la Société, une espérance inébranlable de quelque chose de grand qui se prépare pour elle dans le secret des décrets divins"; F. Lamennais to Countess Senfitt, October 8, 1834, in Paul Bénichou, *Le temps des prophètes*, p. 149.

disappearing, little by little, from the legislation. No more torture, and soon, one might hope, no more death penalty.[16]

Providence governs human history and leads it on the path of religious and moral progress with its invincible force: "when, freeing itself from the old envelope of a forever extinguished past, everything is reborn, everything changes, everything transforms."[17] The agent of the moral and religious renovation must be the people, in which Lamennais sees the presence of God in history.[18] The new prophets of the new epoch of the history of humanity shall be the poets and the artists.[19]

In his youth a supporter of reactionary Catholicism, Lamennais later became a fervent defender of the alliance between Christianity and political liberty. During the Restoration, when France was divided between those who wanted Christianity without liberty, and those who wanted liberty without Christianity, Lamennais defended both liberty and Christianity. He held that Christianity and liberty had a common root, and one was the necessary condition of the other.[20] Although he was aware of the disgraced condition of French Catholicism, he hoped for a religious and moral rebirth through a new alliance between order and progress, faith and science, Christian religion and political liberty. Christianity cannot live without liberty – first of all the liberty of examining the sacred scriptures, and openly discussing religious, moral, and political issues. Over the centuries, human reason has become accustomed to liberty. Hence it would be impossible to destroy it. Even if it were possible, what would be the value of a religion that is an obstacle instead of an encouragement to the progress of humanity?[21]

The evangelical law proclaims the equality and brotherhood of men, Lamennais stressed repeatedly in his writings. Just as it contributed to the dismantling of ancient slavery in the past, Christianity must in modern times

---

[16] "L'esprit humain, en se développant, pénètre de plus en plus dans les profondeurs infinies des vérités divines qui ne changent point, et la société humaine, par un progrès semblable, tend à se spiritualiser de plus en plus, où à se rapprocher de plus en plus de l'Église, qui modifie elle-même ses formes extérieures, ses modes de relation avec la société selon ce progrès [...]. L'esprit de persécution, relégué chez un petit nombre d'hommes, s'éteint et bientôt cédera tout à fait aux justes idées de liberté qui se propagent rapidement et prévalent déjà dans l'opinion publique. Les derniers restes de la barbarie disparaissent peu à peu de la législation. Plus de torture, et prochainement, on doit l'espérer, plus de peine de mort"; Hugues-Félicité-Robert de Lamennais, *De l'avenir de la société*, in Henry de Lubac, S.J., *La postérité spirituelle de Joachim de Flore*, pp. 52–53.

[17] Paul Bénichou, *Le temps des prophètes*, p. 153.   [18] Ibid., pp. 153 and 158, n.128.

[19] "La religion de l'avenir projette ses premières lueurs sur le genre humain en attente, et sur ses futures destinées: l'artiste doit en être le prophète"; Paul Bénichou, *Le temps des prophètes*, p. 165.

[20] Hugues-Félicité-Robert de Lamennais, "Du Catholicisme dans ses rapports avec la société politique," *Oeuvres Complètes de Lamennais, vol. 7*, Paris: Pagnerre Editeur, 1844, pp. 38–39.

[21] Ibid., vol. 7, p. 283.

fight for the termination of modern slavery – that is, political oppression. Only by returning to its roots as a religion that practices charity might Christianity live again in the hearts of millions of human beings, rather than vegetate in the shade of a throne or supply a sad image of itself in public ceremonies. Although they inevitably bring suffering and grief, revolutions that are animated by a true spirit of liberty must be considered as gifts of Providence and signs of God's presence in history. The greatest revolution ever realized, after all, was Christianity. According to Lamennais, the most pressing mission of his times was to spread the spirit of Christianity from the realm of the religious community to the realm of politics. God must support civil and political liberty for the simple reason that He repudiates any power of human beings over human beings.[22]

Lamennais used a Christian language to convey his prophecies of a new temporal order. In his "salute to the future," he wrote that Christian eschatology inspires the hope for a more just society: "World of hope and holy joy, world, not of the mighty [...] but of the weak, of the small [...] no longer of the princes [...] but of the people whose reign has begun, no longer of hatred and domination, but of fraternity and love, I salute this cradle of yours out of which emanates pure light [...] World that, for so many centuries, the children of Adam called a world of justice and liberty, world of peace and cherishing, I salute you."[23] In his *Esquisse d'une philosophie* (1840), he repeated the same vision: "The old world is dissolving, the old doctrines are fading: but amidst this seemingly haphazard and disorderly work, we witness the appearance of new doctrines, a new world coming together; the religion of the future is shining its very first lights on humankind."[24] The "religion of the future" will be the leading force of the new epoch that will at last establish the alliance between Christian religion and liberty: "With broken chains, [the new world] will rise as with its primordial strength, and on such day as this occurs, it will be a great day; this will define an era in which an immense effusion of life has come to bear, where humankind, pushed by an unknown power lighting up within itself, launches into the future with a kind of prophetic hope."[25]

---

[22] Ibid., vol. 7, p. 283.

[23] "Monde d'espèrance et de sainte joie, monde, non plus des grands [...] mais des faibles, des petits [...] non plus des princes [...] mais des peuples dont le règne commence, non plus de haine et de domination, mais de fraternité et d'amour, je salue ton berceau d'où emane une pure lumière [...] Monde que depuis tant de siècles, appelaient les enfants d'Adam, monde de justice et de liberté, de paix et de dilection, je te salue"; quoted by René Remond, *Lamennais et la démocratie*, Paris: Presses universitaires de France, 1948, pp. 21–2.

[24] Hugues-Félicité-Robert de Lamennais, *Esquisse d'une philosophie*, vol. III, Paris: Pagnerre, 1840–1846, p. 273.

[25] "Ces fers brisés, il se lèvera dans sa force première, et ce jour sera grand; il marquera une de ces époques où il semble qu'il se fasse comme une immense effusion de vie, où le genre humain, poussé par je ne sais pas quelle puissance inconnue qui s'éveille en lui, s'élance dans l'avenir, avec une sorte de prophétique espoir"; Paul Bénichou, *Le temps des prophètes*, p. 148.

The signs of the coming of the new epoch are clear, and everyone is aware of them.[26] Christ's prophecy shall become at last true:

The Son swore to send the consoling Spirit, which precedes both He and His Father, and whom they mutually adore; the Spirit will come and reinvent the face of the earth, and this will be as a second creation. Eighteen centuries ago, the Verb spread the divine seed, and it was then fertilized by the Spirit. Today, the earth is tenebrous and cold once again. Our forefathers have watched the sun's decline. And as it lowered into the horizon, the entire human race shuddered. Then, during this night, there came something unknown and with no name. Children of the night, the dusk may be dark, but the Orient is starting to light up again.[27]

Lamennais' appeal to poets to be the prophets of the new religion of humanity was not an isolated instance. Pierre Leroux (1797–1871) – the champion of humanitarianism, exiled after Napoleon Bonaparte's coup of 1851, member of the central committee of the International Workingmen Association – proposed a similar vision: "Yet, you yourselves are the announcers of this new religion [...]. All the while having chained yourselves to this mourning the past, you are abundantly spreading the seeds of renewal, you, eulogists of the former social order and vibrant fanfares all at once, you are – without you, yourselves, seeing the dawn – calling to new life and preluding the destinies promised to humanity."[28] He believed that poetry had the prophetic power of spreading the seeds of the new epoch[29] and interpreted history as progress toward equality, guided by divine Providence that will bring about the ultimate victory over evil, God's kingdom on earth:

There is evil: no matter! The truth is the truth, and erring will not prevail against it. Erring and selfishness will be vanquished; and Satan, who is but erring and selfishness incarnate, will be increasingly relegated into nonbeing, death, and oblivion. God will finally rule the earth when the aim he has set himself in his theodicy – by creating man in his image, and by creating man as opposed to men, meaning humanity – when, I assert this, his ultimate aim has been reached through the growth of man, or of men, or of

[26] "Partout on aperçoit les symptômes d'une ère nouvelle [...] Que nous vivions aujourd'hui à l'une de ces époques où tout tend à se renouveler, à passer d'un état à un autre état, c'est ce que nul, on peut le dire, n'oserait révoquer en doute. Jamais il n'exista de pressentiment plus vif, de conviction plus universelle [...] Tous croient à un changement profond, à une révolution totale prête à s'opérer dans le monde." F. Lamennais to Countess de Senfit, June 22, 1833, Paul Bénichou, *Le temps des prophètes*, p. 415.

[27] "Enfants de la nuit, le couchant est noir, mais l'Orient commence à blanchir"; Lamennais borrows from the *Divine Comedy*, which he translated and commented on, the image of the light of redemption coming from the East; see Henry de Lubac, S.J., *La postérité spirituelle de Joachim de Flore*, p. 58; and Stefania Martini, *Per la fortuna di Dante in Francia*, Pisa: Giardini, 1989.

[28] Pierre Leroux, "Aux philosophes," *Revue encyclopédique* (1831), in Paul Bénichou, *Le temps des prophètes*, p. 339.

[29] Pierre Leroux, "Aux philosophes. De la poésie de notre époque," *Revue encyclopédique* (1831), in Paul Bénichou, *Le temps des prophètes*, p. 338.

human consciousness. It is quite certain that this aim rests in an indefinite and quite mysterious tomorrow: but does this mean that it should reign any less strongly in our souls, and isn't it obvious anyhow that, as we draw closer to this aim, the celestial reign which has been evangelized by Jesus on earth and which had been presented as a mere prophecy by Christianity will be increasingly realized?[30]

Leroux's prophetic ideas had a deep impact on George Sand (her true name was Amantine Aurore Lucile Dupin, 1804–1879), the author of successful romantic novels, ardent republican, socialist, champion of women's emancipation. Inspired by Leroux's articles, she resolved to plunge herself into the study of prophetic tradition in search of the eternal truth that God had promised to humanity. That truth is, for her, the saintly equality that God shall donate to his creatures on earth and in the heavens.[31] The final triumph of equality shall come when the "kingdom of the Holy Spirit" shall replace the Christian religion that had in turn replaced Mosaic law. In *Spiridion*, the novel that she published in 1838–1839 in the *Revue des deux mondes* and, with significant revisions, in 1842, she conveyed her prophetic ideas in the form of a dramatic story in which two monks, Alexis and Angel, find a copy of the lost manuscript of the *Eternal Evangel* allegedly written by John of Parma in 1254:

Witnessing, with our own eyes, such a monument to heresy, Alexis and I were grabbed by an involuntary shudder [...] with what surprise we read its summary on the first page: Religion has three eras, just as there are three in the Holy Trinity. The reign of the Father lasted for the time of Mosaic law. The reign of the Son, meaning Christian religion, must not last forever. The ceremonies and the sacraments in which this religion is enveloped are not set to be eternal. There must come a time when these mysteries end, and then the religion of the Holy Spirit must begin, a religion in which men will no

---

[30] "Le mal existe: qu'importe ! La verité est la verité, et l'erreur ne prévaudra pas point contre elle. L'erreur et l'egoïsme seront vaincus; et Satan, qui n'est autre que l'erreur et l'égoïsme, sera relégué de plus en plus dans le non-être, dans la mort, dans le néant. Dieu *règnera sur la terre* quand le but qu'il s'est proposé dans sa théodicée, en faisant l'homme *à son image*, et en créant, non pas des hommes, mais l'homme, c'est à dire l'humanité, quand, dis-je, ce but final sera atteint, par le développement de la charité humaine, de l'activité humaine, de la connaissance humaine, c'est à dire, par le développement de l'homme, ou des hommes, ou de la conscience humaine. Que ce but soit reculé dans un lointain indéfini et tout à fait mystérieux pour nous, cela est certain: mais doit-il moins pour cela régner dans nos âmes, et n'est-il pas évident d'ailleurs qu'à mesure que nous marcherons vers ce but, de plus en plus aussi se réalisera ce *règne céleste sur la terre* évangélisé par Jésus, et qui, dans la forme où le christianisme l'a présenté n'était qu'une prophétie?"; Pierre Leroux, *De l'humanité*, Paris: Perrotin, 1840, pp. vi–vii. Philippe Faure, a prominent advocate of socialist and republican principles, also held a prophetic vision of history: "Je vais combattre pour la Liberté, / non pour un parti. Mon seul espoir / est dans une action providentielle, / dans une transformation religieuse / pour régénérer la société... / Pardonnez, Divin Jésus, si nous, / disciples de L'Evangile Eternel, / Nous ne savons, comme vous, / préférer le martyre au combat"; Philippe Amédée Faure, *Journal d'un combattant de février*, Jersey: C. Le Feuvre Imprimeur – Libraire, 1859, p. 35.

[31] See Marjorie Reeves and Warwick Gould, *Joachim of Fiore and the Myth of the Eternal Evangel in the Nineteenth and Twentieth Centuries*, Oxford: Oxford University Press, 2002, p. 34.

longer need sacraments, and will gift a purely spiritual worship to the Supreme Being. The reign of the Holy Spirit was predicted by Saint John, and it is this reign, which will succeed to the Christian religion, in the same way that the Christian religion succeeded to the rule of Mosaic law.[32]

The book culminates with the poignant story of Moses comforting Christ who laments the failure of his redemptive message.

Be blessed, be comforted, be strengthened; for you have done great things, and you will long reign on earth [...] And yet a day will come when your law will face the same fate as my own law, when your name will be desecrated as my own, when pontiffs and kings will wield your name and your authority to persecute, to condemn to death, and to deliver to the most horrendous torments the new prophets who have come to carry forth and perfect your doctrine. Thus, go in peace. Such is the law of humankind. The truth can only function when escorted by ignorance and imposture [...]. Let our pride not be troubled for failing to reach the *ideal*. Let it be sufficient that we are on the path. Other prophets, other messiahs will come, and these great souls will never fail humanity's great needs.

Sand ends her novel with a prophecy of redemption that epitomizes the hopes of her time: "O men of the past, who have, like me, witnessed the funeral of a religion without being able to salute the dawn of a new religion [...] how your soul has crumbled under the weight of doubt and weariness! O men of the future [...] remember your brothers, keep their memory alive; [...] invite them to be reborn within you and carry on their work, thus forming an unbreakable chain between the past and the future."[33] In the second edition of the book, 1842, George Sand used even more radical words to characterize the new epoch: "Men of the future, it is your task to bring about the prophecy [...]. It will be the work of a new revelation, a new religion, a new society, a new humanity."[34]

A powerful contribution to early nineteenth-century language of prophetic redemption came from the essay *Comment les dogmes finissent*, published by Théodore Jouffroy (1796–1842) in May 1825 in the "Globe" and then in the volume *Mélanges philosophiques*, (1833).[35] Jouffroy, who had lost his Catholic faith when he was about eighteen years old, describes the crisis of his dogmatic

---

[32] George Sand, *Spiridion*, in Paul Bénichou, *Le temps des prophètes*, p. 94.

[33] "O hommes du passé, qui avez, comme moi, assisté aux funérailles d'une religion, sans pouvoir, saluer l'aurore d'une religion nouvelle [...] combien votre âme a défailli sous les poids du doute et de la lassitude! O hommes de l'avenir [...] souvenez-vous de vos frères, évoquez leur souvenir; [...] faites-les renaître en vous et continuez leur ouvrage, en formant une chaîne invincible entre le passé et l'avenir"; George Sand, *Spiridion*, in Paul Bénichou, *Le temps des prophètes*, p. 95.

[34] "Hommes de l'avenir, c'est à vous qu'il est réserré de realiser cette prophétie [...]. Ce sera l'oeuvre d'une nouvelle révélation, d'une nouvelle religion, d'une nouvelle société, d'une nouvelle humanité"; Paul Bénichou, *Le temps des prophètes*, p. 96.

[35] Théodore Jouffroy, "Comment les dogmes finissent," *Mélanges philosophiques*, Paris: Hachette, 1901. For an excellent edition of "Comment les dogmes finissent," see Théodore Jouffroy, *Le cahier vert. Comment les dogmes finissent. Lettres inédites*, edited by Pierre Poux, Paris: Les Presses Françaises, 1924. On Jouffroy, see Francesco Ruffini, *Ultimi studi sul Conte di Cavour*,

faith and the birth of a true religious faith. He traced, first, in a much-idealized fashion, the different phases of the clash between old catholic dogmas and skepticism; then he sketched the prophecy of a world renovated by a new faith laboriously conquered. The new generation, he claimed, lives a new faith that rejects both fanaticism and skepticism. With its faith in truth and virtue, it shall find a legitimate kingdom of truth, engender in the souls an unspeakable love and enthusiasm.

In Jouffroy's redemptive vision, prophets are entrusted with the mission of awakening the people by instilling in their minds the doubt about existing dogmas.[36] Their force is their faith and their hope: "They have foreseen a new faith; they have bound themselves to this ravishing view with enthusiasm, conviction, and resolution. The hope of new days lives within them; they are its predestined apostles, and it's in their hands that the world's redemption rests."[37] Detached from the vices of their contemporaries, the new prophets can renew and rejuvenate the world.[38] Prophets feel indignation, but do not encourage illusions. They know that their fellow citizens are deeply corrupt. Nonetheless, against servility and corruption they announce the moral truth that foreshadows the new epoch of human history:

So, the legitimate empire of the truth begins again, and there is between it and our natures such a strong sympathy that its return stimulates in our souls an inexpressible love and enthusiasm. He who receives it is changed. He is no longer a man, he is no longer a philosopher: he is a prophet; so dominated is he by the ascendance of the truth, that he forgets himself, that he devotes himself to it, that he is it, that he is the truth incarnate; his actions speak it, his voice commands it; there is no further interest, no other affair; he is the apostle, he will be, if it comes to it, a martyr for the new faith.[39]

The new prophet shall come, Jouffroy assures us at the end of his essay, and his enthusiasm shall pervade the whole society and lead it to accomplish the moral and social rebirth.[40]

Bari: Laterza, 1936, p. 39, and A. Omodeo, *Studi sull'età della restaurazione*, Turin: Einaudi, 1970, pp. 166–172.

[36] "Éveillé par la voix de ces prophètes nouveaux, le peuple endormi dans l'indifférence prête l'oreille, et s'aperçoit qu'il ne croyait pas, ou du moins qu'il croyait sans savoir pourquoi; le doute s'élève en lui, car il ne peut se refuser au bon sens; mais ce doute ne se précise pas d'abord dans son esprit, et n'y pénètre que lentement et à son insu"; Thèodore Jouffroy, "Comment les dogmes finissent," p. 4.

[37] Ibid., pp. 13–14.   [38] Ibid., p. 14.

[39] "Alors recommence l'empire légitime de la vérité, et il y a entre elle et notre nature une sympathise si puissante, que son retour excite dans les âmes un amour un enthousiasme inexprimable. Celui qui l'a reçue est changé. Ce n'est plus un homme, ce n'est plus un philo-sophe, c'est un prophète; il est tellement dominé par l'ascendant de la vérité, qu'il s'oublie lui-même, qu'il se dévoue à elle, qu'il est elle c'est la vérité personnifiée ses actions la parlent, sa voix la commande; il n'a plus d'autre intérêt, plus d'autre affaire; il est l'apôtre, il sera, s'il y a lieu, le martyr de la nouvelle foi"; ibid., pp. 17–18.

[40] Ibid., p. 19.

The writer who asserted with the greatest emphasis that God had entrusted him a providential mission was, however, Lamartine (Alphonse Marie Louis de Prat de Lamartine, 1790–1869). Educated within a conservative milieu, he gradually elaborated republican ideas combined with rigorous Christian principles. His first allusion to his prophetic mission is in a letter from 1821: "leaving Naples, on Saturday January 20th, I was illuminated by a ray coming down from on high."[41] He was referring to the inspiration to write the poem of the history of humanity on which he worked for almost twenty years. Another text that documents his belief that he had received the divine inspiration is his narration of the encounter with the prophetess Lady Stanhope that he published in his *Voyage en Orient*: "It is God – she told him – who brings you here to illuminate your soul; you are of these men with aspiration and good will whom He requires as instruments for the marvelous labors He will soon accomplish among men."[42] God's hand touches a few special individuals when He wants His word to live in history: "Young foreigner, says Lebanon's solitary elder, heir to the biblical prophets, come closer / For many long days now, I have seen you from afar / [...] Always someone bears Elijah's mantle / For God will not let his tongue be forgotten! / It is you whose hand he clutched in the crowd / You, his spirit led onto the path / You, who from the breast of a pious mother, / satiated your thirst for the Lord with ardent grace; / It is you he chose to heed / the voice of the mountain and to repeat its words."[43]

Lamartine declared, on different occasions, to different peoples, that he was destined to accomplish a prophetic mission. Charles Brifaut, a moderate royalist, saluted him as the poet legislator who could renew the world.[44] We also have Lamartine's own statements: "It is obvious, he wrote in 1848, that God has his own ideas for me, for indeed I am a true miracle to my own eyes. I cannot explain, in any other way than through some Divine infusion, the inconceivable popularity to which I am currently privy."[45] Under the guidance of faith and reason, Lamartine set to himself the mission of reviving and accomplishing the redemptive goals that the French Revolution had only partially attained: "His task is no longer to be merely resigned to what has happened since 1789; in a way, it must be revered and more fully realized."[46] In the pamphlet *Sur la politique rationnelle* (1831), his profession of political faith, he establishes a parallel between his own times and the times of early Christianity and proclaims a message of social redemption: "Humanity is young. Its social configuration is old and falling into ruins; immortal chrysalis,

[41] Alphonse de Lamartine, Letter of January 25, 1821, to Aymon de Virieu, *Correspondance de Lamartine*, second edition, vol. 2, edited by Valentine de Lamartine, Paris: Hachette, 1881–1882, p. 147.

[42] Paul Bénichou, *Les mages romantiques*, Paris: Gallimard, 1988, pp. 32–33.   [43] Ibid., p. 36.

[44] Ibid., p. 41.   [45] Ibid., p. 41; see also p. 56.

[46] Alphonse de Lamartine, Letter of October 24, 1830, to Virieu, in Paul Bénichou, *Les mages romantiques*, pp. 43–44.

it is laboriously exiting its primitive envelope to assume its virile form, its mature shape. Such is the truth! We are living in one of the most powerful time periods humankind must endure to move closer to the aim of its divine destiny, a period of renewal, of social transformation similar perhaps to that of the evangelical time period."[47]

Alexis de Tocqueville (1805–1859) too, in his *Democracy in America* (1835 and 1840), reveals a remarkable intellectual debt to the prophetic context in which he lived his youth. He does not assert that he has written his book inspired by God. He states, however, that human beings have worked as instruments of God to bring about the birth of democracy. He also claims that the American democracy reveals God's plan:

This whole book has been written under the impulse of a kind of religious dread inspired by contemplation of this irresistible revolution advancing century by century over every obstacle and even now going forward amid the ruins it has itself created. God does not Himself need to speak for us to find sure signs of His will; it is enough to observe the customary progress of nature and the continuous tendency of events; I know, without special revelation, that the stars follow orbits in space traced by His finger. If patient observation and sincere meditation have led men of the present day to recognize that both the past and the future of their history consist in the gradual and measured advance of equality, that discovery gives this progress the sacred character of the will of the Sovereign Master. In that case effort to halt democracy appears as a fight against God himself, and nations have no alternative to acquiesce in the social state imposed by Providence.

Tocqueville admits he cannot read God's mind, but he refuses to accept the idea that God has not intended for the nations of Europe a future of liberty similar to the one that American democracy has inaugurated: "Am I to believe that the Creator made man to let him struggle endlessly through the intellectual squalor now surrounding us? I cannot believe that; God intends a calmer and more stable future for the peoples of Europe; I do not know His designs but shall not give up believing therein because I cannot fathom them, and should prefer to doubt my own understanding rather than His justice."[48]

English poets and writers also contributed to the revival of prophetic expectations. In *The Prophecy of Dante* (written in 1819 and translated into Italian in 1827), Lord Byron presents Dante as the successor of the "great Seers of

---

[47] "L'humanité est jeune, sa forme sociale est vieille et tombe en ruines; chrysalide immortelle, elle sort laborieusement de son enveloppe primitive pour revêtir sa robe virile, la forme de sa maturité. Voilà le vrai! Nous sommes à une des plus fortes époques que le genre humain ait à franchir pour avancer vers le but de sa destinée divine, à une époque de rénovation, et de transformation sociale pareille peut-être à l'époque évangélique"; Alphonse de Lamartine, *Sur la politique rationnelle*, in Paul Bénichou, *Les mages romantiques*, p. 44.

[48] Alexis de Tocqueville, *Democracy in America*, edited by J. P. Mayer, translated by George Lawrence, New York: Harper Perennial, 2006, pp. 12 and 18.

Israel," as a poet with a deeply "prophetic eye."[49] Italy's cry to God will not go unheard, says Byron's Dante: "And Italy, the martyred nation's gore, / Will not in vain arise to where belongs / Omnipotence and Mercy evermore: / Like a harp string stricken by the wind, / The sound of her lament shall, rising o'er / The Seraph voices, touch the Almighty Mind."[50] Thanks to the prophetic light that God has given him, Byron's Dante foresees the coming of a "mortal Savior who shall set [Italy] free."[51] In the midst of a time filled with mourning, his will be a voice to which Italy will listen. New prophets will come and "shall follow in the path that [he] show[s]."[52] From the multitude of servile poets, one shall rise out of the masses and issue "a higher song of freedom."[53] Although the great minds of Italy have not been able to instill hope for many centuries, the time will come when Italy will be able "to revive / the Grecian forms at last from their decay, / and Roman souls [...]," and finally "give / new wonders to the world."[54]

Also noteworthy was Thomas Carlyle's *On Heroes, Hero-Worship, and the Heroic in History*, a collection of lectures first published in 1841. In the lecture given on May 8, 1840, Carlyle explains that, while a hero is regarded as a God among men, a prophet is the most precious gift that God offers to mortals.[55] A true prophet is an "original" man sent by the "Infinite Unknown" to bring us divine messages. When we listen to him, we perceive that his words are true, that they have a special "radiance."[56] The prophet lives and must live in communication with the "inner fact of things." His statements are revelations that come from the heart of the universe.[57] The prophet's very nature forces him to be honest: "While others walk in formulas and hearsays, contented enough to dwell there, this man could not screen himself in formulas: he was alone with his own soul and the reality of things."[58] A sign of this earnestness is the fact that he informs everyone of the prophetic visions that he has received.[59] As exhibited through the example of Muhammad, a true prophet leads and guides his people to a new "birth from darkness to light."[60] Carlyle clarifies that the prophet is similar to the poet. Both know how to penetrate the sacred mystery of the universe and reveal it to other human beings. While the poet reveals the beauty that we must love, the prophet reveals moral truth "of what we are to do."[61] Given "the depth of sincerity" that likens him to the ancient prophets, Dante is the example of the poet-prophet: his words "come from his

---

[49] *The Prophecy of Dante*, in *The Works of Lord Byron*, vol. 4 (Poetry), second edition, edited by Earnest Hartley Coleridge, London: John Murray-Albemarle Street, 1905, Canto II.8 and Canto III.5.

[50] Ibid., Canto III, pp. 14–19.   [51] Ibid., p. 54.   [52] Ibid., p. 64.   [53] Ibid., pp. 104–105.

[54] Ibid., Canto IV, pp. 44–46, 48–49.

[55] Thomas Carlyle, *On Heroes, Hero-Worship, and the Heroic in History*, edited by David R. Sorensen and Brent E. Kinser, New Haven and London: Yale University Press, 2013, pp. 51–52.

[56] Ibid., pp. 53 and 100.   [57] Ibid., p. 54.   [58] Ibid., p. 60.   [59] Ibid., p. 69.

[60] Ibid., p. 76.   [61] Ibid., pp. 78–79.

very heart." The other example is Shakespeare, who at once knows how to illuminate and ignite. Indeed, he suggests that "wheresoever and whensoever there is an open human soul that will be recognized as true!"[62]

4.2 PROPHETIC POETS AND WRITERS

The prophetic literature arriving from France had a wide and deep impact upon the culture of the intellectual and political leaders of the Italian Risorgimento. Giuseppe Garibaldi kept *Le Nouveau Christianisme* on his nightstand until he passed away.[63] Giuseppe Mazzini knew quite well and often discussed the ideas of Lamennais, George Sand, and Pierre Leroux.[64] Cavour was acquainted with early nineteenth-century French culture and deeply admired Theodore Jouffroy.[65] Despite these links, though, a prophetic literature with a redemptive message emerged in Italy independently from the larger European context. Not surprisingly, the earliest prophetic voices were poets. Their chief source of inspiration was Dante, and, for some, Machiavelli. Their message was national redemption.

Vittorio Alfieri's poems and prose are the earliest texts that indicate the rebirth of a prophetic language of political redemption in Italy. When he describes his urge to denounce Italy's servile spirit and laziness, Alfieri explicitly

---

[62] Ibid., p. 100. A strong prophetic language is present also in the works of the socialist theorists before and after Marx. See Henri De Lubac, *La postérité spirituelle de Joachim de Flore*, vol. II, pp. 337–384.

[63] Lucy Riall, *Garibaldi: Invention of a Hero*, New Haven and London: Yale University Press, 2007, p. 38, and n.20. See also T. Olivari, "I libri di Garibaldi," *Storia e Futuro* 1 (2002): pp. 1–16.

[64] Mazzini highly praised George Sand as a critic of the moral and religious corruption of their times: "Elle a souffert par nous et pour nous. Ella a traversé les crises du siècle. Le mal qu'elle peint n'est pas *son* mal; c'est le *nôtre*: ce n'est pas d'elle qu'il nous vient; il était, il est encore autour de nous, dans l'air que nous respirons, dans les fondements de notre société pourrie, dans l'hypocrisie surtout, qui a étendu son large manteau de comédien sur toutes les manifestations de notre vie [...]. Elle a déchiré d'une main hardie le manteau; elle a mis à nu les plaies rongeantes, et elle nous a crié: *Voilà votre société!*"; Giuseppe Mazzini, *Scritti editi ed inediti*, vol. XCIV, Imola: Cooperativa Tipografico-Editrice Paolo Galeati, 1906–1943, p. 55. See also Ettore Passerin d' Entrèves, "Mazzini e George Sand. Letteratura, religione e politica," *Religione e politica nell'Ottocento europeo*, edited by Francesco Traniello, Rome: Istituto per la storia del Risorgimento Italiano, 1993, pp. 184–193; Giuseppe Mazzini, *Pensieri sulla democrazia in Europa*, second edition, edited by Salvo Mastellone, Milan: Feltrinelli, 2005; Luca Beltrami's "Introduzione," in Giuseppe Mazzini, *Scritti sul romanzo e altri saggi letterari*, Rome: Edizioni di Storia e Letteratura, 2012; Arturo Codignola, *La giovinezza di G. Mazzini*, Florence: Vallecchi, 1926; Leonardo La Puma, *Il socialismo sconfitto: saggio sul pensiero politico di Pierre Leroux e Giuseppe Mazzini*, Milan: Franco Angeli, 1984.

[65] See Francesco Ruffini, *Ultimi studi sul Conte di Cavour*, Bari: Laterza, 1936, pp. 19–69; see also Francesco Ruffini, *La giovinezza di Cavour*, second edition, Turin: Edizioni Di Modica, 1937; Rosario Romeo, *Cavour e il suo tempo (1810–1842)*, Bari: Laterza, 1969, p. 301.

spoke – like Dante – of a divine impulse (*"divino impulso"*).[66] In 1777 he wrote that a ferocious unknown god (*"un dio feroce, ignoto"*) had compelled him to fight against tyranny since the days of his youth.[67] In a later work, *Del principe e delle lettere*, he alludes to a "proud and divine fever of the mind and heart" (*"superba e divina febbre dell'ingegno e del cuore"*). His own conscience was the authority that compelled him to rise above the corruption of his times and to imitate the great examples of the past.[68] In Alfieri's case, the concept of rebirth is particularly appropriate. In fact, he rediscovered and took Dante's idea of the prophet as his model: a severe critic of the moral degeneration of his times who is not afraid of his corrupt compatriots' envy.[69] The other source of Alfieri's prophetic texts was Niccolò Machiavelli. From the "divine Machiavelli," as he liked to call him, Alfieri drew the belief that prophets (along with the heads of religions, the saints, and the martyrs) are "superior men" who "deserve, even from the most irreligious of men, admiration, devotion, and veneration."[70]

Drawing from the *Discourses on Livy*, Alfieri refined the idea that Christian religion is inimical to republican liberty because it teaches human beings to think and live as slaves: "The Christian religion, which is that of almost all Europe, is not in itself unfavorable to a free life, but the Catholic religion is almost incompatible with freedom." It teaches individuals to accept the more-or-less unbounded authority of a single man over the great questions of life. In this way, it renders peoples slaves for all time. Moreover, with the practice of confession and the certain forgiveness of any sin, it encourages continued criminal and immoral behaviors and, as a result, prevents the formation of a true civil morality. To the contrary, Christ's true legacy sustains a free way of life: Jesus Christ, "politically considered as a man, also desired – by teaching through example, truth, and virtue – to restore in his own people, and in many

---

[66] Vittorio Alfieri, *Della Tirannide, Del Principe e delle lettere, Panegirico di Plinio e Traiano, La virtù sconosciuta*, edited by Alessandro Donati, Bari: Laterza, 1927, p. 215.

[67] Ibid., p. 105.

[68] "Se io ardisco pur supplicarvi di rimirarmi con benigno occhio, e di scevrarmi dalla moderna turba dei letterati, una tale audacia in me nasce soltanto dalla mia propria coscienza, che se il destino mi volle pur nato in queste moderne età, per quanto in mio potere è stato, io sono tuttavia sempre vissuto col desiderio e con la mente nelle età vostre e fra voi"; ibid., p. 188.

[69] "O gran padre Alighier, se dal ciel miri / Me tuo discepol non indegno starmi, / Dal cor traendo profondi sospiri, / Prostrato innanzi a' tuoi funerei marmi; / Piacciati, deh! Propizio ai be' desiri, / D'un raggio di tua luce illuminarmi. / Uom, che a primiera eterna gloria aspiri, / Contro invidia e viltà de' stringer l'armi? / Figlio, i' le strinsi, e assai men duol; ch'io diedi / Nome in tal guisa a gente tanto bassa, / Da non pur calpestarsi co' miei piedi. / Se in me fidi, il tuo sguardo a che si abbassa? / Va, tuona, vinci: e, se fra' pié ti vedi / Costor, senza mirar, sovr'essi passa"; Vittorio Alfieri, *Rime* (XIX), in *Opere di Vittorio Alfieri*, edited by Francesco Maggini, Florence: Le Monnier, 1933, p. 55.

[70] Vittorio Alfieri, *Della Tirannide, Del Principe e delle lettere, Panegirico di Plinio e Traiano, La virtù sconosciuta*, pp. 213–214.

others at the same time, by way of a better religion, a political existence independent of the Romans who held them enslaved and debased."[71]

Machiavelli's *Exhortation to Free Italy from the Barbarians* (*Esortazione a liberar l'Italia dai barbari*) was the text that inspired Alfieri's prophetic words in *Del Principe e delle lettere*. He confidently announced that Italy could have a future as a republic, thus becoming free and great once again. Save for vile cowardice, there is no reason to believe that what has been done by human beings in the past can no longer be achieved by other human beings in the present, especially on the same soil. If it is capable of rediscovering itself, if it can enact religious reforms (as northern peoples have done) and resume a lifestyle in accordance with the principles of the true Christian religion, only then can Italy rise again. To help peoples to resurrect, it takes prophets like Moses. The second example of political redeemer is Christ. The voice of the future prophet must be so strong as to redeem those slaves who now languish in silence.[72] As he writes in the invocation to the spirits of the free ancient writers (*"alle ombre degli antichi liberi scrittori"*) that opens the third book, his duty compels him not only to emancipate himself from servitude (*"affinché io uscire possa di servitù"*), but to write and speak in order to emancipate his contemporary fellow writers as well as the writers of future generations.[73]

Alfieri predicted that malign voices will say that his work was too harsh against tyrants, that his verses were boring and could in no way help emancipate a people languishing under the yoke of tyranny (*"null'uom dal rio servaggio scuote"*). Despite knowing that many would deride him, Alfieri did not abandon his mission of denouncing tyranny (*"non io per ciò da un sì sublime scopo / rimuoverò giammai l'animo e l'arte"*). His hope was that his voice would be heard and appreciated by human beings who shall come.[74] For Alfieri, the mission of moral and political emancipation is an injunction of conscience.[75] He writes his strongest prophetic words in the *Misogallo*, a collection of poems and prose composed between 1789 and 1798:

The day will come, the day will return when / by then reborn Italians will stand / armed on the battlefield, not with others' weapons / in scant defense, but to launch themselves against the Gauls. / On their strong side two strong spurs, / their ancient virtue and my words, will they have: / when, remembering that they already were, and that I already was / they will burn with an irresistible flame. / And then armed with that heavenly

---

[71] "Gesù Cristo, politicamente considerato come uomo, volle pur anco, insegnando la verità e la virtù con l'esempio, restituire al suo popolo ed a molti altri ad un tempo, per via di una miglior religione, una esistenza politica indipendente dai romani, che servi ed avviliti li teneano"; ibid., p. 210.

[72] "Tu vanne, e dillo, espertamente audace, / in suon sì forte, che in più maschia etade / vaglia a destar chi muto schiavo or giace"; ibid., p. 109.

[73] Ibid., p. 188.

[74] "Né mie voci fien sempre al vento sparte, / s'uomini veri a noi rinascon dopo, / che libertà chiamin di vita parte"; ibid., p. 3.

[75] Ibid., p. 188.

fury, / inspired in me through the works of their ancestors, / they will make my verses fatal to the Gaul. / I already hear them tell me, 'O Poet of ours, born in / depraved times, you nonetheless shaped these / sublime times that you went about prophesying.[76]

As I shall discuss later in this chapter, these words had a profound impact on the conscience of the Italians who loved liberty.

Ugo Foscolo (1778–1827) too composed prophetic verses. Giuseppe Garibaldi said that Foscolo's *Sepolcri* stirred love of the fatherland in the Italians more than any other poet's verses.[77] Like his mentor Alfieri, Foscolo regarded Dante as the poet who took up the prophetic mission of regenerating the Italian nation. Dante conceived and carried out the project of creating the language and the poetry of a nation; he exposed his country's political wounds; he taught that papal corruption, civil wars among cities, and the consequent introduction of foreign arms would lead to the slavery and disgrace of Italians. Raising himself to a place of honor among moral reformers and the avengers of crimes, he advocated the true Christian religion assisted by the hope of paradise and the terror of hell. For Foscolo, Dante was a man of strong principles who felt compassion for Italy. He composed the *Commedia* sustained by the belief that the undertaking had been commissioned to him by God ("*l'impresa gli fosse stata commessa da Dio*").[78] He most desperately tried to protect the true religion from the shade of the religion allied with the sword. He accepted the grace of apostolic light from St. Peter to work for the reform of the Church by bringing it back to Christ's pure principles.[79] Dante lived in times when "a strong yearning after justice and law instigated the people of Italy to become free."[80] In times full of pseudo-preachers, Dante "was naturally proud; and when he compared himself with his contemporaries, he felt his own superiority and found consolation, as well as unfailing guidance, in his moral conscience."[81]

---

[76] "Giorno verrà, tornerà il giorno, in cui / Redivivi omai gl'Itali, staranno / In campo audaci, e non col ferro altrui / In vil difesa, ma dei Galli a danno. / Al forte fianco sproni ardenti dui, / Lor virtù prisca, ed i miei carmi avranno: / Onde, in membrar ch'essi già fur, ch'io fui, / D'irresistibil fiamma avvamperanno. / E armati allor di quel furor celeste / Spirato in me dall'opre dei lor Avi, / Faran mie rime a Gallia esser funeste. / Li odo già dirmi: O Vate nostro, in pravi / secoli nato, eppur create hai queste / Sublimi età, che profetando andavi"; Vittorio Alfieri, *Il Misogallo*, in *Opere*, vol. I, edited by Francesco Maggini, Milan: Rizzoli, 1940, pp. 743–744.

[77] See Maria Sticco, *La poesia religiosa del Risorgimento*, p. 114. The verses in question are: "E tu, onore di pianti, Ettore, avrai, / Ove fia santo e lagrimato il sangue / Per la patria versato, e finché il Sole / Risplenderà su le sciagure umane."

[78] Ugo Foscolo, "Discorso sul testo e su le opinioni diverse prevalenti intorno alla critica e alla emendazione critica della Commedia di Dante," *Studi su Dante*, edited by Giovanni Da Pozzo, Florence: Le Monnier, 1979, pp. 243–245 and pp. 238–239.

[79] Ibid., pp. 244–245.   [80] Ibid., pp. 70–71.

[81] "Sotto l'usbergo del sentirsi puro / conscienzia m'assicura / la buona compagnia che il suo forte usbergo / prepara a lui che non si sente colpa / e lo incita e non teme" (*Inferno* XXVIII, 17 and *Inferno* XXVIII, 115–117); Ugo Foscolo, "Discorso sul testo e su le opinioni diverse prevalenti intorno alla critica e alla emendazione critica della Commedia di Dante," pp. 140–141.

For Foscolo, love inspired Dante's poetry: "I am someone who, when / Love breathes, takes note of it; and according to the way / in which it is said inside of me, so do I speak" (*"io mi son un che quando / Amore spira, noto; e a quel modo che detta dentro, vo significando"*; *Purgatory* XXIV, 52–54). As a true prophet must be, Dante was both severe and tender with his fellow citizens (*"con sapienza e fortezza"*), even if he was perhaps too harsh against Florence.[82] His *Commedia* was "prophetic poetry" (*"poesia profetica"*)[83] that shaped a new mythology (*"mitologia nuova"*) to replace the corrupt religion of his times.[84] Dante's guide, Virgil, issued the most powerful prophecy of antiquity when he wrote, as we read in *Purgatory* XXII, 70–73: "'The times renew themselves; / justice and humanity's first age return, / and new descendants come down from heaven.' / Through you I was poet, through you I was a Christian too" (*"'Secol si rinnuova, / Torna giustizia e primo tempo umano, / E progenie scende dal Ciel nuova.' / Per te poeta fui, per te cristiano"*).

Inspired by Virgil's prophecy, Dante wants to continue the prophecy of the world's renewal.[85] Brunetto Latini (*Inferno* XV, 82–85) also exhorts Dante to make the proper use of the prophetic and poetic gifts that God has bequeathed to him.[86] Out of anger against his successors, St. Peter orders Dante to reveal the truths that he has learned in the world beyond to future generations.[87] Along with Dante, Foscolo regarded Machiavelli as a prophet of political emancipation.[88] Rallying against the unfair charges that would label him a teacher of tyrants, Foscolo composed splendid verses in defense of Machiavelli. Following in Machiavelli's footsteps, he even intended to write an essay on Italy's servitude ("Della servitù dell'Italia"). Foscolo remarked that religion had become an empty ritual in Italy. Yet, the Christian religion must be defended and reformed by bringing it back to its founding principles, just as Machiavelli had taught. On the foundation of a reformed Christianity, Italy shall become a

---

[82] Ugo Foscolo, "Discorso sul testo e su le opinioni diverse prevalenti intorno alla critica e alla emendazione critica della Commedia di Dante," p. 369. Foscolo stresses that in the centuries of their moral and political servitude, Italians forgot Dante and his prophetic message: "From 1600 to 1730, Dante had no commentators, and a few editions. The Spanish government, and the ascendancy of monks, had enervated the national mind; while the popular taste was corrupted by the poetry which then reigned in Spain. Dante, of whom no edition had been allowed at Rome till the middle of the eighteenth century, could at such a period hope for no toleration. [...] The nation, broken down by every species of slavery, no longer had the faculty of admiring the free and daring exertion of sublime genius"; "Primo articolo della Edinburgh Review (February 1818)," *Studi su Dante*, p. 24.

[83] Ugo Foscolo, "Discorso sul testo e su le opinioni diverse prevalenti intorno alla critica e alla emendazione critica della Commedia di Dante," p. 373.

[84] Ibid., p. 471.   [85] Ibid., pp. 500–501.

[86] "Se tu segui la tua stella, / Non puoi fallire a glorioso porto; / Se ben m'accorsi nella vita bella"; ibid., p. 373.

[87] Ibid., p. 523.

[88] Ugo Foscolo, "Frammenti sul Machiavelli," *Prose politiche e letterarie dal 1811 al 1816*, edited by Luigi Fassò, Florence: Le Monnier, 1933, p. 15.

true Jerusalem (*"una vera Gerusalemme"*).[89] If the determination to redeem themselves from their servile mentality were ever to be instilled in Italians, Foscolo concluded that such an undertaking would require prophets who could elevate themselves to the contemplation of the divine order, interpret God's mind, and reveal His will to their compatriots.

Alessandro Manzoni (1785–1873) was the poet whose verses most power-fully exhorted Italians to mobilize for their redemption. Like other prophetic voices of the past, Manzoni exhibited (even in his juvenile works) a sense of radical revulsion for Italy's moral and political corruption. In the poem *A Francesco Lomonaco, per la vita di Dante*, composed in Paris in 1802, he chastised the cruelty and hypocrisy that Italy had displayed against her best sons, such as Dante and Lomonaco, and that ultimately had forced them to abandon their homeland and wander in foreign countries.[90] He called Italy the "cruel stepmother of gentle souls" (*"di gentili alme madrigna"*) who, herself oppressed by the barbarians, oppresses her citizens (*"Sì da' barbari oppressa opprimi i tuoi"*). She always repents but never changes (*"Pentita sempre, e non cangiata mai"*).[91] A few years later, in 1805–1806, he wrote the poem *In morte di Carlo Imbonati*, and dedicated it to his mother, Giulia Beccaria. In the poem, Manzoni denounces Italy's moral perversion even more severely. He calls his times a "filthy century" (*"secol sozzo"*) in which hypocrisy rules, and in which good people are derided while the wicked are admired and honored.[92] When the spirit of Carlo Imbonati exhorts him to remain distant from the vices of his times (*"segui tua strada; e dal viril proposto / Non ti partir, se sai"*), Manzoni solemnly commits himself to remain forever loyal to the ideals of integrity and virtue.[93]

After he converted to Catholicism, probably around 1810, Manzoni trans-lated his moral critique into a prophetic message of moral redemption under God's guidance. In the hymn *Pentecoste* (1812–1815), he evoked the image of the "Church of the living God" (*"Chiesa del Dio vivente"*) who operates in the world to comfort the grieved. The divine spirit descended upon the Church to make it a "signal to the peoples" (*"segnal de' popoli"*) placed upon a hill (*"Ti collocò sul monte"*), and to give new hope to all those who are oppressed and yearn for justice. The heavens announce new liberties (*"nova franchigia"*) and the coming of a morally renewed humanity (*"genti nove"*) who, free from fear and blandishments, are capable of glorious and virtuous achievements

---

[89] Ugo Foscolo, "Della servitù dell'Italia," *Prose politiche e letterarie dal 1811 al 1816*, p. 228.

[90] "Tal premii, Italia, i tuoi migliori, e poi / che pro' se piangi, e'l cener freddo adori, / e al nome vòto onor divini fai?"; Alessandro Manzoni, "A Francesco Lomonaco per la sua Vita di Dante," *Tutte le opere*, vol. 1, edited by Mario Martelli, Florence: G.C. Sansoni, 1988, p. 26.

[91] Ibid. [92] Alessandro Manzoni, "In morte di Carlo Imbonati," *Tutte le opere*, vol. I, p. 44.

[93] "Questa, risposi, / Qualsia favilla, che mia mente alluma, / custodii, com'io valgo, e tenni viva / finor"; ibid.

("*nove conquiste, e gloria; / Vinta in più belle prove*").[94] When foreign domination becomes unbearable and the people have lost all hope, Manzoni writes in
1814, God shows his powerful arm ("*tuonando, il braccio salvator s'è mos-
tro*") and fights alongside those people who fight with valor.[95] Enthused by the
"Proclama di Rimini" of 1815, when Gioacchino Murat exhorted Italians to
join his battle against the Austrians, Manzoni composed a poem (that remained
unfinished) with which he invoked the God who sustains peoples' struggles for
emancipation. As he did with the Hebrews, God will send a redeemer, a new
Moses. Inflamed with sacred indignation against the oppressors of his fellow
compatriots, the new redeemer will give the oppressed the courage that they
need to attain their independence.[96]

In his ode *March 1821*, Manzoni elaborates his prophetic language around
the idea that God listens to the supplications of oppressed peoples: "If the land
on which you [Germans] moaned oppressed / pushes the bodies of your
oppressors, who told you that sterile, eternal / will the mourning of the
Italian people be? / who told you that God, that God who heard you, / will
be deaf to our moaning?" This is the God of *Exodus*, the God who redeems his
people from their oppressors: "Yes, that God who enclosed in a ruby wave / the
cruel who was chasing Israel / that God who put the mallet into the vigorous
Jael's hand / and guided the blow; / that God who is Father to all the peoples, /
and who never told the Germans: / Go, reap where you have not sown; / Spread
out your claws, Italy is yours."[97] By dedicating the poem to Theodor Körner, a
poet-soldier who fought and died for Germany's independence against
Napoleon, Manzoni made the universalistic message of his appeal quite clear.
In his prophetic writings, Christian values purify the appeal to fight against
hatred, and thereby render the struggle truly emancipatory: a fight intended not
to destroy the oppressor, but to establish an earthly order of justice that is
consistent with God's will.

Manzoni's message of redemption is also visible in *I promessi sposi* (*The
Betrothed*). Here Manzoni masterfully portrays the miserable condition of a

---

[94] "Perché, baciando i pargoli, / la schiava ancor sospira? / e il sen che nutre i liberi / invidïando
mira? / non sa che al regno i miseri / seco il Signor solleva? / che a tutti i figli d'Eva / nel suo dolor
pensò?"; Alessandro Manzoni, "La Pentecoste," *Tutte le opere*, vol. I, pp. 89–91.

[95] Alessandro Manzoni, "Aprile 1814," *Tutte le opere*, vol. I, p. 59.

[96] "Egli è sorto, per Dio! Sì, per Colui / che un dì trascelse il giovinetto ebreo / che del fratello il
percussor percosse; / e fattol duce e salvator de' sui, / degli avari ladron sul capo reo / L'ardua
furia soffiò dell'onde rosse; / Per quel Dio che talora a stranie posse, / certo in pena, il valor d'un
popol trade; / ma che l'inique spade / frange una volta, e gli oppressor confonde; / e all'uom che
pugna per le sue contrade / l'ira e la gioia de' perigli infonde"; Alessandro Manzoni, "Il proclama
di Rimini," *Tutte le opere*, vol. I, p. 101.

[97] "Sì, quel Dio che nell'onda vermiglia / chiuse il rio che inseguiva Israele, / quel che in pugno alla
maschia Giaele / pose il maglio, ed il colpo guidò; / quel che è padre di tutte le genti, / che non
disse al Germano giammai: / va', raccogli ove arato non hai; / spiega l'ugne; l'Italia ti do";
Alessandro Manzoni, "Marzo 1821. Alla illustre memoria di Teodoro Koerner," *Tutte le opere*,
vol. I, p. 100.

people who are oppressed, humiliated, and forced to live at the mercy of foreign masters. Rather than inciting hatred against the oppressors, Manzoni fortifies the oppressed. He teaches them that their aspirations for justice are right and that they must keep faith in God's help. Manzoni does not promise an imminent redemption, but invites his compatriots to rediscover within their souls the moral strength that will make them capable of fighting and winning in the name of a just God. Fra Cristoforo's fierce reaction against Don Rodrigo's arrogant pretension to have Lucia under his control is the most eloquent example of Manzoni's emancipatory message:

At this suggestion, the friar's indignation, which he had held back at pains until then, overflew. All those fine resolutions to remain calm and patient went to the winds: the new man he had become joined up with the old man that he had been; and, in such cases, Fra Cristoforo really counted for two. "Your protection!" he exclaimed, moving back a couple of paces, fiercely positioning himself on his right foot, putting his right hand to his hip, lifting the left with the forefinger pointed towards Don Rodrigo, and fixing on his face two blazing eyes: "Your protection! It is better that you have spoken like this, that you have made to me such a suggestion. You have gone way too far; and I am not afraid of you anymore."

As a true Christian, Fra Cristoforo is indignant because he considers the domination of a man over another man to be an offense before God.

Indignation gives him the strength to resist Don Rodrigo's threats without any fear: "I talk as one should talk to one who is abandoned by God, and can no longer frighten anyone. Your protection! I already knew that that innocent girl is under the protection of God; but now you make me feel this with such a certainty that I no longer need to take care saying this to you. Lucia, I say: and you see how I can pronounce this name with my head high and with steady eyes." Fra Cristoforo knows that Lucia is under God's protection because his God, like in the ode *Marzo 1821*, is the God of *Exodus* – the God who knocks down the powerful with a petrified heart and uplifts the oppressed:

I pity this house: the anathema hangs over it. You will see if God's justice will show respect for these few stones, and will be frightened by a bunch of hectors. You have believed God made a creature in His own image in order to give you the pleasure of tormenting her! You have believed God wouldn't be able to defend her! You have despised His warning! You have judged yourself. Pharaoh's heart was hardened like yours; and God knew how to crush it. Lucia is safe from you; I, a poor friar, can tell you that.[98]

Giacomo Leopardi (1798–1837) was also well aware of poetry's prophetic power. He invokes a prophetic poetry capable of resuscitating the too long corrupted and servile hearts of Italians: indeed, a prophetic poetry that can

---

[98] Alessandro Manzoni, *I promessi sposi*, in *Tutte le opere*, vol. I, pp. 659–660. I am using Alberto Nones' translation from my *As if God Existed. Religion and Liberty in the History of Italy*, Princeton and Oxford: Princeton University Press, 2012, p. 128.

inspire the will to fight for their emancipation: "We want a poet to think and imagine and find; we want the poet to burn, to have a divine mind, to have the impetus and force and greatness of affections and thoughts."[99] Leopardi praises love of country as a force capable of generating and sustaining public and private virtues.[100] At the same time, he believes that love of country was an illusion of the ancients that no longer entices modern peoples. According to him, Cicero was a preacher of illusions that his contemporaries were no longer willing to believe in:

reason had come, and no one cared at all about the homeland, glory, benefits to others and to posterity, etc.; everyone had become egotists, they assessed what was useful to themselves, they took into consideration what could happen – not ardor, not fervor, not greatness of spirit; the example of their ancestors was now trivial in times so different. As such, they lost their freedom, people could not preserve or defend what Brutus had even done with the remnants of illusion; the emperors came, lust and laziness grew more and more, and soon after, with much more philosophy, books, science, experience, and history, they had become barbaric.[101]

While Leopardi maintains that poetry has the power of emancipating peoples from their servile mentality, he did not write prophetically because he did not believe in the possibility of reviving in his compatriots the noble illusion of love of country. Nonetheless, he was just as effective as the most powerful prophets in inspiring Italians to commit themselves to the emancipation of their fatherland.

Prophetic spirit also pervaded the writings of Catholic intellectuals. A prominent example is the Piedmontese nobleman Cesare Balbo (1789–1853). In his *Sommario della storia d'Italia* (1846), he claims that the ideal of Italy's independence is consistent with the Christian faith. Providence wants and sustains it. Studying Italian history to identify the traces of God's

---

[99] "Vogliamo che [un poeta] pensi e immagini e trovi, vogliamo ch'avvampi, ch'abbia mente divina, che abbia impeto e forza e grandezza di affetti e di pensieri"; Giacomo Leopardi, "Discorso di un italiano intorno alla poesia romantica," *Tutte le opere*, vol. 1 edited by Walter Binni, Florence: G.C. Sansoni, 1969, p. 932 (translation is mine); see Fernando Figurelli, "Le due canzoni patriottiche di Leopardi e il suo programma di letteratura nazionale e civile," *Belfagor* 6 (1951): pp. 20–39.

[100] Giacomo Leopardi, *"Zibaldone di pensieri," Tutte le opere*, vol. II, edited by Walter Binni, Florence: G.C. Sansoni, 1969, p. 263.

[101] "Era venuta la ragione, non importava un fico la patria la gloria il vantaggio degli altri dei posteri ec. eran fatti egoisti, pesavano il proprio utile, consideravano quello che in un caso poteva succedere, non più ardore, non impeto, non grandezza d'animo, l'esempio de' maggiori era una frivolezza in quei tempi tanto diversi: così perderono la libertà, non si arrivò a conservare e difendere quello che pur Bruto per un avanzo d'illusioni aveva fatto, vennero gl'imperatori, crebbe la lussuria e l'ignavia, e poco dopo con tanto più filosofia, libri scienza esperienza storia, erano barbari"; Giacomo Leopardi, *Zibaldone di pensieri*, in *Tutte le opere*, vol. II, p. 762; I am using Alberto Nones' translation from my *As if God Existed. Religion and Liberty in the History of Italy*, p. 131.

will therein, Balbo concludes that modern history as a whole is the achievement of Christianity. Nations, indeed the Italian nation more than others, can progress only as long as they remain faithful to Christianity. If they lose their Christian faith, they are bound to decline and perish. The struggle for Italy's independence becomes meaningful and glorious only if it is in Providence's design.[102] God holds Italy's destiny in His hands. Italians must therefore pray for Him to unite and lead them to independence. Before they enter into any battles to fight for their freedom, they must first sincerely invoke God's protection. With remarkable confidence, Balbo announced God's plan for Italy, even if, he qualified, at times Providence does not allow us to decipher His will. He claims that God entrusted Italy with the mission of being the center of the Christian world.[103] For the end-all success of this mission, Italians must learn to be grateful to God for all His valuable gifts; they must learn not to be impatient.[104]

Despite the Church's hostility to prophecy and political emancipation, prophetic messages of liberation also came from within the Catholic clergy. In his *History of Love (Storia dell'amore)* written in 1821–1823 and published in 1834, Antonio Rosmini (1797–1855), a priest from Rovereto, extols Moses as the example of a redeeming prophet who received the divine and indestructible sentiment of charity precisely because he was "directly connected to God (*"a Dio immediatamente congiunto"*).[105] To serve God is to rule (*"servire Dio è regnare"*), and the love of God grants the greatest liberty (*"la somma libertà e padronanza che possa uomo, non che desiderare, ma pensare!"*). As the example of Moses teaches, the love of God allows for triumph over enemies.[106] Rosmini proclaims that God loves just peoples. By submitting themselves to God, just peoples can see the signs of Providence in human history and can accordingly partake in God's power. In his monumental *Teodicea*, Rosmini justifies the way in which God distributes his justice and goodness among different peoples throughout history. God uses the Socratic method: He questions and challenges people, and, in turn, they must accept the noble effort of deciphering His governing mind. Thanks to Providence, life is an always new enchantment (*"incanto sempre nuovo"*) capable of endless creative achievements, and suffering has a transitory role in preparation for greater goods.

---

[102] "Senza sopranaturalità non si spiegano nè il principio, nè il mezzo, nè l'andamento, nè lo scopo del genere umano, non la storia universale; e men che niuna non la storia speciale dell'Italia, sede del miracolo perenne della centralità da diciotto secoli"; Cesare Balbo, *Sommario della storia d'Italia*, tenth edition, Florence: Le Monnier, 1856, p. 68.

[103] "Così l'Italia ebbe da Dio quest'ufficio di centro della Cristianità: un ufficio, come tutti quelli di quaggiù, dotato di diritti e vantaggi, carico di doveri, che vedremo, nella storia seguente, perenni"; ibid., p. 67.

[104] Ibid., p. 440.

[105] Antonio de' Rosmini-Serbati, *Storia dell'amore cavata dalle divine scritture libri tre*, Cremona: Dal Feraboli Tipografo Vescovile, 1834, p. 218.

[106] Ibid., p. 180.

From his faith in Providence, Rosmini elicited a patriotism for Christians to actively participate in public life and work for the triumph of good. Christian faith is a "sweet tyranny" (*"dolce tirannia"*) that might even demand martyrdom for the liberty of one's country.[107] By stressing that Providence operates within individual consciences and that suffering for moral principles has a redeeming force, Rosmini offers his fellow Italians a prophecy of liberation that directly connects love of God with love of country.

When he thought that circumstances were suitable, Rosmini also intervened on political matters. As a Christian who believed that God desires justice, he maintained that God could not therefore possibly tolerate the visible injustice of the foreign domination of Italy. In a speech delivered in Rovereto on September 25, 1823, Rosmini implored God to make Italy aware of her destiny as a teacher of Christian virtue, of liberty, and of love: a calling that should not instill fear, but that will ultimately bring about tranquility and felicity in the world.[108] God's help alone, however, is not sufficient to sustain Italy's political emancipation. Quite crucially, Italians must also emancipate themselves from their subjection to foreign cultures. In his *Constitution according to Social Justice* (*La costituzione secondo la giustizia sociale*) published in 1848, Rosmini again urges his fellow Italians to be themselves, and to give themselves a political constitution in tune with their own history and spirit.[109] Convinced that Italy's unity and independence were part of God's plan, Rosmini forcefully rejects the view that Italy's redemption required sacrificing one's soul. Unlike the God of Machiavelli, Rosmini's God is not prepared to pardon rulers who lose their soul to redeem the fatherland. Still, Rosmini has no doubt that God Himself was ordering the Italians to fight for their emancipation. In God, and with God, Italy will attain its liberation.[110]

Not all the militants of the Risorgimento unambiguously longed for prophetic visions. One such example is Niccolò Tommaseo (1802–1874), a patriot and prolific writer who clandestinely published the *Opuscoli inediti di fra Girolamo Savonarola* in 1835. Even if the title promises a prophetic message, the essay is an attack against prophecy, or, better yet, an attack on prophecies that promised God's help to Italy.[111] Rather than prophetic language, Tommaseo uses the language of natural cataclysms to convey a vision of social change.[112] Despite this different register, he maintains that Christian faith and

---

[107] Maria Sticco, *La poesia religiosa del Risorgimento*, p. 177.   [108] Ibid., p. 178.

[109] Ibid., p. 180.

[110] "Io non dubito che il movimento italiano sia ordinato da Dio al servizio della sua Chiesa"; "Parmi di vedere, dopo tutti i maneggi degli uomini la mano di Dio, onde me ne rallegro." "La religione è il palladio della libertà italiana"; ibid., p. 182.

[111] "Sventurato chi libertà spera da altra forza che dalla propria e da Dio!" *Opuscoli inediti di fra Girolamo Savonarola*, no place, no date, I, p. 12.

[112] Ibid., I, pp. 65–67.

science can teach the true path to Italy's redemption.[113] He invoked new prophets who would detach themselves from the masses in order to be closer to heaven. From these spiritual heights, they would be able to see the new times and be better disposed to lead their fellow compatriots on the road to liberty.[114] By proclaiming that love is the true prophet (*"l'amore è profeta"*), Tommaseo meant that love reveals new visions of emancipation, and inspires the desire of accomplishing great things. Love gives faith, it unites. And thus, no political redemption is possible without love (*"laddove non è amore, ivi non è redenzione, ivi inferno. Amore è redenzione continova"*).[115]

In Tommaseo's conception of love, the foundation of redemption is faith. Faith sustains the struggle of liberty because it provides hope.[116] The Gospel, the apostles, and the fathers of the Church do not forbid "courage and the conscience of magnanimous things." A Christian's duty is to spare grief to others, and remove or relieve it, even at risk of one's own grief and danger; to work to uplift the oppressed, to suffer and fight with them; to point out and reprimand injustices, regardless of who perpetrates them, be they plebeians or princes. Patience teaches how to endure one's own ills, but not to tolerate when others inflict suffering upon their fellow human beings. The Italian revolution must be a "war of religion" that originates from love and faith, not from hatred and prejudice. Only a revolution supported and restrained by the true Christian faith will be liberating and not produce a new tyranny.[117] As a good prophet, Tommaseo affirmed that the true difficulty of a successful Italian revolution would occur after all fighting has ended: that is to say, the preservation of acquired liberty. In the first place, Italians must liberate themselves from the corrupting consequences that centuries of oppression had on their minds and thoughts. While revolutions led by leaders without

---

[113] "Ciascun popolo col dolore riscatta sè stesso: e in questa parola *redenzione* è non solo la fede Cristiana, ma la scienza politica tutta quanta. Patire, migliorare noi stessi, vincere il male dovunque e' si trovi, ricomperarci, risorgere"; ibid., II, p. 109.

[114] "Ad ogni stagione di nuova libertà si raccoglie un uomo, pochi uomini si raccolgono lontan dalla folla; e rinnovano pensando, ricreano pregando, parlando fanno. Perchè dalle alture solitarie meglio si domina il piano: quivi la terra è più prossima al cielo. Quivi si rinfresca l'umana natura appassita, e l'allentata si fa più agile a rimbalzare sotto il tocco potente della voluttà e del dolore. Quivi gli uomini da un pensiero comune stretti, e dalla morta società separati, a lei si congiungono più strettamente che mai, si congiungono come spirito al corpo, per animarla, non per marcire con essa. E nell' amara caligine dei secoli andati apparvero le famiglie del solitarii come fiamma dal rovo; e diedero all'Italia, diedero al mondo libri, terreni, arti, affetti, preghiere ed esempi. Ma non ogni solitudine è ne' silenzii del deserto; e tempo verrà che saran tutti popolati i deserti; e nel popoloso deserto delle città le anime liberatrici saranno chiostro e romitaggio a sè stesse. E tra le folte ombre di nuovi pensieri e alle fresch'acque di nuovi affetti riposeranno, e sulla vetta d'un desiderio altissimo raccorranno le stanche ale; e guarderanno pietose alla devastazione della sottoposta campagna. Istituti nuovi, non nuove religioni, chiede l'Italia, chiede l'umanità; dove meno anguste le regole e sieno più larghe le idee [...] Ma tu risuscita, o Padre, il cadavere abitato già dallo spirito mio; o lo dissolvi; e di vite nuove ripopola il deserto d'Italia"; ibid., II, pp. 30–31.

[115] Ibid., II, p. 31.   [116] Ibid., II, pp. 46–47.   [117] Ibid., II, pp. 185–187.

religious faith may be suitable to other peoples, the Italian revolution can and must only be a political revolution animated by moral and religious ideals.

While Tommaseo's *Opuscoli inediti di fra Girolamo Savonarola* were not Savonarolan at all, other patriots of the Risorgimento did indeed reclaim Savonarola's prophetic legacy. A patriot and former Catholic priest who converted to Protestantism, Camillo Mapei (1809–1853) founded the journal *Savonarola's Echo* (*L'eco di Savonarola*) in London in 1847. A second series of the same journal was released in Italy thanks to the efforts of Salvatore Ferretti (1817–1874), another Protestant who had migrated to London. As Mapei explains in the opening issue, the new journal's mission was the same as that which Savonarola – inspired by God (*"mosso dallo Spirito del Signore"*) – pursued, namely, to contemplate the scriptures and extract principles for Italy's redemption.[118] The words of true prophets, such as Savonarola, have always had beneficial effects upon nations. God has spoken to Italy and has revealed His plan. If correctly understood, God's words will be the font from which great blessings shall flow.[119] Prophets provide and sustain moral force.[120] They teach people how to love liberty and how to work for the unity of the nation. Italy will resurrect and political redemption will come, if Italians obey God's law.[121] Not surprisingly, Moses was yet again the luminous model of the redeeming prophet that Mapei was invoking.[122]

---

[118] Camillo Mapei, *L'eco di Savonarola. Foglio mensile diretto da Italiani cristiani*, London: Partridge and Oakey, 1847, p. 1.

[119] "Come mai, nel mare immenso di dubbii, in cui si trovavano gl' Italiani poteano non ascoltare la voce della ragione, trasgredire il comando di Dio, disprezzare esempii sì grandi e sì luminosi? Come chiuso avrebber il loro cuore ad un Dio che ha parlato! Come non avrebbero ascoltato Colui, cui intendono le inanimate creature, alla voce del quale prese ordine il caos, e ad un cui cenno il sol s' arrestò nel suo corso! Il Creatore ha parlato alla creatura, il sovrano dell'universo si è degnato svelare i suoi disegni, di annunziar la sua volontà ai figli della polvere, agli atomi posti su questo globo, ed eglino avrebbero ricusato istruirsene, gli avrebbero opposta una non curanza che non potrebbesi in modo alcuno spiegare! Nò, la divina misericordia nol permise. Gl' Italiani lesser la Bibbia, gl' Italiani la leggono, e coll'aiuto dell'onnipossente grazia han sentiti e risentiranno i vantaggi, che dalla lettura di essa derivano. Ella è cosa omai riconosciuta generalmente, che, dovunque si permette la lettura e la libera predicazione della parola di Dio, immensi sono i vantaggi che ne risentono le Nazioni; la ricevuta libertà, l'ingentilito costume, lo stato di progresso in cui si ritrovano, ed i beni che da tutto ciò ne derivano ne fanno incontestabil testimonianza"; ibid., p. 32.

[120] "Trovano in essi tutto ciò che può fortificar la lor fede, meditando continuamente le prove della loro origin celeste in quel imponente seguito di rivelazioni e di profezie sempre più sviluppate a misura che il loro adempimento si appressa; quella dottrina sì maestosa e consolante, sì superiore alla ragione egli è vero, ma sì ben fatta pel cuore; quella morale infine avvolta da principio nelle forme e nelle ceremonie proprie ad uomini grossolani, è divenuta in appresso cotanto spirituale e sublime"; ibid., pp. 33–34.

[121] "Se tu siegui l'amico consiglio, / Se dar fede ai miei detti vorrai, / Di tua gloria vetusta vedrai / La bell' era di nuovo fiorir. / Un potere che in male si volve / Nò, dal Cielo ch'è santo, non viene; / Chi per santo e celeste lo tiene, / Ombra alcuna di senno non ha"; "Carme popolare," in *L'eco di Savonarola. Foglio mensile diretto da Italiani cristiani*, pp. 52–54.

[122] "Libera versione del cantico di Mosé," in *L'eco di Savonarola. Foglio mensile diretto da Italiani cristiani*, pp. 83–84.

4.3 GIUSEPPE MAZZINI AND HIS PROPHETIC LEGACY

Without a doubt, the most prominent and effective prophetic voice of the Italian Risorgimento was Giuseppe Mazzini.[123] From his youth, he designated his life's mission to the founding and diffusion of a faith (*"creare una fede"*) that would give his fellow Italians the moral strength to begin the journey of their redemption.[124] He regarded himself as a redeemer, as a new Prometheus who had stolen the light of emancipation from God.[125] God and his conscience were his only guides. Indeed, he was prepared to sacrifice himself to accomplish his mission.[126]

Mazzini interprets his prophetic mission as a total and unmitigated commitment to the principle of duty, free from any inclination for life's pleasures.[127]

---

[123] On Mazzini's prophetic message see Adolfo Omodeo, "Risorgimento senza eroi," *Difesa del Risorgimento*, edited by Adolfo Omodeo, Turin: Einaudi, 1951, pp. 439–446; Ettore Rota, *Le origini del Risorgimento*, vol. 2, Milan: Vallardi, 1948; Maria Sticco, *La poesia religiosa del Risorgimento*; Luigi Salvatorelli, *Il pensiero politico italiano dal 1700 al 1870*, Turin: Einaudi, 1935; Carlo Calcaterra, *Il nostro imminente Risorgimento: gli studi e la letteratura in Piemonte nel periodo della Sampaolina e della Filopatria*, Turin: Società Editrice Internazionale, 1935; Arturo Carlo Jemolo, *Il giansenismo in Italia prima della rivoluzione*, Bari: Laterza, 1928; Francesco Olgiati, *La pietà cristiana. Esperienze ed indirizzi*, Milan: Vita e Pensiero, 1935; Robert T. Handy, "The Influence of Mazzini on the American Social Gospel," *The Journal of Religion* 29 (1949): pp. 114–123; Marcella Pellegrino Sutcliffe, *Victorian Radicals and Italian Democrats*, Woodbridge: Boydell & Brewer, 2014; Martin Wight, *Four Seminal Thinkers in International Theory: Machiavelli, Grotius, Kant, and Mazzini*, Oxford: Oxford University Press, 2004; *A Cosmopolitanism of Nations: Giuseppe Mazzini's Writings on Democracy, Nation Building, and International Relations*, edited by Nadia Urbinati and Stefano Recchia, Princeton: Princeton University Press, 2009.

[124] Ettore Passerin d'Entrèves, "Il romanticismo 'progressivo' di Giuseppe Mazzini negli scritti giovanili (1829–1843)," *Religione e politica nell'Ottocento europeo*, p. 147.

[125] Mazzini's mother powerfully contributed to reinforce his persuasion that he was the chosen prophet of Italian emancipation. "Sei il prediletto di Dio," she wrote to him, "Egli ti trasse illeso dai più mortali frangenti e non ti abbandonerà mai sino alla vittoria finale delle tue idee [...] Io veggo già la tua innocenza coronata in cielo; il tuo nome è destinato a sfolgorare in eterno tra i benefattori dell'umanità. Per me questo è un articolo di fede; è scritto lassù [...] Fede, dunque, costanza, o eroe del sacrificio!"; *La madre di Mazzini. Carteggio inedito del 1834–39*, edited by Alessandro Luzio, Turin: Bocca, 1919, pp. 23–24. On Mazzini's mother and her influence on his prophetic ideas see Adolfo Omodeo, *L'età del Risorgimento italiano*, Messina: G. Principato, 1931; I am citing from the 1946 edition, Naples: Edizioni Scientifiche Italiane, p. 333.

[126] "Il nostro è un segreto fra la nostra coscienza e Dio." And in another letter: "Abbiamo rapito la scintilla all'Eterno, ci siamo posti tra lui e il popolo, abbiamo assunto le parti dell'emancipatore, e Dio ci ha accettato; ora nei pochi anni che ci rimangono, noi non siamo che vittime di espiazione, soffriremo per tutti"; Giuseppe Mazzini, *Epistolario*, vol. II, Florence: G.C. Sansoni, 1902, II, p. 284; "Noi sulla terra non siamo che una missione incarnata" – he writes to Eleonora Ruffini on March 17, 1836 – "adempiamola come se non esistesse che Dio e la nostra coscienza e noi pochi. V'è bisogno di gioia e di felicità per operare come il core ci detta"; *La madre di Mazzini*, pp. 309–310.

[127] "Ricordati sempre che altra è la vita del dovere, altra la vita del cuore. La prima, benché soddisfi la coscienza, non dà gioia mai, amarezza quasi sempre. La seconda è quella degli affetti e

Unwilling to indulge in hope, Mazzini was a prophet whose lifelong companion was grief for the miserable condition of his homeland.[128] For Mazzini, prophets must be heroes who are endowed with an immense moral strength that allows them to continue to fight even when their compatriots ridicule them and refuse to listen to them. But they will be heard in the future. From exile, from their deathbed, from the gallows, they cry to their fellow compatriots: "you shall triumph" (*"voi vincerete"*).[129] He is aware that the task of emancipating a people degraded by centuries of foreign domination, political oppression, and religious corruption – all courtesy of the Church of Rome – is prohibitively hard. Yet, he believes that prophecy can accomplish the task; he is confident that God wants the emancipation of Italy and of all peoples. Mazzini's own prophetic faith in the Italian cause's final victory had immense power in motivating thousands of young Italians to respond to the call and to begin the long journey toward moral and political redemption.

As I have intimated, Mazzini was well acquainted with the European prophetic literature of the early nineteenth century. But Dante was the main source of his conception of the prophet that Italy needed.[130] In the 1826 essay *Of Dante's Love of Country (Dell'amor patrio di Dante)*, written when he was twenty-one, Mazzini described true prophets as exceptional persons who "understand the situation and the needs of their compatriots with just a glance; they are strangers to the vices of their contemporaries, and instead all the more strongly suffer from them; a holy indignation fills them; tormented by a pressing desire to better their brothers and sisters, they issue forth a strong and austere voice that, like a prophet, rebukes people; a voice that is largely unwelcomed by those to whom it is directed, as children do with medicine."[131] Mazzini returned to Dante yet again when he edited and published Ugo Foscolo's commentary on the *Divine Comedy* in 1843. Mazzini claims that Dante composed the *Divina Commedia* to accomplish the prophetic mission to which he had consecrated himself and his work. For Mazzini, Foscolo was correct to believe that "Dante had established himself principally as a reformer of religion, and that the poem was dictated for the prophetic mission to which he rightfully and without fear

---

nessuna cosa può sostituirsi agli affetti"; "Alla sorella Antonietta, 17 marzo 1838," *La madre di Mazzini*, p. 344.

[128] "Diedi un lungo tristissimo addio a tutte le gioie, a tutte le speranze di vita individuale per me sulla terra [...] M'affratellai col dolore e mi ravvolsi in esso come pellegrino nel suo mantello"; *Note autobiografiche*, vol. LXXVII, Edizione Nazionale, Imola: Galeati, 1938, p. 258.

[129] G. Mazzini, "Saggio sopra alcune tendenze della letteratura europea nel sec. XIX," in Giuseppe Mazzini, *Scritti sul romanzo e altri saggi letterari*, pp. 76–77.

[130] See Jessie W. Mario, *Della vita di Giuseppe Mazzini*, Milan: Edoardo Sonzogno, 1886, pp. 46–47. See also *Scritti scelti di Giuseppe Mazzini, con note e cenni biografici di Jessie White V. Mario*, Florence: G.C. Sansoni, 1901, p. xi, where Jessie White Mario cites Carlyle's judgment on Mazzini as the prophet of Italy.

[131] Giuseppe Mazzini, *Dell'amor patrio di Dante*, in *Scritti editi ed inediti di Giuseppe Mazzini*, vol. I, Imola: Cooperativa Tipografico-Editrice Paolo Galeati, 1906, p. 11.

of sacrilege consecrated himself with priestly rites in heaven most high."[132] A few years later, Mazzini further elaborates his ideas on prophets. In addition to their strokes of genius, they are inspired individuals who come forth in each historic era, and who are able to infuse and catalyze generous and divine impulses in their fellow citizens' souls. They are the prophets of a truth that becomes the faith of many, a truth and a faith that make emancipation possible.[133] Mazzini wants to be one such prophet not only to severely castigate his compatriots' moral and political corruption, but also to exhort them to fight and be willing to sacrifice themselves for their redemption.

When national and democratic movements seemed definitively dispersed, Mazzini wrote in 1834 that "the condemnation of the papacy, the empire, the monarchy, and the aristocracy emerges from all the aspirations of the age, from the ideas of the most powerful intellects, from the various succession of systems, from collective European thought"; indeed, it eventually appears in the form "of novels, of plays, of history, of songs, of prophecy."[134] Mazzini offers a prophetic vision of unparalleled, inspiring power to those Italians and European patriots afflicted by defeats and tested by suppression: "The nature of great changes is spontaneity. God alone makes the hours of the world beat. When the times are ripe, He inspires in the people – those who have most suffered and kept their faith intact – the will and courage to win or die for everyone. This is the people who initiates, who arises and fights: whether they triumph or perish, the word of the age unfolds from their ashes or from their victory, and the world is saved."[135] The "prophetic instinct" of peoples raises "the stone from the tomb where they lie," it instills new faith and new hope: "in the midst of the palingenetic signs that fill the earth and sky, among those flashes of the future that flicker everywhere and announce a new synthesis, the voice of thousands will answer: we advance toward freedom; we move in search of the equality and brotherhood that were promised to us."[136]

The duty of revolutionaries is "to translate the thought of God into earthly facts."[137] To those who have lost faith in freedom, Mazzini points out that "the secret of the age lives in the people, and can only be reached by living not just for it, but also with it." The new "Messiah" will be this people who initiates and who "will rise in the power of insurrection, in the presence of the world; great and free, the people is gathered in a single thought, in a single love, and

---

[132] Ugo Foscolo, *La commedia illustrata da Ugo Foscolo*, vol. III, London: Pietro Rolandi, 1843, p. 552.

[133] "In tutti i grandi periodi storici dell'Umanità sorsero uomini ispirati i quali, suscitando i grandi, generosi, divini impulsi dell'anima, mossero guerra agli appetiti materiali, agli istinti dell' egoismo. E trovarono ascoltatori"; Giuseppe Mazzini, *Genio e Tendenze di Thomas Carlyle*, in *Scritti editi e inediti*, vol. XXIX, Imola: Galeati, 1919, p. 113; see Ettore Passerin d'Entrèves, *Religione e politica nell'Ottocento europeo*, pp. 138–147.

[134] Giuseppe Mazzini, "Dell'iniziativa rivoluzionaria in Europa," in Giuseppe Mazzini, *Scritti politici*, edited by Terenzio Grandi and Augusto Comba, Turin: UTET, 2005, p. 390.

[135] Ibid., pp. 395–396.   [136] Ibid., p. 397.   [137] Ibid., p. 398.

recognizes God in heaven and Humanity on earth as its only masters." The "breath of God announcing the sun of humanity to the peoples" calls upon the peoples to awaken, to begin the journey of redemption: "Children of God and of humanity rise up and move. The hour has come. Freedom lives in you: the equality that was expected to be just in heaven now walks today on the earth that you tread, and social redemption rises above individual redemption. Learn how to achieve it; show yourselves equal to the undertaking. Do not doubt its success; do not say: we are weak; when God assigns a mission, he provides the forces necessary to accomplish it."[138] Strengthened "by the law of the world and the breath of God," the peoples will know how to win their redemption.[139]

The foundation stone of Mazzini's prophetic message is his belief that faith gives peoples the strength to translate moral ideals into action. This principle of faith urges human beings to find new and higher political and social forms; it purifies them from egotism; it renders them capable of acting and actualizing moral ideals in the realm of history. For Mazzini, religion is the source of the impulse to achieve harmony between thought and action.[140] Without sincere religious sentiment, there has never been, and never can there be, any redemption:

Man is higher up than the earth that sustains him. He lives on its surface, not in the middle of it. His feet touch the ground, but his forehead faces the sky, as if he wanted to set out for it. Up there, in the highest, splendid in the clear sky or hidden in the midst of stormy clouds, lies his pole star. From the bottom of his soul, he aspires to a future that he at present cannot hope to reach, but which is the goal of any activity of life, the secret of being, the guarantee of progress; and every great epoch of humanity makes that aspiration more intense, and spreads a new light on the concept that man forms about that future. To that light, corresponds a social renovation – a new earth in the image of the new heaven. Historically speaking, I do not know of a single conquest of the human spirit, of even one important step on the way to the improvement of human society, which is not rooted in a strong religious belief; and I say that any doctrine in which the aspiration to the ideal remains neglected – in which, that is, a solution to this supreme necessity of some faith is not found, as the times allow for, and a solution to the eternal problem of the origin and the fate of humanity – is and will always be incapable of actualizing the concept of a new world.[141]

---

[138] Ibid., p. 408.   [139] Ibid., p. 411.
[140] See Carlo Cantimori, *Saggio sull'idealismo di Giuseppe Mazzini*, Faenza: Casa Tipografica Editrice G. Montanari, 1904.
[141] "L'uomo è più in alto della terra che lo sostiene. Ei vive sulla sua superficie e non nel suo centro. I suoi piedi toccano il suolo, ma la sua fronte si volge al cielo come s'ei volesse avviarvisi. Lassù, nell'alto, splendida in un cielo sereno o nascosta fra nuvoli di tempesta, sta la sua stella polare. Dal profondo dell'anima egli aspira ad un avvenire ch'ei non può nella forma presente sperar di raggiungere, ma ch'è l'oggetto d'ogni attività della vita, il segreto dell'essere, la mallevadoria del progresso; e ogni grande epoca dell'umanità rende quell'aspirazione più intensa, e spande una nuova luce sul concetto ch'ei forma di quell'avvenire. A quella luce novellamente diffusa corrisponde un rinnovamento sociale – una nuova terra a somiglianza del nuovo cielo. Io non conosco, parlando storicamente, una sola conquista dello spirito umano, un solo passo

Religion has a much greater value than philosophy with respect to the emancipation of peoples, as evidenced by the French Revolution.[142] Mazzini interpreted the French Revolution as the defeat of dead institutions at the hands of an ideal lived out as a faith, indeed a manifestation of a most genuine religious spirit. For him, the French Revolution was "Luther's work in the political sphere," and therein resides the Revolution's glory and power.[143] The religion that Mazzini pointed out to Italians is a religion of truth and of duty:

importante mosso sulla via di perfezionamento della società umana, che non abbia radici in una forte credenza religiosa; e dico che ogni dottrina nella quale rimanga negletta l'aspirazione all'ideale, nella quale non sia contenuta, quale i tempi la consentono, una soluzione a questa suprema necessità d'una fede, a questo eterno problema dell'origine e dei fati dell'umanità, è e sarà sempre impotente a ridurre in atto il concetto d'un nuovo mondo. Potrà riescire a foggiare magnifiche forme; ma mancherà ad esso la scintilla di vita che Prometeo conquistava alla sua statua dal cielo"; Giuseppe Mazzini, *I Sistemi e la Democrazia*, in *Scritti editi e inediti di Giuseppe Mazzini*, vol. VII, Milan: Daelli Editore, 1864, pp. 326–327. In a letter to Francesco Bertioli of January 1833, Mazzini writes: "I am not a Christian in the sense of believing in the divinity of Christ and like things: I admit of any other revelation than that of the Genius; I believe that religion is an outcome, and an expression of the Society, just like literature, law, politics, etc. [I believe that] religion [is] subject to Progress just like all other things – and in this sense Christianity is the first religion expressing our civilization, i.e., a religion of the modern world as opposed to the ancient – as Christianity in my view has elaborated the Dogma of Equality. And in this sense I am a Christian. Yet, I also believe that Christianity has only preached Equality before God, and one's own *individual* improvement, whereas we are now approaching the age in which Equality must be preached before men, and the improvement must be *social* – and in this sense I am not a Christian. However, as everything occurs progressively, we – a society still under the empire of Catholicism – cannot jump with one leap beyond Christianity and preach the pure Deism which is my religion"; *Scritti editi ed inediti di Giuseppe Mazzini*, vol. V, Imola: Galeati, 1909, p. 216.

[142] Giuseppe Mazzini, *Dal papa al concilio*, in *Scritti editi e inediti di Giuseppe Mazzini*, vol. VII, Milan: Daelli Editore, 1864, pp. 234–235.

[143] Giuseppe Mazzini, *Condizione e avvenire dell'Europa*, in *Scritti editi e inediti di Giuseppe Mazzini*, vol. VIII, Rome: Daelli Editore, 1891, p. 186. Like Mazzini, other patriots worked for a moral and religious reform. An example is the journal *Il Cattolico Cristiano*, published in Malta from 1848 to 1850. As the founder of the paper – Luigi De Sanctis (1808–1869), a former theologian – stressed, the religious reform was necessary for Italy to be able to find her liberty again, and to generate new and better moral habits: "Italy needs a religious reform [. . .] Let the evangelical light appear, and Italy shall be one, shall be free, shall be happy; there cannot be unity, liberty, or happiness unless the principle of brotherhood and love is firmly established; and this principle cannot be firmly established if not through the Gospel [. . .] Let us destroy the papal institutions, which are tyrannical institutions; and inasmuch as the popes have suppressed the Gospel in order to tyrannize, and on its ruins have based their code of oppression, let us overturn this code, and let us edify again the Gospel from its ruins! This is the only way to free Italy forever"; see Augusto Armand Hugon, "Correnti evangeliche tra gli italiani in esilio 1840–1860," *Atti del XXXIII Congresso di Storia del Risorgimento Italiano (Messina, 1–4 settembre 1954)*, Rome: Istituto per la Storia del Risorgimento Italiano, 1958, pp. 29–36.

Truth! The rising Italy does not ask but that, and cannot live but with that. The rising Italy seeks her goal in the present and the norm of her life in the future – a moral criterion, a method of choice between good and evil, between truth and error, without which no responsibility, and hence no liberty, can exist for her. Centuries of servitude, centuries of egotism (which is the only foundation for the life of a slave); centuries of corruption, slowly and shrewdly instilled by a Catholicism deprived of any sense of its mission have spoiled, perverted, nearly erased the instinct for the great and sacred things that God bestowed on Italy. [...] The resurrecting Italy needs to fortify herself by acquiring an awareness of her duties, of her strength, of virtue animated by sacrifice, and of the certainty about the next triumph which is in the logic of things.[144]

For Mazzini, the entire history of mankind was the gradual revelation of divine Providence. Step by step, humanity ascends to the ultimate goal that God has predisposed for it: one civilization is the stepping-stone for the next; one phase concludes and another one begins. Duty and mission are the forms through which human beings conform to the fulfillment of this divine law of progress. This sense of duty and the overall mission are absolutely selfless; they have no allure of rewards and do not carry fallacious illusions of happiness. Once Christianity's task has been resolved in the new religion of progress, and once the era initiated with the French Revolution has ended, a new era that is at once social and religious can be ushered in. God has assigned Italy the task of inaugurating a third and higher form of civilization based upon the association of the world's free peoples.[145] The most powerful and true force of emancipation is the word of God that lives and unceasingly operates in history by virtue of prophets. In *Fede e avvenire*, Mazzini explains his conception of history and social emancipation in a piece that deserves to be cited in full:

No, eternal God! Your word is not accomplished; your thoughts, your thought of the world, are not completely revealed. It creates and will create throughout long centuries inaccessible to human calculation. Those centuries that have passed have revealed but some fragments of your thoughts. Our mission is not concluded. We barely know its origin; we ignore its ultimate purpose: time and our discoveries only broaden its

---

[144] "Il vero! L'Italia nascente non chiede se non quello, non può vivere senza quello. L'Italia nascente cerca in oggi il proprio fine, la norma della propria vita nell'avvenire, un criterio morale, un metodo di scelta fra il bene e il male, tra la verità e l'errore, senza il quale non può esistere per essa responsabilità, quindi non libertà. Secoli di schiavitù, secoli di egoismo, unica base all'esistenza dello schiavo; secoli di corruzione, lentamente e dottamente instillata da un cattolicesimo senza coscienza di missione, hanno guasto, pervertito, cancellato quasi l'istinto delle grandi e sante cose, che Dio pose in essa [...] L'Italia nascente ha bisogno di fortificarsi acquistando conoscenza dei propri doveri, della propria forza, della virtù scossa dal sagrificio, della certezza di trionfo che è nella logica: e voi le date una teorica d'interessi, d'opportunità, di finzioni; un machiavellismo male inteso e rifatto da allievi ai quali Machiavelli, redivivo, direbbe: io aveva innanzi la sepoltura; voi, stolti, la culla d'un popolo. L'Italia nascente ha bisogno d'uomini che incarnino in sé quel vero nel quale essa deve immedesimarsi; che lo predichino ad alta voce, lo rappresentino negli atti, lo confessino, checché avvenga, fino alla tomba [...]"; Giuseppe Mazzini, "A Francesco Crispi (1864)," *Scritti politici*, pp. 983–984.

[145] Adolfo Omodeo, *L'età del Risorgimento italiano*, Naples: VIVARIUM, 1996, p. 337.

boundaries. Our mission moves through the centuries towards destinies unknown to us: it seeks its own law, of which we have just the first contours. From new beginning to new beginning, through the series of its successive incarnations, it purifies and expands the formula of sacrifice; it studies its own path; it learns your faith, eternally in progress.[146]

God marks the hours of the world. When the times are ripe, He inspires the faith, will, and courage that allow His people to be victorious, or die fighting for the cause of liberty.[147] For Mazzini, democracy was not just the exercise of popular sovereignty, but the ethical elevation of the people. He considered the people as a means or medium of "divine revelation."[148] The duty of the republican youth was to nurture faith in the people, to educate them, to redeem them from political servitude and social brutishness, to provide examples of abnegation and sacrifice.[149] National redemption, republican liberty, and religious regeneration were inseparable elements of Mazzini's radically innovative prophetic message. Indeed, his vision was designed in the auspices of inaugurating, under God's protection, a new epoch in humanity's history.

By the end of his life, Mazzini faced a powerful ideological and political offensive against his prophetic vision of political and social emancipation by way of Mikhail Bakunin, the leader of the international anarchist movement. In his 1871 pamphlet *La théologie politique de Mazzini*, Bakunin directly attacks the religious foundation of Mazzini's theory:

The Italian patriot's revolutionary programme had at its core an essentially false principle which, after paralysing and nullifying his most heroic efforts and most ingenious schemes, was bound sooner or later to lure him into the ranks of reaction. That principle is a dual idealism, both metaphysical and mystical, grafted on to the patriotic ambition of the statesman. It is the cult of God and of divine and human authority, it is faith in the messianic destiny of Italy as queen of nations, Rome as capital of the world, it is the political lust for State grandeur and glory, necessarily based upon hardship for the people. Lastly, it is that religion of all dogmatic and absolutist minds, that passion for

---

[146] Giuseppe Mazzini, "Fede e avvenire," *Scritti politici*, p. 458.

[147] "Dio solo batte le ore del mondo. Maturi i tempi, Egli spira nel popolo, che ha più patito e più serbato intatta la propria fede, la volontà e il coraggio di vincere o morire per tutti. È quello il popolo iniziatore. Esso sorge e combatte: trionfi o muoia, si svolge dalle sue ceneri o dal suo trofeo di vittoria la parola dell'epoca e il mondo è salvato"; Giuseppe Mazzini, "Dell'iniziativa rivoluzionaria in Europa (1834)," *Scritti politici*, p. 396.

[148] Adolfo Omodeo, *L'età del Risorgimento italiano*, pp. 336–337.

[149] Ibid., p. 341. An eloquent document of Mazzini's prophetic vision is the oath of the militants of Giovane Italia, the association that he founded in 1831: "Nel nome di Dio e dell'Italia. Nel nome di tutti i martiri della santa causa italiana caduti sotto i colpi della tirannide straniera e domestica. Pei doveri che mi legano alla terra dove Dio m'ha posto e ai fratelli che Dio m'ha dati – Io N.N. credente nella missione commessa da Dio all'Italia, e nel dovere che ogni uomo italiano ha di contribuire al suo adempimento, convinto che dove Dio ha voluto fosse nazione esistono le forze necessarie a crearla – che il popolo è depositario di quelle forze [...] così giuro, invocando sulla mia testa l'ira di Dio [...] s'io tradissi in tutto o in parte il mio giuramento"; Giuseppe Mazzini, *Scritti politici*, pp. 185–186.

uniformity which they call unity, and which is the graveyard of liberty. Mazzini is the last high priest of an obsolescent religious, metaphysical, and political idealism.[150]

Bakunin claims that Mazzini's faith in God has placed him among the ranks of the reactionary and conservative forces led by Napoleon III, Bismarck, the Empress Eugenia, Queen Isabella, and the pope. On the contrary, revolutionaries all over the world are "bold defiers of God, divine order and the principle of authority, but also, and for the self-same reason, the upholders of a human order and human liberty."[151] Bakunin further contends that Mazzini has lost his political and moral leadership over the younger generation of revolutionaries precisely because of his prophetic language. Instead, this generation "draws its inspiration from another spirit, another morality and another love than [does Mazzini], and turns its back on his God."[152] The new and true philosophy of the revolution must carry a materialist and atheist banner, the very principles Mazzini had fought against throughout his life:

He [Mazzini] says that we are materialists and atheists. We have nothing to reply to that, for so we are, and in so far as a feeling of pride is possible for poor individuals who rise like the waves, only to disappear into the vast ocean of the collective life of human society, we glory in it, because atheism and materialism are truth, or rather the real basis of all truth, and because it is truth we want above all, regardless of the practical consequences, and nothing but the truth. Furthermore, we do have this faith – that despite all appearances to the contrary and despite the timid reservations of political and sceptical caution, truth alone can create the practical good of men.[153]

With a witty rhetorical move, Bakunin claims that materialism, not Mazzini's idealism, is the right philosophy of revolutionaries. Bakunin explicitly states that Mazzini is not suited to lead the revolutionary movement precisely because he sincerely believes that he is a prophet inspired by God:

With the doctrinaire, imperative tone characteristic of all founders of new religions, Mazzini asserts and assumes that the materialists are incapable of love, or of pledging their existence to the service of great things. In so saying he is only proving that as a consistent idealist and despiser of humanity in the name of the God whose prophet he genuinely believes himself to be, he has never begun to understand human nature and the historical developments of society, and that if he is not ignorant of history, he singularly fails to understand it.[154]

For Bakunin and his followers, Mazzini's force – his prophetic language – is also his vice. Socialism needs science, a positive science of society and history; it does not need prophecy:

Mazzini condemns socialism; whether as priest or as messianic envoy of the supernal master he is bound to condemn it, since socialism, seen from the moral viewpoint, is the

---

[150] I am citing from Mikhail Bakunin, "The Political Theology of Mazzini," *Selected Writings*, edited by Arthur Lehning, London: Jonathan Cape, 1973, p. 214.
[151] Ibid., p. 215.   [152] Ibid., p. 216.   [153] Ibid., p. 217.   [154] Ibid., p. 221.

advent of human respect to replace the voluntary bondage of divine worship, while seen from the practical scientific viewpoint it is the proclamation of that great principle which, once instilled in the awareness of the people, has become the sole starting-point both for the researches and growth of positivist science and for the revolutionary action of the proletariat.[155]

For Bakunin, the conflict between Mazzini's prophetic republicanism and socialism is and must be irreconcilable:

Since the beginning of his public career, Mazzini has never ceased to repeat to the proletariat of Italy and Europe the following words, which sum up his religious and moral catechism: "Be moral, worship God, accept the moral law I bring you in his name, help me to establish a republic founded on the (impossible) union of reason and faith, divine authority and human liberty, and you shall have power and glory, and furthermore prosperity, liberty and equality." Socialism, on the other hand, speaking with the voice of the International, tells them "that the economic subjection of the man of labour to the monopolizer of the means of labour, that is, the sources of life, lies at the bottom of servitude in all its forms, of all social misery, mental degradation and political dependence; and that, for this reason, the economic emancipation of the working classes is the great end to which every political movement ought to be subordinate as a simple means.[156]

Therefore, science and materialism must be the new intellectual pillars that can sustain the emancipation of the proletariat. Without real knowledge of the conditions or laws of the development of real things on earth, Bakunin insists, no social emancipation is possible. He clarifies: "Since experiment, the properly controlled and scrutinized evidence of our senses, is a necessary condition of real science, we must abandon the idea of knowing anything which is beyond the range of our senses."[157] Evidently beyond the scope of our senses, and thus not at all scientific, prophecy must be discarded as a useless – indeed, detrimental – product of the imagination.

In his masterful 1927 study *Mazzini e Bakunin: Dodici anni di movimento operaio in Italia (1860–1872)*, Nello Rosselli copiously documents how Bakunin's materialistic language conquered the younger generation's hearts and minds. Many of them regarded Mazzini's religion of duty, with his idea of God serving as the foundation of moral principle, as absurd metaphysical concepts. In a socialist newspaper from May 1871, we read: "We young materialists do not care about the future of our soul after our death. God cannot be a nightmare. If he is an impediment, let's just discard it."[158] Another militant claimed: "We cannot follow Mazzini in his journey to heaven. His religious vision contradicts reason. We can no longer accept them." In

---

[155] Ibid., p. 223. [156] Ibid., pp. 224–225. [157] Ibid., p. 230.
[158] I am citing from Nello Rosselli, *Mazzini e Bakunin. Dodici anni di movimento operaio in Italia (1860–1872)*, Turin: Einaudi, 1967, p. 290. The first edition appeared in 1927 (Turin: Fratelli Bocca).

another socialist newspaper from August 1871, we read that Mazzini "has dedicated all his life to the noble cause of the emancipation of Italy and the emancipation of the working classes. Now he is a dying star. He does not want to repudiate his God. His faith condemns him to lose touch with the new needs and new claims of social movements. The new sun is the materialist and atheistic International."[159]

Though tired, disillusioned, and saddened Mazzini devoted his final intellectual and moral energies to fighting the materialist, atheist ideas that were attracting the Italian revolutionary youth. Published in the pamphlet *Mazzini e l'Internazionale* (1871), his article "Gemiti, fremiti e ricapitolazione" counterattacks the new materialistic ideologies by remarking that they are in fact damaging the fight for republican liberty.[160] Mazzini then eloquently explains that forcibly and violently replacing the domination of capitalism with the domination of the proletariat is not emancipation at all. For Mazzini, the oppressed classes can attain emancipation only if they prove themselves to be morally better than their dominators, and if they also strive for the emancipation of all humanity.[161] Civil war may be necessary to attain social redemption, but, at all times, it must be under the guidance of moral law and never be inspired by a thirst for revenge.[162] Mazzini insists that materialism inevitably sustains the cults of force, material interests, and appetites. In opposition to the materialists, he restates his idea that the foundation of humanity's true moral emancipation must be the idea of God: a God who calls us to dedicate our lives to the sacred mission of social progress sustained by the principle of duty.[163] Along with the idea of a God who wants humanity to live in freedom, Mazzini also reaffirms that social and political emancipation requires prophets who inspire people, not scientists who proclaim purported social laws that would supposedly bring about the kingdom of justice on earth. Mazzini proclaimed the same words for fifty years. Equally stable and solid was his faith behind

---

[159] Ibid., p. 294.

[160] *Mazzini e l'Internazionale*, Rome: Amministrazione della Roma del Popolo, 1871, p. 20.

[161] "Noi non possiamo e non dubbiamo vincere se non a patto d'esser migliori dei vinti – se non a patto di respingere energicamente il Male s'anche fregiato dei nostri colori e di sostituire al presente un assetto di cose più benefico a *tutti* e che, non rinegando alcuna delle grandi conquiste operate dall'Umanità, le *modifichi* tutte a seconda delle aspirazioni attuali sulla via del Progresso e *aggiunga* ad esse, come fine dell'Epoca nuova e consacrazione alla generale tendenza verso l'unità *morale* dell'umana famiglia, il termine Associazione"; ibid., p. 21.

[162] Ibid., p. 22.

[163] "L'ispirazione dell'anima, la scienza, la tradizione dell'Umanità, la voce di quanti furono grandi davvero d'intelletto e virtù, c'insegnano che Dio, creandoci, ci chiamava a compiere una missione, a raggiungere un fine – che questo fine è PROGRESSO – che unico metodo a conquistarlo è l'Associazione che l'esistenza di questo fine, di questo disegno provvidenziale preordinato, costituisce per noi tutti un Dovere – che dall' adempimento del Dovere dipende tutto il nostro avvenire qui sulla Terra e altrove, per noi e per gli altri verso i quali siamo capaci di bene"; ibid., pp. 32–33.

those words. Ultimately, they lost the power to move and mobilize, and by the end of his life, he was a defeated prophet.

Mazzini's prophetic language, however, moved a small minority of generous souls.[164] Among them, I must at least cite Goffredo Mameli. A poet-martyr and the author of Italy's national anthem, Mameli died at the age of twenty-one on July 6, 1849, while fighting under Garibaldi's command to defend the Roman Republic.[165] In his poetry, Mameli combines Mazzini's message of redemption with biblical references. In *Dio e il popolo*, for instance, he compares Italy's redemption with the Jews' emancipation from slavery in Egypt.[166] In order to gain their redemption, Italians must become "new believers" (*"nuovi credenti"*) who fight for the ideals of unity, liberty, and humanity (*"Unità, Libertà, Umanità"*). With powerful verses, Mameli reworks the central tenet of prophetic language, namely that God leads the fight of those peoples who strive to break the chains of servitude.[167] Mameli invokes Mazzini's God of humanity (quite similar to Manzoni's conception of God as the father of all peoples): a God who wants all peoples to live in freedom in their respective homelands. Mameli exhorted his compatriots to fight on behalf of the God of humanity. With the words of the *Book of Revelation*, he reassures them that the times are right for Italy's resurrection (*"tempus enim prope est"*). By attaining its own emancipation, Italy will serve a greater purpose in God's plan to renew and redeem the whole earth.[168] Understood as a mystical unity sustained by God's inspiration, the people are the driving force behind the redemption. The poet-prophet's duty is therefore to give meaning to the martyrdom of patriots. To accomplish this task, Mameli resorts yet again to the *Old Testament*: "May their memory be blessed forever, and may life sprout from their bones lying in their place of rest" (*"Ut sit memoria illorum in benedictione. / Et ossa eorum pullulent in loco suo"*; *Ecclesiasticus* XLVI.14). A just God will reward their sacrifice.[169]

---

[164] See Adolfo Omodeo, *L'età del Risorgimento italiano*, p. 341.

[165] As Giosué Carducci remarked in a speech commemorating Mameli's death, "il Mameli aveva accolto nell'intelletto e nel cuore il pensiero di Giuseppe Mazzini"; G. Carducci, "Commemorazione di G. Mameli," *Opere*, vol. VII, Bologna: Zanichelli, 1893, p. 431.

[166] "Ed Egitto è ogni suol di servaggio / Israello son tutte le genti, / È Sionne pei nuovi credenti / Unità, Libertà, Umanità"; Goffredo Mameli, "Dio e il popolo," in Maria Sticco, *La poesia religiosa del Risorgimento*, p. 334. See also Goffredo Mameli, *La vita e gli scritti*, edited by A. Codignola, Venice: La Nuova Italia, 1927.

[167] "Perchè quando sorge il popolo / Sovra i ceppi e i re distrutti, / come il vento sovra i flutti / passeggiare Iddio lo fa. / Che se il popolo si desta, / Dio combatte alla sua testa, / il suo fulmine gli dà," in Maria Sticco, *La poesia religiosa del Risorgimento*, p. 334.

[168] "Salve, fatale Italia! / Però che quando Iddio / vuol rinnovar la terra, / ti crea, ti lancia in guerra, / ti affida l'avvenir"; Goffredo Mameli, "Salve, o Risorta!," in Maria Sticco, *La poesia religiosa del Risorgimento*, p. 336.

[169] "Col sangue del Divino / Trafitto, un cherubino / raccolse quel sospir, / Lo serba nel gran calice / col gemito dei forti, / col sangue delle vittime, / dei santi che son morti / pel Vero pei fratelli / ai preti ai re ribelli: / nel giorno del giudicio, / saetta pei potenti / rugiada pei credenti / sul mondo il

Another story worth citing is that of Gabriele Rossetti (1783–1854). Forced to escape the Neapolitan Kingdom after the 1820 rebellion, he arrived in London, where he became a professor of Italian language and literature at King's College. In 1846, he composed a short poem titled *Il veggente in solitudine*. Rossetti implores God to intervene and help lead poor Italy into a new era in which the worship of liberty and the worship of Christ would go hand in hand – a new era in which the earth shall become the image of heaven.[170] When the will of the people is the will of God, the people become invincible.[171] In his longer poem *Dio e l'uomo* (1849), Rossetti proclaims the imminent arrival of the new age during which a new Moses shall finally ensure perfect harmony between the people and its rulers, as well as among all nations. God is the source of the moral law that will inevitably triumph, and will pave the way to Italy's liberty and to the brotherhood of all peoples.[172] Obstacles, pain, and defeats in the struggle for political emancipation are all signs of God's intention to test and reinforce the virtue of those peoples he loves. Rossetti claims that it is utterly vain to try to halt God's redeeming plan. Those who want to oppose it do nothing more than ultimately reinforce the peoples' determination to make God's law triumph on earth.[173]

Mazzini's writings greatly inspired Ippolito Nievo (1831–1861), a patriot and writer who fought with Garibaldi in Sicily. In the *Confessioni di un italiano* (*Confessions of an Italian*), his major work that originally appeared with the title *Le confessioni di un ottuagenario* in 1867, Nievo offers us a precious sense of his belief in the power of prophetic language. The novel's chief message is that a sincere faith provides the strength required to resurrect from moral and political vileness. Carlo Altoviti, the story's main character, conveys Nievo's prophetic message when he confesses his faith in Italy's redemption:

Now faith is disappearing, and science – alive and full – is not yet with us. Why then should we glorify these times that even the most optimistic call times of transition?

---

verserà"; Goffredo Mameli, "Ai fratelli Bandiera," in Maria Sticco, *La poesia religiosa del Risorgimento*, p. 338.
[170] "Deh ti mova gran Verbo di Dio / dell'Italia l'immenso dolor; / Scriva nella sua storia Italia bella, / qui per me ricomincia era novella, / culto di libertà culto di Cristo! / [. . .] Cristo regna; la reggia e la Chiesa / son difesa del popolo fedel, / e la terra contempla riflessa / in se stessa l'immagin del ciel"; Gabriele Rossetti, "Il veggente in solitudine," in Maria Sticco, *La poesia religiosa del Risorgimento*, p. 346.
[171] "Universal desio / sempre divien poter. / Spesso è il voler di Dio / d'un popolo il voler"; ibid., p. 349.
[172] "O mortal, dei mali tuoi / ti dovresti rallegrar: / Dio non visita che i suoi / per poterli esercitar. / Quando soffri, esulta pure: / di che gemere puoi tu? / E non sai che le sventure / scuola son della virtù?"; Gabriele Rossetti, "Inno al mattino," in Maria Sticco, *La poesia religiosa del Risorgimento*, p. 365.
[173] "Se ostacol preteso / tardarne il successo, / l'ostacol stesso / più rapido il fè; / chi stolto si oppone / l'evento assicura: / l'intera natura / lo compie per te"; Gabriele Rossetti, "Quel che fu, quel che è, quel che sarà," in Maria Sticco, *La poesia religiosa del Risorgimento*, p. 357.

Honor the past and speed up the future, but live in the present with the humility and determination of one who knows he is impotent, but still feels the need to make sense of life. Raised without the beliefs of the past and without faith in the future, I sought everywhere, in vain, a place of repose for my thoughts. And finally, I understood that justice is the goal of human life, and man the minister; and that history expiates by counting up the sacrifices on behalf of humanity. Old in years, I rest my head on the pillow of the grave and offer these words to those who no longer believe, but still wish to use their minds in this age of transition.[174]

Nievo was fully aware that his were times of spiritual weakness. In a letter of August 1850, he highlights the contrast between moral baseness and material and technical progress.[175] No effective effort of emancipation is possible without a true moral faith:

It is the festering of such bad habits under the sparkling tinsel of civilization that makes will become mere wishing; facts become words; words, chit-chat; science, purely utilitarian; harmony, impossible; conscience, venal; life vegetative, dull and intolerable. How can we expect millions of men to conduct a great national drive lasting one, two, ten or twenty years, when not one of them is capable of keeping up that drive for three straight months?[176]

Only individuals who have emancipated themselves – individuals who have released themselves from disenchantment and despair, who have attained a solid faith in spiritual and eternal values, who have chosen duty as their life's guiding principle – can help resurrect a morally dead people.

The few who begin the journey of emancipation must believe in the power of justice and must instill the same faith in their compatriots:

Justice is among us, above us, inside us. It punishes us and it rewards us. Justice alone is the great unifier of things; it offers souls happiness in the great soul of humanity. Yes, these are ill-defined sentiments, and we know not when they may become ideas, but they come from the heart and send poetry to the mind of certain men, and I am one; poetry, however, that lives and becomes flesh, verse by verse, in the annals of history. They are the feelings of a soul tested by life's trials, yet budding already in that sense of joy and sacredness that made me, a mere boy, bend my knee before the majesty of the universe![177]

---

[174] Ippolito Nievo, *Le Confessioni d'un italiano*, edited by Simone Casini, Milan-Parma: Guanda, 1999, pp. 138–139; English translation Ippolito Nievo, *Confessions of an Italian*, edited by Lucy Riall, translated by Frederika Randall, London: Penguin, 2014, pp. 70–71. On Nievo, see the excellent essay by Valeria Giannetti, *Il futuro lume del remoto vero. Ippolito Nievo e la religione dell'ideale*, Florence: Cesati, 2017.

[175] Ippolito Nievo, "Lettere," *Tutte le opere*, vol. VI, edited by Marcella Gorra, Milan: Mondadori, 1981, pp. 160–161.

[176] Ippolito Nievo, *Le Confessioni*, p. 105; English translation, p. 51.

[177] "La giustizia è fra noi, sopra di noi, dentro di noi. Essa ci punisce e ci ricompensa. Essa, essa sola è la grande unitrice delle cose che assicura la felicità delle anime nella grand'anima dell'umanità. Sentimenti mal definiti che diverranno idee quando che sia; ma che dai cuori ove nacquero tralucono giù alla mente d'alcuni uomini, ed alla mia; sentimenti poetici ma di quella poesia che vive, e s'incarna verso per verso negli annali della storia; sentimenti d'un

Justice is a divine and eternal principle, but only just, wise, and virtuous individuals can sow it on earth and create a new history under its guidance:

Justice, truth and virtue: three fine things, three words, three ideas that could captivate a soul and drive it to madness or death: but who would ever bring them down to earth, as Socrates put it? This was the thorn in my side, and it caused me great pain, although I did not understand it very clearly. New institutions and new laws will make new men. But even supposing that was true, who would give us these fine institutions, these excellent laws? Certainly not the foolish and inept governments of the time. Who, then? New people – just, virtuous and wise.[178]

The new, just, and wise prophets who can lead the struggle for moral and political emancipation must be aware that Italy's redemption is part of God's providential plan. They must believe that they are indeed serving "that wondrous Providence that is perfecting our moral order" (*"quella meravigliosa Provvidenza che va perfezionando l'ordine morale"*). With their prophetic insight, they understand to be a sacred truth the reality that divine reason alone moves, pushes, and calms humanity's immensity and diversity.[179] Having faith in divine reason as the governor of humanity's history, Nievo frames a powerful prophecy: "What I see now, many will soon see, and, in the end, everyone. Concord in thought leads to concord in deeds. The truth does not go down like the sun, but rises towards the eternal midday. Every clairvoyant spirit that flies up there shines its prophetic light on a hundred other spirits."[180] Pisana, the other chief character alongside Carlo Altoviti in Nievo's novel, pronounced the sacred words of *homeland* and *family* with "an almost religious and prophetic authority." Her words saved Carlo from his existential despair and reopened the sentiments of faith and hope in his soul. Nievo assures that redemption is possible if the new prophets can capably teach the truth.[181] The ideal he identifies is the city of the spirit, a New Jerusalem where harmony and justice triumph at last: the kingdom of society's free and collective thought.[182] Nievo's novel well represents the spirit of the Risorgimento, and in it reverberate those prophetic voices that had spoken throughout Italy's history.

---

animo provato dal lungo cimento della vita, ma che già covavano in quel senso di felicità e di religione che a me fanciullo fece piegar le ginocchia dinnanzi alla maestà dell'universo!"; Ippolito Nievo, *Le Confessioni*, pp. 191–192; English translation, p. 99.

[178] Ippolito Nievo, *Le Confessioni*, pp. 573–574; English translation, p. 335.

[179] "Una ragione sola sommove, spinge ed acqueta quest'umanità varia ed immensa"; Ippolito Nievo, *Le Confessioni*, pp. 1394–1395; English translation, p. 793.

[180] "Quello che ora veggo io, molti lo vedranno in appresso, e tutti da ultimo. La concordia dei pensieri mena alla concordia delle opere; e la verità non tramonta mai ma sale sempre verso il meriggio eterno. Ogni spirito veggente che sale lassù risplende a cento altri spiriti colla sua luce profetica!"; Ippolito Nievo, *Le Confessioni*, p. 1193; English translation, p. 681.

[181] Ippolito Nievo, *Le Confessioni*, p. 1348; English translation, p. 768.

[182] Ippolito Nievo, *Le Confessioni*, p. 718; English translation, p. 419.

Giuseppe Garibaldi, the most famous hero of the Italian Risorgimento, was neither a philosopher nor a writer. It would be utterly mistaken, however, to portray him only as a patriot and military chief. He was also an inspiring moral figure with a strong religious sentiment.[183] Raised in Nice, a town that oscillated between the rigors of Jansenism and the religiosity of the Counterreformation, Garibaldi accepts Christianity's moral content but completely rejects the dogmas, rites, and politics of the Catholic Church. In his first trips to Rome, he calls it a city that was: "capital of the world, [...] cradle of that holy religion whose first apostles were masters of the nations, emancipators of the peoples, but which was then handed over to foreign domination by their fallen, debased, and merchant-like successors – real scourges for Italy."[184] That said, though, Garibaldi makes careful distinctions among the clergy. With regard to Don Giovanni Verità – the parish priest of Modigliana who helped Garibaldi to escape to Tuscany, hence saving his life after the fall of the Roman Republic – he writes: Verità was a "true priest of Christ, and by Christ I mean here the virtuous man and the legislator, not that Christ made God by the priests and used by them to cover the fallaciousness of their existence."[185]

Garibaldi derives the idea of Christ as man, legislator, and emancipator of peoples from Saint-Simon's *Le Nouveau Christianisme*, a book he became familiar with in 1831. As I have noted, Saint-Simon interpreted Christianity through a social perspective. He claimed that Christ was not so much the son of God as the charismatic leader of the liberation of the peoples. As such, the kingdom of heaven on earth is the result of the struggle against all forms of tyranny. Garibaldi fully accepts Saint-Simon's view. Next to this conception of Christ the man, Garibaldi places the God of truth and reason. At the Congress of Peace in Geneva on September 9, 1867, he presents a motion to adopt the "religion of God," by which he means "the religion of truth and reason." At the same time, Garibaldi emphasizes the necessity of destroying the religious tyranny carried out by priests. Although acclaimed by all the Congress's participants, he faced the hostility of Geneva's Catholics, who organized a protest in front of his hotel. Reflecting upon the Congress, Garibaldi yet again remarks that the new religion of God will open a new chapter in the history of liberty. In Geneva, he writes to a correspondent: "The representatives of the honest part of the peoples shook their hands, and they laid the foundations of the cult of

---

[183] See Lucy Riall, *Garibaldi. The Invention of a Hero*; Alfonso Scirocco, *Garibaldi. Battaglie, amori, ideali di un cittadino del mondo*, Rome and Bari: Laterza, 2007; Dino Mengozzi, *La morte e l'immortale da Garibaldi a Costa*, Manduria: Lacaita, 2000.

[184] Giuseppe Garibaldi, *Memorie*, edited by Ernesto Nathan, Turin: Società tipografia editrice nazionale, 1907, pp. 26–27. I am using Alberto Nones' translation from my *As if God Existed. Religion and Liberty in the History of Italy*, p. 152.

[185] Giuseppe Garibaldi, *Memorie*, pp. 300–301. *As if God Existed. Religion and Liberty in the History of Italy*, p. 153.

justice and truth, which finally must prevail on earth, [and this will be] when the nations will understand that their money must be invested in useful works and not for buying cuirasses, bombs, mercenaries, and spies."[186]

Garibaldi believed in the prophetic idea of a God who intervenes and helps peoples who fight for their emancipation. On August 4, 1848, he writes to his mother that "God shall help and protect us," for the holy cause of the Italian people cannot perish.[187] Italians must gain their liberty with God's help and with their swords.[188] When he witnessed the devastating defeat of Piedmontese armies in the darkest days of 1849, he shared with his wife Anita that his sense of despair was consoled by an unfailing faith in God.[189] As he was sailing to Sicily from Villa Spinola on April 30, 1860, he wrote to the king of Piedmont stating that, while aware of the inherent dangers of his plan to conquer the Neapolitan Kingdom, he was still counting on God's help and his volunteers' valor.[190] In a letter dated July 31, 1875, Garibaldi frames the idea of Rome as the beacon of religious renovation inspired by the ideal of truth.[191] Like the God of Mazzini, Garibaldi's God favors all peoples fighting for independence.[192] In 1864, he pens that God would bless all the peoples of Europe if they went to Poland's aid.[193] On December 19, 1867, in a letter to Anton Giulio Barrilli, a militant of Greece's independence, he stresses that

---

[186] Alfonso Scirocco, *Garibaldi. Battaglie, amori, ideali di un cittadino del mondo*, Roma-Bari: Laterza, 2007, p. 361.

[187] Giuseppe Garibaldi, *Epistolario di Giuseppe Garibaldi. Con documenti e lettere inedite, (1836–1882)*, vol. I, edited by Enrico Emilio Ximenes, Milan: Alfredo Brigola and C., 1885, p. 18.

[188] "Noi siamo alla vigilia dell'ultima guerra, non lenta, non fiacca, non proditoria, ma rapida, sincera, implacata. Levatevi forti dei vostri diritti calpesti, del vostro nome schernito, del sangue che avete sparso, levatevi in nome dei martiri invendicati, della libertà e della patria saccheggiata, vituperata dallo straniero, forti come uomini parati a morire! Non chiedete vittoria che a Dio e al vostro ferro; non isperate nei vuoti simulacri, ma nella giustizia, non confidate che in voi. Chi vuole vincere vince"; Giuseppe Garibaldi, "'Proclama agli italiani,' Genoa, October 18, 1848," ibid., p. 21.

[189] "Roma prende un aspetto imponente, attorno ad essa si raduneranno i generosi e Dio ci aiuterà!"; "Giuseppe Garibaldi to Anita, April 19, 1849," ibid., p. 30.

[190] "Giuseppe Garibaldi to the King Vittorio Emanuele, April 30, 1860," ibid., p. 92.

[191] "Roma deve aprire il suo terzo periodo di incivilimento umanitario, ed in nessuna parte del mondo vi è un terreno meglio preparato. Queste popolazioni, dominate moralmente e materialmente dagli impostori, ne hanno veduto più da vicino le turpitudini e più di ogni altra sono disposte a gettarsi nel campo del Vero e non nella riforma del *Culto dei morti*, come voi ben dite"; "Giuseppe Garibaldi to Pietro Sbarbaro, July 31, 1878," ibid., p. 116.

[192] "Dio non deve permettere più a lungo lo strazio delle sue creature"; "Giuseppe Garibaldi to a Hungarian patriot, December 2, 1862," ibid., p. 216.

[193] "Oggi sono i popoli liberi che devono mettere l'ordine nel mondo, turbato dalle velleità moribonde del dispotismo. Non abbandonate la Polonia! Se tutti l'aiuteremo debitamente avremo adempito ad un sacro dovere, ed il mondo potrà costituirsi conforme al benessere dell'umana specie, allora benedetta da Dio"; "Giuseppe Garibaldi to the Peoples of Europe, February 15, 1864," ibid., p. 225.

comforting and lending a hand to the oppressed is a Christian mission.[194] When the Reformist League of English Workers nominated him honorary president, Garibaldi indicated that the glorious mission of his times was to replace the irreligion of misery, deprivation, and tyranny, with the true religion of God, father and savior of all, and a true brotherhood of nations.[195]

Garibaldi perceives the presence of God in the perfection of the universe. He believes in the immortality of the soul and in the ennobling idea that the individual spirit, small as it may be, is part of the grand spirit that presides over the world.[196] Despite his radical anticlericalism, he exhorted Italian priests to rediscover and teach the true Christian principles of equality and brotherhood. In obedience to these principles, he urges them to become militants of the cause of Italian liberty.[197] If Italian priests truly interrogated their hearts, where the voice of God speaks and reveals our duties, they would understand that their sacred mission is to educate the Italian people in the religion of truth.[198] Until his last days, Garibaldi maintained that only the religion of truth emancipates individual conscience and thus creates the conditions for humanity's moral redemption.[199] Had Garibaldi proclaimed his religion of truth when he

---

[194] "Porgere la mano e una parola di conforto ai caduti, agli oppressi, non è forse la vera missione dell'uomo sulla terra, l'applicazione sublime dei santi insegnamenti del Redentore?"; "Giuseppe Garibaldi to Anton Giulio Barrilli, direttore del *Movimento*, December 19, 1866," ibid., p. 289.

[195] "Vera religione di Dio, padre e Salvatore di tutti, e la vera fratellanza delle nazioni"; "Giuseppe Garibaldi to Colonel Chambers, May 20, 1867," ibid., p. 297.

[196] "Istruirli nella religione del vero! Ecco il modo più ovvio o certo per condurre la gioventù sulla retta via, a noi tracciata dalla coscienza, emanazione di Dio. Quando parlo di Dio, non crediate ch' io voglia insegnarlo. Io non millanto tale impudenza, essa è la base dell'edificio pretino, e che trascina il prete alla menzogna ed alla violenza. Gettando l'occhio nello spazio e l'immaginazione nell'infinito, io vi scorgo le opere dell'Onnipotente, e l'armonia matematica con cui esse vi sono disposte e vi si muovono mi accennano l'esistenza del Reggitore. Con questa fede, non potendo circoscrivere l'essere mio in una esistenza materiale che mi ripugna, e per appagare l'innato istinto dell'immortalità dell'anima, amo spaziare nell'idea nobilitante, benefica, che l'infinitamente piccolo spirito mio possa esser parte dello Spirito, infinitamente immenso, che presiede all'Universo. Io vi ripeto: non insegno, accenno alle mie credenze, ed ove mi sostituisca un meglio, non tralascerò d'abbracciarlo. Comunque sia togliere la gioventù all'educazione del prete, è dovere di tutti, senza di che il progresso umano è impossibile. Dio è il bene. I preti nel mondo, ed in Italia massime, rappresentano il male, quindi non possono essere ministri di Dio"; "Giuseppe Garibaldi to Angiolo Michelini, December 6, 1864," ibid., p. 259.

[197] Giuseppe Garibaldi, "Indirizzo ai Sacerdoti italiani, Caprera, March 6, 1862," ibid., pp. 180–181.

[198] Giuseppe Garibaldi, "Altro indirizzo ai sacerdoti, Caprera, March 8, 1862," ibid., p. 181.

[199] On March 28, 1882 Garibaldi urged the people of Palermo to embrace the religion of truth: "Forma quindi nel tuo seno, ove palpitano tanti cuori generosi, un'Associazione col titolo 'Emancipatrice dell'intelligenza umana', e la di lei missione sia quella di combattere l'ignoranza, svegliare il libero pensiero e mandare perciò tra lo plebi delle città o delle campagne a sostituire alla menzogna la religione del Vero"; "Giuseppe Garibaldi al popolo di Palermo," ibid., p. 333. See also his letter of March 27, 1867, written to Pietro Preda: "Ho letto il vostro libro *Rivelazione e Ragione*, e sono con voi. Noi siamo della religione del vero, ed è questa che sostituiremo a quella del prete che è la menzogna. Libertà di ragione, ecco la bandiera che

was the commander of an army of volunteers, he would have been precisely the armed prophet that Machiavelli envisioned. Italy would have benefited greatly from such a figure. But Garibaldi could not – or did not want to – announce a redeeming vision with the voice of the prophet.

While Garibaldi was the military hero, the prophetic words of Giuseppe Verdi's operas, in particular *Nabucco*, became the inspiring force of the Risorgimento. *Nabucco* premiered at Milan's Scala theater on March 9, 1842. To properly appreciate the redeeming pathos of the opera, we must consider the context in which it was conceived. He composed the music for the libretto written by the acclaimed Temistocle Solera at a time when Verdi was a severely tired, defeated, disconsolate man. Despite this despondency, Verdi found within himself the strength to create music for a people that desired to redeem itself with the help of God. He immediately understood that the biblical narration of *Exodus* lies beneath the words of the chorus "Va, pensiero": the long flight through the desert is the journey to a homeland, a journey that at the same time represents the internal transformation through which slaves become a nation. And to become a nation, the Jews must emancipate themselves from their servile mentality and acquire the conscience and duties of a free people. They pray that God will grant them a new emancipatory prophecy:

> Go, thought, on wings of gold; / Va, pensiero, sull'ali dorate;
> Go, settle upon the slopes, the hills, / Va, ti posa sui clivi, sui colli,
> Where soft and mild smells / Ove olezzano tepide e molli
> The sweet air of the native land! / L'aure dolci del suolo natal!
> Greet the banks of the Jordan, / Del Giordano le rive saluta,
> Zion's toppled towers. / Di Sionne le torri atterrate.
> Oh, my country so beautiful and lost! / Oh mia patria sì bella e perduta!
> Oh, memory so dear and fateful! / Oh membranza sì cara e fatal!
> Golden harp of the prophetic seers, / Arpa d'ôr dei fatidici vati,
> Why do you hang mute from the willow? / Perché muta dal salice pendi?
> Rekindle the memories in the heart / Le memorie nel petto raccendi,
> Speak to us of the time gone by! / Ci favella del tempo che fu!
> Either similar to Solomon from the fates, / O simìle di Solima ai fati
> Draw a sound of sad lamentation, / Traggi un suono di crudo lamento,
> Or else let the Lord inspire you with a harmony / O t'ispiri il Signore un concento
> Which shall instill virtue in our suffering! / Che ne infonda al patire virtù!

opponiamo al cattolicismo, il quale ha per tanti secoli abbrutito la creatura umana. Con lavoro assiduo d'intelligenza e di affetto, si sostituisca dunque alla menzogna il vero, al pregiudizio la retta ragione, l'educazione all'ignoranza, l'apostolato della volgarizzazione della scienza alla superstizione. In ciò il trionfo della virtù sul vizio, del bene sul male, il trionfo dell'emancipazione della coscienza, che è quello della dignità umana. Il vostro libro coopera efficacemente a questo trionfo; e la umanità ve ne sarà riconoscente"; "Giuseppe Garibaldi al signor Preda ex frate," ibid., pp. 295–296.

The prophet Zaccaria responds to the people's invocation:

> "Who raises lamentations / of cowardly women to the Eternal God? /
> Oh arise, anguished brothers, / The Lord speaks through my lips! /
> I discern in the darkness of the future... / The ignoble chains shall be
> broken!... / The wrath of the Lion of Judah / Already falls on the
> treacherous sand!"[200]

This was a prophecy addressed to an oppressed people determined to be free. To have a sense of the emancipatory power of Verdi's music, no words are more appropriate than those penned by his chief biographer Massimo Mila:

every hint was immediately grasped. Imagine when they were sung *coram populo* by the chorus of La Scala, and emphasized by such music, which moved the soul of the audience, put a lump in their throat, and made their eyes grow dim with tears, instilling even in the laziest a new warmth of national brotherhood and solidarity in the devotion to a common ideal. This strange Italian fatherland, which had existed in poetry and in the arts long before it was born as a geographical reality and within the conscience of the citizens, found in Verdi's melody one of its most plastic and concrete ways in which to stir the fantasy of the people.[201]

4.4 THE AUTUMN OF THE RISORGIMENTO AND THE BIRTH OF THE REPUBLIC

When King Vittorio Emanuele II proclaimed Rome the capital of the Kingdom of Italy in 1871, the prophecy of Italian independence and unity became true,

---

[200] "Oh, chi piange? Di femmine imbelli / Chi solleva lamenti all'Eterno? / Oh sorgete, angosciati fratelli, / sul mio labbro favella il Signor / Del futuro nel buio discerno... / ecco rotta l'indegna catena!... / Piomba già sulla perfida arena / del leone di Giuda il furor." Verdi himself, not Temistocle Solera, the author of the libretto, wanted a prophecy of liberation in *Nabucco*: "This reminds me of a comical scene I had with Solera some time before: in the third act he had put a little love duet between Fenena and Ismaele: I didn't like it, for it cooled the action and, it seemed to me, detracted from the biblical grandeur which characterized the drama: one morning when Solera was at my place, I pointed this remark out to him: but he wouldn't say I was right, not so much because he didn't agree as because it bothered him to re-do a finished work: we argued back and forth our reasons: I stuck to my point and so did he. He asked me what I wanted in place of the duet, and I suggested he could write a prophecy of Profeta Zaccaria. He did not think the idea was bad, and, through 'ifs' and 'buts', said he would have thought about it and write something. That was not quite what I wanted, for I knew that many days would have passed before Solera would have resolved to write a verse. I locked the door, put the key in my pocket, and, half joking, half seriously, told Solera: 'You don't get out of here if you've not written the prophecy: here is the Bible, you've got all the words ready in there. All you have to do is to put them into verse'. Solera, whose character was quick to anger, didn't take well that idea of mine. A flash of fury gleamed in his eyes. I passed an uncomfortable minute, for the poet was well-built and could have made quick work of the stubborn maestro that I was. But all of a sudden, he sits down and, a quarter of an hour later, the prophecy was written!"; Massimo Mila, *Verdi*, edited by Pietro Gelli, Milan: Rizzoli, 2000, p. 194.

[201] Ibid., p. 101.

at least in part. In the newborn kingdom, prophetic voices lost the force
they had during the Risorgimento. Very distrustful of ideals and prophecies,
the moral and intellectual mood was instead keen on facts, science, and
power. In his *Storia d'Italia dal 1871 al 1915* (*A History of Italy from
1871 to 1915*), published for the first time in 1928, Benedetto Croce described
the moral and intellectual spirit of the time in a passage that deserves to be
cited in full:

In 1871, after the establishment of the capital of the kingdom in Rome, Italy was
conscious that a whole series of aims, which had long been pursued, were now fully
realized, and that she had reached the close of a period of history. Italy at last possessed
independence, unity, and liberty: that is to say, the way lay open to her for the free
development both of people and of the nation, of individual personalities and the
national personality. This had been the true significance of the romantic national
movements of the nineteenth century, which were closely connected with the winning
of civil and political liberty. Now there was nothing left to ask in this respect, and, for
the time being at any rate, Italy could rest content. But every close of a period of history
brings with it the death of something, however much the end may have been sought and
desired, however essential it may be to the work which was so clearly envisaged and so
energetically brought to completion; and, like all death, it is encompassed by an atmos-
phere of regret and melancholy. There were now no more youthful strivings and heart
burnings after an ideal that was new, lofty, and far removed from realization; no more
dreams, boundless as the ocean, shining with beauty and fascination; no more bitter-
sweet torment of thwarted love; no more trembling hopes, as in 1848 and 1859; no more
generous rivalries and renunciation of individual ideas in order to unite in a common
purpose; no more understandings, whether tacit or avowed, between republicans and
monarchists, Catholics and free-thinkers, ministers and revolutionaries, king and conspirators, all alike being dominated and inspired by devotion to the patriotic cause; no
more outbursts of rejoicing from one end of Italy to the other as in 1870, when the
oppressed breathed again and exiles returned, and the inhabitants of the various provinces, who were at last all Italians, met as brothers. Men even went so far as to regret the
dangers, labors, sufferings which they had endured, the battles, the persecutions, the
breathless escapes in which they had taken part, the trials, the condemnations,
the imprisonments. Many felt that the best part of their life was ended, and all, including
the King himself in a speech from the throne, said that the heroic age of the new Italy
was over while the ordinary era of practical work had begun, that prose had succeeded
to poetry.[202]

---

[202] "Nel 1871, fermata la sede del regno in Roma, si ebbe in Italia il sentimento che un intero
sistema di fini, a lungo perseguiti, si era a pieno attuato, e che un periodo storico si chiudeva.
L'Italia possedeva ormai indipendenza, unità e libertà, cioè le stava dinanzi aperta la via al
libero svolgimento così dei cittadini come della nazione, delle persone individuali e della
persona nazionale; ché tale era stato l'intimo senso del romantico moto delle nazionalità nel
secolo decimo nono, strettamente congiunto con l'acquisto delle libertà civili e politiche. Non si
aveva altro da chiedere per quella parte, almeno per allora, e si poteva tenersi soddisfatti. Ma
ogni chiudersi di periodo storico è la morte di qualche cosa, ancorché cercata e voluta e
intrinseca all'opera chiaramente disegnata ed energicamente eseguita; e, come ogni morte, si
cinge di rimpianto e di malinconia. Non più giovanili struggimenti di desiderio e divampanti

The documents of that period largely confirm Croce's assessment. On October 18, 1870, Alberto Blanc, general secretary of the Ministry of Internal Affairs, wrote from Rome to Marco Minghetti (1818–1886), an eminent liberal politician who was twice prime minister:

> Our Italian genius is going to take on its own new and original form of expression here. The endearing habits formed in exile, the attachments of the heart felt by the generation that is in its prime today for those who were its teachers in youth, the conceptions formed in a series of progressive stages by the nation during the last fifty years, Guelphism, Liberal Catholicism, the collaboration of Italy and the papacy in politics, the alliance of the Latin races, all these will be preserved as touching souvenirs and as proofs of our good faith and our good will in each of the situations through which we have passed – but let us break the hold they have on our ideas and our actions in the present. Germany, following in the steps of England and America, has gained such a lead on the rest of the world that we shall have to hurry our pace and pursue reality, leaving behind affections, dreams, and the sentimental ideal, and grasp hold vigorously of the only things that are solid and secure: positive science, productivity, and the force that comes from both. It pleases me to repeat to you these things that you yourself have been saying for a long time now, because here in Rome I sense a spirit and a setting which, although not endowed with any incontrovertible moral or intellectual superiority, ought to sustain, so it seems to me, a more serious and elevated standard for our political and social action than what we had in Florence, and a less exclusive one than what we found in Turin. This effect of sober enthusiasm, of ardor tempered with reflection, of confidence without boastfulness, of the honest desire to do much and do it well, all of which I observe here, are felt by everyone, all the Italians from the other parts of the country have felt it too. Let us endeavor to make sure that it is not an illusion. [...] Happy the one who shall find himself at the vital points in the magnificent dawn that is commencing for Italy.[203]

---

ardori per un ideale nuovo ed alto e remoto; non più sogni ondeggianti e sconfinati, così belli nella vaghezza del loro scintillio; non più acre e pur dolce tormento dell'amore contrastato; non più trepidar di speranze come nel quarantotto e nel cinquantanove; non più gare generose e rinunzie ai proprî concetti particolari per raccogliersi in un fine comune, e accordi taciti o aperti di repubblicani e di monarchici, di cattolici e di razionalisti, di ministri e di rivoluzionari, di re e di cospiratori, e dominante e imperiosa in tutti religione della patria; non più scoppi di giubilo come nel sessanta da un capo all'altro d'Italia, e il respirare degli oppressi e il ritorno degli esuli e l'affratellarsi delle varie popolazioni, ormai tutte italiane. Il rimpianto, come suole, avvolgeva perfino i pericoli, i travagli, i dolori sostenuti, le battaglie a cui si era partecipato, le persecuzioni, l'affannoso trafugarsi, i processi, le condanne, le carceri e gli ergastoli. Molti sentivano che il meglio della loro vita era stato vissuto; tutti dicevano (e disse così anche il re, in uno dei discorsi della Corona) che il periodo 'eroico' della nuova Italia era terminato e si entrava in quello ordinario, del lavoro economico, e che alla 'poesia' succedeva la 'prosa.'" Benedetto Croce, *Storia d'Italia dal 1870 al 1915*, Rome and Bari: Laterza, 1973, pp. 3–4; English translation from Benedetto Croce, *A History of Italy*, translated by Cecilia M. Ady, Oxford: Clarendon Press, 1929, pp. 1–2.

[203] Federico Chabod, *Storia della politica estera italiana dal 1870 al 1896*, vol. I, Bari: Laterza, 1971, pp. 23–24; English translation from Federico Chabod, *Italian Foreign Policy: The Statecraft of the Founders, 1870–1896*, translated by William McCuaig, Princeton: Princeton University Press, 1996, p. 5.

In 1872, Pasquale Villari (1827–1917), the acclaimed historian and Minister of Education from 1891 to 1892, composed an essay on the problem of schools and the social question that provides us with a precise picture of the skepticism and distaste for ideals, illusions, and prophecies that pervaded the intellectual spirit of post-Risorgimento Italy. He noted that Italians seemed to feel old and lacked a youthful moral energy. They had attained national independence and political unification, but, Villari remarked, they were incapable of attaining the moral regeneration that national independence was hoped to have generated or at least encouraged.[204] The regeneration of a people is a great moral, social, and intellectual task. Laws alone cannot redeem a people, only the proper spirit can.[205] On October 16, 1894, Ferdinando Martini (1841–1928), a professor at the Scuola Normale of Pisa, wrote a letter to Giosuè Carducci that captures the consequences of prophetic spirit's decline in post-Risorgimento Italy:

Political revolutions which are not accompanied by a religious renewal lose sight of their origin and their earliest aims, and finish up by releasing all the worst instincts in the plebs. But after the evil that *we*, all of us, dear Giosuè, have done, are we in a position to provide the remedy? To whom should we preach? We, bourgeois Voltaireans, are the ones that have brought into being the unbelievers, while the pope took care of the bad believers. Now, when the plebeians cry out for chicken in the pot, because they no longer believe in the *beyond*, shall we go forth and speak to them about God, whom yesterday we denied? They will not believe us: I speak of the lower classes in the cities and the villages; those of the countryside do not know what to make of a God without a church, without rites, without priests. The tomb is an insufficient reward for all the evil we (not you and I, we as a class) have done in our thoughtless pride. We chose to tear down without knowing how to build up anything. According to the chatter of the pedagogues, the school was supposed to substitute for the church. A fine substitution! I commend it to you.[206]

Giosuè Carducci (1835–1907) understood that the prophetic discourse which had animated and sustained the Risorgimento was now distant and weak. On the occasion of the proclamation of the Kingdom of Italy in 1861, Carducci celebrated the Risorgimento as a glorious redemption that Italians had won with faith, hope, and charity. But the Battle of Aspromonte – where the Piedmontese troops stopped Garibaldi and his volunteers as they were marching toward Rome in 1862 – marks the end of the will to fight. The full redemption and triumph of liberty will perhaps take place in the distant

---

[204] Pasquale Villari, *La scuola e la quistione sociale in Italia*, Florence: Nuova Antologia, 1872, pp. 1–3.

[205] "Potremmo avere di essa solo un'ombra effimera e fittizia: le leggi, i codici, i regolamenti, tutto quello che si scrive sulla carta, nulla di ciò che è nello spirito, e che solo può redimere"; ibid., p. 36.

[206] Federico Chabod, *Storia della politica estera italiana dal 1870 al 1896*, vol. I, pp. 286–287; English translation, p. 233.

future.[207] Carducci believes that Italians do not want and cannot continue the struggle for freedom.[208] Yet, instead of accepting the decline of the Risorgimento's prophetic spirit, he made a committed effort to revive it with his poems, writings, and speeches. Carducci maintained that heroes and martyrs could inspire the living to carry out great and noble actions, to resist the corruption that was rampant in the newly united and independent Italy. In commemoration of the tenth anniversary of Giuseppe Mazzini's death, Carducci wrote in 1882:

So here it is: I am a materialist in my own way, a bit incoherent. Inconsistency, moreover, is in all physical and human things, and more so in the phenomena of the spirit: otherwise art and philosophy would not exist. That the Shah of Persia, for example, or a Milanese critic could completely and entirely die out and be forgotten is not just a certainty, but also a good thing. But I am not really convinced that all of Giuseppe Mazzini died, that all of Dante died. The religion of heroes is too profound within me: and like them, benevolent stars shine upon the firmament of my thought. Thus, I am not far from believing or hoping or at least imagining that, somewhere in serene space, these heroes undyingly correspond to this need, to this dash of loving senses and thoughts, which are raised by them and then return to them along with the alternating and continuous overflow of our souls towards the shores of the ideal. O Gods of the country, protect all those who are good and save them from the mud, which raises more and more![209]

Like the biblical prophets, Carducci shudders with indignation against his compatriots who, out of cowardice and indolence, either forget the great souls who dedicated their lives to the homeland's rebirth, or are unable to do anything but commemorate them with empty rituals:

Today the dead are neglected. We read these words in a book by Giuseppe Mazzini that is under our eyes. And, according to this view, they do not seem true. Almost saved from death, the body of the father of the country seemingly waits in the cemetery of Staglieno. In its immortal peace, it asks visitors: What have you done for a year now? We have given many speeches at assemblies; we have written many articles for the newspapers; we

---

[207] "Ah, hatred is grave and sterile, / my heart is tired of going on; / shine and smile upon me, o pure / light of the future! / Smile! Our children, / who are born to see you, / are entrusted by me to you: may they live / blessedly in your light. / May crowns and lappets fall to the ground! / May the iniquitous sword be in pieces! / May justice and freedom / alone reign in the world! / O goddesses, into perpetual / darkness, will these eyes / close, and they will search for / your dominion in vain"; Giosuè Carducci, "Dopo Aspromonte," in Maria Sticco, *La poesia religiosa del Risorgimento*, p. 473. On Carducci as the last poet-prophet, see Luigi Russo, *Carducci senza retorica*, Bari: Laterza, 1957, pp. 189–190.

[208] Luigi Russo, *Carducci senza retorica*, p. 202.

[209] Appearing first in *Cronaca Bizantina*, vol. 2, n.5, Rome, March 1, 1882, this speech was then published in *Edizione nazionale delle opere di Giosuè Carducci*, vol. XIX, Bologna: Zanichelli, 1942, pp. 13–14. See also Edoardo Ripari's excellent essay "Un nuovo Dio per l'Italia: Giosuè Carducci e la religione civile," *Voci dall'800*, edited by Ivan Pozzoni, Villasanta: Limina Mentis, 2011, vol. II, pp. 193–216.

have engraved many inscriptions on stones. And then? And then, to tell the truth, we also supported the monument, and the sum is, quite honestly, significant. There is more. Upon the news of the father of the country's death, the displays of suffering and of love of the country were so great and solemn that one could not imagine more. In those days, all of Italy seemed to become Mazzinian... Yes, but only for it to return, the next day, to being skeptical and opportunistic, to laughing at everything – with exceptions made, of course, for the respect owed to those who have cash and for the obligatory admiration of those who have power [...]. The commemoration of Giuseppe Mazzini's virtues? Oh please. Rather, let's imitate them according to our strengths. The commemoration of his deeds made for his homeland and humanity? And who doesn't know about these deeds? Rather, let us prepare ourselves to fulfill these vows. Let us educate ourselves, let us restore ourselves, and let us discipline ourselves. The times are pressing.[210]

Carducci wants Italians to rediscover the idea of God in the depths of their consciences. In a speech given on September 30, 1894 in San Marino, he states that God is

the highest vision to which peoples can rise in the strength of their youth; God, the sun of sublime minds and passionate hearts – just as the sun of the planets passes through the fabled constellations – passes through the forms of religions: the only and universal god is the god of the peoples. In fact, as the eyes and vows of the strong are almost naturally lifted and raised up to him in the sky, which seems to be his abode, and seek him and invoke him as an avenger and a judge, while their arms draw swords against tyrants and oppressors, he is all the more pleased with the peoples because, in so doing, they live, work, and fight for freedom. And he is the one who blows triumph through Joshua's trumpets; he is the one who pushes the ships of Themistocles into the Aegean; he is the one who informs uneasy Rome about the oppressed kings on Lake Regillus; he is the one who strikes fear into Barbarossa's horse at Legnano; and it is to him, both before and after victory, that even Washington's most pure and crowned forehead bows.

When the divine idea shines steady and serene, Carducci concludes, "there and then do cities rise and flourish; where and when it falters and darkens, there and then do cities decline and fall. God was with the beginning and foundation of our republic, that is to say, its citizens."[211]

With the stern voice of the prophet, Carducci exhorts us to remember that the homeland was resurrected through the work of generous souls who had faith in God, the father of all peoples. In an 1889 address given to students of the University of Padua, he thunderously proclaims: "May they not come to provoke us, to deny us the ideal, to deny us God. Scoundrels! The ideal was accumulated so much in our fathers' souls and ours that, by simply being released and thus dazzling the false prophets, it found a people unto itself; it

---

[210] On March 10, 1873, the piece "Un anno dopo" appeared in the joint edition – titled *Alleanza e Voce del Popolo commemorano Giuseppe Mazzini* – of Bologna's democratic-republican newspapers *L'Alleanza* and *Voce del Popolo*. It was later published in *Edizione nazionale delle opere*, vol. XIX, pp. 4–5.

[211] Giosuè Carducci, *Edizione nazionale delle opere*, vol. VII, pp. 364–365.

renewed a nation, it marked the fate of a history." In the poem "Per il monumento di Dante a Trento," which is dated September 20, 1896, Carducci imagines that God entrusts Dante with the protection of Italy while waiting for his mission to be fulfilled.[212] At God's order, Dante must return in order to expel false gods and create a new paradise.[213] Here Carducci expresses an invocation, not a prophecy. He does not urge his compatriots to rediscover the spirit of the Risorgimento; he encourages them to pin their hopes on Dante. A year later, Carducci dedicates touching verses to Dante, who himself knelt in the small church in Polenta in the hills of Romagna. While he hears the bells sounding the *Ave Maria* and inviting the faithful to pray, he still entreats God, not the God who exhorts and guides peoples to struggle and sacrifice for emancipation, but the God who brings calm and provides inner peace.[214]

In early twentieth-century Italy, no one wanted to be a prophet more than Gabriele D'Annunzio. In the tragedy *La gloria*, which was performed for the first time in 1899, D'Annunzio outlines the myth of a prophet who obtains the strength to instill hope in the masses from the deep and mysterious forces of the universe. Ruggero Flamma, the tragedy's protagonist, declares:

We too have touched the earth, we have questioned the earth, we have stretched out over her, we have heard the rumbling of her springs under burning heat and in her depths... She wants to be broken, moved, shaken, afflicted. But she is still so rich that she can nourish the seed of the highest hope. And if we had only brought her this seed, wouldn't our work as sowers already be fruitful? Our land hopes. Do you not feel the anguish of divine hope in the depths of that crowd which rumbles down there like a lost herd? If we had only ignited this anguish in her, then we would have already given a vital testament of ourselves.[215]

It is from the earth that Ruggero comes to understand the terrible truth that infuses a new faith which demands sacrifice: "Born in me through contact with the earth, that truth spreads everywhere; it penetrates deeply, disturbs, agitates, stirs. Its nobility is in its origin; the proof of its resistance is in the breadth of its path. Throughout the centuries, does the right of humanity's sacrifices not break out of every new truth – the same sacrifices which are necessary for these truths to affirm themselves? My very faith makes me the bearer and herald of that terrible right."[216] And he, in turn, must reveal the truth that the earth has

---

[212] "God places Italy in your hands / so that you can keep guard over her, / while the perfection of time still comes to be"; Giosuè Carducci, "Per il monumento di Dante a Trento," in Maria Sticco, *La poesia religiosa del Risorgimento*, p. 480.

[213] "Go, strike and cast out all false gods, / until he calls you to be up with him again / in what you create, a new paradise"; ibid.

[214] Giosuè Carducci, "La chiesa di Polenta (1897)," in Maria Sticco, *La poesia religiosa del Risorgimento*, p. 481.

[215] Gabriele D'Annunzio, *La gloria*, Act I, Scene IV, Milan: Fratelli Treves Editori, 1899, pp. 48–49.

[216] Ibid., pp. 50–51.

revealed to him. He cannot be silent: "Ah, do you remember when this house was quiet? A great ocean of unexpressed thoughts continuously all around me... Now I am 'the One who expresses' and 'the One who raises humanity's cry.' Silence is forbidden to me. My house is protected by the people. My name belongs to the wind. Listen."[217]

In the poem D'Annunzio writes to support and celebrate the war in Libya, he even brings the Libyan Sibyl into play: "And from the Libyan Sibyl, / under the sky turned by the Titan, / God's judgment is unsealed for us." In the speeches he makes in favor of entry into the war, D'Annunzio introduces himself as the poet who knows how to read the oracle's response, and he instills it into people's hearts. On May 5, 1915, he addresses the people of Genoa and proclaims: "O comrades, isn't the oracle we are waiting for already engraved within our hearts? Is it not already fixed at the summit of our united will? What do you want? In ancient times, a great king was once so bold as to hasten and force the response of an ambiguous priestess by locking her in his merciless arms. Tomorrow a very great people, with its own powerful grip, will get the judgment it desires."[218] The prophet's mission here is to reawaken sleeping souls and urge them to war. In this speech given before the monument commemorating the departure of the Expedition of Garibaldi's Thousand from Quarto during the night of May 5, 1860, D'Annunzio reveals the words of the prophets inscribed on the stones:

If ever stones cried out in the dreams of the prophets, behold here what this monument commands during this our vigil. It is a commandment raised over the sea. It is a mount of severe will at whose summit two wings open and a garland twists. It is huge and powerful like a decuman wave, O sailors, like that wave that rises more forcefully after the nine which preceded it and before the nine that are to follow it: the great wave, which carries and calls for courage.[219]

Ethereal spirits and heroes – to whom the poet, once again, knew how to listen – call the people to war:

And lofty spirits tell us that Michelangelo's *Night* has awakened and that his *Dawn*, with her foot and elbow donned in stone, is shaking off her pain and already leaping into the sky from the Eastern Alps. Heroes rise from their tombs and move toward her; their ripped flesh binds again whole; they are armed now with the same weapons that took their lives; they are now equipped with the same force that once conquered them: all for her, who now releases the feathers of Victory from her great shoulders. We will remake white flags from their funeral wrappings. Now, from a distance, doesn't the wing bone

---

[217] Ibid., p. 59.

[218] Gabriele D'Annunzio, *Per la più grande Italia: orazioni e messaggi*, Milan: Fratelli Treves Editori, 1920, p. 11. D'Annunzio chooses these words for the volume's epigraph: "Wake the sleeping and announce to those already awake: 'The days are near. Let us march out to high war!'"

[219] Ibid., p. 15.

look like the edge of an altar raised by martyrs' euphoria? And, inside, is there not a cavity similar to the grave of sacrifice for blood and flame?[220]

Confined to bed due to injuries sustained during an emergency landing on January 16, 1916 while aboard a plane belonging to the nascent Italian air force, D'Annunzio writes on narrow strips of paper that contain a single line – an imitation of the ancient sibyls who wrote their responses on leaves. With the help of his daughter Renata, he puts these prophetic phrases together in *Notturno*, which was first published in 1916 and then again as a definitive edition in 1921 after the short-lived Fiume enterprise had concluded. In this work, D'Annunzio presents himself as "an Egyptian scribe sculpted in basalt" whose body is in dissolution.[221] Immobility and temporary blindness strengthen his prophetic qualities: "All the matter of my life – all the sum of my knowledge – is reforged in my wounded eye. Continually in anguish, it is inhabited by an evocative fire."[222] He writes that he feels "overwhelmed by a cry higher than any other," that he has lost his voice in the pause. It seems that the imperious cry demands something more than just mere words.[223] It demands prophetic words that will proclaim never before heard truths: "Listen. Listen. I will tell you very serious things that you do not know. Be silent. Listen to me, then you will all jump to your feet."[224] Everyone will jump and stand up for the homeland, the *patria*: that name which produces a rousing shiver in the prophet's body and which, from that body, then spreads to the body of the people.

In *Per l'Italia degli italiani*, D'Annunzio compares himself to Orpheus and brings Lazarus and Christ into frame: "I am the blindfolded Orpheus who, at the gates of Hades, waits to be transformed into Lazarus, who is aware of that mystery towards which the crucified Jesus threw out his last cry." He asserts that "an indefatigable sibyl, chose to reside in the nave of [his] spirit, rather than under the vault of the Sistine Chapel, and today writes on his paper: 'O Gabriel, through my will, the Sun has stopped on the pinnacle of your reason and shines; and gilds every thought' [...]. Every accent reechoes, every image flashes again, every divination reseals itself. Immobile but omnipresent, I witness the new myth that is born from the faith and pain of my blindfolded self."[225] In his 1926 *Libro ascetico della Giovane Italia*, he proclaims that a god shines in his soul:

Art is a sacrifice, the most eminent of sacrifices. It is a sacrifice and, should the work reveal what people had never before seen or imagined, it is also a prophecy. I was given

---

[220] Ibid., p. 17.
[221] Gabriele D'Annunzio, *Notturno*, Milan: Mondadori, 1995, p. 3. See Timothy C. Campbell, "Remembering D'Annunzio and il Duce: Modern Prophecy in Italy," *Quaderni d'Italianistica* XXVII (2006): pp. 89–108.
[222] Ibid., p. 11.   [223] Ibid., p. 59.   [224] Ibid., p. 62.
[225] Gabriele D'Annunzio, *Per l'Italia degli italiani*, Milan: Bottega di poesia, 1923, pp. 26–27.

this gift of expression that, in the history of spirit, in the history of all ages and all languages, no one has ever had equally. That is why I was able to draw out of myself both the man who was afflicted within and the god who flashed when I was at my best. To fertile young people, I am more of an example than a teaching: an example is better than words.[226]

D'Annunzio writes that he knows how to listen to God's revelations: "Over fleeting and voracious history, this figure culminates as an impregnable flower in the perennial novelty of myth. Even throughout our long suffering, our God desired to provide abundant proof of our privileged blood!"[227] The poet knows "our God's secret design," and, in God's name, he issues the command for the people to stand up and to fight new and more glorious battles.[228] D'Annunzio claims to have derived prophetic light from everything: the earth, stones where prophets engraved their words, sibyls, oracles, lofty messengers, heroes, Egyptian scribes, Orpheus, a god, God. But these revelations – which indifferently come from sibyls, from oracles, from the earth, or from God – remain but poetic ploys that strike the audience's imagination and delight their ears. They are not prophecies. They may inspire applause, but they do not transform consciences; they do not sternly point out the path of duty. With the air of a demagogue, D'Annunzio believes Italians are now far from the patriotism of the Risorgimento that held humanity, the Italian homeland, and political freedom together.[229] Instead, they yearn for a country that conquers and for a leader to follow. They have become nationalists, and D'Annunzio gives them what they want to hear. In turn, they proclaim him their poet.

In 1899's *La gloria*, D'Annunzio had already outlined the cornerstones of the nationalist idea founded on devotion to a leader and on a cult of force:

I believe in the Leader that I have chosen for myself; I believe that Ruggero Flamma is capable of proving people wrong tomorrow. Found anywhere, in any field, every sign of virile energy, of masculine will and poise, of crude sincerity, lifts my heart; especially since such signs are rare in a time filled with vociferations and contortions. Leaving behind the solitude of our studies and laboratories, my companions and I entered the struggle, for we had foreseen the imminent appearance of a dominating and creative idea for which we wanted to be obedient and lucid instruments: the reconstitution of the City, of the Fatherland, of Latin Strength.[230]

---

[226] Gabriele D'Annunzio, *Il libro ascetico della Giovane Italia*, Milan: L'Olivetana, 1926, p. xii.
[227] Gabriele D'Annunzio, *Per la più grande Italia: orazioni e messaggi*, pp. 21–22.
[228] Ibid., pp. 29–30.
[229] On D'Annunzio's nationalism and nationalism more generally, see: Renzo De Felice, *D'Annunzio politico, 1918–1938*, Bari: Laterza, 1978; Filippo Sallusto, *Nazionalismo italiano, nazionalismo francese: Gabriele D'Annunzio e Roberto Forges Davanzati*, Canterano: Aracne, 2018, pp. 29–73.
[230] Gabriele D'Annunzio, *La gloria*, Act I, Scene II, pp. 27–28.

The restoration of the homeland's greatness requires violence and blood:

In order to live, do you understand? In order to exist! The necessity of violence grasps us, it presses us. No work can be done without blood spilled on a people. Nor could we ever stop the momentum already in motion. Instead, we must accelerate it; we must make it swift, brief, unanimous, victorious; we must really implement it now in preparation for an even greater trial that is nevertheless near. Do you understand? The time has come even for those who continue to deny it, just like a dying person who does not want to die.[231]

In the poems that he composes in order to contribute to this nationalist intoxication, D'Annunzio openly blesses slaughter and massacre. He writes these verses as the epigraph to a collection of poems written to glorify the war in Libya: "May you one day witness the Latin sea cover itself in slaughter while at war for you, / may you see laurels and myrtles bend as they form your crowns, / O reborn ever anew, O flower of all the races, / aroma of all the earth. Italy, Italy, / sacred to the new dawn / with plow and bow." With war and conquest, Italy will finally become great: "Thus, divine Italy, under your / just sun and in the darkness, armed / and cautious, with palladium on your gun carriages, / I see you move toward your new life, / make strength out of your silence, / and turn your wounds into greatness. / In my night, above my pain, / this supreme image spreads out. / Enclose it in the strength of your heart."[232] Benedetto Croce finely wrote:

In D'Annunzio, where there is no false goodness and false heroism – that is to say, products of the same imagination that covers snakes with flowers – the only remnants of morality and true heroism are found in attitudes or gestures, a smile, clear eyes, a forgiving hand, a priestly forehead; in sum, the statue and not the soul: a statue which never softens from its stiffening and which seems unaware that, besides attitudes, there is virtue, which is not an attitude; beyond gestures, there is duty, which is not a gesture. Like his sculptor Lucio Settala, D'Annunzio too can say: "I do not sculpt souls."[233]

---

[231] Ibid., Act I, Scene IV, p. 47.

[232] Gabriele D'Annunzio, "Libro IV," *Merope: laudi del cielo, del mare, della terra e degli eroi*, Milan: Fratelli Treves Editori, 1912, p. 180.

[233] Benedetto Croce, "Note sulla letteratura italiana nella seconda metà del secolo XIX: VII, Gabriele D'Annunzio," *La Critica* 2 (1904): pp. 20–21. In the first decades of the twentieth century, harsh voices arose in Italian culture against D'Annunzio, who claimed to be the advocate of the nation's redemption. It is worth quoting Giuseppe De Robertis: "This mishap of Gabriele exploded a bit after exile. Once he set foot in Italy, he got a taste for it. He spoke and spoke, in a stupefying way, like a cicada! [...] The homeland is fine; but D'Annunzio no – this dandy who seems to have deliberately begun his career as a civil poet with the *Odi navali* in order to claim, presumably, to have the first say today [...]. Now, by God; this Italy that D'Annunzio speaks of [...] has not been seen by me; I don't see it even with all the sun's brilliance. I could say that I have never seen it [...]. Going from Carducci to D'Annunzio is an exteriorization [...]. D'Annunzio never said a single, necessary word [...,] he falsified reality. [...] He wanted to go back to the Greeks and the Romans [...]. He mentions the usual names – both Garibaldi and other Garibaldians, all of whom feel so far removed from us with this mathematical war [...]. He played games of deception in the name of the present moment, in the

But sculpting souls is precisely the mission of the true prophets of emancipation whom D'Annunzio tried to imitate, albeit with the poses of a mediocre actor.

Indifference, disillusion, and disenchantment are the words we often read in the political literature of post-Risorgimento Italy. The belief that had sustained the struggle for independence's solidarity was that God wanted an Italy free and united; the motto of the Italians after 1871 was much more individualistic, "every man for himself, and God for us all" ("*chacun pour soi, Dieu pour tous*"). There was no room for Mazzini's prophecy of the brotherhood of peoples in this united and independent Italy. The new political and intellectual leadership regarded it as a puerile and dangerous dream. In a speech given in Parliament in 1894, Francesco Crispi, who was one of Garibaldi's Mille, explained that the representatives of the left were wrong when they repeated Mazzini's words from 1854: "In forty years, such and so much progress has been made, that the matters that, for us young people, for us conspirators, once made us raise our spirits and prepare ourselves for great struggles, are no longer felt today."[234] In this same speech, he cited the Mazzinian ideal of the free and strong humanity that was to be achieved through the unity of free nations, but it was a poor rhetorical move. The idea that the nation and political liberty are inseparable, and that the liberty of the nation must go together with the liberty of all nations, were no longer Crispi's principles, nor were they the principles of most of the Italian intellectual and political elite. "Man must style himself according to the changing circumstances of the times, to different

---

name of Italy [. . .]. Thus, he gave false speeches based on old patterns that, in turn, anyone and everyone would know how to give: with a worn-out style, rhetorical illuminations, and common comparisons"; G. De Robertis, "D'Annunzio ha parlato," *La Voce*, August 15, 1914; also, in *La cultura italiana del '900 attraverso le riviste*, vol. III, edited by A. Romano, Turin: Einaudi, 1960, pp. 555–562. Equally eloquent are Aldo Palazzeschi's words in *Due imperi... mancati* (1920): "Gabriele D'Annunzio opens and closes the unfortunate season of war. As it was carried out, Italy's war is nothing more than a D'Annunzian boast, but without sense, without skill, without profit. And he has embellished it throughout all his days: he has decked it with flowers, adorned it with hymns, odes and songs, speeches, invocations, imprecations, inaugurations, commemorations and adventures of every kind; on land and in the air, under and above water, as if it were a great gymnastic match, a tournament in which the muscles and lungs had to have a delightedly complete outburst. All this without even asking what kind of war it would be like or that had to be fought; without the slightest care for the men upon whom this war was imposed, nothing. Heads held high! March on! Such men still see the people as the plebs of long ago, and they live in the drunken thrill of resurrecting Leonidas, the Punic Wars, centaurs, Roman eagles, the wings of victory, the scraps of extinct grandeur, as if centuries and millennia had not passed over this humanity. Scrape it all off, and do you know what you will find? A cavalry officer. Creatures who live outside of reality and detached from life, creators of emptiness"; Aldo Palazzeschi, *Due imperi... mancati*, Milan: Linea d'ombra edizioni, 1994, pp. 150–152.

[234] "In quarant'anni si è fatto tale e tanto progresso, che le questioni che, a noi giovani, a noi cospiratori, ci facevano sollevare l'animo e preparare alle grandi lotte, oggi non si sentono più"; Federico Chabod, *Storia della politica estera italiana dal 1870 al 1896*, vol. I, p. 75; English translation, p. 65.

conditions" (*"l'uomo deve acconciarsi alle mutate circostanze dei tempi, alle condizioni diverse"*), Crispi proclaimed along with Machiavelli – but this was Machiavelli deprived of his prophetic message.[235]

Scholarly works also corroborated the sense that *fin-de-siècle* Italian culture and mentality was becoming increasingly distant from prophets of emancipation. In the preface to the second edition of his monumental study *La vita e i tempi di Girolamo Savonarola* of 1882 (the first edition appeared in 1859), Pasquale Villari praised Savonarola as a religious reformer who "devoted his energies to the moral renovation of mankind," and who understood virtue to be "the assured basis of religion, and the source of true liberty."[236] Villari also openly expressed, however, his skepticism about Savonarola's prophetic qualities.[237] The fact that many intelligent Florentines believed Savonarola to have been inspired by God was the consequence of their Renaissance mentality – when learned people had lost true religious faith but believed in occult arts, miracles, wonders, aerial spirits, and prophecies. Savonarola claimed that scripture was the only basis of his preaching. Yet, Villari clarifies that Savonarola searched the scriptures for proof of the visions, voices, and forewarnings that his elated fantasy had revealed to him.[238] Savonarola was a prophet only in the sense that he clearly understood that Italy's political weakness and the corruption of the papacy and clergy were on the brink of bringing complete ruin both to the Italian states and to the Church. For Villari, Savonarola deserves to be remembered and honored not because he was a prophet, but for his struggle and his martyrdom for religious and moral reform.[239]

[235] Ibid., pp. 75 and 282; English translation, p. 65.

[236] "Ma dev'essere una religione quale la voleva il Savonarola, che santifichi con la morale, la libertà e la patria, favorendo ogni civile progresso: una Chiesa amica dello Stato. Ed i sacerdoti che questa Chiesa costituiscono e rappresentano, chiamati a guidare il popolo, debbono, egli diceva, colle opere, rappresentare, personificare la dottrina che predicano a parole"; Pasquale Villari, "Girolamo Savonarola e l'ora presente. Conferenza tenuta in Firenze da Pasquale Villari il 10 giugno 1897," *La storia di Girolamo Savonarola e de' suoi tempi*, vol. I, Florence: Le Monnier, 1930, p. LXXV.

[237] "Un dubbio lasciano certo nell'animo del lettore moderno i miracoli e molte strane profezie, a cui non possiamo prestare fede alcuna"; ibid., p. XL.

[238] Pasquale Villari, *La storia di Girolamo Savonarola e de' suoi tempi*, vol. I, pp. 126–127.

[239] "Il Savonarola si trovò in un momento solenne della storia del mondo. Egli vedeva chiaramente e fu in ciò profeta davvero, che le condizioni d'Italia, che la condotta, la corruzione del papa e del clero erano arrivate a tale da minacciare certa rovina allo Stato ed alla Chiesa. Una riforma in questa era perciò divenuta inevitabile. Se non si faceva dentro di essa, si sarebbe fatta al di fuori, spezzandone l'unità. Questo era ciò che egli voleva evitare con tutte le sue forze, e però raccomandava la riforma interiore, serbando l'incolumità delle dottrine, e minacciava futuri guai se ciò non si faceva subito. La sua voce fu soffocata nel sangue; e la Riforma di Lutero trionfò, l'unità della Chiesa cristiana fu spezzata, l'Italia fu flagellata come era stato dal Savonarola profetato"; Pasquale Villari, "Girolamo Savonarola e l'ora presente. Conferenza tenuta in Firenze da Pasquale Villari il 10 giugno 1897," *La storia di Girolamo Savonarola e de' suoi tempi*, vol. I, pp. LIX–LX.

Even Mazzini, the acknowledged prophet of the Risorgimento, earned criticism. In her biography *Della vita di Giuseppe Mazzini* (1885), Jessie White Mario worships Mazzini as the prophet of Italian regeneration and of a republican Italy yet to come. But she also remarks that Italians had already forgotten his true message of political and social emancipation.[240] Questioning the effective impact of Mazzini's ideas on the Risorgimento, the eminent historian Gaetano Salvemini (1873–1957) criticizes Mazzini for his lack of intellectual rigor and his habit of subordinating reason to sentiment. Salvemini goes on to state in his 1905 essay that the weakest part of Mazzini's political theory was precisely his prophetic vision, namely that God had entrusted Italy the mission of opening a new era in human history. Equally ill-conceived was Mazzini's belief that the republic corresponds to God's design ("*la repubblica non era, evidentemente, nei disegni di Dio*"). Nonetheless, Salvemini recognizes Mazzini's immense charismatic power and stresses that Mazzini's ideas – his principle of duty, his persuasion that political and social emancipation demands sufferance, and his vision of social solidarity and a brotherhood of nations – were of perennial value. While the Italians could still look at Mazzini as a father and a brother, as a source of inspiration and consolation, his ideas ultimately were very distant from the contemporary ones.[241]

Over the centuries, Italian poets had composed prophetic words that sustained the hopes and struggles for political emancipation. Another poet, Giosuè Carducci (1835–1907), vividly expresses the sense that prophetic sentiments had lost their force in post-Risorgimento Italy. On the proclamation of the Kingdom of Italy in 1861, Carducci praises the Risorgimento as a glorious redemption that Italians had achieved not through brute force or cunning, but through their faith, hope, and charity. He also stresses, though, that the Battle of Aspromonte – where the Piedmontese troops halted Garibaldi and his volunteers as they were marching to Rome in 1862 – marks the end of the will to fight. For Carducci, the redemption and the triumph of liberty became hopes for a very distant future.[242] Italians were neither willing nor capable to fight for

---

[240] Jessie White Mario, *Della vita di Giuseppe Mazzini*, Milan: Società Editrice Sonzogno, 1896, pp. xi–xii.

[241] Gaetano Salvemini, *Il pensiero religioso politico sociale di Giuseppe Mazzini*, Messina: A. Trimarchi, 1905. I am referencing the third edition, Gaetano Salvemini, *Mazzini*, Rome: La Voce, 1920, pp. 163–164.

[242] "Oh, grave è l'odio e sterile, / Stanco il mio cuor de l'ire; / Splendi e m'arridi, o candida / Luce de l'avvenire! / Arridi! i nostri parvoli / Che a te veder son nati / Io t'accomando: ei vivano / Del raggio tuo beati. / A terra i serti e l'infule! / In pezzi, o inique spade! / Solo nel mondo regnino / Giustizia e libertade! / O dee, ne la perpetua / Ombra si chiuderanno / Quest'occhi, e il vostro imperio / In van ricercheranno"; Giosuè Carducci, "Dopo Aspromonte," in Maria Sticco, *La poesia religiosa del Risorgimento*, p. 473. On Carducci as the last poet-prophet, see Luigi Russo, *Carducci senza retorica*, Bari: Laterza, 1957, pp. 189–190.

the ideals of political and social redemption.[243] In the poem "For the monument of Dante" (*Per il monumento di Dante a Trento*) written on September 20, 1896, he imagines God entrusting Italy to Dante's tutelage, and encouraging him to wait for the perfection of times to come.[244] Dante must arrive upon God's command, and then expel all false divinities and create a new paradise.[245] Here Carducci voices an invocation, not a prophecy. He does not exhort his fellow Italians to rediscover the Risorgimento's spirit; he invites them to put their hopes in Dante. A year later, Carducci pens moving words for Dante who once knelt in the little church of Polenta in the hills of Romagna, but once again he does not urge Italians to resume the struggle for moral regeneration. He instead appeals to God, who pacifies him as he finds inner peace and listens to bells calling the faithful to pray their evening *Ave Maria*.[246]

A few prophets appeared in remote corners of Italy and announced radically egalitarian messages. The best example is Davide Lazzaretti (1834–1878), the "prophet of Mount Amiata." Lazzaretti's story is particularly interesting because he was a fervent patriot of the Risorgimento who later founded a popular movement dedicated to the pursuit of republican liberty. He proclaimed that he was inspired by God and that God would sustain his efforts to found a new Zion on earth.[247] On his flag he wrote "Long live the Republic, kingdom of God" (*"Viva la repubblica regno di Dio"*).[248] He preached in his church on Mount Labbro between 1869 and 1870, and more than two thousand peasants followed him. In *My struggle with God* (*La mia lotta con Dio*, 1876), Lazzaretti affirmed that God had revealed to him and to him alone secrets of the utmost importance for humanity's future. He saw a vision of seven new cities, one of which was situated atop Mount Amiata where he had established his community. He called his followers "brothers and patriots" (*"fratelli e patrioti"*), and he invoked God's blessing upon the beautiful Italian fatherland that all peoples admire (*"nostra bella patria, ammirata da tutti i popoli della terra"*). For Lazzaretti, the entrance of Italian troops into Rome on September 20, 1870 was a sign of God's desire to punish corrupt prelates who had perverted Christ's message.[249] He advocated a

---

[243] Luigi Russo, *Carducci senza retorica*, p. 202.

[244] "Italia Dio in tua balía consegna / Sí che tu vegli spirito su lei / Mentre perfezïon di tempi vegna"; Giosuè Carducci, "Per il monumento a Dante a Trento," in Maria Sticco, *La poesia religiosa del Risorgimento*, p. 480.

[245] "Va, batti, caccia tutti falsi dèi, / Fin ch'egli seco ti richiami in alto / A ciò che novo paradiso crei"; ibid.

[246] Giosuè Carducci, "La chiesa di Polenta (1897)," in Maria Sticco, *La poesia religiosa del Risorgimento*, p. 481.

[247] See Giacomo Barzellotti, *David Lazzaretti di Arcidosso detto il santo. I suoi seguaci e la sua leggenda*, Bologna: Zanichelli, 1885, p. 9.

[248] Ibid., p. 10.

[249] "Lasciamo correre le vicende come piace alla provvidenza [...] Iddio ha voluto permettere ciò che oggi avviene per umiliare la superbia, la finzione e la inumanità dei coloro, che mal corrispondono al suo divin ministero"; ibid., p. 165.

theocratic democracy where religion and state are one and the same, with the sovereign power emanating from God and the people. When Lazzaretti decided to descend from Mount Labbro at the head of a large procession of followers on August 18, 1878, he asked his brothers whether they wanted the republic. After they all responded affirmatively, he said: "The republic begins today in the world, but it shall not be the republic of 1848; it shall be the Kingdom of God" (*"la repubblica incomincia da oggi in poi nel mondo; ma non sarà quella del'48; sarà il regno di Dio"*). "Viva la repubblica" – long live the republic – were the last words he spoke before the Carabinieri opened fire on the procession and killed him.[250]

Around the same time, socialist militants resorted to prophetic language disguised as a scientific language to exhort Italian workers to organize and fight for their social redemption.[251] They proclaimed that their vision of the new order was the consequence of the scientific knowledge of the laws of social life. Filippo Turati, the acknowledged leader of the Italian Socialist Party which he helped found in 1892, declared that the socialist principle would change the face of the world and transform herds of slaves into free persons (*"il principio che muterà la faccia del mondo e farà di mille mandre di schiavi un popolo solo di liberi"*). In his view, the redemption of the proletariat would be the last phase of history and usher in the redemption of all humanity.[252] The leaflets that socialist organizers distributed to persuade workers to join the movement asserted even more emphatically that the triumph of socialism was the necessary outcome of the objective tendency of capitalist society. A handbook for socialist speakers stressed that everything confirms the inevitable process of social transformation (*"fatale andare"*).[253] Socialism's advent was not

---

[250] Ibid., p. 237.

[251] See Oddino Morgari, *L'arte della propaganda socialista*, Milan: Lotta di Classe Editrice, 1896; Ettore Ciccotti, *Psicologia del movimento socialista. Note ed osservazioni*, Bari: Laterza, 1903; Enrico Decleva, "Anticlericalismo e religiosità laica nel socialismo italiano," *Prampolini e il socialismo riformista. Atti del convegno di Reggio Emilia, ottobre 1978*, Rome: Modo operaio-Edizioni Avanti, 1979, pp. 259–279; Malcolm Sylvers, "L'anticlericalismo nel socialismo italiano dalle origini al 1914," *Movimento operaio e socialista* 16 (1970): pp. 175–189; Arnaldo Nesti, *"Gesù socialista." Una tradizione popolare italiana 1880–1920*, Turin: Editrice Claudiana, 1974; Ettore Passerin d'Entrèves, "Il socialismo alla De Amicis nella Torino di fine Ottocento," *Il Mulino* 24 (1975): pp. 85–93; Gabriele Turi, "Aspetti dell'ideologia del PSI (1890–1910)," *Studi Storici* 21 (1980): pp. 61–94; Franco Andreucci, "La diffusione e la volgarizzazione del marxismo," *Il marxismo nell'età della Seconda Internazionale*, Turin: Einaudi, 1979, pp. 5–58. On the prophetic content of socialist theories before and after Marx and Engels, see Henry de Lubac, *La postérité spirituelle de Joachim de Flore. De Saint-Simon à nos jours*, pp. 336–384.

[252] "La redenzione del proletariato, ultimo porto della lotta odierna, sarà al tempo stesso la redenzione dell'umanità tutta quanta"; Filippo Turati, "La moderna lotta di classe," *Il paradiso socialista: La propaganda socialista in Italia alla fine dell'Ottocento attraverso gli opuscoli di "Critica sociale,"* edited by Rossano Pisano, Milan: Franco Angeli, 1986, pp. 87–91.

[253] "L'avvento del socialismo è una fatalità storica. Perché il socialismo è una fatalità storica? Le prove: i fenomeni della vita sociale, la tendenza del moderno capitalismo all'accentramento,

presented as the fulfillment of a prophecy. Rather, it was presented as the outcome of objective social forces that workers had to follow – an approach that contributed powerfully to instilling socialist faith in workers' hearts and minds. However, it was a vulnerable mode of propaganda and education. Since this faith was (supposedly) based on facts, as soon as these facts stubbornly contradicted hopes, the faith began to pale and fade.

Nonetheless, a few socialist militants resorted to prophetic language that took inspiration from Christianity. The most effective of them was Camillo Prampolini (1859–1930), the respected socialist apostle of Reggio Emilia. Prampolini elaborated the Christian idea of the kingdom of God within his prophetic discourse of socialist redemption.[254] In typical prophetic style, Prampolini made it clear that God wants His kingdom to triumph on earth. This does not mean that the kingdom of God will come at His command. On the contrary, Prampolini explains that it will come only if the oppressed have faith in it.[255] Times are ripe for the kingdom's coming when, and if, workers truly believe in it and want it. The kingdom of God shall come to put an end to poverty, oppression, war, and the exploitation of human beings over other human beings.[256] If proletarians organize and reinforce a sense of brotherhood among themselves, the blessed world of solidarity announced by Christ will triumph over injustice.[257] Prampolini insisted that redemption will come only

innumerevoli pubblicazioni d'autori delle più disparate opinioni confermano il *fatale andare* della società verso un ordine di cose diverso dall'attuale"; "Piccolo manuale dell'oratore socialista ad uso degli operai e dei contadini (1896)," *Il paradiso socialista*, pp. 290–291.

[254] "No [...] evidentemente queste disuguaglianze derivano solo dall'ignoranza e dalla malvagità degli uomini. Dio non può volerle. Certamente, Dio le condanna. Certamente, Dio vuole che gli uomini vivano come fratelli – distribuendosi in pace e giustizia la ricchezza comune – e non già vivano come lupi in lotta l'uno contro l'altro, godendo gli uni della miseria degli altri. Dunque – diceva Gesù ai suoi compagni – noi dobbiamo far guerra a questo doloroso e brutto regno dell'ingiustizia in cui siamo nati; noi dobbiamo volere, fortemente volere il regno della giustizia, dell'uguaglianza, della fratellanza umana, perché questo è il regno che Dio vuole fra gli uomini; noi dobbiamo persuadere i nostri fratelli che esso è possibile e non è un sogno. Dobbiamo trasfondere in loro la nostra fede, e il 'regno di Dio' si avvererà"; Camillo Prampolini, *Predica di Natale*, Reggio Emilia: Tipografia operaia, 1897, p. 4.

[255] Ibid., p. 5.

[256] "È venuto il tempo in cui il sogno di Cristo può essere finalmente realizzato. Basta che i lavoratori lo vogliano"; ibid.

[257] "Se i lavoratori dei campi e delle città si daranno la mano; se avranno fede nella giustizia; se comprenderanno che gli uomini sono uguali e che per conseguenza nessuno ha diritto di dirsi padrone di un altro e di vivere a spese altrui, ma tutti hanno l'obbligo di prendere parte al lavoro necessario alla vita di tutti; se per vivere umanamente – cioè per diventare liberi, per non aver padroni e godere insieme l'intero frutto delle loro fatiche – i lavoratori, invece di vivere isolati e di farsi concorrenza, metteranno in pratica il precetto di Cristo: 'amatevi gli uni cogli altri siccome fratelli,' e formeranno dovunque le loro organizzazioni; allora, davanti alla loro crescente e sempre più capace organizzazione, le ingiustizie sociali scompariranno come si dileguano le tenebre dinanzi al sole che nasce. E sorgerà così il mondo buono e lieto della solidarietà umana agognato da Cristo, il 'regno di Dio'"; ibid., pp. 5–6.

from faith in justice. The working classes must organize, learn, educate themselves, fight, resist, suffer.[258] Human progress is necessary and continuous. In
the past there were slaves, then servants; today there is the proletariat; tomorrow there will be free workers. In full agreement with classical prophetic
language, Prampolini asserted that the oppressed shall achieve their redemption
only when they feel the duty to fight oppression and exploitation (*"voi l'avrete
quando sentirete il dovere di non lasciarvi opprimere e sfruttare"*).[259]

Although the socialists failed in bringing about the kingdom of justice and
brotherhood, they did succeed in instilling a sense of self-dignity and civic
consciousness in the hearts and minds of many artisans, workers, and peasants.
They also built and preserved institutions of solidarity, schools for workers,
libraries, leagues, and cooperatives to sustain a slow but steady process of social
and intellectual emancipation. Even before the king of Italy Vittorio Emanuele
III shamefully called Mussolini to form a new government in 1922, the first and
foremost goal of the fascists was to devastate the hard work of socialist
militants with inhuman ferocity. In addition to destroying liberty, fascism's
mission was to accomplish a religious reform, as the regime's ideologists
proclaimed. By religious reform, they meant to instill a new faith that would
have provided Italians with the moral strength needed to attain national greatness.[260] Part of this ideological strategy was the effort to enlist the
Risorgimento's prophets as forerunners of Mussolini's regime. Already in
1923, Giovanni Gentile published *The Prophets of the Italian Risorgimento*
(*I profeti del Risorgimento italiano*) and claimed that Mazzini and Gioberti
were champions of the Risorgimento's prophetic promise, which had now been
fulfilled in Mussolini.[261]

In Gentile's wake, long lines of propagandists zealously mobilized to build a
fascist prophetic tradition. In 1927, Arturo Marpicati, the future chancellor of
the Academy of Italy and the deputy secretary of the National Fascist Party,
declared Foscolo a prophet of the Italy that fascism has now redeemed:

---

[258] Camillo Prampolini, "Come avverrà il socialismo," *Il paradiso socialista*, p. 171.

[259] Ibid., p. 172.

[260] See Emilio Gentile, *Le religioni della politica: fra democrazie e totalitarismi*, Rome and Bari:
Laterza, 2001; English translation, Emilio Gentile, *Politics as Religion*, Princeton: Princeton
University Press, 2006.

[261] The two essays that form the short book, Gentile explains in the preface, had been published
separately in 1919. He decided to reissue them in a volume because Mazzini and Gioberti were
the spiritual leaders of the Risorgimento "nel suo periodo eroico, quando fu posto il problema
della nostra esistenza nazionale e se ne additò la soluzione a mo' di profezia." The prophecy of
the Risorgimento, he remarked, had not been achieved on September 20, 1870 when the Italian
troops entered into Rome, and not even with the victory in World War I, but when Mussolini
founded the new Italy. On the first page of the book we read the following inscription: "A
BENITO MUSSOLINI / ITALIANO DI RAZZA / DEGNO DI ASCOLTARE / LE VOCI DEI
PROFETI / DELLA NUOVA ITALIA"; Giovanni Gentile, *I profeti del Risorgimento italiano*,
Florence: Vallecchi, 1923.

"If true Italy will one day come to be, I will have a pious judge," wrote the Poet to a friend. And the Italy of today would certainly be and is, in fact, the one that he imagined: strong with its own beautiful weapons, united, victorious, hardworking, a candid advocate of ideas and principles regarding the State, strength, humanity [...] which were also Foscolo's ideas, the fruit of his profound thought. Indeed, the Italy of today is pious and infinitely grateful and devoted to a writer who – through his immortal works, blood, and exile – so loved her, dreamed of her, desired her, and paved the way for her. In 1927, Italy's sailors brought a large laurel wreath to the Poet's house in Zakynthos. The Duce wrote on a tricolor ribbon that adorned it: To Ugo Foscolo, from the Italy that He envisaged.[262]

Dante was promptly added to the ranks of the prophets of Fascism. A leading figure in fascist cultural politics, Emilio Bodrero exclaims in a 1931 issue of the journal *Nuova Antologia*: "Only today can we understand Dante as Italian and Imperial, because such is Benito Mussolini's Fascism: Italian and Imperial; only today can we recognize Dante as the prophet of our destiny."[263] Not even poor Leopardi could escape being enlisted into the army of fascism's prophets. Deaf to the text's ironic tone, the regime's illustrious exegetes claimed that Leopardi's *Paralipomeni della Batracomiomachia* exalted an Italy which would return to be the queen and dominatrix of the world for the third time.[264] In 1934, it was Petrarca's turn. In an article in *Gli annali della Cattedra Petrarchesca*, Arrigo Solmi reads Petrarca's *Africa* as the prophecy of a victorious war in Ethiopia. He writes: "Today, in the pride of our new history, with the laurel of victory in a just war, with fascism's prestige and strength renewed for the fortune of the Fatherland, with the resurrected power of a vast Empire made victorious by virtue of ingenuity and arms, we [...] recognize the Poet's prescient genius."[265] In 1938, with an admirably sober language, Carlo Calcaterra celebrated Alfieri as the prophet of the victorious Duce:

Just as eagles can always leap from the heights of spirit, so too can "the new man" always rise from the immeasurable depths of a great people that is stirring before the gates of the future: "the new man" who synthesizes all of our aspirations and, through his genius, turns them into reality [...] Just as the much needed Hero first came to us from the ardent blood of Romagna, overcoming death and giving life, so too has our Leader been able to climb from the hills of Monferrato into the light of Europe and conquer an empire in just a few months. The eagles of which our poets speak possess these spiritual wings; the new men of Italy are made with this inflexible and polished metal.[266]

---

[262] I am citing from: Stéphanie Lanfranchi, "'Verrà un dì l'Italia vera...': poesia e profezia dell'Italia futura nel giudizio fascista," *California Italian Studies* 2.1 (2011): p. 3.

[263] Ibid., p. 8. In February 1918, just a few months after the defeat at the Battle of Caporetto, Gentile gave a speech at the Casa di Dante in Rome. He exalted Dante as the prophet of the idea that there cannot be political life without religious faith, or rather without absolute devotion to an idea. See "La profezia di Dante," *Studi su Dante*, Florence: Le Lettere, 1990, pp. 174–175.

[264] Stéphanie Lanfranchi, "'Verrà un dì l'Italia vera...': poesia e profezia dell'Italia futura nel giudizio fascista," p. 7.

[265] Ibid.   [266] Ibid., pp. 11–12.

Indeed, it is difficult to imagine a more evident falsification of the writer who, at the dawn of the Risorgimento, had celebrated the supreme value of moral freedom that never bows to any master.

Even in the years of the totalitarian regime, some free voices still spoke up in order to rediscover the true nature of prophecy. In his 1928 monograph on Ugo Foscolo, Marco Fubini (1900–1977) denounces the use and abuse of searching for precursors. Fubini writes that the poet-prophet is "destined, like all precursors, to remain halfway: on this side of the Promised Land, neither completely in the past, nor completely in the future." He invites literary scholars to avoid anachronisms that distort the interpretation of the historical and cultural context within which a text is born – distortions that ultimately misrepresent a text's meaning.[267] In his magnificent 1942 book *Dante e la cultura medievale*, Bruno Nardi (1884–1968) reminds Italians that true prophets are servants of a moral ideal, never slaves of a regime: "Dante was a true prophet, not because his plans for political and ecclesiastical reform were implemented (rather, given the natural course of events, we recognize that they were impractical, as they indeed proved to be), but because, like all great prophets, he knew how to look beyond the events taking place before his own eyes, and point to an eternal ideal of justice as the standard for measuring not only people's moral stature, but also the value of their actions."[268] Despite the undertakings of serious scholars, fascism inflicted irreparable damage on the Italian prophetic tradition. As I will try to show later, our prophets were no longer able to inspire moral redemption and social emancipation.

While Gentile labeled the prophets of the Risorgimento as forerunners of Mussolini's regime, Piero Gobetti (1901–1926) became aware of the need of a prophetic language opposed to the fascist ideologists' discursive elaborations. Gobetti rediscovered Alfieri's message and sought to revive it because it taught "a more spiritual religiosity, a heroic morality which guides the life and action of men and peoples." In Alfieri's creed, Gobetti found a religion and a God who command human beings to be free, and who demands people to manifest the spirit of sacrifice that sustains revolutionary movements. Italy could never be free without strong minds driven by a natural impulse to "search for glory in the highest endeavors," without the "just and noble wrath of the justly enraged and enlightened peoples."[269] Gobetti emphasized that this revolutionary morality bolstered by religious spirit was the only path to redemption from fascist tyranny: "We are not men if we are not free. The matter is not to conquer liberty by means of reforms or through the utilitarianism of moderates and

---

[267] Marco Fubini, *Ugo Foscolo: saggio critico*, Turin: Fratelli Ribet, 1938, p. 8.

[268] Bruno Nardi, *Dante e la cultura medievale*, Bari: Laterza, 1948, p. 415. See also: Carla Chiummo, "Dante in veste post-risorgimentale (1870–1900)," *Studi Rinascimentali* 8 (2010): pp. 57–66.

[269] Piero Gobetti, "Risorgimento senza eroi," *Scritti storici, letterari e filosofici*, edited by Paolo Spriano, Turin: Einaudi, 1969, p. 75.

philanthropists; the political liberty of Alfieri arises from inward liberty, intended as strong feelings. This idea is the political program of Alfieri, the announcement of a revolution that one still waits for in Italian history."[270] Like Alfieri, Gobetti recognized the intellectual roots of a religion of liberty in the prophets of the *Old Testament*. Such a religion is apt to inspire a people of citizens determined to fight for liberty because they feel compelled to do so – not because victory is a certain outcome. Gobetti explained that the religion of liberty is a religion that "is no longer comfort for the weak but rather certainty for the strong": a religion that excludes interests and calculations and requires *"fanaticism* from the initiators, enthusiasm of sincerity."[271]

Carlo Rosselli's (1899–1937) writings also indicate the anti-fascist camp's awareness that a new prophetic spirit was necessary to defeat Fascism. A theorist of liberal socialism, Rosselli was the founder of the anti-fascist movement "Justice and Liberty" (*"Giustizia e Libertà"*), and was ultimately assassinated by Mussolini's henchmen. Aware of the anti-Christian character of Nazism, he hoped in a "more Christian European conscience" that would take moral values more to heart. He therefore firmly condemned Hitler in the name of that conscience. Rosselli believed that the crisis of the contemporary world was a religious crisis, and that the religion of those who fought against Fascism and Nazism had to be the spiritual heir of Christianity. According to him, the old God died in the Spanish Civil War because the Catholic Church used God's name to sustain fascist regimes. The anti-fascists' defeat marked the defeat of the last religious human beings who believed that "to live one needs reasons to live for": the last remaining individuals "who believe[d] in a God, the last who evidently testified that man is not an animal of prey or for slaughter." Brought about by the victory of Fascism and Nazism, and by the death of the old God, the religious crisis could only be resolved with the new religion that inspired the anti-fascist and anti-Nazi struggle. Rosselli wrote that this religion "is precisely the embodiment of that enthusiasm, the popular and social organization (in Greek, the ecclesiastical organization) of what has set the heart of so many thinkers and martyrs throbbing since the origins of the modern world [...], and of what has flashed through us in an unforgettable moment of our youth as the only beauty for which alone it is worth living and dying."[272]

Fascism had prevailed, Rosselli claimed in *Liberal Socialism* (*Socialismo liberale*) – published in France in 1930 but written in 1929, when he was under

---

[270] Ibid., pp. 75–76.
[271] Ibid., p. 132 and p. 128. Norberto Bobbio has correctly remarked that Gobetti elaborates the concept of "religion of liberty" ten years before Croce did. See "Ritratto di Piero Gobetti," *Italia fedele. Il mondo di Gobetti*, Florence: Passigli, 1986, p. 29.
[272] Carlo Rosselli, "Polemica sulla Chiesa," in Carlo Rosselli, *Scritti dall'esilio*, edited by Costanzo Casucci, Turin: Einaudi, 1988, p. 213.

police confinement on the island of Lipari – because too few Italians valued the inner liberty that comes from the sense of duty:

It is a sad thing, but true, that the education of man in Italy, the formation of the basic moral cell – i.e. the individual – is in large part still to be done. Most people lack the jealous and profound sense of autonomy and responsibility, because of misery, indifference, secular renunciation. Centuries of serfdom got the average Italian to oscillate between servile habit and anarchic revolt. He lacks the concept of life as struggle and mission, the notion of liberty as moral duty, the awareness of his own and the other's limits.[273]

As a possible remedy to the moral weakness of the Italians he outlines the contours of a new prophetic vision. He claims that a new socialist movement should draw its inspiration from "Greek rationalism and the messianism of Israel." The former encompasses a love of liberty, a respect for individual autonomy, and a harmonious and detached conception of life; the latter teaches an entirely down-to-earth sense of justice, a myth of equality, and a spiritual torment that forbids all indulgence.[274] Both visions were necessary to remedy the moral weakness of Italians:

The Italian problem is essentially a problem of liberty. A problem of liberty in its comprehensive meaning: at the individual level, it is a problem of spiritual autonomy, emancipation of conscience; at the social level, i.e., at the level of the construction of the state and of the relationships between groups and classes, it is a problem of organization of liberty. Without free persons, there can be no free State. Without emancipated consciences, there can be no emancipation of classes. The circle is not vicious. Liberty begins with the education of man and ends with the triumph of a State of free citizens, with equal rights and duties a State in which the liberty of each is condition and limit of the liberty of all.[275]

Who but prophets like those of the *Old Testament* could help Italians resuscitate the moral strength they needed to regain liberty?

When the fascist regime was at the peak of its strength, Benedetto Croce published his most eloquent pages to explain that prophets are necessary for the redemption of a morally and politically enslaved people. In 1928, he stressed that faith in liberty could be resurgent through the work of new prophets who would challenge the grim religions of irrationality, might, and race. "Moral enthusiasm," he wrote, "comes and goes." At times it is energetic and at other times it relaxes in leisure and in forgetfulness. Therefore, in a laic society as in the society of the Church, it is necessary that from time-to-time apostles, martyrs and saints intervene. Of course, these cannot be artificially created, and one needs to count on Providence, which, just like it has always sent them

---

[273] Carlo Rosselli, *Socialismo liberale*, edited by John Rosselli, Turin: Einaudi, 1997, p. 111; English translation from Carlo Rosselli, *Liberal Socialism*, edited by Nadia Urbinati, Princeton: Princeton University Press, 1994, p. 103.
[274] Carlo Rosselli, *Liberal Socialism*, p. xv.   [275] Ibid., p. 103.

on earth, will continue to do so."[276] In his *Storia d' Europa nel secolo XIX*, written a few years later in 1932, Croce claimed that the moral strength which inspired and guided liberal, democratic, and national movements, was a "religion of liberty." This religion unified and harmonized the long history of liberty, and demonstrated its force with the examples of its "poets, theorists, orators, journalists, propagandists, apostles, and martyrs." It has shaped people's souls and has driven them to action and sacrifice: "The heroic figure, who spoke to the hearts, was that of the poet-soldier, the intellectual who can fight and die for his idea; a figure who did not just remain in the raptures of imagination and educational paradigms but rather appeared in the flesh on the battlefields and on the barricades throughout Europe. The missionaries had crusaders of liberty as their fellows."

According to Croce, not even the totalitarian state can eradicate the religion of liberty from human conscience: "So that when the question is raised whether liberty will enjoy what is known as the future, the answer must be that it has something better still: it has eternity. And today, too, notwithstanding the coldness and the contempt and scorn that liberty meets, it is in so many of our institutions and customs and our spiritual attitudes, and operates beneficently within them." Faith in the power of the religion of liberty inspired Croce to issue his extraordinary prophecy of a finally unified Europe:

Meanwhile, in all parts of Europe we are watching the growth of a new consciousness, of a new nationality (because, as we have already remarked, nations are not natural data, but historical states of consciousness and historical formations). And just as, seventy years ago, a Neapolitan of the old kingdom or a Piedmontese of the subalpine kingdom became an Italian without becoming false to his earlier quality but elevating it and resolving it into this new quality, so the French and the Germans and the Italians and all the others will raise themselves into Europeans and their thoughts will be directed towards Europe and their hearts will beat for her as they once did for their smaller countries, not forgotten but loved all the better.[277]

---

[276] "L'entusiasmo morale ora si avviva ora si smorza, ora balza energico ora si distende nell'abitudine e nel comodo e nel lasciare andare; e che perciò occorre, nella società laica come già in quella della Chiesa, che di volta in volta apostoli e martiri e santi intervengano, i quali non si può di certo fabbricarli artificialmente, ma bisogna confidare nella Provvidenza, che, come li ha sempre mandati sulla terra, cosí li manderà ancora. Parecchi pensano perciò che il problema fondamentale dei nostri tempi sia religioso; e così penso anch'io, con questa determinazione, per altro, che religioso è il problema di ogni tempo, e che non si tratta punto d'inventare pel nostro una nuova religione, ma di sempre rinsaldare ed approfondire la religione esistente, quella che una volta si chiamava la religione insita o naturale, e ora si potrebbe chiamare storica"; Benedetto Croce, *Etica e politica*, Bari: Laterza, 1943, p. 309. I am using Alberto Nones' translation from my *As if God Existed. Religion and Liberty in the History of Italy*, p. 219.

[277] "Per intanto, già in ogni parte d'Europa, si assiste al germinare di una nuova coscienza, di una nuova nazionalità (perché, come si è già avvertito, le nazioni non sono dati naturali, ma stati di coscienza e formazioni storiche); e a quel modo che, or sono settant'anni, un napoletano dell'antico Regno o un piemontese del regno subalpino si fecero italiani non rinnegando l'esser loro anteriore ma innalzandolo e risolvendolo in quel nuovo essere, così francesi e tedeschi e

Croce's prophetic words touched the minds of Italian anti-fascists, among them Piero Calamandrei. An outstanding Florentine legal theorist, writer, and anti-fascist militant, Calamandrei recognized in his diaries of 1940–1945 that a struggle of emancipation against fascism needs prophets who can convert Italian hearts to faith in liberty stronger than fascists' faith in the Duce. On May 7, 1940, he writes: "In order to resist the overwhelming deviationism of that call to the basest bestial appetites, as those of conquest and violence, one would need a heroic Christianity, with martyrdoms and tortures. One must implant a human ideal that can be communicated to the masses, for no *rational* reasons exist to usefully fight among the people Nazism's elementary and barbaric creed."[278] A few days later, he reflects again on the necessity of a faith that could oppose Nazism:

Personally, I am neither a believer nor a practicing Christian; but I have morals that are the remains of Christian religion. How can I defend a civilization which is based on these remains, if not by doing my best to prevent the source of these remains from drying up among that people? What other faith can we oppose to the savage faith of the Germans bewitched by Hitler (a faith capable of leading men to death and of resisting against those savages), if not the Christian faith based on the certainty of the afterlife? If one does not want to abdicate in front of the invaders by renouncing to fight, if one does not want to foment in all the peoples the savage fury of nationalism in order to respond to the other nationalisms, one cannot but cultivate in the people a belief in the afterlife that makes us defend here goodness, charity, and liberty, and that gives the strength to die for these ideals.[279]

When the fall of France was imminent, Calamandrei felt the urge to pray: "If I could pray, today I would pray on my knees for France."[280] The moral and political alternatives were clear: either the Christian faith or the domination of force.

The imbeciles and the wicked are always right. When one says that justice in the end prevails, one says a perfectly nonsensical sentence: the fact is that we reasoning men in the end find the way to demonstrate that justice is on the side of those who have triumphed. If there is no God, in the world nothing counts but force. Without God, morals are an illusion, a deception. Whoever believes in justice without believing in the afterlife is a vile hypocrite who refuses to look at reality to the bottom.[281]

italiani e tutti gli altri s'innalzeranno a europei e i loro pensieri indirizzeranno all'Europa e i loro cuori batteranno per lei come prima per le patrie più piccole, non dimenticate già, ma meglio amate"; *Storia d'Europa nel secolo XIX*, p. 358; English translation, Benedetto Croce, *History of Europe in the Nineteenth Century*, New York: Harcourt, Brace and Company, 1933, p. 360.

[278] Piero Calamandrei, *Diario 1940–1945*, vol. I, edited by Giorgio Agosti, Florence: La Nuova Italia, 1982, pp. 158–159. On Calamandrei, see Norberto Bobbio, "Ricordo di Piero Calamandrei," *Belfagor* 13 (1958): pp. 589–602.

[279] Piero Calamandrei, *Diario 1940–1945*, vol. I, pp. 162–163.   [280] Ibid., p. 167.

[281] Ibid., p. 185.

When injustice triumphs in the world without any shame or restraint, the moral strength to resist can only come from Christian prophetic visions. On January 25, 1945, he remarked that "religion is a faith in justice more than a faith in joy and personal eternity. Christian religion makes the centuries end in a great judgment: in order to tolerate the sufferance of life, one cannot but hope that all infamous acts come to an end and to a sentence."[282] Continuing to entertain hope even in the darkest days, Calamandrei returns to the moral lessons of the Risorgimento.

I also read Settembrini's *Ricordanze*: Settembrini is a naïve man and not of great stature, but what a character! Today there are no longer men of that temperament: coherent and courageous, capable of facing a death or life sentence just not to say a less than dignified word, just to reject even the smallest compromise with their conscience. Among us, even among the best ones, at least among those of the circle I know, such men no longer exist, even the honest men are more skillful, but less fierce. How could one of us [...] face with serenity what Settembrini endured twice? Perhaps the difference is the following: that he firmly believed in God, in the afterlife, and we do not. Ours are noble spirits, but limp and disheartened: we feel our country's tragedy, but this gives us more sadness and discouragement than active indignation.[283]

Even if they felt the power of prophecy, neither Calamandrei nor other anti-fascist leaders attempted to mold and deliver a prophetic language of emancipation. The Italian Resistenza was a struggle for emancipation without prophets. Although prophets were lacking, profound religious inspiration abounded, and it is in this spirit that Calamandrei masterfully identifies the meaning of the Resistenza. While some people talked of a "collective soul" and others of "Providence," he wrote, everyone should have been talking of God: "of this unknown God who is inside each of us." The Resistenza had a "religious character" because religion means "seriousness of life, commitment for moral values, coherence between thought and action."[284] For Calamandrei and others, how and why a people – or at least the best of them – could resurrect from the moral death of servile life was a "miraculous and mysterious" event. It was indeed miraculous and mysterious, but it was, I say hesitantly, the reverberation of the prophetic light of

---

[282] Ibid., vol. II, pp. 292–293.   [283] Ibid., vol. II, pp. 315–316.

[284] "Qualcuno ha parlato di 'anima collettiva', qualcuno ha parlato di 'provvidenza': forse bisognerebbe parlare di Dio: di questo Dio ignoto che è dentro ciascuno di noi, che parla contemporaneamente in tutte le lingue: 'L'Arabo, il Parto, il Siro / il suo sermon l'udì'. Quando io considero questo misterioso e miracoloso moto di popolo, questo volontario accorrere di gente umile, fino a quel giorno inerme e pacifica, che in una improvvisa illuminazione sentì che era giunto il momento di darsi alla macchia, di prendere il fucile, di ritrovarsi in montagna per combattere contro il terrore, mi vien fatto di pensare a certi inesplicabili ritmi della vita cosmica, ai segreti comandi celesti che regolano i fenomeni collettivi, come le gemme degli alberi che spuntano lo stesso giorno, come certe piante subacquee che in tutti i laghi di una regione alpina affiorano nello stesso giorno alla superficie per guardare il cielo primaverile, come le rondini di un continente che lo stesso giorno s'accorgono che è giunta l'ora per mettersi in viaggio"; Piero Calamandrei, *Passato e avvenire della Resistenza*, Milan: Grafica Milano, 1954, reprinted in Piero Calamandrei, *Uomini e città della Resistenza*, Rome and Bari: Laterza, 2011, pp. 14–15.

the Risorgimento. The anti-fascist militants and the historians who called the Resistance a second Risorgimento were correct.[285]

On June 2, 1946, Italian citizens voted to institute the first Italian Republic that encompassed the entire territory of the nation. Furnishing Italy with a new constitution that replaced the monarchy, the Constituent Assembly (June 25, 1946–January 31, 1948) had the opportunity to provide a prophetic foundation of the new Republic. Giorgio La Pira (1904–1977) was the proponent of such a prophetic vision for the new Italy. He was a man of sincere Christian faith who committed himself to the grand task of reviving Savonarola's prophetic mission. In 1940, while living in the convent of San Marco in Florence (where Savonarola also lived), La Pira delved into the tradition of Christian republicanism and reclaimed the idea of God as the origin of the moral law that imposes on us the duty to love and defend liberty. In the supplement to the first issue of the clandestine journal *Vita Cristiana* (*Christian Life*), La Pira writes that the desire for liberty is the most vital among humankind's desires. The more it is violated, the more it is invigorated. La Pira saw liberty as an impregnable fortress within which man's personality is steadily clasped.[286] Civilization took a giant step on the day when it posed the principle of the rule of law as the basis of juridical and political constructions. La Pira highlighted it as a truly "Copernican discovery [...] essential for the maintenance of justice and order." He further noted that "this very sacred principle has been violated by those who replaced the law with arbitrary power" and who introduced the "mysticism of the state," the gravest heresy of the times. Instead of worshiping the true God, certain individuals adore one thing: the state, the race, the proletariat, the nation, etc. But to be adored, this "thing" must be personified, whence the attribution of rational and strong-willed faculties that are typical of the human person and, in essence, of God.[287] Under the veil of the state's mysticism, atheist Communism and pagan Nazism have banned God, persecuted the Church, oppressed liberty, and destroyed the human person. On the contrary, Christian faith imposes the responsibility to fight against any form of totalitarianism as religious duty. La Pira's Christian vision of liberty inspired him to take the bold step of proposing that the Constituent Assembly approve a preamble to the Constitution containing the Universal Declaration of Human Rights and an invocation to God. Drawing on the concept of "not the state for the individual but the individual for the state," La Pira asserted that the "totalitarian state was essentially a radical denial of the human person's value as it had been elaborated throughout the whole history of Christian civilization based on the Gospel and the highest human reflections." To provide the Republic with a

---

[285] See for instance Vittorio Foa, *Lettere della giovinezza*, edited by Federica Montevecchi, Turin: Einaudi, 1998, p. 243.

[286] Giorgio La Pira, *Principî*, January–February 1940, supplement to the first issue of *Vita Cristiana*, p. 1.

[287] Ibid., pp. 3–4.

solid foundation, the Constitution should affirm the principle that "man's nature is spiritual" and thus transcend all temporal values. According to La Pira, such a philosophical foundation was necessary: "This spiritual and religious root of man is the only ground on which it is possible to firmly construct the building of natural rights – sacred and imprescriptible."[288]

In total opposition to fascism's dogmas, he proposed the following preamble:

Having experienced through the painful tyranny of the totalitarian fascist state how the disregard and defiance of man's and the fundamental human communities' natural rights truly are the biggest causes of public tragedies, the Italian people decide to list these sacred and indefeasible rights in a solemn declaration as the preliminary act of their new democratic and republican life. Aware of the great problems of renewal that present times raise, we aim, with this declaration and the Constitution that accompanies it, to create a social and political order that conforms to the high dignity of the human person and human brotherly solidarity, and that thereby guarantees everybody his place and function in the well-ordered national community. We thus regain our place within Christian civilization – ferment and essence of our history and culture – and within the community of peoples who love liberty, labor, justice, and peace. We consequently proclaim, in the sight of God and the human community, the following declaration of the rights of man.[289]

La Pira further clarified the Constitution's religious significance in a speech given at the sitting of September 9, 1946: "I believe that it is essential – in building our new state – to proclaim in the Constitution's opening declaration the spiritual nature of the person, through which his imprescriptible natural rights are legitimated."[290] La Pira wanted the Republic to affirm the rights of the individual person before God because only a state founded on this principle could be an alternative to the fascist state that had transformed the Duce into a divinity. His proposal evokes the example of Savonarola, who persuaded the Florentine political elite in 1494 to declare God to be the "king of Florence." La Pira most likely believed that, if Italians did in fact place the Republic under God's tutelage, then they would not repeat the tragic mistake of permitting a man to become the new god of Italy.

Whereas Savonarola succeeded in persuading the Great Council to accept his proposal to declare Christ the "king of Florence," La Pira failed to persuade the Constituent Assembly to accept his invocation to God. The most powerful critique of La Pira's proposal came from Concetto Marchesi (1878–1957). A Marxist and eminent Latinist, Marchesi noted that there was a dominant religion in Italy, Catholicism. For him, proclaiming the religious nature of the democratic state would have implied the affirmation of an absurd and disrespectful principle. Marchesi also feared that providing the republican state with a religious foundation would have raised the radical opposition of the Vatican

---

[288] *Assemblea Costituente Commissione per la Costituzione Prima Sottocommissione, Relazione del Deputato La Pira Giorgio, sui principi relativi ai rapporti civili*, p. 15.
[289] Ibid., p. 19.   [290] Ibid., 14.

and the great majority of the Catholic population. He claimed that the Church would not tolerate another religion in Italy, cautioned "not [to] take the name of the Lord in vain" and concluded that God must remain out of the constitution. While Palmiro Togliatti, the general secretary of the Communist Party, intervened and shifted the discussion from philosophical and theological questions to political ones, the socialist Giovanni Lombardi underscored that, along with the Christian faith, a secular faith also existed. Lombardi asserted that the Constitution should recognize only the latter to the detriment of the former.[291]

The Constituent Assembly resumed the discussion of La Pira's preamble on December 22, 1947. When the Assembly was ready to move to the final vote on the entire text of the constitution, La Pira took the floor to claim, as he had done at the beginning of the Constituent Assembly's proceedings, that the constitution should have a preamble with the invocation to God: "As my colleagues already know, last night I presented to the presidency the proposal that the constitutional text be preceded by a short phrase of a spiritual nature, which said: 'In the name of God, we, the Italian people, adopt the present Constitution.'" La Pira explained that the proposed phrase was not a specific profession of faith, and therefore everyone should have been able agree on it: the Mazzinians, with their principle of "God and People"; the Liberals, because the neoliberalism of the time also accepted this point; and the Marxists, who had the considerable tendency to separate dialectical materialism from historical materialism. Through his proposal, La Pira intended to solidify the belief that a common point of contact existed for all creatures, that there always is a superior reality. He concluded: "Therefore, if, above any political points, we all could unanimously cleave to this phrase, it would really be a triumph of faith."[292] As he realized that his proposal would have divided the Assembly and public opinion, La Pira withdrew it. Under the circumstances, La Pira's choice was commendable. Nonetheless, had the Constituent Assembly accepted La Pira's preamble, the Republic born after the tragedy of fascism would have been a prophetic republic based on a religion of liberty.

---

[291] Ibid., pp. 16–17.

[292] "Si direbbe 'in nome di Dio il popolo si dà la costituzione' [...] Voglio dire, in sostanza, che c'è un punto di convergenza per ogni creatura, c'è sempre una realtà superiore, e quindi per questa ragione, se noi potessimo, concordemente, al di sopra di ogni questione politica, ancorarci a questa formula, sarebbe veramente uno spettacolo di fede"; Assemblea Costituente CCCXLVI, "Resoconto sommario della seduta antimeridiana di lunedì 22 dicembre 1947," p. 3577.

5

EPILOGUE

Just as Eugenio Montale was writing the verses I have cited below[1] – in which he foresees the end of any kind of prophecy – Pier Paolo Pasolini,[2]

[1] The poem "Laggiù" ("Down Below") is in the collection *Satura* and dated December 16, 1969, four days after the bombing at the Banca Nazionale dell'Agricoltura headquarters in Milan's Piazza Fontana. Through a poem that has the semblance of a prophecy, Montale instead announces the end of prophecy itself: "La terra sarà sorvegliata / da piattaforme astrali / Più probabili o meno si faranno / laggiù i macelli / Spariranno profeti e profezie / se mai ne furono / Scomparsi l'io il tu il noi il voi / dall'uso / Dire nascita morte inizio fine / sarà tutt'uno / Dire ieri domani / un abuso / Sperare – flatus vocis non compreso / da nessuno / Il Creatore avrà poco da fare / se n'ebbe / I santi poi bisognerà cercarli / tra i cani / ... / Gli angeli resteranno inespungibili / refusi" ("Space stations will maintain surveillance / over the earth / Down below massacres will be / more or less likely / Prophets will disappear, prophecies too / if there ever were any / I you we will all become / obsolete words / Birth death beginning end will all / be the same word / Hope – a *flatus vocis* understood / by nobody / The Creator will have little to do / if he ever did / You'll have to look for saints / among the dogs / ... / Angels will remain printer's errors / that can't be corrected"). Eugenio Montale, *Satura 1962–1970*, translated by William Arrowsmith, edited by Rosanna Warren, New York: W.W. Norton & Company, 1998, pp. 187–188.

[2] For this last section dedicated to Pier Paolo Pasolini, I would like to call attention to the intellectual debt owed to Giacomo Jori who, in addition to *Pasolini. La vita e le opere*, Turin: Einaudi, 2001, provided me with time and precious words that I hope to have put to good use in the following pages. I also owe a debt of gratitude to Maria Teresa Venturi for her thorough study *"Io vivo nelle cose e invento, come posso, il modo di nominarle": Pier Paolo Pasolini e la lingua della modernità*, Florence: Firenze University Press, 2020. In the first part of her work, Venturi comments on and explores themes that I only mention. In my initial conception of this project, the volume would have concluded with the Constituent Assembly. My wife Gabriella Argnani pointed out to me that not considering Pier Paolo Pasolini would have been an unforgivable mistake. I thank her for such a precious suggestion and for having guided me through Pasolini's soul, words and work, and the criticism surrounding the last one.

another great poet, was writing "Patmos,"[3] a poem composed in perfect prophetic style.[4]

Pasolini was born in Bologna on March 5, 1922, and was brutally killed on the seaside of Ostia during the night of November 1, 1975. His body so mangled as to be unrecognizable was found by chance, covered in dust and mud, so present in his artistic production from the 1950s onwards.[5] In this circumstance the mud and dust have taken on a positive value: it is as if they had veiled and protected the dignity of the defenseless body of the poet who had sung them. Pasolini's murder has never been fully explained.[6] Two volumes were among the objects discovered during the police investigation of Pasolini's car: Friedrich Nietzsche's *On the Future of Our Educational Institutions*[7] and an issue of the magazine *Il politecnico (The Polytechnic)*.[8] Page corners were folded to mark two articles in the magazine: Giorgio Caproni's "*Viaggio fra gli esiliati di Roma*"

---

[3] Pier Paolo Pasolini, "Trasumanar e organizzar," *Tutte le poesie*, vol. 2, edited by Walter Siti, Milan: Mondadori, pp. 124–132. According to tradition, Patmos is the place where John the Apostle received the visions exposed in the *Book of Revelation*.

[4] On the day of the Piazza Fontana bombing, Pier Paolo Pasolini was at Alberto Moravia's home in Milan with the movie director Michelangelo Antonioni.

[5] See Pier Paolo Pasolini, *Ragazzi di vita*, Milan: Garzanti, 1955, *Una vita violenta*, Milan: Garzanti, 1959 and the movies *Accattone* (1961) and *Mamma Roma* (1962).

[6] Without any ascertained dynamics or any clear motives, Pasolini's tragic end is a story that will remain alive forever. Pasolini himself is a living and vital presence in hidden ways: the force with which he affects our social and cultural life – and, for many of us, our private lives too – is inconsumable. With unsurpassed art, he knew how to transform his life, his death, and even his body into poetry, "a good that is not consumed." Pasolini's murder, the investigations, the trials, and sentencings belong entirely to the impressive group of Italian mysteries. During these last forty-seven years, much ink has been used to tell of the lynching and slaughter perpetrated against his body, and to advance hypotheses regarding the motive, instigators, and murderers. Nothing certain has emerged, except for the indisputable fact that those responsible have never really been sought. I allow myself one observation: no poet, man or woman of letters, or artist that I know of suffered what Pasolini suffered. No one has been subjected to a series of accusations or trials like those to which he was subjected: 310 judicial proceedings, from July 7, 1947, to the day of his death, almost one per month. Although he was acquitted judicially, it was never fully so in most news outlets and in the sphere of public opinion, as emphasized by Laura Betti in *Pasolini: cronaca giudiziaria, persecuzione, morte*, Milan: Garzanti, 1977. On the subject, it is interesting to see the documentary *Whoever Says the Truth Shall Die*, www.youtube.com/watch?v= 5mwKpi2psS4. I wonder if his main fault might have been the simplicity with which he knew how to listen and observe, the candor with which he was able to sing and represent reality. Or I wonder if it might also have been his being radically against the outlaw that he recognized in bourgeois individuals that "do not commit any crime that is not conscious, contrary to true barbarians, to animals"; Pier Paolo Pasolini, "Il sogno del centauro, Incontri con Jean Duflot (1969–1975)," "Elogio della barbarie," "Nostalgia del sacro," *Saggi sulla politica e sulla società*, edited by Walter Siti, Milan: Mondadori, 1999, p. 1488. To understand the cultural climate in which Pasolini lived, I refer to Anna Tonelli, *Per indegnità morale*, Rome and Bari: Laterza, 2015.

[7] The edition that Pasolini had was published by Adelphi in 1975. There are many page corners folded in the book.

[8] *Il politecnico*, no. 36, September 1946.

("Journey among the Outcasts of Rome") on page 140, and Concetto Marchesi's *"Nella scuola la nostra salvezza"* ("Our Salvation is in Education") on page 376. Pasolini was murdered while he was reflecting on education, the path to emancipation that he so loved and had practiced with great passion and dedication throughout his life, especially as a young professor in the countryside of Friuli[9] (a place whose language he treasured and where he felt like a native son) and during his first years in Rome.[10] At Pasolini's funeral in Rome, Alberto Moravia remarked, "First of all, we have lost a poet, and in the world there are not many such poets. Only three or four are born in a century."[11] When his remains returned to Casarsa della Delizia, in Friuli, to be buried, in the Church of Santa Croce, David Maria Turoldo said of his friend and his brother Pasolini, who met his ruin because of his great humanness, that he was a great poet of the people, a voice of the people.[12] Indeed, he was a poet and, as a poet, he also dedicated himself to his boundless works of painting, prose, cinema, essay writing, theater, and linguistics. To underscore just how much Pasolini's work drew on Dante,

[9] From a very young age, Pasolini took the problem of education to heart. After September 8, 1943, he and some friends founded a school in San Giovanni di Casarsa, near Versuta, where he took refuge with his mother, Susanna Maria Colussi. A primary school teacher, she looked after the younger children, and Pasolini and his friends taught the older ones. In one of the diaries he entrusted to his cousin Nico Naldini (thanks to whom we can now read them), Pasolini noted: "Non credo di essermi mai dato agli altri con tanta dedizione come a quei fanciulli durante la lezione di italiano e di storia" ("I don't think I've ever given myself to others with such dedication as I did to those children during their Italian and history lessons"). In the autumn of 1944, Pasolini and some friends also founded the Academiuta di lenga furlana, whose official magazine, *Stroligùt*, published five issues. See Pier Paolo Pasolini, *Poesie e pagine ritrovate*, edited by Andrea Zanzotto and Nico Naldini, Rome: Lato Side Editori, 1980.

[10] An air of education lurks in many of Pasolini's writings, but I maintain that the pages of *Lettere Luterane* are the most sublime from this point of view. On Pasolini and education see also Roberto Carnero and Angela Felice, *Pasolini e la pedagogia*, Venice: Marsilio, 2016. The close bond between Pasolini and Friuli emerges in chiaroscuro throughout his life and often passes through the "lenga furlana" (Friulian language) of the peasants *"di ca da l'aga"* (on this side [the right bank] of the Tagliamento river), the landscapes, the flowers. Heartbreaking are the words he dedicates to those places when writing to the poetess and teacher of Spilimbergo Novella Aurora Cantarutti, on November 17, 1954: "Sono passato per il Friuli: e l'ho visto tutto ròso e inzuppato dall'autunno, pieno del vecchio ineffabile amore. Davanti al Friuli dovrei ricominciare tutto dacapo e, a pensarci, qualcosa mi prende alla gola: un senso insieme di morte e di vita. Se vivrò dovrò pure tornare" (I passed through Friuli: and I saw it all threadbare and soaked in the wetness of autumn, full of the old ineffable love. In front of Friuli, I would have to start all over again and, thinking about it, something takes hold of my throat: a sense of both death and life); Pier Paolo Pasolini, *Le lettere*, edited by Alessandra Giordano and Nico Naldini, Milan: Garzanti, 2021, p. 874.

[11] See https://video.repubblica.it/spettacoli-e-cultura/pasolini-maestro-corsaro/216709/215893.

[12] "Perché noi siamo un popolo che canta anche quando ha da piangere. È quella la nostra natura migliore, come quella di tuo figlio, grande poeta del popolo, voce del popolo" ("Because we are a people who sing even when there is something that we should cry for. That is our best nature, like that of your son, the great poet of the people, the voice of the people"); David Maria Turoldo, "Chiediamo scusa d'esistere," *Pasolini in Friuli 1943-1949*, edited by *Corriere del Friuli* and the Comune di Casarsa della Delizia, Udine: Arti Grafiche Friulane, 1976, pp. 67-70.

one should read "*La volontà di Dante a esser poeta*" ("The Will of Dante To Be a Poet") and "La divina Mimesi" ("Divine Mimesis"). Released posthumously in November 1975,[13] the latter consists of a rewriting of the first two cantos of the *Divine Comedy*. Rewriting the *Divine Comedy* was "an idea that accompanied him, or perhaps it would be better to say that it hounded him, starting in the final years of the 1950s."[14] It has been correctly noted that the memory of Dante "is continuous, pervasive, in Pasolini's prose and poetry."[15] Like Dante, Pasolini was a civic poet.[16] The idea of words as weapons, and the conviction that poetry is "a good that is not consumed" but the eternal word that transcends humanity and the things of this world, "ascesis in which, rather than praying,"[17] the forms of world beyond are sung, both emerge time and time again in the prophetic language that I have examined in the preceding chapters. They are concepts that Pasolini receives from Dante.[18] "Dante does not have any clues or signposts, but instead possesses a secret key: a prodigious instrument that penetrates the dark areas of existence and sparks light amidst the most unfathomable mysteries. Dante has poetry."[19] Pasolini also possesses the same prodigious instrument. The close link between these two authors – the authors who begin and conclude my journey into prophetic language as an instrument of emancipation – leads me to dedicate but a few, final pages to Pasolini.

---

[13] Pier Paolo Pasolini, *La divina Mimesis*, Turin: Einaudi, 1975.

[14] Riccardo Bruscagli, "Dante e Pasolini," lecture given on March 24, 2010 at Teatro La Pergola, Florence. www.leggeredante.it/2010/Pasolini/Introduzione.pdf.

[15] Ibid.

[16] The eighth work of section "VI. A Desperate Vitality" of *Poesia in forma di rosa* (*Poem in the Shape of a Rose*) begins with Pasolini's indication of the theme treated in the following: "(Funereal conclusion, with synoptic table – for use by the lady creating the 'piece' – of my career as a poet and a prophetic look at the sea of future millennia)." It goes on: "[...] Then came the Resistance / and I / fought with the weapons of poetry, / I reinstated Logic and became / a civic poet. / [...] I can write only in prophecies / rapt by Music / in an excess of seed or pity. / [...] That is how / I can write Themes and Threnodies / and Prophecies too; / as a civic poet, oh yes, always!"; English translation from *The Selected Poetry of Pier Paolo Pasolini*, edited and translated by Stephen Sartarelli, Chicago: University of Chicago Press, 2014, pp. 354–357. For Pasolini, being a civil poet means being aware of the strength that poetry has in the formation of consciences, and thus taking responsibility for this. Poetry, therefore, can no longer consist only in stylistic freedom that expresses irrational and immediate intuition, or the revelations of the unknown (as had happened with decadent poets). Stylistic freedom must be tempered by the responsibility of the poet-citizen, of the militant intellectual. Once again in Pasolini's idea of poetry, two opposing ideas, freedom and responsibility, are called to coexist and mutually enrich each other.

[17] Pier Paolo Pasolini, *Le lettere*, edited by Antonella Giordano and Nico Naldini, Milan: Garzanti, 2021, p. 1393. Giacomo Jori suggested this beautiful text to me.

[18] See Emanuela Patti, *Pasolini after Dante: The Divine Mimesis and the Politics of Representation*, London: Routledge, 2016.

[19] The citation is taken from the first page of Michela Mastrodonato's wonderful and impassioned article "Dall'Archiano di Bonconte al Tevere di 'Ragazzi di vita': dialogo fluviale fra Dante e Pasolini sulla vita, la morte e la rondinella," *Una goccia nel mare*, Atti del XXII Congresso Aipi, Florence: Franco Cesati Editore, 2016, pp. 182–192.

I take my first steps into the world of Pasolini with great and deep trepidation, precisely in the year in which we commemorate the hundredth anniversary of his birth. His writings reveal a man who felt himself to be a prophet: a man who, like many of the authors I have discussed, was able to read the meaning of events.[20] He wrote quite sincerely that he had experienced mysticism, albeit unknowingly, and had started to believe "in miracles and prophecy" (*"al miracolo e alla profezia"*) in 1944 when he was only twenty-two.[21] Pasolini was delicate and gaunt, direct but with an allusive and imaginative language. He was an artist who knew he lived in a "void of history" and "from the extreme edge" saw "Post history":

I am a force of the Past. / My love lies only in tradition. / I come from the ruins, the churches, / the altarpieces, the villages / abandoned in the Apennines or foothills / of the Alps where my brothers once lived. / I wander like a madman down the Tuscolana, / down the Appia like a dog without a master. / Or I see the twilight, the mornings / over Rome, the Ciociaria, the world, / as the first acts of Post history / to which I bear witness, for the privilege / of recording them from the outer edge / of some buried age. / Monstrous is the man / born of a dead woman's womb. / And I, a fetus now grown, roam about / more modern than any modern man, / in search of brothers no longer alive.[22]

He was a troublesome and complex man who did not fear contradictions, just as the best exemplars in the tradition of medieval mysticism.

Pasolini's path is a spiritual journey tangent to space and time,[23] in the dimension of truth.[24] The essence of the poet and his strength are collected in

---

[20] A great deal of Pasolini's work is studded with recurring words of prophetic language. Here are some examples where Pasolini explicitly refers to prophecy: "Like a prophet of the 1600s / an alternative of lust / and of holiness, of servility, and of radical rejection! [...]" ("Poema per un verso di Shakespeare," IV, Una disperata vitalità, *Poesia in forma di rosa*, taken from *Tutte le poesie*, vol. 1, edited by Walter Siti, Milan: Mondadori, p. 1167); "Let all that I have known, by grace / or by will / stop being wisdom. / It is of no use for an old boy / to fly into the skies of the Sahara or of Arabia. I will know. History is prophecy / I say crazily. [...] / [Wisdom,] you will go away in a verse, / thwarted by prophecy" (Poema per un verso di Shakespeare," IV, Una disperata vitalità, *Poesia in forma di rosa*, taken from *Tutte le poesie*, vol. 1, edited by Walter Siti, Milan: Mondadori, p. 1170); "But now let us conjure up some prophecies" ("L'enigma di Pio XII," Poesie su commissione, *Trasumanar e organizzar*, taken from *Tutte le poesie*, vol. 2, edited by Walter Siti, Milan: Mondadori, p. 25).

[21] Pier Paolo Pasolini, *Poesie e pagine ritrovate*, p. 46.

[22] "Poesie mondane," June 10, 1962, *Poesie in forma di rosa*. English translation from *The Selected Poetry of Pier Paolo Pasolini*, pp. 310–313.

[23] "Eyes do not distinguish / a day from the centuries [...] Do so that you do not forget / my most pure desires / with the dawn that brightens / and then quickly darkens." Pier Paolo Pasolini, "Oscuri e invincibili, Poesie disperse e inedite," appendix to *L'Usignolo della Chiesa Cattolica* in *Tutte le poesie*, vol. 1, edited by Walter Siti, Milan: Mondadori, p. 522. On the complex idea of time that emerges from Pasolini's works, see the excellent volume of Luciano De Fiore, *Risposte pratiche risposte sante: Pasolini, il tempo e la politica*, Rome: Castelvecchi, 2018.

[24] "And I know myself to be incorrigible in pursuing my mania for truth / (I do not know if it is a matter of truth, or of love for truth: but that it is a mania / is certain: perhaps self-harm, perhaps attachment to my fate, / as one chosen and destined to select between vulgarity and idealism),"

the oxymoron[25] "desperate vitality," the title of a section in his *Poesia in forma di rosa* (*Poem in the Shape of a Rose*). Poetry must withstand confrontations with both history and the absolute; it must keep realism and irrationality together.

In a 2015 interview given on the occasion of the fortieth anniversary of the poet's death, Dacia Maraini states that Pasolini "clashed with his time and with society, but he was not a man of private conflicts."[26] In "Frammento," he recounts the only time that he exercised "any physical or moral violence" (a disruptive statement in its candor, if we consider the accusations that have marked his life), against "a group of fascists" who had attacked him while he was going to the premiere of *Mamma Roma*.[27] He recounted that matter, saying that, rather than "being ashamed," he felt "a real satisfaction" for having "struck first" and, as was his "sacred right," for having filled the revealed "face" of the "enemy" "with slaps."[28] He also maintains that he did not use violence to respond to the violence he suffered, rather he did so because he was "exasperated" by the violence inflicted against those "comrades" who were with him.

After a *j'accuse* brought against the Italian bourgeoisie stricken by destructive symptoms, "Frammento" ends with the idea of "necessary and fittingly evangelical violence" when the "marketplace" takes over the "Temple." Pasolini spoke of "truth felt with great precision."[29] He observed reality in an

Pier Paolo Pasolini, "Trasumanar e organizzar," *Trasumanar e organizzar*, in *Tutte le poesie*, vol. 2, edited by Walter Siti, Milan: Mondadori.

[25] Franco Fortini explains that Pasolini often uses the rhetorical figure of synoeciosis, "quella sottospecie dell'oxymoron, [...] con la quale si affermano, d'uno stesso soggetto, due contrari" ("that subspecies of oxymoron. [...] by which two opposites of the same subject are affirmed"); Franco Fortini, *Attraverso Pasolini*, Turin: Einaudi, 1993, p. 22. Synoeciosis creates a correlation between two opposites in such a way that, rather than eliminating themselves or finding a synthesis between the two, they intensify one another and give meaning and strength to each other.

[26] See https://video.repubblica.it/spettacoli-e-cultura/pasolini-maestro-corsaro/216709/215893.

[27] Pier Paolo Pasolini, "Frammento," *Scritti corsari*, with a preface by Alfonso Belardinelli, Milan: Garzanti, 1975, p. 239. Pasolini confirms his nonviolence in the letter, and confession, he writes to Don Giovanni Rossi on December 26, 1964. He does not mention violence among those sins that he attributes to himself. The letter is included in Pier Paolo Pasolini, *Le lettere*, edited by Antonella Giordano and Nico Naldini, Milan: Garzanti, 2021, pp. 1297–1298.

[28] Pier Paolo Pasolini, "Dialoghi con Pasolini," *Vie Nuove*, no. 40, vol. XVII, 1962.

[29] "I know. / I know the names of those responsible for the 'coup' (and which in reality is a series of 'coups' set in place under a system to protect power) / [...] I know all these names and I know all the facts (attacks on institutions and massacres) of which they are guilty. / *I know. But I have no evidence. I don't even have clues.* / I know because I am an intellectual, a writer, who seeks to follow everything that happens, to know everything that is written about it, *to imagine all that which is not known* or that remains silent; who organizes even distant facts, who *puts together disorganized and fragmented pieces of an entire, coherent political framework which restores logic in those places where arbitrariness, madness, and mystery seem to rule.* All this is part of my job and of its *instinct*..." (italics are mine). Pier Paolo Pasolini, "Che cos'è questo golpe?,"

unscrupulous fashion; he threw himself into it as if to be crushed by it; he wanted to touch it, to know it intimately, to become one with it. But his gaze upon the world was not of the miraculous kind: "not natural, not secular," "shapeless and non-confessional," but religious.[30] It was an "irresistible need to admire nature and people, to recognize profundity where others catch sight only of the lifeless, mechanical appearance of things."[31] He believed that miracles existed as a "subjective reality" and that they were the "innocent and naïve explanation of the true mystery that resides in people, of the power hidden within humanity."[32] Through his study of the mystics, Pasolini discovered that "only those people who believe in myths are realists, and vice versa," because "that which is mythical is nothing but another expression of realism."[33] He said of himself that he had no hope and that he had never lost any illusions. He called himself an "unarmed ideological freedom fighter" – whereas ideology was represented by the illusions that he claimed to have never lost, those illusions that substantiate the "neither conventional nor confessional poetic religion" that had come down to him from his mother Susanna.[34] While the "Gospel of Christ" for Pasolini "replenishes, integrates, regenerates," it "does not console." He asked rhetorically, "What is one to do with consolation?" He believed in the original purity of human beings – a purity that, until the end of the 1960s, he saw in what remained of the peasant world, in the underclass, and in very high culture.

Pasolini viewed average culture – bourgeois mass culture that prevents people from knowing that they do not know, a culture that in reality closes the door on "the atrocity of doubt" ("atrocità del dubbio") and its "unpleasant sensitivity" ("sottigliezza sgradevole") – as corruption and the objective of a humanity that had transformed into a "machine" and become headless in the process. Perhaps, in the case of Pasolini, it is more correct to say heartless, that heart which Ochwìa Biano, the chief of the Taos Pueblo, indicates to Carl Gustav Jung as the place of thought.[35]

Corriere della sera, September 14, 1974. Then with the title "14 novembre 1974. Il romanzo delle stragi," in Pier Paolo Pasolini, *Scritti corsari*, pp. 88–93.

[30] "III B facciamo l'appello," a program directed by Enzo Biagi, RAI Teche, 1971.

[31] Pier Paolo Pasolini, "Il sogno del centauro. Incontri con Jean Duflot (1969–1975) – Il malinteso," *Saggi sulla politica e sulla società*, p. 1422.

[32] Ibid., p. 1423.   [33] Ibid., pp. 1461–1462.

[34] Ibid., p. 1421. See also Pier Paolo Pasolini, "Pasolini su Pasolini, Conversazione con Jon Halliday [1968–1971]. Il background pasoliniano," *Saggi sulla politica e sulla società*, p. 1288.

[35] Carl Gustav Jung, *Ricordi, sogni e riflessioni*, edited by A. Jaffè, Milan: Rizzoli, 1978, p. 297. Pasolini himself confirms this idea: "Then comes the film, and to understand the film [according to Pasolini, cinema is a universal language that 'represents reality through reality' and this allows him to 'always live at the level of reality'] one must have more heart than head [...]" (Pier Paolo Pasolini, *Il caos*, Tempo, n.40, October 4, 1969).

In the interview *"Siamo tutti in pericolo"* ("We are all in danger") that he granted to Furio Colombo on November 1, 1975, between four and six in the afternoon, just a few hours before his murder, Pasolini affirmed that he believed in "magical thinking" because he believed "that hitting the same nail over and over again can make a house collapse."[36] Like the prophets, he knew that "the few who made history are those who said no, not the courtiers and assistants of cardinals." He knew that "the refusal to function must be great, not small, total, not on this or that point, 'absurd,' not common sense."[37] He also knew that he should fight with the tools that society makes available, the very one he wanted to defeat.

A man and an artist traversed by contradiction, Pasolini challenged power openly, without any fear, with the illusion of being able to win. What to most people seems naïve was Pasolini's strength, the strength of those who believe – that strength masterfully conveyed in the story of the so-called multiplication of loaves and fish in the Gospel of John. In the Gospel passage, there is no word that refers to the idea of multiplication, but rather an emphasis on how the twelve baskets were filled "with the leftover pieces of five barley loaves":

One of the disciples, Andrew, the brother of Simon Peter, then told him, "There is a boy here who has five barley loaves and two fish; but what is this for so many people?" Jesus responded, "Make them sit down." There was much grass in that place. Thus, they sat down and there were about five thousand people. Then Jesus took the loaves and, after giving thanks, distributed them to those who were seated, and he did the same with the fish, for as long as the people wanted some. And when they were satisfied, he said to the disciples, "Gather the leftover pieces so that nothing will be wasted." They gathered them and filled twelve baskets with the pieces of the five barley loaves left over from all those who had eaten.[38]

The disciples did not understand the power of that boy's gesture who deprived himself of food for the sake of others. Nor did the disciples understand the reach of belief. On the contrary, Jesus of Nazareth did not have doubts. Believing it could feed five thousand people, the boy gave everything he had, and then it did in fact feed the masses. Five loaves and two fish were not only enough for everyone, but a large quantity of food was left over. The strength of

---

[36] "Siamo tutti in pericolo" ("We are all in danger"), an interview granted by Pier Paolo Pasolini to Furio Colombo on November 1, 1975. With Colombo's permission, it was reprinted in *l'Unità* on May 9, 2005. It is also included in *Saggi sulla politica e sulla società*, pp. 1723–1730.

[37] See also Pier Paolo Pasolini, "Lettere Luterane," *Saggi sulla politica e sulla società*, p. 561. "Remember that I, your teacher, do not believe in this history and this progress. It is not true, however, that we move onward. Very often both individuals and society regress or worsen. In such cases, transformation must not be accepted. [...] Regression and deterioration are not to be accepted: perhaps with indignation or anger, that, contrary to their appearance, are profoundly rational acts in this specific case. It is necessary to have the strength of total criticism, of rejection, of desperate and useless condemnation."

[38] *John* 6:8–13.

a believer bursts into the world and can transform it. Pasolini believed this to be true, and so too did all those who ever used prophetic language.

Pasolini had "nostalgia for the poor and true people who fought to overthrow [their] master without becoming that master." He longed for "the pure and direct revolution of oppressed people with the sole purpose of setting themselves free and being placed in command of their own selves." He imagined that "one such moment [could] still come in Italian history and in the history of the world." He imagined that the best of what he conceived for the world's future could be inspired by one of his poems. But he knew and saw that this world was not the world of his present. For Pasolini, the present was "hell."[39] The "tragedy" was evidenced by the fact that he no longer saw "human beings" but "strange machines that bump into one another." Pasolini was alone against the world, and he tells us about the solitude he experienced even at a very young age.[40] In the poem "*Supplica a mia madre*" ("Plea to My Mother"), he mentioned soulless bodies from which he desired love, a love that he desired in vain: "And I don't want to be alone. I have an infinite / thirst for love, for bodies pure and soulless." So too does he allude to the heart-wrenching loneliness to which he was condemned: "This is why the life you blessed / me with will always be condemned to loneliness."[41] In the collection of poetry *L'Usignolo della Chiesa Cattolica*, he also writes poignant verses out of the pain felt due to this condemnation to loneliness: "[...] You, alone / granted solitude to one / who, in your shadow, / felt too great a love / for the world."[42]

He loved "fiercely and desperately," and love, expressed in all its forms, characterized his existence and determined its tragic end. Love seems to be his "harmony." Verses – not of hate, but of love – rise from the massacred self of which his body is a symbol, of which his voice with its stable vibrations is a symbol: a voice that is youthful and convinced by the "unalterable sweetness" of which the poet Pasolini could not have been unaware.[43] Otherwise, screams emerge from him.

---

[39] Pier Paolo Pasolini, "Il sogno del centauro. Incontri con Jean Duflot (1969–1975) – L'apocalisse secondo Pasolini," *Saggi sulla politica e sulla società*, p. 1448.

[40] "Questo sarà compreso meglio solo se si tiene conto della reale solitudine in cui io vivevo [...]" ("This will be better understood only if one considers the real solitude that I was living in [...]"); Pier Paolo Pasolini, *Poesie e pagine ritrovate*, p. 46.

[41] "Supplica a mia madre," *Poesia in forma di rosa*. English translation from *The Selected Poetry of Pier Paolo Pasolini*, pp. 314–317.

[42] Pier Paolo Pasolini, "Memorie," *L'Usignolo della Chiesa Cattolica*, in *Tutte le poesie*, vol. 1, edited by Walter Siti, Milan: Mondadori, pp. 457–460. English translation from *The Selected Poetry of Pier Paolo Pasolini*, pp. 110–111. The relationship between Pasolini and his mother is extremely complex and heavy. Oddly, though, I have not found much literature on the subject. On the power exercised by mothers on sons in Mediterranean cultures, see Daniela Bini, *Portrait of the Artist and His Mother in Twentieth-Century Italian Culture*, Teaneck: The Fairleigh Dickinson University Press Series in Italian Studies, 2020. A chapter is dedicated to Pier Paolo Pasolini and Susanna Maria Colussi.

[43] He defines himself as such several times. See Pier Paolo Pasolini, "Il sogno del centauro. Incontri con Jean Duflot (1969–1975) – L'apocalisse secondo Pasolini," *Saggi sulla politica e sulla società*, pp. 1403–1550.

It is impossible to say what kind of scream / mine is: true, it's terrible – / so much so that it distorts my features / making them like the jaws of an animal – / but, in some way, it is also joyful / so much so that it makes me become like a child again. / It is a scream let out to call someone's attention / or to ask for help; but also, maybe, to damn this someone. / It is a scream that wants people to know, / in this deserted place, that I exist, / or yet, not only that I exist, / but that I know. It is a scream / that, from anxiety's depth, / bears some vile accent of hope; / or a scream of absurd absolute certainty, / in which pure desperation echoes. / In any case, this is certain: whatever / my scream might mean, / it is destined to outlive every possible ending.[44]

The restlessness of the last prophetic poet, who still moves those who come into contact with him, is well encapsulated in the contrast between his body and his voice.

Pasolini went through the dark streets of the city and mingled with the bottom of the heap. He did not feel part of "the beautiful band of intellectuals, sociologists, experts, and journalists – all with the noblest of intentions" – who are like "those puppets that make children laugh hard because they have their bodies turned to one side and their head to the other." On the contrary, he was a man who placed on his shoulders "all the weight of confronting himself, by himself, with truth," that truth which he knew firsthand because he had descended into hell and seen "other things, more things." He did not ask to be believed but noted that his interlocutors "always had to change the subject at hand in order to not face the truth." Pasolini paid the price for the life that he lived. He revealed that he had gone down to hell and knew things "that do disturb other people's complacency." But he warned, "Be careful, hell is rising and coming for you."[45]

---

[44] Pier Paolo Pasolini, *Teorema*, Milan: Garzanti, 1968.

[45] Many times, Pasolini mentions hell as imminent or present. To understand his thought better, see Pier Paolo Pasolini, "Il sogno del centauro. Incontri con Jean Duflot (1969–1975) – L'apocalisse secondo Pasolini," *Saggi sulla politica e sulla società*, p. 1448. *"Is the present therefore the time of ambiguity, the time of decadence?* Hell. *How do you explain that the impression of an imminent apocalypse grows in each of your films? Teorema, Porcile, Medea ... they deal more and more with parables about the end of the world?* The end of 'a' world, rather. *As a Marxist, do you think it is sufficient to limit yourself to making a list of the signs, the symptoms of the catastrophe of a world? Darkness and the gloomy complexity of the universe that you express by way of 'myth' remain connected to the world of sin, of guilt ...* Marxists or not, we are all involved in this end of a world. Society has not solved the mystery of its existence any more than Oedipus did. I look at the shaded side of reality because the other side does not yet exist" (interviewer's questions are in italics and Pasolini's responses are written in normal script).

Selected Bibliography of Primary Sources

Accetto, Torquato. *Della dissimulazione onesta*. Edited by Salvatore Nigro. Turin: Einaudi, 1997.

Albergati, Fabio. *La repubblica regia*. Bologna: Vittorio Benacci, 1627.

Albert the Great. *Quaestio de prophetia: Visione, immaginazione, dono profetico*. Edited by Anna Rodolfi. Florence: Edizioni del Galluzzo, 2009.

Alfieri, Vittorio. *Della Tirannide, Del Principe e delle lettere, Panegirico di Plinio e Traiano, La virtù sconosciuta*. Edited by Alessandro Donati. Bari: Laterza, 1927.

Alighieri, Dante. *Convivio*. Translated by Richard H. Lansing. New York: Garland, 1990.

Dantis Alagherii epistolae: The Letters of Dante. Edited by Paget Toynbee. Oxford: Clarendon Press, 1920.

The De Monarchia of Dante Alighieri. Edited by Aurelia Henry. Boston and New York: Houghton, Mifflin and Company, 1904.

The Divine Comedy, Inferno. Translated by Charles S. Singleton. Princeton: Princeton University Press, 1970.

The Divine Comedy, Paradiso. Translated by Charles S. Singleton. Princeton: Princeton University Press, 1975.

The Divine Comedy, Purgatorio. Translated by Charles S. Singleton. Princeton: Princeton University Press, 1973.

Ammirato, Scipione. *Discorsi sopra Cornelio Tacito*. Florence: Filippo Giunti, 1594.

Arendt, Hannah. *Eichmann in Jerusalem. A Report on the Banality of Evil*. New York: Viking Press, 1964.

Atkinson, James B. and David Sices, eds. *Machiavelli and his Friends: Their Personal Correspondence*. DeKalb: Northern Illinois University Press, 1996.

Bakunin, Mikhail. "The Political Theology of Mazzini." *Selected Writings*. Edited by Arthur Lehning. London: Jonathan Cape, 1973.

Balbo, Cesare. *Sommario della storia d'Italia*. Tenth edition. Florence: Le Monnier, 1856.

Bartoli, Riccardo. "I Diritti dell'uomo. Catechismo Cattolico-democratico del cittadino. Riccardo Bartoli M[inore] O[sservante] sacerdote reggiano." *La Religione amica della democrazia. I cattolici democratici del Triennio rivoluzionario (1796–1799)*. Edited by Vittorio E. Giuntella. Rome: Studium, 1990.

Barzellotti, Giacomo. *David Lazzaretti di Arcidosso detto il santo: i suoi seguaci e la sua leggenda*. Bologna: Zanichelli, 1885.

Battista, Giuseppe. "L'apologia della menzogna." *Delle giornate accademiche. Dedicate all'Illustriss. e Eccell. Sig. Francesco Marino Caracciolo, Principe d'Avellino*. Venice: Presso Combi, e LaNoù, 1673.

Berti, Silvia, ed. *Trattato dei tre impostori. La vita e lo spirito del Signor Benedetto de Spinoza*. Turin: Einaudi, 1984.

Besozzi, Gian Pietro. *Discorsi intorno alla vita di san Paolo apostolo*. Milan: Paolo Gottardo Pontio, 1573.

Biagi, Enzo. "III B facciamo l'appello." Television program. RAI Teche, 1971.

Bocalosi, Girolamo. "Dell'educazione democratica da darsi al popolo italiano." *Giacobini italiani*. Vol. II. Edited by Delio Cantimori and Renzo De Felice. Bari: Laterza, 1964.

Boccaccio, Giovanni. *De genealogia deorum*. Translated by Charles G. Osgood in Boccaccio on Poetry. Princeton: Princeton University Press, 1930.

Boccalini, Traiano. *Ragguagli di Parnaso e pietra del paragone politico*. Vol. 1, Ragguaglio LXXVII. Edited by Giuseppe Rua. Bari: Laterza, 1910.

Bocchi, Achille. *Symbolicarum Quaestionum, De universo genere, quas serio ludebat*. Bologna: Apud Societatem Tipographiæ Bononiensis, 1574.

Bonaventura, Federico. *Della ragion di stato et della prudenza politica*. Edited by Nicola Panichi. Rome: Edizioni di Storia e Letteratura, 2007.

Bonini, Filippo Maria. *Il Ciro politico*. Venice: Niccolò Pezzana, 1658.

Botero, Giovanni. *Della Ragion di Stato Libri Dieci, con Tre Libri delle Cause della Grandezza, e Magnificenza delle Città*. Venice: i Gioliti, 1589.

De regia sapientia libri tres. Milan: Apud Pacificum Pontium, 1583.

The Reason of State. Edited by Robert Bireley. Cambridge: Cambridge University Press, 2017.

Brucioli, Antonio. *Dialogi*. Venice: Gregorio de Gregori, 1526.

Dialogi. Vol. I. Venice: Giovannantonio e i fratelli da Sabbio, 1528.

La Biblia la quale in sè contiene i sacrosanti libri del Vecio e Nuovo Testamento, i quali ti apporto Christianissmo Lettore, nuovamente tradotti de la Hebraica e Greca verità in Lingua Toscana. Venice: no publisher, 1541.

Prediche del reverendo padre fra Gieronimo da Ferrara per tutto l'anno nuovamente con somma diligentia ricorrette. Venice: no publisher, 1540.

Tomo terzo de' sacrosanti libri del Vecchio Testamento tradotti dalla Ebraica verità in Lingua Italiana & con breve & catholico commento dichiarati per Antonio Brucioli. Venice: Alessandro Brucioli e frategli, 1546.

Bruno, Giordano. *Oeuvres complètes de Giordano Bruno*. Vol. II. Translation by Y. Hersant. Paris: Les Belles lettres, 1994.

Calamandrei, Piero. *Diario 1940–1945*. Edited by Giorgio Agosti. Florence: La Nuova Italia, 1982.

Uomini e città della Resistenza. Rome-Bari: Laterza, 2011.

Campanella, Tommaso. *Articuli prophetales*. Edited by Germana Ernst. Florence: La Nuova Italia, 1977.

Lettere. Edited by Germana Ernst. Florence: Olschki, 2010.

Carducci, Giosuè. *Edizione nazionale delle opere di Giosuè Carducci*. Bologna: Zanichelli, 1942.

Carlyle, Thomas. *On Heroes, Hero-Worship, and the Heroic in History*. Edited by David R. Sorensen and Brent E. Kinser. New Haven and London: Yale University Press, 2013.

Cattin, Giulio. *Il primo Savonarola. Poesie e prediche autobiografiche dal codice Borromeo*. Florence: Olschki, 1983.

Cepàri, Virgilio. *Essercitio della presenza di Dio*. Rome: Alessandro Zannetti, 1621.

Cerretani, Bartolomeo. *Dialogo della mutatione di Firenze*. Edited by Raul Mordenti. Rome: Edizioni di Storia e Letteratura, 1990.

Coleridge, Earnest Hartley, ed. *The Works of Lord Byron*. Vol. 4 (Poetry). Second Edition. London: John Murray-Albemarle Street, 1905.

Croce, Benedetto. *A History of Italy*. Translated by Cecilia M. Ady. Oxford: Clarendon Press, 1929.

Etica e politica. Bari: Laterza, 1943.

History of Europe in the Nineteenth Century, translated by Henry Furst, New York: Harcourt, Brace and Company, 1933.

La rivoluzione napoletana del 1799: biografie, racconti, ricerche. Bari: Laterza, 1948.

"Note sulla letteratura italiana nella seconda metà del secolo XIX: VII, Gabriele D'Annunzio." *La Critica* 2 (1904): pp. 1–28, 85–110.

Storia della età barocca in Italia: Pensiero. Poesia e letteratura. Vita morale. Bari: Laterza, 1957.

Storia d'Europa nel secolo XIX. Bari: Laterza, 1932.

Storia d'Italia dal 1870 al 1915. Rome-Bari: Laterza, 1973.

Cuoco, Vincenzo. *A Historical Essay on the Neapolitan Revolution of 1799*. Edited by Bruce Haddock and Filippo Sabetti. Toronto: University of Toronto Press, 2014.

Saggio storico sulla rivoluzione di Napoli. Edited by Antonino De Francesco. Rome-Bari: Laterza, 2014.

Curcio, Carlo. *Utopisti e riformatori sociali del Cinquecento*. Bologna: Zanichelli, 1941.

Utopisti italiani del Cinquecento. Rome: Colombo, 1944.

D'Annunzio, Gabriele. *Il libro ascetico della Giovane Italia*. Milan: L'Olivetana, 1926.

La gloria. Milan: Fratelli Treves Editori, 1899.

Merope: laudi del cielo, del mare, della terra e degli eroi. Milan: Fratelli Treves Editori, 1912.

Notturno. Milan: Mondadori, 1995.

Per la più grande Italia: orazioni e messaggi. Milan: Fratelli Treves Editori, 1920.

Per l'Italia degli italiani. Milan: Bottega di poesia, 1923.

da Crema, Battista. *Opera utilissima de la cognitione et vittoria di sé stesso [...] componuta per il reverendissimo Battista da Crema maestro di scientia spirituale pratica et perfettione, christiano rarissimo*. Milan: Gottardo da Ponte, 1531.

Specchio interiore opera divina, per la cui lettione ciascuno devoto potrà facilmente ascendere al colmo della perfettione. Milan: Dal Calvo, 1540.

Via de aperta verità. Venice: Bastiano Vicentino, 1532.

Della Porta, Giovan Battista. *La fisionomia dell'huomo et la celeste. Libri sei*. Venice: Nicolò Pezzana, 1668.

de Lamartine, Valentine, ed. *Correspondance de Lamartine*. Second Edition. Vol. 2. Paris: Hachette, 1881–1882.

de Lamennais, Hugues-Félicité-Robert. *Esquisse d'une philosophie*. Vol. III. Paris: Pagnerre, 1840–1846.

de Lubac, Henry. *La posterité spirituelle de Joachim de Flore*. Paris: Lethielleux, 1979–1981.

de' Rosmini-Serbati Antonio. *Storia dell'amore cavata dalle divine scritture libri tre*. Cremona: Dal Feraboli Tipografo Vescovile, 1834.

de Saint-Simon, Henri. *Le Nouveau Christianisme*. Paris: Au bureau du Globe, 1832.

da Sezze, Carlo. *Opere complete*. Edited by Raimondo Sbardella. Rome: Isola del Liri, 1967.

de Tocqueville, Alexis. *Democracy in America*. Edited by J. P. Mayer. Translated by George Lawrence. New York: Harper Perennial, 2006.

di Cino Rinuccini, Filippo. *Ricordi storici di Filippo di Cino Rinuccini dal 1282 al 1460 colla continuazione di Alamanno e Neri suoi figli fino al 1506: seguiti da altri monumenti inediti di storia patria estratti dai codici originali ... con documenti ed illustrazioni*. Edited by Giuseppe Aiazzi. Florence: Stamperia Piatti, 1840.

di S. Paolo, Simone. *Riforma dell'huomo*. Florence: Stamperia di Piero Martini, all'insegna del lion d'oro, 1695.

di Passerano, Alberto Radicati. *A Parallel between Muhamed and Sosem, the Great Deliverer of the Jews by Zelim Musulman: in a Letter to Nathan Rabby*. London: J. Harbert, 1732.

Twelve Discourses concerning Religion and Government Inscribed to all Lovers of Truth and Liberty. Second Edition. London: no publisher, 1734.

Fancelli, Manlio, ed. *Orazioni politiche del Cinquecento*. Bologna: Zanichelli, 1941.

Fehrenbacher, Don E. and Virginia Fehrenbacher, eds. *Recollected Words of Abraham Lincoln*. Stanford: Stanford University Press, 1996.

Ficino, Marsilio. *Epistolae*. Venice, 1495.

Foscolo, Ugo. "Della servitù dell'Italia." *Prose politiche e letterarie dal 1811 al 1816*. Edited by Luigi Fassò. Florence: Le Monnier, 1933.

"Discorso sul testo e su le opinioni diverse prevalenti intorno alla critica e alla emendazione critica della Commedia di Dante." *Studi su Dante*. Edited by Giovanni Da Pozzo. Florence: Le Monnier, 1979.

La commedia illustrata da Ugo Foscolo. Vol. III. London: Pietro Rolandi, 1843.

"Primo articolo della Edinburgh Review (February 1818)." *Studi su Dante*. Edited by Giovanni Da Pozzo. Florence: Le Monnier, 1979.

Fourier, Charles. *Teoria dei quattro movimenti. Il nuovo mondo amoroso*. Turin: Einaudi, 1971.

Galdi, Matteo. "Saggio d'istruzione pubblica rivoluzionaria." *Giacobini italiani*. Vol. I. Edited by Delio Cantimori and Renzo De Felice. Bari: Laterza, 1964.

Garibaldi, Giuseppe. *Epistolario di Giuseppe Garibaldi. Con documenti e lettere inedite (1836–1882)*. Edited by Enrico Emilio Ximenes. Milan: Alfredo Brigola and C., 1885.

Memorie. Edited by Ernesto Nathan. Turin: Società tipografia editrice nazionale, 1907.

Giannone, Pietro. *Istoria civile del Regno di Napoli*. Vol. X. Milan: Società Tipografica de' Classici Italiani, 1823.

Opere di Pietro Giannone. Edited by Sergio Bertelli and Giuseppe Ricuperati. Milan-Naples: Riccardo Ricciardi, 1972.

Giannotti, Donato. "Della Repubblica Fiorentina." *Opere politiche e letterarie di Donato Giannotti*. Vol. I. Edited by Filippo Luigi Polidori. Florence: Le Monnier, 1850.

Giuntella, Vittorio E. *La Religione amica della democrazia. I cattolici democratici del Triennio rivoluzionario (1796–1799)*. Rome: Studium, 1990.

Gobetti, Piero. "Risorgimento senza eroi." *Scritti storici, letterari e filosofici*. Edited by Paolo Spriano. Turin: Einaudi, 1969.

Gregory, Tullio. *Theophrastus redivivus. Erudizione e ateismo nel Seicento*. Naples: Morano, 1970.

Guicciardini, Francesco. *Dialogue on the Government of Florence*. Edited and translated by Alison Brown. Cambridge: Cambridge University Press, 1994.

"Estratti savonaroliani." *Scritti autobiografici e rari*. Edited by Roberto Palmarocchi. Bari: Laterza, 1936.

Maxims and Reflections of a Renaissance Statesman (Ricordi). Edited and translated by Mario Domandi. Gloucester (MA): Peter Smith, 1970.

Opere di Francesco Guicciardini. Edited by Emanuella Lugnani Scarano. Turin: UTET, 1983.

Storia d'Italia. Edited by Emanuella Lugnani Scarano. Turin: UTET, 2013.

The History of Italy. Edited and translated by Sidney Alexander. New York and London: The Macmillan Company and Collier-Macmillan, 1969.

Guicciardini, Luigi. *Del Savonarola ovvero Dialogo tra Francesco Zati e Pieradovardo Giachinotti il giorno dopo la battaglia di Gavinana*. Florence: Olschki, 1959.

Gusta, Francesco. "Saggio critico sulle crociate." *Le dolci catene. Testi della contro-rivoluzione cattolica in Italia*. Edited by Vittorio E. Giuntella. Rome: Istituto per la Storia del Risorgimento Italiano, 1988.

Harrington, James. "The Commonwealth of Oceana." *The Political Works of James Harrington*. Edited by John G. A. Pocock. Cambridge: Cambridge University Press, 1977.

Jouffroy, Thèodore. "Comment les dogmes finissent." *Mélanges philosophiques*. Paris: Hachette, 1901.

Le cahier vert. Comment les dogmes finissent. Lettres inédites. Edited by Pierre Poux. Paris: Les Presses Françaises, 1924.

Jung, Carl Gustav. *Ricordi, sogni e riflessioni*. Edited by A. Jaffè. Milan: Rizzoli, 1978.

l'Aurora, Enrico Michele. "All'Italia nelle tenebre l'aurora porta la luce." *Giacobini italiani*. Vol. I. Edited by Delio Cantimori and Renzo De Felice. Bari: Laterza, 1964.

Landino, Cristoforo. *Comento sopra la Comedia*. Vol. 1. Edited by Paolo Procaccioli. Rome: Salerno, 2001.

La Pira, Giorgio. *Principî*, January–February 1940, supplement to the first issue of *Vita Cristiana*.

"Relazione del Deputato La Pira Giorgio sui principi relativi ai rapporti civili." Assemblea Costituente Commissione per la Costituzione Prima Sottocommissione.

"Resoconto sommario della seduta antimeridiana di lunedì 22 dicembre 1947." Assemblea Costituente CCCXLVI, p. 3577.

Leopardi, Giacomo. "Discorso di un italiano intorno alla poesia romantica." *Tutte le opere*. Edited by Walter Binni. Florence: G.C. Sansoni, 1969.

Tutte le opere. Edited by Walter Binni. Florence: G.C. Sansoni, 1969.

Leroux, Pierre. *De l'humanité*. Paris: Perrotin, 1840.

Lessing, Gotthold Ephraim. "Die Erziehung des Menschengeschlechts." *Nouveau Christianisme. Lettres d'Eugène Rodrigues sur la religion et la politique*.

L'éducation du genre humain de Lessing traduit, pour la première fois de l'allemand par Eugène Rodrigues. Paris: Au Bureau du Globe, 1832.

Lincoln, Abraham. "Address to the New Jersey Senate, Trenton, New Jersey, February 21, 1861." *Speeches and Writings 1859–1865.* Vol. 2. Edited by Don E. Fehrenbacher. New York: The Library of America, 1989.

"Letter to Albert G. Hodges, April 4, 1864." *Speeches and Writings 1859–1865.* Vol. 2. Edited by Don E. Fehrenbacher. New York: The Library of America, 1989.

"Letter to Eliza P. Gurney, September 4, 1864." *Speeches and Writings 1859–1865.* Vol. 2. Edited by Don E. Fehrenbacher. New York: The Library of America, 1989.

"Meditation on the Divine Will." *Speeches and Writings 1859–1865.* Vol. 2. Edited by Don E. Fehrenbacher. New York: The Library of America, 1989.

"Portion of Last Speech in Campaign of 1858, Springfield, Illinois." *Speeches and Writings 1832–1858.* Vol. 1. Edited by Don E. Fehrenbacher. New York: The Library of America, 1989.

"Second Inaugural Address." *Speeches and Writings 1859–1865.* Vol. 2. Edited by Don E. Fehrenbacher. New York: The Library of America, 1989.

Livy. *Ab urbe condita,* English and Latin, Cambridge (MA): Harvard University Press, 1919.

Manzoni, Alessandro. *Tutte le opere.* Vol. 1. Edited by Mario Martelli. Florence: Sansoni, 1988.

Machiavelli, Niccolò. *Discourses on Livy.* Edited by Harvey C. Mansfield, Chicago: Chicago University Press, 1996.

Florentine Histories. Edited by Laura Banfield and Harvey C. Mansfield. Princeton: Princeton University Press, 1988.

Il Principe. Edited by M. Martelli in *Tutte le opere.* Florence: Sansoni, 1971.

Machiavelli. The Chief Works and Others. Edited by Allan Gilbert. Durham (NC) and London: Duke University Press, 1969.

Teatro. Andria, Mandragola, Clizia. Edited by Pasquale Stoppelli. Rome: Salerno Editrice, 2017.

The Art of War. Edited and translated by Christopher Lynch. Chicago and London: The University of Chicago Press, 2003.

The Historical Political and Diplomatic Writings of Niccolò Machiavelli. Translated by Christian E. Detmold. Boston: James R. Osgood and Company, 1882.

The Prince. Edited by Harvey C. Mansfield. Chicago and London: The University of Chicago Press, 1998.

Tutte le opere. Edited by M. Martelli. Florence: Sansoni, 1971.

Macrobius. *Commentary on the Dream of Scipio.* Edited by W. H. Stahl. New York: Columbia University Press, 1952.

Commento al Somnium Scipionis. Edited by Mario Regali. Pisa: Giardini, 1983.

Malvezzi, Virgilio. *Davide perseguitato.* Venice: Filippo Alberto, 1636.

Mapei, Camillo. *L'eco di Savonarola. Foglio mensile diretto da Italiani cristiani.* London: Partridge and Oakey, 1847.

Marchetti, Giovanni. "Che importa ai preti (1798)." *Le dolci catene. Testi della controrivoluzione cattolica in Italia.* Edited by Vittorio E. Giuntella. Rome: Istituto per la Storia del Risorgimento Italiano, 1988.

Mazzini, Giuseppe. *Epistolario.* Vol. II. Florence: G.C. Sansoni, 1902.

"Gemiti, fremiti e ricapitolazione." *Mazzini e l'Internazionale.* Pamphlet. Rome: Amministrazione della Roma del Popolo, 1871.

Note autobiografiche. Scritti editi ed inediti. Vol. LXXVII. Imola: Cooperativa Tipografico-Editrice Paolo Galeati, 1938.

Pensieri sulla democrazia in Europa. Second edition. Edited by Salvo Mastellone. Milan: Feltrinelli, 2005.

Scritti editi ed inediti. Imola: Cooperativa Tipografico-Editrice Paolo Galeati, 1906–1943.

Scritti editi e inediti di Giuseppe Mazzini. Vol. VII. Milan: Daelli Editore, 1864.

Scritti editi e inediti di Giuseppe Mazzini. Vol. VIII. Rome: Daelli Editore, 1891.

Scritti politici. Edited by Terenzio Grandi and Augusto Comba. Turin: UTET, 2005.

Scritti sul romanzo e altri saggi letterari. Rome: Edizioni di Storia e letteratura, 2012.

Mila, Massimo. *Verdi.* Edited by Pietro Gelli. Milan: Rizzoli, 2000.

Montale, Eugenio. "Laggiù (16.XII,1969)." *L'opera in versi.* Edited by R. Bettarini and G. Contini. Turin: Einaudi, 1980.

"Laggiù / Down Below." *Satura 1962–1970.* Edited by Rosanna Warren. Translated by William Arrowsmith. New York: W.W. Norton & Company, 1998.

Morgari, Oddino. *L'arte della propaganda socialista.* Milan: Lotta di Classe Editrice, 1896.

Muzzarelli, Alfonso. "Delle cause dei mali presenti e del timore de'mali futuri e suoi rimedi. Avviso al popolo cristiano." *Le dolci catene. Testi della controrivoluzione cattolica in Italia.* Edited by Vittorio E. Giuntella. Rome: Istituto per la Storia del Risorgimento Italiano, 1988.

Nardi, Bruno. *Dante e la cultura medievale.* Bari: Laterza, 1948.

Nesi, Giovanni. *Oraculum de novo saeculo.* Florence: Lorenzo Morgiani, 1497.

Nievo, Ippolito. *Confessions of an Italian.* Edited by Lucy Riall. Translated by Frederika Randall. London: Penguin, 2014.

Le Confessioni d' un italiano. Edited by Simone Casini. Milan-Parma: Guanda, 1999.

Tutte le opere. Edited by Marcella Gorra. Milan: Mondadori, 1981.

Nifo, Agostino. *Parva Naturalia Augustini Niphi Medices philosophi suessani*, Venetiis, Hieronymus Scotus, 1550.

Sui sogni. Milan-Udine: Mimesis Edizioni, 2016.

Olgiati, Francesco. *La pietà cristiana. Esperienze ed indirizzi.* Milan: Vita e pensiero, 1935.

Pagani, Antonio. *La tromba della militia christiana.* Venice: Francesco Ziletti, 1585.

Palmieri, Vincenzo. "La libertà e la legge considerate nella libertà delle opinioni e nella tolleranza de' culti religiosi." *La Religione amica della democrazia. I cattolici democratici del Triennio rivoluzionario (1796–1799).* Edited by Vittorio E. Giuntella. Rome: Studium, 1990.

Pasolini, Pier Paolo. "Dialoghi con Pasolini," *Vie Nuove* XVII, no. 40 (1962).

Lettere 1955–1975. Edited by Antonella Giordano and Nico Naldini. Milan: Garzanti, 2021.

Poesie e pagine ritrovate. Edited by Andrea Zanzotto and Nico Naldini. Rome: Lato Side Editori, 1980.

Saggi sulla politica e sulla società. Edited by Walter Siti. Milan: Mondadori, 1999.

Scritti corsari. Milan: Garzanti, 1975.

Teorema. Milan: Garzanti, 1968.

The Selected Poetry of Pier Paolo Pasolini. Edited and translated by Stephen Sartarelli. Chicago: University of Chicago Press, 2014.

Petrarca, Francesco. *Canzoniere.* Edited by Giancarlo Contini. Turin: Einaudi, 1964.

Epistolae rerum familiarum. Vol. II. Edited by Vittorio Rossi. Florence: Sansoni, 1934.

The Complete Canzoniere. Translated by A.S. Kline. *Poetry in translation*, 2001.

Petrocchi, Massimo. *Storia della spiritualità italiana.* Vol. I. Rome: Edizioni di Storia e Letteratura, 1978.

Pomponazzi, Pietro. *Apologia.* Edited by Vittoria Perrone Compagni. Florence: Olschki, 2011.

De incantationibus. Edited by Vittoria Perrone Compagni and Laura Regnicoli. Florence: Olschki, 2011.

Prampolini, Camillo. *Predica di Natale.* Reggio Emilia: Tipografia operaia, 1897.

Pucci, Francesco. "Forma d'una republica catholica." *Per la storia degli eretici italiani del secolo XVI in Europa.* Edited by Delio Cantimori and Elizabeth Feis. Rome: Reale Accademia d'Italia, 1937.

Lettere, documenti e testimonianze. Vol. I. Edited by Luigi Firpo and Renato Piattoli. Florence: Olschki, 1955.

Ranza, Giovanni Antonio. "Della vera chiesa istituita da Gesù Cristo." *Giacobini italiani.* Vol. I. Edited by Delio Cantimori and Renzo De Felice. Bari: Laterza, 1964.

Rosselli, Carlo. *Liberal Socialism.* Edited by Nadia Urbinati. Princeton: Princeton University Press, 1994

Scritti dall'esilio. Edited by Costanzo Casucci. Turin: Einaudi, 1988.

Socialismo liberale. Edited by John Rosselli. Turin: Einaudi, 1997.

Rucellai, Giovanni. *Giovanni Rucellai e il suo Zibaldone.* Edited by Alessandro Perosa. London: The Warburg Institute, University of London, 1960.

Russo, Vincenzio. "Pensieri politici." *Giacobini italiani.* Vol. I. Edited by Delio Cantimori and Renzo De Felice. Bari: Laterza, 1964.

Savonarola, Girolamo. *Apologeticus de ratione poeticae artis.* Translated by Stanley Meltzoff in *Botticelli, Signorelli and Savonarola, Theologia Poetica and Painting from Boccaccio to Poliziano.* Florence: Olschki, 1987.

Compendio di rivelazioni e Dialogus de veritate prophetica. Edited by Angela Crucitti. Rome: Angelo Belardetti, 1974.

Le lettere di Girolamo Savonarola, ora per la prima volta raccolte e a miglior lezione ridotte da Roberto Ridolfi. Edited by Roberto Ridolfi. Florence: Olschki, 1933.

Lettere e Scritti apologetici. Edited by Roberto Ridolfi, Vincenzo Romano, and Armando F. Verde. Rome: Angelo Belardetti, 1984.

Prediche sopra Aggeo con il Trattato circa il reggimento e governo della città di Firenze. Edited by Luigi Firpo. Rome: Angelo Belardetti, 1965.

Prediche sopra Amos e Zaccaria, edited by Paolo Ghiglieri. Rome: Angelo Belardetti, 1971–1972.

Prediche sopra Giobbe. Edited by Roberto Ridolfi. Rome: Angelo Belardetti, 1957.

Prediche sopra i Salmi. Edited by Vincenzo Romano. Rome: Angelo Belardetti, 1969–1975.

Prediche sopra Ruth e Michea. Edited by Vincenzo Romano. Rome: Angelo Belardetti, 1962.

Selected Writings of Girolamo Savonarola. Religion and Politics, 1490–1498. Translated and edited by Anne Borelli and Maria Pastore Passaro. New Haven and London: Yale University Press, 2006.

Sermoni sopra il salmo "Quam bonus." Edited by Claudio Leonardi. Rome: Angelo Belardetti, 1999.

Trattato in difesa e commendazione dell'orazione mentale. Edited by Mario Ferrara in *Operette spirituali*. Vol. 1. Rome: Belardetti, 1976.

Spinoza, Baruch. *Tractatus teologico-politicus*. Leiden; New York: E.J. Brill, 1989.

Thomas Aquinas. *Le questioni disputate. Testo latino dell'Edizione leonina e traduzione italiana, vol. II, La verità, Questioni (10–20)*. Edited by Roberto Coggi. Bologna: Edizioni Studi Domenicano, 1992.

Questiones Disputatae. Translated by James V. McGlynn, S.J. Chicago: Henry Regnery Company, 1953.

Somme théologique: La Prophétie. Second edition. Edited by Paul Synave, O.P., and Pierre Benoit, O.P. Paris: CERF, 2005.

Summa Theologiae. Translated by Fathers of the English Dominican Province. New York: Benziger Bros, 1947–1948.

Tommaseo, Niccolò. *Opuscoli inediti di fra Girolamo Savonarola* [No place, no date].

Urbinati, Nadia and Stefano Recchia, eds. *A Cosmopolitanism of Nations: Giuseppe Mazzini's Writings on Democracy, Nation Building, and International Relations*. Princeton: Princeton University Press, 2009.

Vanini, Giulio Cesare. *Tutte opere*. Edited by Francesco Paolo Raimondi and Mario Carparelli. Milan: Bompiani, 2010.

Varchi, Benedetto. *Storia fiorentina*. Edited by Gaetano Milanesi. Florence: Le Monnier, 1857.

Verde, Armando F. *Lo Studio Fiorentino. 1473–1503. Ricerche e documenti*, IV: *La vita universitaria*. Vol. 2. Florence: Olschki, 1985.

Villari, Pasquale. *La storia di Girolamo Savonarola e de' suoi tempi*. Vol. I. Florence: Le Monnier, 1930.

Voltaire. *Dictionnaire philosophique*. Paris: Garnier, 1878.

von Albertini, Rudolf. *Firenze dalla repubblica al principato. Storia e coscienza politica*. Turin: Einaudi, 1970.

Walzer, Michael. *Exodus and Revolution*. New York: Basic Books, 1985.

The Revolution of the Saints: A Study in the Origins of Radical Politics. Cambridge (MA) and London: Harvard University Press, 1965.

Zuccolo, Ludovico. *Dialoghi*. Venice: Marco Ginammi, 1625.

Discorso dello amore verso la patria. Venice: Evangelista Deuchino, 1631.

Selected Bibliography of Secondary Sources

Ambrosini, Federica. *L'eresia di Isabella: Vita di Isabella da Passano, signora della Frattina (1542–1601)*. Milan: Franco Angeli, 2005.

Andreucci, Franco. "La diffusione e la volgarizzazione del marxismo." *Il marxismo nell'età della Seconda Internazionale*. Turin: Einaudi, 1979, pp. 5–58.

Audisio, Emanuela, Pasolini maestro corsaro. Italy: 3D Produzioni, 2015. Online: https://video.repubblica.it/spettacoli-e-cultura/pasolini-maestro-corsaro/216709/215893. Accessed December 17, 2021.

Baldini, A. Enzo, ed. *Botero e la ragion di Stato: Aatti del Convegno in memoria di Luigi Firpo*. Florence: Olschki, 1992.

Barnavi, Élie and Miriam Eliav-Feldon. *Le périple de Francesco Pucci: Utopie, hérésie et vérité religieuse dans la Renaissance tardive*. Paris: Hachette, 1988.

Baron, Hans. "The 'Prince' and the Puzzle of the Date of Chapter 26." *Journal of Medieval and Renaissance Studies* 21 (1991): pp. 84–102.

Barr, Colin. "Giuseppe Mazzini and Irish Nationalism, 1845–70." *Giuseppe Mazzini and the Globalization of Democratic Nationalism, 1830–1920*. Edited by Christopher A. Bayly and Eugenio F. Biagini. Oxford: Oxford University Press, 2008.

Barzellotti, Giacomo. *David Lazzaretti di Arcidosso detto il santo: I suoi seguaci e la sua leggenda*. Bologna: Zanichelli, 1885.

Bausi, Francesco. *Machiavelli*. Rome: Salerno Editrice, 2005.

"Petrarca, Machiavelli, il Principe." *Niccolò Machiavelli: politico, storico, letterato: Atti del Convegno di Losanna, 27–30 settembre 1995*. Edited by Jean-Jacques Marchand. Rome: Salerno Editrice, 1996, pp. 41–58.

Bayle, Pierre. *Dictionnaire historique et critique*. Vol. 3. Edited by Pierre Brunel. Amsterdam, 1740.

Ben-Aryeh, Debby Nirit. *Renaissance Florence in the Rhetoric of Two Popular Preachers: Giovanni Dominici (1346–1419) and Bernardino da Siena (1380–1444)*. Florence: Brepols, 2001.

Bénichou, Paul. *Le temps des prophètes: Doctrines de l'âge romantique*. Paris: Gallimard, 1977.

Les mages romantiques. Paris: Gallimard, 1988.

Benoit, Pierre. "Révélation et Inspiration." *Revue Biblique* 70 (1963): pp. 321–370.

Bercovitch, Sacvan. *The American Jeremiad.* Madison (WI): University of Wisconsin Press, 1978.

Berns, Thomas. "Prophetic Efficacy: The Relationship between Force and Belief." *The Radical Machiavelli. Politics, Philosophy and Language.* Edited by Filippo Del Lucchese, Fabio Frosini, and Vittorio Morfino. Brill: Leiden-Boston, 2015, pp. 207–218.

Betti, Laura. *Pasolini: cronaca giudiziaria, persecuzione, morte.* Milan: Garzanti, 1977.

Biagi, Enzo. "III B facciamo l'appello." Television program. RAI Teche, 1971.

Bini, Daniela. *Portrait of the Artist and His Mother in Twentieth-Century Italian Culture.* Teaneck: The Fairleigh Dickinson University Press Series in Italian Studies, 2020.

Blenkinsopp, Joseph. *A History of Prophecy in Israel.* Louisville (KY): Westminster John Knox Press, 1996.

Bloomfield, Morton W. "Recent Scholarship on Joachim of Fiore and His Influence." *Prophecy and Millenarianism: Essays in Honour of Marjorie Reeves.* Edited by Ann Williams. Burnt Hill: Longman, 1980, pp. 21–52.

Bobbio, Norberto. "Introduzione." *Scritti di Leone Ginzburg.* Turin: Einaudi, 1964.

Italia civile. Florence: Passigli, 1986.

Italia fedele. Il mondo di Gobetti. Florence: Passigli, 1986.

Maestri e compagni. Florence: Passigli, 1984.

"Ricordo di Piero Calamandrei." *Belfagor* 13 (1958): pp. 589–602.

Bolzoni, Lina. "Prophétie littéraire et prophétie politique chez Tommaso Campanella." *La prophétie comme arme de guerre des pouvoirs (XV–XVII siècles).* Paris: Presses de la Sorbonne Nouvelle, 2000, pp. 251–263.

"Una pretesa di libertà. Poesia, magia, profezia in Tommaso Campanella." *Storia della letteratura italiana, Vol. V, La fine del Cinquecento e il Seicento.* Edited by Enrico Malato. Rome: Salerno Editrice, 1997, pp. 869–903.

Bongi, Salvatore. "Francesco da Meleto un profeta fiorentino a' tempi del Machiavello." *Archivio storico italiano* 3 (1889): pp. 62–70.

Bonora, Elena. *I conflitti della Controriforma. Santità e obbedienza nell'esperienza religiosa dei primi barnabiti.* Florence: Casa Editrice Le Lettere, 1998.

Boralevi, Lea Campos. "Classical Foundational Myths of European Republicanism: The Jewish Commonwealth." *Republicanism: A Shared European Heritage.* Vol. 1. Edited by Martin van Gelderen and Quentin Skinner. Cambridge: Cambridge University Press, 2002, pp. 247–261.

Bregstein, Philo, *Whoever Says the Truth Shall Die.* Hilversum, Holland: VARA TV Production, 1981. Online: https://www.youtube.com/watch?v=5mwKpi2psS4. Accessed December 17, 2021.

Brown, Allison. "Savonarola, Machiavelli, and Moses: A Changing Model." *Florence and Italy. Renaissance Studies in Honour of Nicolai Rubinstein.* Edited by Peter Denley and Caroline Elam. London: Westfield College (University of London Committee for Medieval Studies), 1988.

Bruscagli, Riccardo. "Dante e Pasolini." Lecture. Teatro La Pergola. Florence: March 24, 2010. Online: http://www.leggeredante.it/2010/Pasolini/Introduzione.pdf. Accessed December 12, 2021.

Buber, Martin. *Kingship of God.* New York: Harper & Row, 1967.

Bull, Malcolm, ed. *Apocalypse Theory and the Ends of the World.* Oxford: Basil Blackwell, 1995.

Bull, Malcolm. *The Prophetic Faith*. New York: Harper & Row, 1949.

Burdach, Konrad. *Riforma Rinascimento Umanesimo. Due dissertazioni sui fondamenti della cultura e dell'arte della parola moderne*. Translated by Delio Cantimori. Florence: Sansoni, 1986.

Cacciari, Massimo and Paolo Prodi. *Occidente senza utopia*. Bologna: Il Mulino, 2016.

Cadoni, Giorgio. "Qualche osservazione su Machiavelli e Savonarola." *La Cultura* 2 (2007): pp. 263–278.

"Tale stato non può stare così..." *Savonarola e la politica*. Edited by Gian Carlo Garfagnini. Florence: SISMEL, 1997.

Caffiero, Marina. *La nuova era. Miti e profezie dell'Italia in rivoluzione*. Genoa: Agorà, 1991.

Calcaterra, Carlo. *Il nostro imminente Risorgimento: gli studi e la letteratura in Piemonte nel periodo della Sampaolina e della Filopatria*. Turin: Società Editrice Internazionale, 1935.

Campbell, Timothy C. "Remembering D'Annunzio and Il Duce: Modern Prophecy in Italy." *Quaderni d'Italianistica* XXVII (2006): pp. 89–108.

Canone, Eugenio. "Ispirati da quale Dio? Bruno e l'espressione della sapienza." *Bruniana & Campanelliana* 11 (2005): pp. 389–409.

Cantimori, Carlo. *Saggio sull'idealismo di Giuseppe Mazzini*. Faenza: Casa Tipografica Editrice G. Montanari, 1904.

Cantimori, Delio. *Eretici italiani del Cinquecento e Prospettive di storia ereticale italiana del Cinquecento*. Edited by Adriano Prosperi, Turin: Einaudi, 2009.

Prospettive di storia ereticale. Bari: Laterza, 1960.

"Visioni e speranze di un ugonotto italiano." *Rivista Storica Italiana* 62 (1950): pp. 199–217.

Canziani, Guido and Gianni Paganini, eds. *Theophrastus redivivus*. Florence: La Nuova Italia Editrice, 1981.

Capitani, Ovidio. "Per il significato dell'attesa della nuova età in Niccolò da Cusa." *L'attesa dell'età nuova nella spiritualità della fine del Medioevo. Atti del III Convegno storico internazionale (Todi, 16–19 ottobre 1960)*. Spoleto: Fondazione Cisam, 1962, pp. 198–216.

Caravale, Giorgio. *Il profeta disarmato: L'eresia di Francesco Pucci nell'Europa del Cinquecento*. Bologna: Il Mulino, 2011.

Carter, Nick. *Britain, Ireland and the Italian Risorgimento*. London: Palgrave Macmillan, 2015.

Cervelli, Innocenzo. "Savonarola, Machiavelli e il libro dell'Esodo." *Savonarola. Democrazia tirannide profezia, Atti del terzo Seminario di studi, (Pistoia, 23–24 maggio 1997)*. Edited by Gian Carlo Garfagnini. Florence: SISMEL-Edizioni del Galluzzo, 1998, pp. 243–329.

Chabod, Federico. *Italian Foreign Policy: The Statecraft of the Founders, 1870–1896*. Translated by William McCuaig. Princeton: Princeton University Press, 1996.

Per la storia religiosa dello Stato di Milano durante il dominio di Carlo V. Note e documenti. Bologna: Zanichelli, 1938.

Storia della politica estera italiana dal 1870 al 1896. Vol. 1. Bari: Laterza, 1971.

Chiummo, Carla. "Dante in veste post-risorgimentale (1870–1900)." *Studi Rinascimentali* 8 (2010): pp. 57–66.

Ciccotti, Ettore. *Psicologia del movimento socialista. Note ed osservazioni*. Bari: Laterza, 1903.

Ciliberto, Michele. *L'occhio di Atteone: nuovi studi su Giordano Bruno.* Rome: Edizioni di Storia e Letteratura, 2002.
   Niccolò Machiavelli. Ragione e pazzia. Rome and Bari: Laterza, 2019.
Claeys, Gregory. "Mazzini, Kossuth, and British Radicalism, 1848–1854." *Journal of British Studies* 28, no. 3 (Summer 1989): pp. 225–261.
Codignola, Arturo. *La giovinezza di G. Mazzini.* Florence: Vallecchi, 1926.
Cohn, Norman. *The Pursuit of the Millennium: Revolutionary Millenarians and Mystical Anarchists in the Middle Ages.* London: Maurice Temple Smith, 1970.
Cohn, Samuel. *Lust for Liberty: The Politics of Social Revolt in Medieval Europe, 1200–1425: Italy, France and Flanders.* Cambridge (MA): Harvard University Press, 2006.
Colish, Marcia L. "Republicanism, Religion, and Machiavelli's Savonarolan Moment." *Journal of the History of Ideas* LX (1999): pp. 597–616.
Collins, Adela Y. "Ascents to Heaven in Antiquity: Toward a Typology." *A Teacher for All Generations: Essays in Honor of James C. VanderKam.* Vol. 2. Edited by Erich F. Mason. Leiden: Brill, 2012, pp. 553–572.
   "The Uses of Apocalyptic Eschatology." *Fourth Ezra and Second Baruch: Reconstruction After the Fall.* Edited by Matthias Henze and Gabriele Boccaccini. Leiden: Brill, 2013.
Collins, John J. "From Prophecy to Apocalypticism: The Expectation of the End." *The Encyclopedia of Apocalypticism. Vol. 1: The Origins of Apocalypticism in Judaism and Christianity.* Edited by John J. Collins. New York: Continuum, 1998, pp. 129–161.
   "Introduction: Towards the Morphology of a Genre." *Semeia* 14 (1979): pp. 1–20.
   "Prophecy to Apocalypticism: The Expectation of the End." *The Encyclopedia of Apocalypticism, Vol. 1: The Origins of Apocalypticism in Judaism and Christianity.* New York: Continuum, 1998.
   "Temporality and Politics in Jewish Apocalyptic Literature." *Apocalyptic in History and Tradition.* Edited by Christopher Rowland and John Barton. London: Sheffield Academic Press, 2002.
   The Apocalyptic Imagination. New York: Crossroad, New York 1984.
Compagni, Vittoria Perrone. "'Evidentissimi avvertimenti dei Numi': Sogni, vaticini, profezie in Pomponazzi." *Annali del Dipartimento di Filosofia (Nuova Serie)* XVII (2011): pp. 21–59.
Cornill, Carl Heinrich. *The Prophets of Israel: Popular Sketches from Old Testament History.* Translated by Sutton F. Corkran. Chicago: The Open Court Publishing Company, 1973.
Cosenza, Mario Emilio. *Francesco Petrarca and the Revolution of Cola di Rienzo.* Chicago: The University of Chicago Press, 1913.
D'Addario, Arnaldo. *Aspetti della Controriforma a Firenze.* Rome: Pubblicazioni degli Archivi di Stato, 1972.
Dall'Aglio, Stefano. "L'altra faccia dello pseudoprofeta Francesco da Meleto scrivano della SS. Annunziata di Firenze." *Bibliothèque d'Humanisme et Renaissance* LXVII (2005): pp. 343–351.
Darsey, James. *The Prophetic Tradition and Radical Rhetoric in America.* New York: New York University Press, 1997.
Dasgupta, Rabidra K. "Mazzini and Indian Nationalism." *East and West* 7, no. 1 (Spring 1956): pp. 67–70.

Decleva, Enrico. "Anticlericalismo e religiosità laica nel socialismo italiano." *Prampolini e il socialismo riformista. Atti del convegno di Reggio Emilia, ottobre 1978.* Rome: Modo operaio-Edizioni Avanti, 1979, pp. 259–279.

d'Entrèves, Ettore Passerin. "'Il romanticismo 'progressivo' di Giuseppe Mazzini negli scritti giovanili (1829–1843)." *Religione e politica nell'Ottocento europeo.* Edited by Francesco Traniello. Rome: Istituto per la storia del Risorgimento Italiano, 1993.

"Il socialismo alla De Amicis nella Torino di fine Ottocento." *Il Mulino* 24 (1975): pp. 85–93.

"Mazzini e George Sand. Letteratura, religione e politica." *Religione e politica nell'Ottocento europeo.* Edited by Francesco Traniello. Rome: Istituto per la storia del Risorgimento Italiano, 1993, pp. 184–193.

De Felice, Renzo. *D'Annunzio politico, 1918–1938.* Bari: Laterza, 1978.

De Fiore, Luciano. *Risposte pratiche risposte sante: Pasolini, il tempo e la politica.* Rome: Castelvecchi, 2018.

De Grazia, Sebastian. *Machiavelli in Hell.* Princeton: Princeton University Press, 1989.

Delcorno, Carlo. "Forme della predicazione cattolica fra Cinque e Seicento." *Cultura d'élite e cultura popolare nell'arco alpino fra Cinque e Seicento.* Edited by Ottavio Besomi and Carlo Caruso. Basle-Boston-Berlin: Birkhäuser, 1995.

de Lubac, Henry. *La posterité spirituelle de Joachim de Flore.* Paris: Lethielleux, 1979–1981.

De Mattei, Rodolfo. *Il pensiero politico italiano nell'età della Controriforma.* Milan-Naples: Ricciardi, 1982.

De Petris, Alfonso. *Riletture dell'Apocalisse: Riconsiderazioni sull'idea del Regno.* Florence: Olschki, 2007.

De Robertis, Giuseppe. "D'Annunzio ha parlato." *La cultura italiana del '900 attraverso le riviste.* Vol. III. Edited by Angelo Romano. Turin: Einaudi, 1960, pp. 555–562.

De Sanctis, Francesco. Conferenze su Machiavelli. Edited by Maria Teresa Lanza in *L'arte, la scienza e la vita: nuovi saggi critici, conferenze e scritti vari.* Turin: Einaudi, 1972.

History of Italian Literature. Edited by Joan Redfern. New York: Harcourt, 1931.

"Schopenauer e Leopardi." *Leopardi.* Edited by Carlo Muscetta and Antonia Perna. Turin: Einaudi, 1969.

Dionisotti, Carlo. "La testimonianza del Brucioli." *Machiavellerie.* Turin: Einaudi, 1980.

Dooley, Brendan. *Morandi's Last Prophecy and the End of Renaissance Politics.* Princeton and Oxford: Princeton University Press, 2002.

Ebgi, Raphael, ed. *Umanisti italiani.* Turin: Einaudi, 2016.

Edelheit, Amos. *Ficino, Pico and Savonarola: The Evolution of Humanist Theology 1461/2–1498.* Leiden and Boston: Brill, 2008.

Eliav-Feldon, Miriam. "Secret Societies, Utopias, and Peace Plans: The Case of Francesco Pucci." *Journal of Medieval and Renaissance Studies* 14 (1984): pp. 139–158.

Ernst, Germana. "Ancora sugli ultimi scritti politici di Tommaso Campanella." *Bruniana & Campanelliana* 5 (1999): pp. 131–153.

"Aspetti dell'astrologia e della profezia in Galileo e Campanella." *Novità celesti e crisi del sapere.* Edited by Paolo Galluzzi. Florence: Giunti, 1983, pp. 255–266

Il carcere, il politico, il profeta. Saggi su Tommaso Campanella. Pisa-Rome: Istituti editoriali e poligrafici internazionali, 2002.

"'L'alba colomba scaccia i corbi neri': Profezia e riforma in Campanella." *Storia e figure dell'Apocalisse fra'500 e'600.* Edited by Roberto Rusconi. Rome: Viella, 1996, pp. 107–125.

"'L'aurea età felice': Profezia, natura e politica in Tommaso Campanella." *Tommaso Campanella e l'attesa del secolo aureo. Atti della III Giornata Luigi Firpo.* Florence: Olschki, 1998, pp. 61–88.

Profezia (*prophetia*). *Enciclopedia Bruniana e Campanelliana.* Vol. 1. Edited by Eugenio Canone and Germana Ernst. Pisa: Istituti editoriali e poligrafici internazionali, 2006.

"'Redeunt Saturnia regna': Profezia e poesia in Tommaso Campanella." *Bruniana & Campanelliana* XI.2 (2005): pp. 429–449.

"Vocazione profetica e astrologica in Tommaso Campanella." *La città dei segreti. Magia, astrologia e cultura esoterica a Roma.* Edited by Fabio Troncarelli. Milan: Franco Angeli, 1985, pp. 136–155.

Esposito, Mario. "Una manifestazione d'incredulità religiosa nel medioevo: il detto dei 'Tre Impostori' e la sua trasmissione da Federico II a Pomponazzi." *Archivio Storico Italiano* 89 (1931): pp. 3–48.

Fassò, Luigi, ed. *Prose politiche e letterarie dal 1811 al 1816.* Florence: Le Monnier, 1933.

Faure, Philippe Amédée. *Journal d'un combattant de février.* Jersey: C. Le Feuvre Imprimeur – Libraire, 1859.

Febvre, Lucien. "Un abuso e il suo clima sociale: la scomunica per debiti in Franca Contea." *Studi su Riforma e Rinascimento e altri scritti su problemi di metodo e geografia storica.* Edited by Delio Cantimori. Translated by Corrado Vivanti. Turin: Einaudi, 1966, pp. 205–231.

Fenzi, Enrico. "Per Petrarca politico: Cola di Rienzo e la questione romana in Bucolicum Carmen V, Pietas pastoralis." *Bollettino di italianistica* 1 (2011): pp. 49–88.

Ferretto, Silvia. "'Una chiesa rinnovata' e 'un popolo fatto tutto santo': La visione del Cristianesimo tra riflessione teologica e millenarismo in Francesco Pucci." *Archivio Storico Italiano* 165 (2007): pp. 77–120.

Ferrone, Vincenzo. *La società giusta ed equa: Repubblicanesimo e diritti dell'uomo in Gaetano Filangieri.* Bari and Rome: Laterza, 2003.

Figurelli, Fernando. "Le due canzoni patriottiche di Leopardi e il suo programma di letteratura nazionale e civile." *Belfagor* 6 (1951): pp. 20–39.

Filangieri, Gaetano. *Scienza della legislazione.* Milan: Giuseppe Galeazzi Regio Stampatore, 1791.

Firpo, Luigi. "Appunti campanelliani, XXI. Le censure all' 'Atheismus trionfato.'" *Giornale Critico della Filosofia Italiana* 30 (1951): pp. 509–524.

"Il Campanella astrologo e i suoi persecutori romani." *Rivista di filosofia* 30 (1939): pp. 200–215.

Il processo di Giordano Bruno. Edited by Diego Quaglioni. Rome: Salerno Editrice, 1993.

"L'utopia politica nella Controriforma." *Contributi alla storia del Concilio di Trento e della Controriforma.* Edited by Eugenio Garin. Florence: Vallecchi, 1948.

Ricerche campanelliane. Florence: Sansoni, 1947, pp. 134–173.

Fitzgerald, Brian. *Inspiration and Authority in the Middle Ages: Prophets and their Critics from Scholasticism to Humanism.* Oxford: Oxford University Press, 2017.

Foa, Vittorio. *Lettere della giovinezza.* Edited by Federica Montevecchi. Turin: Einaudi, 1998.

Formichetti, Gianfranco. "Il De siderali fato vitando di Tommaso Campanella." *Il mago, il cosmo, il teatro degli astri: saggi sulla letteratura esoterica del Rinascimento.* Edited by Gianfranco Formichetti. Rome: Bulzoni, 1985, pp. 199–217.

Fortini, Franco. *Attraverso Pasolini.* Turin: Einaudi, 1993.

Fubini, Marco. *Ugo Foscolo: saggio critico.* Turin: Fratelli Ribet, 1938.

Garfagnini, Gian Carlo. "Alle origini dell'impegno politico savonaroliano: la profezia." *Una città e il suo profeta. Firenze di fronte a Savonarola.* Edited by Gian Carlo Garfagnini. Florence: SISMEL, 2001.

"Il messaggio profetico di Savonarola e la sua recezione. Domenico Benivieni e Gianfrancesco Pico." *Studi savonaroliani. Verso il V centenario.* Edited by Gian Carlo Garfagnini. Florence: SISMEL, 1996.

"La polemica antiastrologica del Savonarola ed i suoi precedenti tomistici." *Filosofia scienza astrologia nel Trecento europeo.* Edited by Graziella Federici Vescovini and Francesco Baroncelli. Padua: Il Poligrafo, 1992.

"La predica savonaroliana per una società in crisi." *Savonarola rivisitato [1498–1998].* Edited by Massimiliano G. Rosito. Florence: Città di Vita, 1998.

Gargano, Alfonso, ed. *I preti della libertà.* Naples: Magmata, 2000.

Garin, Eugenio. "Da Campanella a Vico." *Dal Rinascimento all'Illuminismo. Studi e ricerche.* Pisa: Nistri-Lischi, 1970, pp. 79–117.

"L'attesa dell'età nuova e la 'renovatio.'" *L'attesa dell'età nuova nella spiritualità della fine del Medioevo. Atti del III Convegno storico internazionale (Todi, 16–19 ottobre 1960).* Spoleto: Fondazione Cisam, 1962, pp. 9–35.

L'età nuova. Ricerche di storia della cultura dal XII al XVI secolo. Naples: Morano, 1969.

Garrone, Alessandro Galante. *I miei maggiori.* Milan: Garzanti, 1984.

Gaston, Vivien. "The Prophet Armed. Machiavelli, Savonarola, and Rosso Fiorentino's Moses Defending the Daughters of Jethro." *Journal of the Warburg and Courtauld Institutes* 51 (1988): pp. 220–225.

Gatti, Hilary. "The Sense of an Ending in Bruno's *Eroici furori.*" *Essays on Giordano Bruno.* Princeton: Princeton University Press, 2011.

Gentile, Emilio. *Le religioni della politica: fra democrazie e totalitarismi.* Rome and Bari: Laterza, 2001.

Politics as Religion. Princeton: Princeton University Press, 2006.

Gentile, Giovanni. *I profeti del risorgimento italiano.* Florence: Vallecchi, 1923.

"La profezia di Dante." *Studi su Dante.* Florence: Le Lettere, 1990.

Giannetti, Valeria. *Il futuro lume del remoto vero. Ippolito Nievo e la religione dell' ideale.* Florence: Cesati, 2017.

Giglioni, Guido. "Voci della sibilla e voci della natura: divinazione oracolare in Girolamo Cardano." *Bruniana & Campanelliana* 11 (2005): pp. 365–387.

Gilbert, Felix. "Contarini on Savonarola: An Unknown Document of 1516." *Archiv für Reformationsgeschichte* 59 (1968): pp. 145–150.

"Cristianesimo, Umanesimo e la bolla 'Apostolici Regiminis' del 1513." *Rivista Storica Italiana* 79 (1967): pp. 976–990.

"Florentine Political Assumptions in the Period of Savonarola and Soderini." *Journal of the Warburg and Courtauld Institutes* 20 (1957): pp. 187–214.

Ginzburg, Carlo. *Il nicodemismo. Simulazione e dissimulazione religiosa nell'Europa del '500.* Turin: Einaudi, 1970.

Gregory, Tullio. *Theophrastus redivivus. Erudizione e ateismo nel Seicento.* Naples: Morano, 1970.

Greil, Marcus. *The Shape of Things to Come.* New York: Farrar, Straus and Giroux, 2006.

Guidi, Guidobaldo. "La politica e lo stato nel Savonarola." *Studi savonaroliani. Verso il V centenario.* Edited by Gian Carlo Garfagnini, Florence: SISMEL, 1996.

Lotte, pensiero e istituzioni politiche nella repubblica fiorentina dal 1492 al 1512. Florence: Olschki, 1992.

Gutterman, David. *Prophetic Politics and Christian Social Movements.* Ithaca (NY): Cornell University Press, 2005.

Haberken, Phillip. "Prophetic Rebellions: Radical Urban Theopolitics in the Era of Reformations." *The Routledge History Handbook of Medieval Revolt.* Edited by Justine Firnhaber-Baker and Dirk Schoenaers. London and New York: Routledge, 2017, pp. 349–369.

Hammarskjöld, Dag. *Jalons.* Paris: Editions du Félin, 2010.

Handy, Robert T. "The Influence of Mazzini on the American Social Gospel." *The Journal of Religion* 29, no. 2 (Spring 1949): pp. 114–123.

Hankins, James. *Plato in the Italian Renaissance.* Vol. 2. Leiden and New York: E.J. Brill, 1990.

Hardouin, Jean. *Acta conciliorum et epistolae decretales ac constitutiones summorum pontificum.* Vol. IX, 1576. Paris: Ex typographia regia, 1715.

Hefele-Hargenröther-Leclerq. *Histoire des Concils d'après les documents originaux.* Paris: Letouzey et Ané, 1917.

Herzig, Tamar. *Savonarola's Women: Vision and Reform in Renaissance Italy.* Chicago and London: Chicago University Press, 2008.

Heschel, Abraham J. *The Prophets.* New York: Harper & Row, 1962.

Hugon, Augusto Armand. "Correnti evangeliche tra gli italiani in esilio 1840–1860." *Atti del XXXIII Congresso di Storia del Risorgimento Italiano (Messina, 1–4 settembre 1954).* Rome: Istituto per la Storia del Risorgimento Italiano, 1958, pp. 29–36.

Inglese, Giorgio. "'Italia' come spazio politico in Machiavelli." *The Radical Machiavelli.* Edited by Filippo Del Lucchese, Fabio Frosini, and Vittorio Morfino. Leiden and Boston: Brill, 2015, pp. 73–80.

Jameson, Fredric. *Postmodernism, or the Cultural Logic of Late Capitalism.* Durham, NC: Duke University Press, 1991.

Jemolo, Arturo Carlo. *Il Giansenismo in Italia prima della rivoluzione.* Bari: Laterza, 1928.

Kateb, George. *Lincoln's Political Thought.* Cambridge (MA) and London: Harvard University Press, 2015.

Kuntz, Marion Leather. "Guillaume Postel and the World State: Restitution and the Universal Monarchy, Part I." *History of European Ideas* 4 (1983): pp. 299–323.

"Guillaume Postel and the World State: Restitution and the Universal Monarchy, Part II." *History of European Ideas* 4 (1983): pp. 445–465.

The Anointment of Dionisio: Prophecy and Politics in Renaissance Italy. The Pennsylvania State University Press: University Park, PA, 2001.

Lanfranchi, Stéphanie. "'Verrà un dì l'Italia vera...': poesia e profezia dell'Italia futura nel giudizio fascista." *California Italian Studies* 2, no. 1 (2011). Online: https://escholarship.org/uc/item/2m5817bv. Accessed December 12, 2021.

Lantschner, Patrick. *The Logic of Political Conflict in Medieval Cities: Italy and Southern Low Countries, 1370–1440.* Oxford: Oxford University Press, 2015.

La Puma, Leonardo. *Il socialismo sconfitto: saggio sul pensiero politico di Pierre Leroux e Giuseppe Mazzini.* Milan: Franco Angeli, 1984.

Lastraioli, Chiara. "Utopies célestes et terrestres dans la production d'Antonio Brucioli." *MORUS – Utopia e Renascimento* 8 (2012): pp. 231–245.

Lazzerini, Luigi. "Machiavelli e Savonarola. L' 'Esortazione alla penitenza' e il 'Miserere.'" *Rivista di storia e letteratura religiosa* 44 (2008): pp. 385–402.

Teologia del miserere. Da Savonarola al Beneficio di Cristo 1490–1543. Turin: Rosenberg & Sellier, 2013.

Lea, Henry C. *A History of Auricular Confession and Indulgences in the Latin Church.* Philadelphia: Lea Bros. & Co., 1896.

Ledda, Giuseppe, ed. *Poesia e profezia nel'opera di Dante, Atti del Convegno internazionale di Studi Ravenna, 11 novembre 2017.* Ravenna: Centro Dantesco dei Frati Minori Conventuali, 2019.

Leonardi, Claudio. "Committenze agiografiche nel Trecento." *Patronage and Public in the Trecento: Proceedings of the St Lambrecht Symposium, Abtei St. Lambrecht, Styria, 16–19 July 1984.* Edited by Vincent Moleta. Florence: Olschki, 1986, pp. 37–58.

"Girolamo Savonarola profeta di San Marco." *La chiesa e il convento di San Marco a Firenze.* Vol. 1. Florence: Giunti, 1989.

"Intellectuals and Hagiography in the Fourteenth-Century." *Intellectuals and Writers in Fourteenth-Century Europe: The J.A.W. Bennett Memorial Lectures, Perugia, 1984.* Edited by Piero Boitani and Anna Torti. Tubingen: Narr, and Cambridge: Brewer, 1986, pp. 7–21.

"La crisi della cristianità medievale, il ruolo della profezia e Girolamo Savonarola." *Verso Savonarola. Misticismo, profezia, empiti riformistici fra Medioevo ed Età moderna. Atti della III Giornata di Studi (Poggibonsi, 30 aprile 1997).* Edited by Gian Carlo Garfagnini and Giuseppe Picone. Florence: SISMEL, 1999.

"La profezia di Savonarola." *Girolamo Savonarola. L'uomo e il frate. Atti del XXXV Convegno storico internazionale (Todi, 11–14 ottobre 1998).* Spoleto: Centro Italiano di Studi sull'Alto Medioevo, 1999.

"La spiritualità del Savonarola: l'arte del ben morire." *Una città e il suo profeta. Firenze di fronte al Savonarola.* Edited by Gian Carlo Garfagnini. Florence: SISMEL, 2001.

"Savonarola e la politica nelle prediche sopra l'Esodo e nel Trattato circa el reggimento e governo della città di Firenze." *Savonarola e la politica.* Edited by Gian Carlo Garfagnini. Florence: SISMEL, 1997.

Lettieri, Gaetano. "Nove tesi sull'ultimo Machiavelli." *Humanitas* 72 (2017): pp. 1034–1089.

Luzio, Alessandro, ed. *La madre di Mazzini. Carteggio inedito del 1834–39.* Turin: Bocca, 1919.

Mameli, Goffredo. *La vita e gli scritti.* Edited by Arturo Codignola. Venice: La Nuova Italia, 1927.

Manselli, Raoul. "Dante e l'"Ecclesia spiritualis." *Dante e Roma: atti del Convegno di studi, Roma 8–9–10 aprile 1965,* Florence: Le Monnier, 1965.

"L'attesa dell'età nuova ed il gioachimismo." *L'attesa dell'età nuova nella spiritualità della fine del Medioevo. Atti del III Convegno storico internazionale (Todi, 16–19 ottobre 1960).* Spoleto: Fondazione Cisam, 1962, pp. 145–170.

"Pietro di Giovanni Olivi ed Ubertino da Casale (a proposito della Lectura super Apocalipsim e dell'Arbor vitae crucifixae Jesu)." *Studi Medievali* IV (1965): pp. 95–122.

"Ricerca sull'influenza della profezia nel basso medioevo." *Bullettino dell'Istituto Storico Italiano per il Medio Evo e Archivio Muratoriano* 82 (1970): pp. 1–12.

Manuel, Frank E., ed. *Utopias and Utopian Thought*. Boston: Houghton Mifflin, 1996.

Manzotti, Fernando. "Riccardo Bartoli." *Dizionario Biografico degli Italiani*. Vol. VI. Rome: Istituto della Enciclopedia Italiana, 1964, pp. 588–590.

Marcel, Raymond. "Le fureur poétique et l'Humanisme florentin." *Mélanges Georges Amati: création et vie intérieure. Recherches sur les sciences et les arts*. Paris: Centre National de la Recherche Scientifique, 1956, pp. 177–193.

Mario, Jessie White. *Della vita di Giuseppe Mazzini*. Milan: Edoardo Sonzogno, 1886.

Scritti scelti di Giuseppe Mazzini, con note e cenni biografici di Jessie White V. Mario. Florence: G.C. Sansoni, 1901.

Martelli, Mario. "Da Poliziano a Machiavelli: sull'epigramma 'Dell'Occasione' e sull'occasione." *Interpres* 2 (1979): pp. 230–254.

"Firenze." *Letteratura italiana. Storia e geografia, II, L'età moderna, I*. Turin: Einaudi, 1988, pp. 132–140.

"La logica provvidenzialistica e il capitolo XXVI del 'Principe.'" *Interpres* 4 (1981–1982): pp. 262–383.

"Machiavelli e Savonarola." *Savonarola. Democrazia tirannide profezia, Atti del terzo Seminario di studi, (Pistoia, 23–24 maggio 1997)*. Edited by Gian Carlo Garfagnini. Florence: SISMEL-Edizioni del Galluzzo, 1998, pp. 67–89.

"Savonarola poeta." *Una città e il suo profeta. Firenze di fronte al Savonarola*. Edited by Gian Carlo Garfagnini. Florence: SISMEL, 2001.

Martin, John. *Venice's Hidden Enemies: Italian Heretics in a Renaissance City*. Berkeley: University of California Press, 1993.

Martini, Stefania. *Per la fortuna di Dante in Francia*. Pisa: Giardini, 1989.

McCormick, John. "Prophetic Statebuilding: Machiavelli and the Passion of the Duke." *Representations* 115 (2001): pp. 1–19.

McQueen, Alison. *Political Realism in Apocalyptic Times*. Cambridge: Cambridge University Press, 2018.

Mengozzi, Dino. *La morte e l'immortale da Garibaldi a Costa*. Manduria: Lacaita, 2000.

Mila, Massimo. *Verdi*. Edited by Pietro Gelli. Milan: Rizzoli, 2000.

Morghen, Raffaello. *Dante profeta: tra la storia e l'eterno*. Milan: Jaca Book, 1983.

Morisi Guerra, Anna. *Apocalypsis nova. Ricerche sull'origine e la formazione del testo dello pseudo-Amadeo*. Rome: Istituto Storico Italiano per il Medioevo, 1970.

Nardi, Bruno. *Dante e la cultura medievale*. Bari: Laterza, 1948.

Nelson, Eric. *The Hebrew Republic. Jewish Sources and the Interpretation of European Political Thought*. Cambridge (MA) and London: Harvard University Press, 2010.

Nesti, Arnaldo. "Gesù socialista." *Una tradizione popolare italiana 1880–1920*. Turin: Editrice Claudiana, 1974.

Niccoli, Ottavia. *La vita religiosa nell'Italia moderna. Secoli XV–XVIII*. Rome: Carocci, 2008.

Profeti e popolo nell'Italia del Rinascimento. Rome and Bari: Laterza, 1987.

Prophecy and People in Renaissance Italy. Princeton: Princeton University Press, 1990.

"The End of Prophecy." *Journal of Modern History* 61 (1989): pp. 667–682.

Olivari, Tiziana. "I libri di Garibaldi." *Storia e Futuro* 1 (2002): pp. 1–16.

Omodeo, Adolfo. *L'età del Risorgimento italiano*. Messina: G. Principato, 1931.

"Risorgimento senza eroi." *Difesa del Risorgimento*. Turin: Einaudi, 1951, pp. 439–446.

Studi sull'età della restaurazione. Turin: Einaudi, 1970.

Ossola, Carlo. "La parola mistica." *Mistici italiani dell'età moderna*. Edited by Giacomo Juri. Turin: Einaudi, 2007.

Ossola, Carlo, Silvia Ciliberti, and Giacomo Jori, eds. *Gli angeli custodi: storia e figure dell'amico vero*. Turin: Einaudi, 2004.

Palazzeschi, Aldo. *Due imperi ... mancati*. Milan: Linea d'ombra edizioni, 1994.

Pandolfi, Tullio. "Gian Matteo Giberti e l'ultima difesa della libertà d'Italia negli anni 1521–1525." *Archivio della Reale Società Romana di storia Patria* 31 (1911): pp. 131–237.

Panichi, Alessio. *Il volto fragile del potere. Religione e politica nel pensiero di Tommaso Campanella*. Pisa: ETS, 2015.

Parel, Anthony. *The Machiavellian Cosmos*. New Haven: Yale University Press, 1992.

Patti, Emanuela. *Pasolini after Dante: The Divine Mimesis and the Politics of Representation*. London: Routledge, 2016.

Petersen, Rodney L. *Preaching in the Last Days: The Themes of the 'Two Witnesses' in the Sixteenth and Seventeenth Centuries*. New York and Oxford: Oxford University Press, 1993.

Peterson, David S. "Religion, Politics, and the Church in Fifteenth-Century Florence." *Girolamo Savonarola: Piety, Prophecy, and Politics in Renaissance Florence*. Edited by Donald Weinstein and Valerie R. Hotchkiss. Dallas: Bridwell Library, 1994.

Petrocchi, Massimo. *Storia della spiritualità italiana*. Vol. I. Rome: Edizioni di Storia e Letteratura, 1978.

Pettit, Philip. *Republicanism: A Theory of Freedom and Government*. Oxford: Oxford University Press, 1998.

Pisano, Rossano, ed. *Il paradiso socialista: La propaganda socialista in Italia alla fine dell'Ottocento attraverso gli opuscoli di "Critica sociale."* Milan: Franco Angeli, 1986.

Podestà, Gian Luca. *Il tempo dell'Apocalisse: vita di Gioacchino da Fiore*. Rome and Bari: Laterza, 2004.

Polecretti, Cynthia L. *Preaching Peace in Renaissance Italy: Bernardino of Siena and His Audience*. Washington, DC: CUA Press, 2000.

Polizzotto, Lorenzo. "Prophecy, Politics and History in Early Sixteenth-Century Florence: The Admonitory Letters of Francesco d'Antonio de' Ricci." *Florence and Italy: Renaissance Studies in Honour of Nicolai Rubinstein*. Edited by Peter Denley and Caroline Elam. London: Westfield College-University of London Committee for Medieval Studies, 1988.

The Elect Nation: The Savonarolan Movement in Florence (1494–1545). Oxford: Oxford University Press, 1994.

Procyk, Anna. *Giuseppe Mazzini's Young Europe and the Birth of Modern Nationalism in the Slavic World*. Toronto: University of Toronto Press, 2019.

Prosperi, Adriano. *America e apocalisse e altri saggi.* Rome: Istituti editoriali e poligrafici internazionali, 1999.

L'eresia del Libro Grande: storia di Giorgio Siculo e della sua setta. Milan: Feltrinelli, 2011.

Tribunali della coscienza. Turin: Einaudi, 1996.

Reeves, Marjorie. "Dante and the Prophetic View of History." *The World of Dante.* Edited by Cecyl Grayson. Oxford: Oxford University Press, 1980, pp. 44–60.

The Influence of Prophecy in the Later Middle Ages: A Study in Joachimism, Notre Dame: University of Notre Dame, 2011. First published 1969 by Oxford University Press.

"The Third Age: Dante's Debt to Gioacchino Fiore." *L'età dello spirito e la fine dei tempi in Gioacchino da Fiore e nel gioachimismo medievale. Atti del II Congresso Internazionale di Studi Gioachimiti, 6–9 settembre 1984.* Edited by Antonio Crocco. San Giovanni in Fiore: Centro Internazionale Studi Gioachimiti, 1986, pp. 127–139.

Reeves, Marjorie and Warwick Gould. *Joachim of Fiore and the Myth of the Eternal Evangel in the Nineteenth Century.* Oxford: Oxford University Press, 1987.

Remond, René. *Lamennais et la démocratie.* Paris: Presses universitaires de France, 1948.

Riall, Lucy. *Garibaldi: Invention of a Hero.* New Haven and London: Yale University Press, 2007.

Ridolfi, Roberto. *Studi savonaroliani.* Florence: Leo Olschki, 1935.

Ripari, Edoardo. "Un nuovo Dio per l'Italia: Giosuè Carducci e la religione civile." *Voci dall'800.* Vol. II. Villasanta: Liminamentis, 2011, pp. 193–216.

Roberts, Timothy. "The Relevance of Giuseppe Mazzini's Ideas of Insurgency to the American Slavery Crisis of the 1850s." *Giuseppe Mazzini and the Globalization of Democratic Nationalism, 1830–1920.* Edited by Christopher A. Bayly and Eugenio F. Biagini. London: British Academy, 2008.

Rodolfi, Anna. "Il ruolo delle immagini sensibili nella dottrina della conoscenza profetica di Alberto Magno." *Annali del Dipartimento di Filosofia 2005.* Florence: Florence University Press, 2006, pp. 79–107.

"Sogno e profezia in Alberto Magno." *Scientia, fides, theologia. Studi di filosofia medievale in onore di Gianfranco Fioravanti.* Edited by Stefano Perfetti. Pisa: ETS, 2011, pp. 193–215.

Romeo, Giovanni. *Inquisitori, esorcisti e streghe nell'Italia della Controriforma.* Florence: Sansoni, 2003.

Romeo, Rosario. *Cavour e il suo tempo (1810–1842).* Bari: Laterza, 1969.

Rosselli, Nello. *Mazzini e Bakunin. Dodici anni di movimento operaio in Italia (1860–1872).* Turin: Einaudi, 1967. First published 1927 by Fratelli Bocca.

Rota, Ettore. *Le origini del Risorgimento.* Vol. 2. Milan: Vallardi, 1948.

Roth, Cecil. *The Last Florentine Republic.* New York: Russell & Russell, 1968.

Rotondò, Antonio. "Jacopo Brocardo." *Dizionario Biografico degli Italiani.* Vol. XIV. Rome: Istituto dell'Enciclopedia Italiana, 1972, pp. 384–389.

Rowland, Ingrid D. *Giordano Bruno: Philosopher and Heretic.* New York: Farrar, Straus and Giroux, 2008.

Rubinstein, Nicolai. "Savonarola on the Government of Florence." *The World of Savonarola. Italian Elites and Perceptions of Crisis.* Edited by Stella Fletcher and Christine Shaw. Aldershot and Burlington: Ashgate, 2000.

Ruffini, Francesco. *La giovinezza di Cavour*. Second edition. Turin: Edizioni Di Modica, 1937.

Ultimi studi sul Conte di Cavour. Bari: Laterza, 1936.

Rusconi, Roberto. "Profezia e profeti in Occidente, dal secondo medioevo alla prima età moderna. Dallo scrittoio alla piazza ovvero dalla penna alla spada." *Carisma profetico: fattore di innovazione religiosa*. Edited by Giovanni Filoramo. Brescia: Morcelliana, 2003.

The Last Florentine Republic. New York: Russell & Russell, 1968.

Russo, Luigi. "I poeti-numi del 1848." *Belfagor* 3 (1948): pp. 129–142.

Carducci senza retorica. Bari: Laterza, 1957.

Machiavelli. Bari: Laterza, 1949.

Sallusto, Filippo. *Nazionalismo italiano, nazionalismo francese: Gabriele D'Annunzio e Roberto Forges Davanzati*. Canterano: Aracne, 2018.

Salvatorelli, Luigi. *Il pensiero politico italiano dal 1700 al 1870*. Turin: Einaudi, 1935.

Salvemini, Gaetano. *Mazzini*. Third edition. Rome: La Voce, 1920.

Sannino, Anna Lisa. "L'altro 1799." *Cultura antidemocratica e pratica politica controrivoluzionaria nel tardo Settecento napoletano*. Naples: ESI, 2002.

Sasso, Gennaro. "Del ventiseiesimo capitolo del 'Principe', della provvidenza e di altre cose." *La Cultura* 22 (1984): pp. 249–309.

"Il 'Principe' ebbe due redazioni?" *La Cultura* 29 (1981): pp. 52–109.

Machiavelli e gli antichi e altri saggi. Vol. I. Milan: Riccardo Ricciardi, 1987.

Niccolò Machiavelli. Il pensiero politico. Bologna: Il Mulino, 1993.

Scarfoglio, Domenico. *Lazzari e giacobini. Cultura popolare e rivoluzione a Napoli nel 1799*. Naples: L'ancora, 1999.

Schenk, Gerrit J. "Dis-astri. Modelli interpretativi delle calamità naturali dal medioevo al Rinascimento." *Le calamità ambientali nel tardo Medioevo: realtà, percezioni, reazioni*. Edited by Michael Matheus. Florence: Florence University Press, 2010, pp. 23–75.

Scirocco, Alfonso. *Garibaldi. Battaglie, amori, ideali di un cittadino del mondo*. Rome and Bari: Laterza, 2007.

Scott, John T. "The Fortune of Machiavelli's Unarmed Prophet." *The Journal of Politics* 80 (2018): pp. 615–629.

Shulman, George. *American Prophecy. Race and Redemption in American Political Culture*. Minneapolis: University of Minnesota Press, 2008.

Skinner, Quentin. *Liberty before Liberalism*. Cambridge: Cambridge University Press, 1988.

"Thomas More's Utopia and the Virtue of True Nobility." *Visions of Politics, Vol. 2, Renaissance Virtues*. Cambridge: Cambridge University Press, 2002, pp. 213–244.

Sorge, Valeria. *Tra contingenza e necessità. L'ordine delle cause in Pietro Pomponazzi*. Milan and Udine: Mimesis, 2010.

Spini, Giorgio. *Ricerca dei libertini. La teoria dell'impostura delle religioni nel Seicento italiano*. Florence: La Nuova Italia, 1983.

Una "testimone della verità". Eleonora de Fonseca Pimentel tra impegno civile e riflessione etico-religiosa. Naples: La Città del Sole, 2007.

Stephens, John N. *The Fall of the Florentine Republic 1512–1530*. Oxford: The Clarendon Press, 1983.

Sticco, Maria. *La poesia religiosa del Risorgimento*. Milan: Vita e Pensiero, 1945.

Sutcliffe, Marcella Pellegrino. _Victorian Radicals and Italian Democrats._ Woodbridge: Boydell & Brewer, 2014.

Sylvers, Malcolm. "L'anticlericalismo nel socialismo italiano dalle origini al 1914." _Movimento operaio e socialista_ 16 (1970): pp. 175–189.

Synave, Paul and Pierre Benoit. _Prophecy and Inspiration: A Commentary on the Summa Theologica II-II, Questions 171–178._ Translated by Thomas L. Sheridan and Avery R. Dulles. New York: Desclée, 1961.

Tarrant, Neil. "Concord and Toleration in the Thought of Francesco Pucci, 1578–81." _The Sixteenth Century Journal_ 46 (2015): pp. 983–1003.

Tinelli, Elisa. "Le utopie del secondo Cinquecento e del primo Seicento, come renovatio laica dell'ideale della fuga mundi." _Quaderni di Storia_ 90 (2019): pp. 157–175.

Tirinnanzi, Nicoletta. "Filosofia, politica e magia nel Rinascimento: l'esperienza di Giordano Bruno." _Giordano Bruno nolano e cittadino europeo._ Grottaglie: CRSEC e Scorpione editrice, 2004, pp. 31–59.

Tognetti, Giampaolo. "Venezia e le profezie sulla conversione dei Turchi." _Venezia e i Turchi: scontri e confronti di due civiltà._ Edited by Anna Della Valle. Milan: Electa, 1985.

Torrell, Jean-Pierre, O.P. _Recherches sur la théorie de la prophètie au Moyen Âge XIIe – XIVe siècles._ Fribourg: Éditions Universitaires, 1992.

Toussaint, Stephanie. "Profetare alla fine del Quattrocento." _Studi savonaroliani._ Edited by Gian Carlo Garfagnini. Florence: SISMEL, 1996.

Trinkaus, Charles. _In Our Image and Likeness: Humanity and Divinity in Italian Humanist Thought._ Notre Dame: University of Notre Dame Press, 1995.

Tucker, Robert C. "The Theory of Charismatic Leadership." _Daedalus_ 97 (1968): pp. 731–756.

Turchetti, Mario. "Savonarola: la tirannide secondo un profeta." _Savonarola. Democrazia tirannide profezia, Atti del Seminario (Pistoia, 23–24 maggio 1997)._ Edited by Gian Carlo Garfagnini. Florence: SISMEL, 1998.

Turi, Gabriele. "Aspetti dell'ideologia del PSI (1890–1910)." _Studi Storici_ 21 (1980): pp. 61–94.

Turoldo, David Maria. "Chiediamo scusa d'esistere." _Pasolini in Friuli 1943–1949._ Edited by Corriere del Friuli and the Comune di Casarsa della Delizia. Udine: Arti Grafiche Friulane, 1976, pp. 67–70.

Tuscano, Pasquale. _Del parlare onesto. Scienza, profezia e magia nella scrittura di Tommaso Campanella._ Naples: Edizioni Scientifiche Italiane, 2001.

Valerio, Adriana. "Il profeta e la parola: La predicazione di Domenica da Paradiso nella Firenze post-Savonaroliana." _Studi savonaroliani: verso il V centenario._ Edited by Gian Carlo Garfagnini. Florence: Sismel, 1996, pp. 299–307.

——— "L'altra rivelazione: L'esperienza profetica femminile nei secoli XIV-XVI." _Donne, potere e profezia._ Edited by Adriana Valerio. Naples: D'Auria, 1995, pp. 136–162.

——— "La predica sopra Ruth, la donna, la riforma dei semplice." _Una città e il suo profeta: Firenze di Fronte al Savonarola._ Edited by Gian Carlo Garfagnini. Florence: SISMEL, 2001, pp. 261–262.

Vasoli, Cesare. _Civitas Mundi: Studi sulla cultura del Cinquecento._ Rome: Edizioni di Storia e Letteratura, 1996.

——— _Filosofia e religione nella cultura del Rinascimento._ Naples: Guida, 1988.

"Giovanni Nesi tra Donato Acciaioli e Girolamo Savonarola." *I miti e gli astri.* Naples: Guida, 1977, pp. 51–128.

"Il messaggio profetico di Savonarola e la sua recezione. Domenico Benivieni e Gianfrancesco Pico." *Studi savonaroliani. Verso il V centenario.* Edited by Gian Carlo Garfagnini. Florence: SISMEL, 1996.

"Il pensiero politico della Scolastica." *Storia delle idee politiche economiche e sociali* II.2 Turin: UTET (1983): pp. 367–462.

"La profezia di Francesco da Meleto." *Umanesimo e ermeneutica.* Padua: Cedam, 1963, pp. 27–80.

"L'attesa della nuova era in ambienti e gruppi fiorentini del Quattrocento." *L'attesa dell'età nuova nella spiritualità della fine del Medioevo. Convegni del centro di studi sulla spiritualità medievale.* Todi: Accademia Tudertina, 1962, pp. 370–432.

"L'influenza di Gioacchino da Fiore sul profetismo italiano della fine del Quattrocento e del primo Cinquecento." *Il profetismo gioachimita tra Quattrocento e Cinquecento: Atti del III Congresso Internazionale di Studi Gioachimiti (S. Giovanni in Fiore, 17–21 settembre 1989).* Edited by Gian Luca Podestà. Genoa: Marietti, 1991.

"Quasi sit Deus": Studi su Marsilio Ficino. Lecce: Conte, 1999.

Tra "maestri" umanistici e teologi: studi quattrocenteschi. Florence: Le Lettere, 1991.

Venturi, Franco. *Saggi sull'Europa illuminista. I. Alberti Radicati di Passerano.* Turin: Einaudi, 1954.

Venturi, Maria Teresa. *"Io vivo nelle cose e invento, come posso, il modo di nominarle": Pier Paolo Pasolini e la lingua della modernità.* Florence: Firenze University Press, 2020.

Verde, Armando F. *Lo Studio Fiorentino. 1473–1503. Ricerche e documenti, IV: La vita universitaria.* Vol. 2. Florence: Olschki, 1985.

"Savonarola lettore e commentatore del testo sacro." *Una città e il suo profeta. Firenze di fronte al Savonarola.* Edited by Gian Carlo Garfagnini. Florence: SISMEL, 2001.

Verdon, Timothy and John Henderson, eds. *Christianity and the Renaissance: Image and Religious Imagination in the Quattrocento.* Syracuse, NY: Syracuse University Press, 1990.

Villari, Pasquale. *La scuola e la quistione sociale in Italia.* Florence: Nuova Antologia, 1872.

La storia di Girolamo Savonarola e de' suoi tempi. Vol. I. Florence: Le Monnier, 1930.

Viroli, Maurizio. *As if God Existed: Religion and Liberty in the History of Italy.* Princeton and Oxford: Princeton University Press, 2012.

Machiavelli's God. Translated by Anthony Shugaar. Princeton and Oxford: Princeton University Press, 2010.

Niccolò's Smile: A Biography of Machiavelli. New York: Farrar, Straus and Giroux, 2000.

Redeeming The Prince: The Meaning of Machiavelli's Masterpiece. Princeton and Oxford: Princeton University Press, 2014.

Viti, Paolo. "Savonarola e i libri." *Una città e il suo profeta. Firenze di fronte al Savonarola.* Edited by Gian Carlo Garfagnini. Florence: SISMEL, 2001.

Voci, Anna Maria. "Per l'interpretazione della canzone 'spirto gentil' di Francesco Petrarca." *Romanische Forschungen* 91 (1979): pp. 281–288.

von Albertini, Rudolf. *Firenze dalla repubblica al principato. Storia e coscienza politica.* Turin: Einaudi, 1970.

Walker, Daniel P. *Spiritual and Demonic Magic from Ficino to Campanella.* London: Warburg Institute, University of London, 1958.

Walmesley, Charles. *Storia generale della Chiesa cristiana dalla sua nascita all'ultimo stato di trionfo nel cielo tratta principalmente dall'Apocalisse di S. Giovanni Apostolo. Opera di Mr. Pastorini trasportata da un monaco benedettino della Congregazione di S. Mauro dall'idioma inglese al francese, e resa ora per la prima volta all'italiana favella.* Cesena: Eredi Biasini all'insegna di Pallade, 1794–1795.

Walzer, Michael. *Exodus and Revolution.* New York: Basic Books, 1986.

In God's Shadow: Politics in the Hebrew Bible. New Haven: Yale University Press, 2012.

The Revolution of the Saints: A Study in the Origins of Radical Politics. Cambridge (MA) and London: Harvard University Press, 1965.

Weber, Max. *Ancient Judaism.* New York: Free Press, 1952.

The Theory of Social and Economic Organization. Edited by Talcott Parsons. Translated by A.M. Henderson and Talcott Parsons. Glencoe (IL): The Free Press, 1947.

Weinstein, Donald. *Savonarola and Florence. Prophecy and Patriotism in the Renaissance.* Princeton: Princeton University Press, 1970.

West, Cornel. *Prophesy Deliverance! An Afro-American Revolutionary Christianity.* Louisville (KY)-London: Westminster John Knox Press, 1982.

Wight, Martin. *Four Seminal Thinkers in International Theory: Machiavelli, Grotius, Kant, and Mazzini.* Oxford: Oxford University Press, 2004.

Witt, Ronald G. "Coluccio Salutati and the Conception of the 'Poeta Theologus' in the Fourteenth Century." *Renaissance Quarterly* XXX (1977): pp. 538–563.

Yates, Frances. *Giordano Bruno and the Hermetic Tradition.* London: Routledge and Kegan Paul, 2004.

Zarri, Gabriella. "Disciplina regolare e pratiche di coscienza: le virtù e i comportamenti sociali in comunità femminili." *Disciplina dell'anima, disciplina del corpo, e disciplina della società tra medioevo ed età moderna.* Edited by Paolo Prodi. Bologna: Il Mulino, 1994, pp. 257–278.

"Potere carismatico e potere politico nelle corti italiane del Rinascimento." *Poteri carismatici e informali: chiesa e società medioevali.* Edited by Agostino Paravicini Bagliani and André Vauchez. Palermo: Sellerio, 1992, pp. 175–191.

Index

(page numbers in bold and italic refer to footnotes)